# THE REED READER

Also by Ishmael Reed

# THE REED READER

## ISHMAEL REED

BASIC
BOOKS

A MEMBER OF THE PERSEUS BOOKS GROUP

Excerpts from *The Free-Lance Pallbearers*, *Yellow Back Radio Broke-Down*, *The Last Days of Louisiana Red*, *The Terrible Twos*, *Reckless Eyeballing*, and *The Terrible Threes* are reprinted courtesy of Dalkey Archive Press.

Excerpts from *Mumbo Jumbo* and *Flight to Canada* are reprinted courtesy of Scribner, a division of Simon & Schuster, Inc.

*Japanese by Spring* is available from Penguin Putnam, Inc.

Published by Basic Books,
A Member of the Perseus Books Group

Designed by Mark McGarry

Library of Congress Cataloging-in-Publication Data

Reed, Ishmael, 1938–
    [Selections. 2000]
    The Reed reader / Ishmael Reed.
        p. cm.
    ISBN 0-465-06893-6 (cloth); ISBN 0-465-06894-4 (pbk.)
        1. Afro-Americans—Literary collections.  I. Title.
PS3568.E365 A6 2000
813'.54—dc21

                                                                    00–23106

FIRST PAPERBACK EDITION
01  02  03  /  10  9  8  7  6  5  4  3  2  1

*In Memory of Robert C. Maynard*

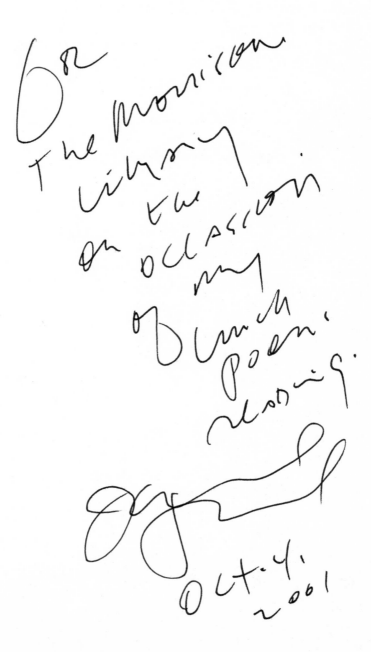

For
The Morrison
Library
on the
occasion
my
Branch
Poem
reading.

[signature]

Oct. 4.
2001

My Dad loves to signify; he was born to signify.

TENNESSEE REED

## CONTENTS

I have been writing fiction and nonfiction on and off since my late teens. My first short story was influenced by Nathanael West's style in *A Cool Million* and *The Dream Life of Balso Snell*, which I'd ordered from a book club called the Reader's Subscription. My story, "Something Pure," was also influenced by the acerbic wit of H. L. Mencken, whose work I read while working at Buffalo's Grosvernor Library, where I also first read James Baldwin's books. I was 18 and enrolled at Millard Fillmore College, the night school division of the University of Buffalo. I'd registered there because the grades I'd received in a technical school which I attended for two years were too low, and the high grades I'd earned at an academic high school, where I spent my last two years, were not enough to offset them. I'd had no business being in a technical school, since I had no mechanical aptitude, and so I spent most of my time in the band room, playing second violin with a string quartet as well as trombone. I wrote "Something Pure," a satire about the commercialization of religion, as an assignment from my instructor, a Mr. Scott. He brought it to the attention of other English professors, who offered me a full four-year scholarship.

But when my stepfather refused to list his assets, I was denied the scholarship. "These folks want to know all your business," he said. I was furious with him at the time, but later began to understand his position. He was a Southern black, and too often blacks had had their property stolen—and were treated like slaves—as a result of signing documents they didn't understand.

An assembly line worker at the Chevrolet plant, he was illiterate but, eventually, taught himself to read and became a leader of his church. I squeaked by financially until my junior year with assistance from a New York State loan program and my earnings from my job at the downtown library.

After dropping out of college in 1960, I wrote for a militant newspaper called *The Empire Star*. The *Star* was founded by A. J. Smitherman, who fled Tulsa, Oklahoma after a massacre of black people began there on May 31, 1921. A. J. Smitherman, a fearless, "pistol-packing" newspaper editor, was one of two anti-lynching African Americans who aroused the mob's anger. The number of people killed has been estimated at somewhere between 200 and 300, but that figure may rise, since a new mass grave has been recently discovered. As with hundreds of lynchings of black men, this particular white mob was energized by a rumor that a black man had assaulted a white woman. But this turned out to be a cover for the Mob's real intention—that of punishing Blacks who inhabited a prosperous section of Tulsa known as "The Black Wall Street." This was to be the first American community bombed from the air. Smitherman was indicted on the trumped-up charge of inciting a riot. Because he refused to disclose Smitherman's whereabouts, the mob cut off his brother's ear. I had been a helper at Smitherman's office when I was 13 and wrote a Jazz column for the paper. By the time I came back to the *Star*, in the early sixties, a young firebrand, Joe Walker, had become editor, and the two of us put out the whole newspaper. We shook up the town, writing about segregated schools, police brutality and local politics.

I think it was from listening to Blue Note and Prestige records during my teens and talking with Wade Legge, a young Be-Bop pianist who performed with Charles Mingus and Dizzy Gillespie, that I became convinced that New York was the place for me, if I wanted to meet people who were as hip as I thought I was. In Buffalo I used to sit in a place on Franklin Street called Cafe Encores with the *Village Voice* and read about people like Ted Joans, the most successful Jazz poet among the Beats. But finally it was Malcolm X, with whom I'd had some one-on-ones, as well as the encouragement of a screenwriter who read a play of mine while standing at the bar at Chumley's on Bedford Street during a weekend visit to New York, that helped me make the decision. A few months later I left Buffalo.

In 1962, I moved to New York and supported myself at different jobs in hospitals, in a factory and as a clerk in the New York State Department of Labor. I attended meetings of the Umbra Society, a group of African American writers who met weekly at the Lower East Side apartment of Tom Dent.

Among them were David Henderson, Calvin Hernton, Askia Muhammed Toure, Charles and Raymond Patterson, Lorenzo Thomas, Norman Pritchard. From time to time, I'd find myself in the company of literary celebrities. Norman Mailer, James Baldwin, Ralph Ellison, John A. Williams, Langston Hughes and Amiri Baraka. I was encouraged by writers like Gloria Oden and Gilbert Sorrentino, then an editor at Grove Press, who wrote an enthusiastic letter about my first novel. I was a green bumpkin in those days. I remember, within a few months after arriving in New York, standing at the bar at the White Horse Inn (one of Dylan Thomas's watering holes, I had read somewhere), and in walked Edward Albee and Tennessee Williams. I went up and down the bar telling the patrons that the two famous playwrights had entered the bar. And I went about town showing people Sorrentino's letter so often that the print began to fade. During my five years in New York, I was regarded as provincial by jaded New Yorkers. The late alto saxophonist C Sharp used to kid me by calling me "Buffalo." The trumpeter Kenny Dorham, with whom I used to drink at a downtown joint called the Port of Call, told me that I would never make it as a writer in New York.

Manhattan was a writers' town, where words were regarded with reverence and verbal inventiveness was admired. From time to time I worked on the *Daily News* Straw Poll, asking the public their views about the elections, and it seemed that as soon as you stepped into Manhattan, the witty answers began. There were book parties where you would rub elbows with famous authors and critics. The town was electric with exciting debate. You could go uptown and see Muhammad Ali at a Muslim event, or downtown and attend the opening of a gallery show.

Since Tom Dent was a prominent member of the Civil Rights Movement, I met some of its stars. Charlayne Hunter Gault, James Meredith and A. D. King visited our meetings. I'd run into Malcolm from time to time, and wrote a poem in his honor called "Fanfare for an Avenging Angel." It was terrible, but he said it reminded him of Dante and Virgil's poetry.

In 1965, I began working on my first novel, *The Free-Lance Pallbearers*. Langston Hughes and Walter Lowenfels were among the first to assist me in having my work included in hardcover books. Hughes published my poem "The Feral Pioneers" in his book *The Poetry of the Negro*. I sent him some of Lucille Clifton's poems and he published those too. He introduced me to Anne Freedgood, who was responsible for my book being published by Doubleday. *The Free-Lance Pallbearers* started out as a realistic novel, but it was impossible to write that kind of book in the Lower East Side of the 1960s, where artists,writers and musicians were breaking new ground. In each succeeding draft the novel became more and more surreal.

*The Free-Lance Pallbearers* uses some of the mechanics of the Gothic novel, but it also borrows from popular culture, using a mixing and sampling technique that would characterize most of my later work. I think that this technique might be the constant in African American culture, that of making something whole from scraps. I would later describe this method as the gumbo style.

The main influence on *Pallbearers* was Voltaire's *Candide*. I was also reading F. M. Esfandiary's *The Beggar*, Charles Wright's *The Wig* and Kenneth Patchen's *The Journal of Albion Moonlight* at the time. The central character, Bukka Doopeyduk, a true believer in the prevailing philosophy, which is based upon the evacuation habits of a dictator, struggles with day-to-day domestic problems in a land so dominated by one man that it takes its name from him, its leader, Harry Sam. The excerpt reprinted here glances at the complicity between the university, some leaders of the black political movement and the state during the Vietnam war. It also takes an irreverent swipe at the Catholic Church, not only as a look backward at the anti-clerical writers of the Renaissance but also because of the endorsement of the war by leading figures of the American Catholic Church, including Cardinal Spellman, who was Vicar of the Armed Forces. If during the writing of *The Free-Lance Pallbearers*, I thought that the Catholic Church was monolithic, I was relieved of that idea after befriending some Jesuits at Creighton University in Omaha, including Father Lee Lubbers and my late dear friend Father Ted Cunningham. They taught me that there was probably more rebellion within the church than any coming from without.

Within five years of leaving Buffalo, *The Free-Lance Pallbearers,* was published. Still in my twenties, I was not sophisticated enough to be cool about it. I was not used to such adulation and the perks that went along with being a published author. The great dinners at the Doubleday town house. The admiration of beautiful women. Being recognized in public. Told that every line I wrote was great. To be young, gifted and black in New York of the 1960s was to be overwhelmed with much affection. If I had remained there, I would have been loved and admired to death. One of the reasons I left, in the summer of 1967, for Los Angeles, was because my working-class background taught me to be suspicious of too much affection. I returned to New York for a couple of summers, but for all practical purposes, I'd permanently relocated to California.

I spent a lonely summer of 1967 in an apartment in the Echo Park Canyon section of Los Angeles, working on my second book, *Yellow Back Radio Broke-Down*. In New York, I was constantly reminded of the fact that I wasn't the brightest guy around, but I was alert enough to size up the literary situation. The politics were left wing. The *New York Times Magazine* printed favorable notices about Eldridge Cleaver, and the *New York Review of Books* published a diagram for making a Molotov cocktail. Black books, or "riot" books as they were called in private, were hot in the 1960s, and some frustrated writers from other racial backgrounds claimed that white liberal critics were giving a free pass to books of questionable literary quality by black authors.

This certainly wasn't true of my early novels. One prepublication review of my first novel said that the book should be flushed down the toilet along with its author. As for my second novel, *Yellow Back Radio Broke-Down*, many readers couldn't get past the title. The title came from Lorenzo Thomas's "Modern Plumbing Illustrated," published in *The East Side Review*. I wanted to break down—that is, deconstruct—the Western novel (which had been called the Yellow Back in the 1890s) into its individual parts. *Yellow Back Radio Broke-Down* also shows my growing interest in African American religion, but, like *Pallbearers*, it uses forms of popular culture like vaudeville. All one has to do is to compare the slapstick of the excerpts from *Yellow Back* with that of the modernist prose being written in New York at the time, which was humorless, clunky, convoluted and intensely Eurocentric, to discover how much my generation departed from the literary norms of the 1950s.

One critic said that I was living proof that the bacteria of the pop culture had entered the literary world. To him, the literary world was one based upon what he would have called traditional European culture. I wasn't a European, I was an American. My work was more likely to be influenced by popular culture than by the "classics." In *Yellow Back*, a black cowboy, whose character is inspired by the Loup Garou legend of Haiti and the Louisiana Bayou, enters a Western town and causes such havoc that the ranchers have to call in the Pope for relief. As I was cutting and pasting characters in those days, the character also recalled a cowboy icon of my youth, Lash Larue, who disciplined his enemies with a whip. In Buffalo, black kids like me learned about good and evil from cowboys like Larue and Roy Rogers. The scenes reprinted in *The Reed Reader* show my interest in a different reading of history from that found in the average American school curriculum. *Yellow Back* got mixed reviews. I was delighted when it received a favorable review in a rodeo magazine published in the West. I've never ridden a horse. This book was faithful to the form of the Yellow Backs in another way; they were usually written by dudes from the East, like me.

If *The Free-Lance Pallbearers* and *Yellow Back Radio Broke-Down* received little notice, my third novel, *Mumbo Jumbo*, drew and continues to draw much attention. In it, I employed the techniques of the previous novels, including parallel texts and discontinuous jumping-around Jazz-like narrative. I also used photos and graphics which added still another dimension to the plot line. In the early seventies, before an audience at Sarah Lawrence I called it my *Ragtime* novel. I was conscious of rhythm when I wrote it and, as a student of Jazz, I understand that rhythm—not wonderful-sounding complex chords, or 2, 5, 1 progressions—is at the root of Jazz. Most critics, when they praise writing for approaching the rhythms of Jazz, don't know what they're talking about, and such critical rubbish merely reveals the facile approach that some use when analyzing African-influenced American forms. Most Jazz criticism is a form of white-collar crime.

My reading of the 1920s "Jazz Age" as a manifestation of a psychic plague, and a comment by James Weldon Johnson that the early ragtime songs "jes grew," got me going. I named the plague "Jes Grew," and the excerpt reprinted here traces the origin of the plague to New Orleans. Continuing my fascination with popular forms, as this novel was germinating in my mind in 1969, I taught a course at the University of Washington at Seattle in which I used a "detective novel" written by Chester Himes; the intuitive approach employed by my "detective," Papa LaBas, was based upon that of Himes's characters.

At first I thought that Papa LaBas ("Papa" being the title accorded to Haitian houngans, or priests) was a carryover from the West African Eshu, who is called by a number of names by the Yoruba, and whose twin aspect is Elegbera-Elegbaa, but after studying the indigenous language of western Nigeria, for ten years, it has occurred to me that, stylistically, and in demeanor, this character more closely resembles Iku, who, in the indigenous literature, is said to be *eniti ile re mbe lagbedemeji aiye on orun* (an entity whose residence lies between earth and heaven). His Haitian manifestation is Baron Samedi.

This excerpt from *Mumbo Jumbo* also reveals my problems with Christianity, Judaism and Islam, and my belief that they are intolerant of other religions. This belief explains why I would write admiringly, in *Mumbo Jumbo*, of Julian the Apostate Emperor, who attempted to restore the Greek religion after Christianity had taken hold among the Roman upper classes. His complaining about the Christians smashing art which they considered "pagan" is similar to the Muslims invading African countries and India and destroying indigenous art and Buddhist temples. (Arab scholar Dr. Sam Hamod assures me that such doings are not inspired by the teachings of Muhammad.) In contrast, Buddhism and West African religion I've found to be very tolerant.

My next novel, *The Last Days of Louisiana Red*, featured my continued interest in the career of Marie LaVeau, whose history I'd found in Robert Tallant's books. I was told recently by New Orleans historian Marie Osbey that Marie LaVeau was born in Haiti and came to New Orleans in search of her husband. This explains why the HooDoo Queen or the Widow Glapion, whose New Orleans gravesite is still visited by thousands, included African religion in her "business." In this novel the practitioners of the old religion are arrayed against Mini the Moocher, a character from the Cab Calloway song which has coded references to Afro-American religion. I'd criticized the black nationalists for insisting upon "positive" portraits, exclusively, of African Americans, and true to form, the late Addison Gayle, Jr. and Houston Baker hit me for rendering some popular revolutionaries as descendants of the Amos and Andy stereotypes. I was using stereotypes to make serious points, a technique that would be popularized by artists and ironists like Joe Overstreet, Betye Saar and Robert Colescott and one could add, Louis Armstrong, Charles Mingus and Adrienne Kennedy. *The Last Days of Louisiana Red* also developed my use of drawing materials from different cultures, a constant in African American religion. And so not only will you find HooDoo mythology in the book but also my take on Sophocles' *Antigone*. Teachers who adopted *The Last Days of Louisiana Red* for their courses wrote to tell me that the book inspired their students to read Sophocles.

With *Louisiana Red*, I was confronted with a new group who would insist that characters of their gender be treated with deference. To depart from this latest of a series of "blueprints" required of African American writers would invite the label "misogynist," which, in time, would be like being called a communist in the '50s; you couldn't work. This new crowd had infinitely more clout than the black nationalists, and they could place stiff impediments in the path of a writer's career. Having lived this long, I've found that the best way to deal with such opposition, which resorts to censorship, boycotts, slander and innuendo, is to wait them out.

Though I have had and continue to have cordial relations with most black feminists, the fact that a few cast me as a sexist for my portrait of Minnie in *Lousiana Red* became, in the view of white middle-class feminist critics and scholars, as well as white males who became born-again black feminists, a feud between Ishmael Reed and all black women. Margo Jefferson accused me of sexism, based on her reading of *The Last Days of Louisiana Red*, and is still blasting me, though she recently pined, erotically, over John Wayne, in a column in the *New York Times*. Had she forgotten that "the Duke" said he was all for women's liberation as long as they had dinner ready when he got home? In 1998, this Pulitzer Prize–winning *Times* critic threatened me with violence during my appearance on a New York University panel sponsored by the Black Genius series, a creation of novelist Walter Mosley. I found this odd because in her critique of *Louisiana Red* she opposed scenes in which violence was committed against women. (I was well aware that women could be just as ugly in their actions as men; when I was a kid, I was slapped around by white and black women for "trying to be cute" or "acting smart." I would tackle such middle-class feminist hypocrisy in my novel *Reckless Eyeballing*.)

Chapter 34 from *The Last Days of Louisiana Red* finds Papa LaBas on another case. In this situation, blacks who are hustling "revolution," with the encouragement of white liberal dabblers, are attempting to combat the forces of African-American tradition, here coded as "The Business." One of the liberals, Maxwell Kasavubu, has a dream in which he becomes characters in Richard Wright's novel *Native Son*. A spy is also undermining Ed Yellings, the master of Solid Gumbo Works, in his household, posing as a nanny.

In 1975, I received the Rosenthal Award from the National Institute of Arts and Letters as a result of their selecting *The Last Days of Louisiana Red* as the best noncommercial novel of the year. (To the consternation of some of my publishers, "noncommercial" has become my middle name.) After the ceremony, we gathered in a reception area at which many of the most famous American writers were present. I heard someone shout, "Ishmael Reed, you ain't nothin' but a gangster and a con artist." I turned to see Ralph Ellison, dressed in an expensive-looking blue suit, being led away by his wife, who was obviously embarrassed. Mr. Ellison was inebriated. I was speechless, but maybe I had it coming. When I first met Ellison in the mid-sixties at a salon sponsored by arts patron Pana Grady at the elite Dakota apartments on Manhattan's Upper West Side, I had asked him whether he'd written a great book, as the critics had said, or whether it was praised because Freudianism was the vogue. He walked away.

I had used *Invisible Man* in a class at the University of California at Berkeley and, after a close reading, concluded that Ellison had nodded to the values of the New York intelligentsia in his anti-Stalinism, Marxism, Existentialism,

Freudianism, anti-(Black) Nationalism and Modernism. His criticism of Black Historical Colleges recalled that of W. E. B. Dubois, who also believed that uncritically mimicking the ideas of white writers and thinkers would, in his words, "wed" one to the truth. Ellison congratulated Richard Wright for being "guided" by Freud and Marx. High culture for both meant the culture of European white men and their American imitators, and though he and his friends get called "the New York Intelligentsia," not one of them has contributed an original idea to world thought. Instead, they have a history of paying blind obeisance to European hand-me-down theories and rewarding only those who share their values.

The Ellison Jrs. and the other members of the cult may find it difficult to believe but John A. Williams and John O. Killens wrote books that were just as good as *Invisible Man*. Both authors were more prolific. Formalistically, Amiri Baraka, N. H. Pritchard and Ted Joans were further advanced than Ellison. Ernest Gaines's work is closer to the Blues, and Melvin Tolson was a superior Modernist and Gwendolyn Brooks a superior craftsperson. Toni Cade Bambara and J. J. Phillips are superior intellectuals.

So why was Ellison lionized? There are a number of reasons. The New York Literary Establishment was afraid of the competition from a wave of young 1960s African American writers. One of the few pieces he published after *Invisible Man* was a hit at Amiri Baraka, printed in the NYI's house organ, *The New York Review of Books*. And so part of Ellison's job was to keep the natives down, a designated role that he played for forty years. But Ellison's supporters also denied him the options they reserved for themselves. They could be separatists and integrationists, insiders and outsiders, ethnic and universal, whenever they pleased. Ellison could only be an American.

I thought about the Ellison outburst for years afterward, and I decided that in New York one could follow one of two models. One could surround oneself with groupies who followed the leader's path, that of coasting for a lifetime on little work and beating down the younger generation with sneers and one-liners, except for a handful of sycophants, or one could be a Langston Hughes, who encouraged and assisted the younger generation. One could write to please one's patrons or like John A. Williams, Chester Himes and John O. Killens tell the truth and be marginalized as a result.

The Ellison cult, with enormous academic and publicity support, is based upon the notion that black talent is rare, and that wherever it does appear, it's inferior. One of his Jrs. announced recently that Ellison viewed black literature as inadequate. When I interviewed Ralph Ellison, I asked him his opinion of a number of novels written by African American writers of the younger generation. He hadn't read any of them. And while Ellison's supporters dismiss those black writers who dared to question some of his literary and political theories as demagogues, or as "black militants," it is his supporters who are the demagogues because they give little indication that they have actually read the views of the Ellison opposition. I doubt whether even a few of them have read Larry Neal's articulate and cogent essay in *Black Fire*, edited by Amiri Baraka and Neal and titled "And Shine Swam On." Neal's challenge to the Ellisonian aesthetic is well argued. For Ellison's literary chickenheads, to challenge the "modernist master" is to be a "black militant" and therefore easily dismissed.

When I first met Malcolm X in 1961, for the first of what would be several lengthy conversations, our initial exchange was about history. Jimmy Lyons, a Buffalo disc jockey, in preparing for the show on which I would interview Malcolm, suggested that we discuss American history. I said to Malcolm X, like a smart aleck, that he would probably consider Black History to have been distorted. "It's cotton-patch history," he fired back. That really sat me down! He was right, of course. His comment took me back to the history I'd learned in school. The illustrations in our text books of Africans having a grand time, playing the banjo and dancing. Slavery was seen as one big party. A famous historian, in a class I took at the University of Buffalo, said that the "underground railroad," the network of friendly stops that would shepherd fugitive slaves to the North, was pretty much a myth. It wasn't until later that I learned on my own that Buffalo was an important stop—the last one before Canada—on the underground railroad. Researching my novel *Flight to Canada*, I discovered that William Wells Brown, an early African American novelist and agitator, had lived near the Buffalo church that I attended as a youngster.

Working on *Flight to Canada* introduced me to slave narratives and other materials that acquainted me with a history of the United States that I hadn't known and enabled me to see that much of the education I'd received was, as Malcolm X said, "cotton-patch" history. I wasn't surprised to learn years later, while reading Kenneth C. Davis's *Don't Know Much About the Civil War*, that the teaching of the Civil War has traditionally been based upon Margaret Mitchell's novel *Gone With the Wind*. I doubt whether any of those historians who've accused the Afrocentrics of making up history have objected. American journalists are often as obtuse as the historians. Recently, a journalist dismissed the wish of some African Americans to change the name of their school from Nathan B. Forrest as an exercise in political correctness, the phrase that's routinely used nowadays to dismiss any challenge to status quo readings of history. This Associated Press story, which was printed in the *New York Times*, defended Forrest as a smart guerilla warrior. Nowhere in the story was there a mention of the fact that soldiers under General Forrest's command massacred more than 300 black men, women and children, at Fort Pillow, Tennessee, even though they'd surrendered. After the war, Forrest became the first Grand Wizard of the Ku Klux Klan! I wrote the *Times* to set the record straight. The letter was not published.

Armed with information about slavery and the Civil War that hadn't been covered during my "education," I gleefully set about writing *Flight to Canada*. The passage excerpted here spoofs the fake Southern aristocracy and the cynicism of Abraham Lincoln and refers to four slaves who represent the different approaches used by Africans to deal with the situation in which they found themselves. Arthur Swille is a multinational tycoon who is above politics: He profits from the war, by financing both the Confederacy and the Union. In the scene, Swille is being attended by his faithful slave, Uncle Robin, who is questioned by Swille about some slaves who've run away, including Raven Quickskill, who was a sort of trustee of Swille's plantation prison. Their interview is interrupted by a visit from Abraham Lincoln, who is seeking financial aid for the Union cause.

*Flight to Canada* was published in 1976. I didn't publish another novel until 1982. During that period, I began collecting essays for a book and wrote plays. My first play, *Mother Hubbard,* was based upon my first novel, *The Free-Lance Pallbearers.* Staged readings of the play were held at Dartmouth, directed by Professor William Cook and at the Actors Studio in New York, where the character of Rudolph Greene, the house husband, was played by Clarence Williams III. My first book of essays, *Shrovetide in Old New Orleans,* was published in 1978. If, as Mel Watkins said, the book showed the author "Floating like a butterfly and stinging like a bee," by the time I returned to writing novels, I had developed a killer instinct.

In 1979, after residing in "liberated zones" and the suburbs for a number of years, I moved to an Oakland neighborhood of the sort that is described by the media as "tough" and "inner city." My writing was affected by this change. Appalled at what I found there—criminal operations permitted to go on unchecked, denial of services that are taken for granted in affluent white neighborhoods, people, whose behavior is blamed for their plight by intellectual sluts, trying their best to fend for themselves—my writing became more direct, especially those works that were based upon my experiences in this district. My play, *Hubba City,* about the Oakland drug crisis, is an example of this change. Though my former interests would appear in my novels and sometimes in my poetry, I was no longer distant, careening through a literary Milky Way, but was standing at Ground Zero as well.

With *The Terrible Twos,* published in 1982, I also began what I call my "Writin' Is Fightin'" period. I found that most of the people living in this "inner-city" area are decent and law abiding, but the actions of a small minority are seized upon by politicians, the media and an army of nasty, cruel op-ed writers, self-loathing ex-ethnics who get paid for lazily recycling the same old tired stereotypes, yet they dare to call inner-city residents lazy and idle. There's nothing like living at "Ground Zero" to understand the lay of the land. Something that you can't assess from Harvard or from Martha's Vineyard, or from an espresso cafe in Greenwich Village or Monterey.

*The Terrible Twos* and *The Terrible Threes,* though disguised as innocent Christmas novels, took on the mean-spirited Age of Reagan, which saw the abandonment of the poor, and the introduction of crack cocaine into the black communities so that the government might achieve some foreign policy goals, a situation from which black neighborhoods are finally slowly recovering.

In *The Terrible Twos,* Dean Clift, an apolitical former fashion model, is made president by Big Business. He goes into mourning after his wife is electrocuted while lighting the White House Christmas tree. Experiencing a deep funk—"a dark night of the soul"—he is escorted to the American underworld by Saint Nicholas, where he encounters ex-politicians whose deeds have brought them eternal punishment. Some of them implore him to help the downtrodden so that he might escape their fate. After he delivers a speech endorsing the Bill of Rights, the 26th Amendment is invoked by Rev. Clement Jones and his puppet president, Jesse Hatch. A zombie Santa Claus who is manipulated by a radical but fake Rastafarian makes a socialist-sounding speech before outraged department store owners and politicians. There is also a conspiracy underway called Operation Two Birds. *The Terrible Twos* uses fantasy and science fiction and recalls the social realist style, but most readers and critics understood that I was writing about the present. If some readers found those novels of the 1980s *(The Terrible Twos, Reckless Eyeballing* and *The Terrible Threes)* hard to take—one writer said that reading Ishmael Reed was like having a kidney stone—it's perhaps because they were written from another neighborhood. A neighborhood where I could look out the window and view the consequences of the mean-spirited Reagan period on African Americans. The excerpt printed here includes the Santa Claus speech, and the president's visit to the American underworld.

*Reckless Eyeballing* was written in the spirit of Ghede, a descendant of the Yoruba Iku, whose task is to show "each man his devil." In the book, Ian Ball, a black playwright, has to cater to New York feminists in order to get his play staged. Tremonisha Smarts is appointed his dramaturg and helps him edit his play so that all material offensive to feminists is removed. Also included in the plot are the activities of a "Flower Phantom" who wanders through the novel shaving the heads of feminists, a practice used in France and elsewhere to punish women who collaborated with the Nazis. The novel does a send-up about the conflict between blacks and Jews, and though some characters make philo-Semitic speeches and others make anti-Semitic speeches, the novel was accused of promoting anti-Semitism in the *New York Times* by Michiko Kakutani, who regularly praises novels with racist features. This critic also came down hard on what she considered the novel's misogyny, even though she has published worshipful interviews with some of the most notorious of white male sexist novelists, John Updike and Saul Bellow. *Reckless Eyeballing* tackled the hypocrisies and contradictions of the feminist movement, and powerful members of that movement and their followers struck back. White feminists at the Louisiana State University in Baton Rouge threatened a boycott of my appearance there, but the boycott failed when it was discovered that none of the protestors had read my books. In the late eighties, as a result of *Reckless Eyeballing*, I was left for literary roadkill, and ironically, it was a group with whom I'd feuded during the 1960s, the Chicago nationalists, who supported me during this period.

Though I had been smeared as a hater of black women, it was black women who defended me as well. Producers Gail Reid and Nora Vaughn of the Bay View Opera House and the Black Repertory Theatre staged my plays. And *Hubba City*, which was dismissed by a San Francisco white male critic as misogynist, was staged in Washington, D.C., through the efforts of black media feminists. Two black writers, Gwen Carmen and J. J.Phillips, debated white feminists, who stuck me with the "M" word. When white San Francisco feminists demanded that playwright Ntozake Shange condemn me, she refused.

Finally, Henry Louis Gates, Jr., who was recently called by *The Economist* "the chief interpreter of African American culture to the white establishment," did a hit piece on me as a sexist, after he'd accused Richard Wright and

Ralph Ellison of the same crime. I figured he'd become the grand inquisitor of black male misogynists in order to deflect criticism from angry black feminists, like Michele Wallace, who had complained that he'd become the number one black feminist, as a result of his presiding over the growing number of black feminist cultural projects. He and his colleagues had done considerable bad-mouthing of black men as misogynists in order to finagle feminist sales, and course adoptions, but when First Sexist was caught with his pants down, Gates and his friends promised President Clinton that they'd go to the wall for him. The neo-liberal and neo-conservative publications who invented them aren't concerned about the inconsistencies of their Talented Tenth as long as they mimic the editorial line that the problems of the black "underclass" are a result of their personal behavior, a point of a view that has about as much thought as a chicken's. Gates can't get through a speech without citing 35-year-old grandmothers living in the projects, even though the black out-of-wedlock birth rate is the lowest since 1960. In his PBS series on Africa, he emphasized the African supply side of the slave trade so as to convince the targeted market of his cultural products that they were guilt-free merchandise. The neo-conservatives who praised this TV series for its "painful" truths about the African supply side of the slave trade are among those who usually blame the drug problem on the demand side. Moreover, when presented with an opportunity to present the demand side of the trans-Atlantic slave trade and its consequences, Ken Burns, producer of the pro-Confederate "The Civil War," said that viewers would find the issue of slavery "boring."

I've chosen chapters 18–22 from *Reckless Eyeballing* in which Ian Ball is awaiting the audience's response to his play about Ham Hill (Emmett Till) and the vindication of a woman whom he has recklessly eyeballed. ("Reckless eyeballing" is the Southern term for a black man who looks at a white woman the wrong way, sometimes with dire consequences; its existence is another reason why racism should be examined by trained professionals, like Drs. Allen Pouissant and Michael LeNoir, instead of pundits and public intellectuals out to market their ideological goods.) The play has been rewritten so that it accommodates the values of feminists. In Chaper 19, Ball views the play that is being shown on the theatre's main stage. *Eva's Revenge,* which portrays Hitler's mistress as an incipient feminist, has been made the theatre's main attraction by the feminist producer, Becky French. In Chapter 21, Ball discovers that, for his bowing to the wishes of the feminists, his name has been removed from the Sex List, the 1980s version of the Black List, which rates male playwrights according to their degree of misogyny.

In *The Terrible Threes* I continue to explore the co-dependent relationship between Black Peter and Saint Nicholas begun in *The Terrible Twos*. Black Peter and Saint Nicholas are part of the Christmas pageant in the Netherlands and elsewhere. During the course of the novel, Peter assists people with their personal problems. In two of the chapters included in this book, he rescues a Japanese American literary groupie and a turkey, continuing my use of animal characters begun in *Mother Hubbard*. The imposter Black Peter appears in a hotel scene, and discovers that the real Black Peter has returned. The fake Black Peter gets credit for his miracles. Nola Payne, a Supreme Court Justice, is visited by the ghost of Judge Taney, of Dred Scott fame, and like Dean Clift, has a change of mind. Though *The Terrible Threes* samples Dickens, a book called *Dreds*, which I was introduced to during a teaching stint at Dartmouth, as well as the plays of Plautus, also influenced the writing of the *Terribles*. According to *Dreds*, Rastafarianism believes that individuals may be redeemed, and some Plautine plays end in reconciliation. In a review I considered a clear case of literary sabotage, the book was dismissed by an Ellison, Jr., in the *New York Times* as not making sense.

At the age of fifty I decided never again to place myself in a position where my success or failure was determined by the whims of whatever messianic clique was wielding power in American literary circles. The result was a novel that took my writing into a new direction: *Japanese by Spring*. While attending a conference on African American literature in Paris, during the early 1990s, I participated in a press conference where I said that Paris was no longer the center of world culture and that an artist could find as much inspiration in Tokyo or Accra. This remark was greeted with groans from the French in the audience but applause from the rest of the Europeans attending the press conference. I had been studying Japanese and Yoruba since 1989, but had no idea, when I blurted out this remark, how I would get to Japan or Africa. Before the end of the 1990s, I was to travel to both places. *Japanese by Spring* was the novel that took me across the border away from the literary planters and their black slave catchers. It earned me a tour of Japan, where the novel was greeted warmly. Japanese readers were delighted when I autographed their books in Katakana.

In February 1999 I visited Nigeria and renewed friendships which I had made during a trip to Ghana in 1996, including the grand old man of Nigerian letters, Cyprian Ekwesi, whom, along with other African writers, I have published in my Zine, *Konch*. On my last day in Lagos I read poems I had written in their language. During the nineties, as a result of my trips to Nigeria and Japan,

I began to realize that I had wasted energies by engaging in local literary brawls. Brawls confined to a small ring. I had been like the physicist's fish, swimming in a pond with no awareness of other dimensions tugging at it. Those critics who had knocked me during my career had done me a favor. It was because of them that I became a world-class writer.

*The Reed Reader* also includes a sampling of my nonfiction, poetry and plays. "The Fourth Ali," my report on the second Muhammad Ali–Leon Spinks fight, was commissioned by Rudy Langlais, a former editor at the *Village Voice*. This assignment gave me an opportunity to travel to one of my favorite cities. The Big Easy. I spent my time attending prefight ceremonies and ordering up food to my room from the restaurant located next door to the hotel. Being a fight fan and a news junkie were two obsessions I inherited from my stepfather, so it was probably inevitable that I would cover a fight. Instead of giving a blow-by-blow description of the combat, I tried to show the atmosphere surrounding the fight. I left the description of the fight to the trainers, whom I interviewed after the fight.

"Shrovetide in Old New Orleans," which is also the title to a book of my essays published in 1978, was based on an assignment from *Oui*, which some would call a "girlie" magazine. I was provided with a car and an expense account which, in my mind, required me to produce the best copy I was capable of. Looking back on this assignment, I can understand why some of my companions during this visit, Toni Morrison, Rudy Lombard and the late Toni Cade Bambara and Tom Dent, might have been annoyed with me. Morrison, Bambara and Gloria Smart, James Baldwin's sister, were living in the French Quarter. I was nervous and tense, uptight, trying to nail down the story of Mardi Gras while attempting to be social. It didn't work out, and Tom Dent and I got into some testy exchanges. I was abrupt and cross at times. I could see why my spleenishness would turn off my companions, all of whom went on to accomplish great deeds. Toni Morrison won the Nobel Prize for literature. Toni Cade Bambara produced a great novel, *The Salt Eaters*. Tom Dent, before his death, published *Southern Journey* and Rudy Lombard ran for Mayor of New Orleans. After many trials and errors, I learned how to write an essay.

I think some of the New Orleans writers became annoyed with my forays into their town and writing about their culture. Can't blame them. This delicious city was noted for its diversity long before the word became popular. People of all backgrounds and skin colors. From the wealthy in their mansions on Charles Street to the people who live off po'boy sandwiches. Walking down Canal Street, a few months ago, I decided that the passersby were among the pool that Jerry Springer tapped for his show. If you travel through Louisiana, Tennessee and the state of Washington, you can get a glimpse of those people whom the media hide from their consumers, the white underclass. In Alaska, they live in trailer camps and compete with the natives for resources.

"God Made Alaska for the Indians" appeared in the book of essays with the same name. This essay came about as a result of one of those strange coincidences that writers often experience. I visited a high school in San Francisco that was so tough that when I came out to get into my car, I found a coat hanger that had been used in an unsuccessful attempt to steal my car. While talking to the students, in the library, I noticed some books about the myths of the Tlingit Indians of the Northwest, carvers of those beautiful totem poles which have fascinated people all over the world. Later, I did further research on these myths and took a stab at using the myth of the Raven in *Flight to Canada*. A friend of mine, Bob Callahan, had a friend, Andy Hope, a Tlingit "Big Man," who said that he'd read *Flight to Canada* and wanted me to visit Alaska. I did. "God Made Alaska for the Indians" is about this trip. This was in 1979, and it was the beginning of a period in which I developed contacts with writers from different ethnic groups. These contacts culminated in the production of my anthology *Multi-America*, which includes the work of Italian Americans, Irish Americans, German Americans, Asian Americans, Native Americans and African Americans.

The essay "Airing Dirty Laundry," which was published in a book of essays bearing the same name, was my response to the denigration of African Americans by the media. I came to the conclusions reached in this essay almost by accident. In my first book of essays, *Shrovetide in Old New Orleans*, I, like many African American intellectuals before and since, including both Booker T. Washington and W. E. B. DuBois, had addressed the "pathologies" among what's been called the "black underclass." That changed when I was invited to respond to Pete Hamill's "Letter to a Black Friend" in *Esquire* magazine. During my preparation for writing this article, I discovered that the so-called pathologies ascribed to the "black underclass" existed in other ethnic groups, including Hamill's own: Irish Americans. Hamill accused the black underclass of drinking too much liquor, yet he later published a book about his problems with alcohol entitled *A Drinking Life*.

After examining the media since the publication of "Airing Dirty Laundry," I've come to several conclusions. One, as long as there are money and ratings in it, African Americans will continue to be scapegoated for the social problems of the country, regardless of facts which show these problems to be as widespread in other groups. Two, though it's trendy to say that to attack African Americans requires courage and a defiance of politically correct standards, attacking blacks is all that we get from Hollywood, TV and the news media, all segregated operations: the "pathologies" that exist in other communities are concealed by a code of silence, while those among African Americans are on public display, daily, especially those of black men. Finally, the less white one is in American society, the more difficulties one will experience in everyday life.

This book includes two essays that address the dilemma of African American males in American Society: an introduction to Eldridge Cleaver's book *Soul on Ice*, and "Bigger and O.J.," an examination of how O. J. Simpson and Bigger Thomas were treated by the media and the criminal justice system. The situation of black men and women as well as darker people all over the world is ignored by those who dominate the cultural life of this country. They can only see white. It's not that blacks and people of color are invisible to them. They simply can't see. Even someone as gifted and astute as George Orwell, whose "Politics and the English Language" was a major influence on my writing, ignored the fact that for millions of people the world over 1984 had been happening for hundreds of years. Big Brother has always been a problem for African Americans. Government agencies still try to sting black politicians; my play *Savage Wilds* is about the entrapment of Marion Barry, at the time mayor of Washington, D.C., —of which sting even the conservative columnist William Safire said, "Never before has the United States government stooped so low." The reason that black kids are ten times as likely to go to jail for committing the same crime as white kids is because they are subjected to more surveillance and what Jerome Miller calls "Search and Destroy" missions.

The *Reader* also includes the play *Hubba City*, about elderly members of a neighborhood Crime Alert program and their struggles with a crack dealer. In fiction and drama one is allowed to speculate and so this play tackles the subject of government complicity in the introduction of crack into black neighborhoods, a fact later verified by journalist Gary Webb. Massachusetts Senator John Kerry also claims that key government agencies knew that the Reagan and Bush administrations were aligning themselves with drug dealers. This play also enabled me to discuss a factor that contributed to the decline of crime rates all over the United States. The participation by black citizens in the effort to take back their neighborhoods while the media gives all of the credit to the police.

Besides the sheer enjoyment of working in the theatre, I began writing plays to create roles for black actors that would challenge their talents and provide them with opportunities missing on the mainstream stage and in the movies. Beginning with a staged reading of my play *Mother Hubbard* at the Actors Studio in 1981, five plays have been staged in New York, Oakland and San Francisco.

While much of my recent writing comes under the category of "writin' is fightin'," when I write poetry I am taking my soul out for a sail. I've been writing poetry since I was a young person and this volume includes a sampling of work written over the years. Some of the poetry and songs have been set to music and produced on record by Kip Hanrahan. They can be found on *Conjure I*, and *Conjure II Cab Calloway Stands in for the Moon*, both distributed by Rounder Records. One of the high points in my literary career was when I toured Europe with the Ishmael Reed Band. Jack Bruce of Creme and the venerable Little Jimmy Scott sang my songs and poetry and David Murray and Billy Bang performed them.

Despite my kvetching and grouching and b-word-ing, I have been more successful than most writers black, white, red, yellow and brown, and within the last few years, I have received recognition that was denied artists whose work is as good or even superior to mine. My main complaint is that voiced by many writers. The role that middlepersons have played in preventing me from reaching an audience. Forty years of boxing on paper has been what a modernist might call a blissful agony for me, but the issue I complained about in the 1960s is still a problem of the African American writer. Powerful interests still define the scope of the African American culture. In the 1990s, the impudent and defiant aspects of Afro American culture are considered to be uncool and have been replaced by the quiet and less "anxious." Powerful tastemakers still appoint "czars" of so-called minority literatures.

*The Reed Reader* is a sampling of fiction, nonfiction, poetry, songs and theatre published and performed since the 1960s. Since writing is a lifetime pursuit, and great artists are rare, this volume is a midcareer report on the progress of a pretty good writer who has written day after day, and year after year, plodding along and giving the craft his best, and sometimes his worst, shot. Although there has been pressure on me to produce what the trade calls a "blockbuster," I have been lucky to have editors who've risked their careers by giving me the freedom to write the kind of books I felt most comfortable writing. I have taken risks. Some of the techniques I have employed have succeeded and some have fallen flat on their faces. But there have been far more victories than defeats. As people of my generation used to say: It's been a gas.

ISHMAEL REED
Oakland, California
November 17, 1999

THE REED READER

**NOVELS**

## AN OLD WOMAN KIDNAPS CHECKERS

AND I ran until I stumbled over a man who was lying face down in the street. My heels spun as I flew into a row of garbage cans causing the lids to tumble clanging into the gutter. In front of the spent form rested a giant ball of light manure. Thinking that the man might be ill, I went over to him and tugged at his armpits. Lying next to his body was a piece of luggage upon which were pasted stickers with the names of several Western capitals. Aroused, he slowly turned over and rubbed his eyes. I recognized him at once! It was my old professor from the Harry Sam College, U2 Polyglot, working out some empirical problems of his paper, "The Egyptian Dung Beetle in Kafka's 'Metamorphosis.'"

"Bukka, my boy," he said as he sat upright in the street. "What are you doing outdoors during this grave crisis? All citizens have been advised to remain inside with their shades drawn and their fingers crossed."

"I was on my way home before I fell into you, professor," I answered.

He lit a pipe which he removed from the luggage at his side and continued to examine me. "My boy," he finally said, "you look a little weak. I mean, those pointed ears and hooves. What are you trying to do, get on a quiz show or something?"

I told him of the setbacks I had received since leaving the Harry Sam College: the fights with Fannie Mae; my physical and spiritual deterioration; my increasing doubts as to the validity of the Nazarene discipline.

When he heard the last of these downcomings, the pipe nearly fell from his lips. "You've not kept up with the faith! That indeed is serious. You must get right down on your knees and repeat after me."

The thinned tweed of U2 Polyglot's knees met the street and I knelt next to him as he chanted: "HARRY SAM does not love us. If he did, he would come out of the John and hold us in his lap. We must walk down the street with dem signs in our hands. We must throw back our heads and loosen our collars. We must bawl until he comes out of dere and holds us like it was before the boogeyman come on the scene and everybody went to church and we gave each other pickle jars each day and nobody had acne or bad breath and cancer was just the name of a sign."

The professor—after the manner of the Nazarene Bishops—lifted his nose from the street with great dignity. He then looked both ways and whispered into my ear: 'Look, Bukka. I know that you've been afflicted with the hoodoo. That's no disgrace; why in the 'bad ol days' they took the hoodooed, bound their paws, gagged them and made them lie on straw mats. But in this enlightened period, we take a more scientific view of this disease and that my boy is precisely what it is—a disease and not a curse."

He shook his head sadly, then said, "The life of a scholar has its ups and downs, Bukka. We try to lift the spiritual sights of mankind and what do we get? These piddling allowances from the state for projects in the humanities, such as the one in which I'm now engaged. The grant I received for pushing this goddamn ball all over Europe is not enough to keep me in good pipe tobacco—so I've taken to a little hustlin'* on the side. You see, there's this ol woman with two bricks for breasts who was taking conjure lessons through the mail under the Mojo Power Retraining Act. The other day while experimenting she came upon a recipe for allaying the symptoms and even curing advanced stages of hoodoo fever. I've been selling the stuff like hotcakes in Europe, scene of mysterious hoodoo epidemics and I get five per cent on each bottle sold."

He removed a bottle from the luggage which I tried to wrest from his hand, so eager was I to return to my normal self.

"Not so fast," he said, gripping the bottle. "That'll be five mazumas."

I shoved the bills into his hand which he totaled, licking his thumb after each count. I unscrewed the bottle's cap and poured the solution down my throat. I became itchy and nauseous. Convulsing and retching, I held my hips

---

* Readers will note that U2 Polyglot is quite adept at the use of slang. This is because his position at the Harry Sam College was that of Chairman of the Department of American Studies.

with crossed arms. My nostrils bristled from the sharp odor of the fluid and hair began to fall away from my body. Fangs dropped from my mouth, and falling into the street, broke into fine crystals. My feet began to shake involuntarily as if stricken.

"Thank you, professor," I said to U2 Polyglot, as I began to feel a new lease on life.

"That's all right," he said, lighting up his benevolent eyes, those soft eyes which looked like chick-peas. I still have faith that you will become a fine Nazarene Bishop, one of these days; I only hope that I will be able to follow your career."

I was about to bid him farewell when suddenly a jeep full of Screws pulled up next to the ball whose greenish-brown flakes shone in the moonlight. One Screw stood up in the vehicle as soon as it screeched to a halt and aimed a turkey musket at our heads.

"What is this crap?" he shouted. "Why aren't you citizens indoors like everybody else? Haven't you been informed of the curfew?"

I was scared to death, but the professor seemed unperturbed as the Screw's fingers fidgeted with the trigger of the turkey musket. U2 Polyglot removed some officious-looking papers bearing the greenish-brown seal of HARRY SAM from his vest pocket. The Screw's eyes popped after he inspected them. He grinned meekly, then snapped to a stiff salute and clicked his heels. "Forgive me, Your Excellency, for interfering with a top-secret project."

"That's all right," U2 Polyglot replied. "We must all be on guard against enemies of HARRY SAM."

The Screw saluted, then shouted something to the other four who were huddled together in the back seat of the jeep. The vehicle jerked forward then backward and skidded around the corner on two wheels.

"Well, Bukka," the professor said. "I have to get back to work. Take it easy, kid." With this said, he lodged his nose in the ball of manure and with aplomb and correctness began pushing it down the street. I waved, until U2 Polyglot became a dark speck on the horizon. The projects were settled in heavy gloom. Hundreds of candles flickered behind the yellow curtains of the narrow cubicles. The sirens wailed throughout the area, and men holding flashlights trotted through the streets. The Nazarene apprentices from the universities—looking like sick dust mops—were dispensing coffee and doughnuts to the volunteers. I went into my apartment and turned on radio station UH-O. Reports of the crisis in the Harry Sam John were coming in from all over the world:

Because of the grave crisis in the Harry Sam John, the Pope has called in all Bingo cards. Appearing on the balcony of his Vatican apartment and waving his crooked finger over a restless throng, the Pontiff said that "Under no circumstances would last week's Bingo results be revealed."

A milling crowd booed as the Swiss guards rolled wheelbarrows up to the Sistine Chapel and dumped tons of Bingo cards. Early-morning raids were staged in key Latin American cities as bootleg Bingo games were broken up. On Mulberry Street in Lower Manhattan, mobs pelleted police, hooted and cursed as they yelled: "Give us Bingo or shoot us." Although a spokesman has said that last week's Bingo results are walled up in a secret room in the Vatican protected by three Spanish cardinals, informed sources here say they've been passed on to the American ambassador. They are: B6, I16, N26, FREE, G33, O43. The State Department has issued a flat denial.

I shut off the radio and began to repair the house which was still in shambles from my strife with Fannie Mae. The lamps were overturned. Ashtrays lay scattered on the rug and chairs were broken into splinters. Dead plants lay in soiled spots near broken vases. I stretched my arms, yawned, then went into the kitchen and downed a bottle of beer. I then went into the bedroom, removed my clothes, curled up into a ball, threw the covers over my head and went to sleep.

At about twelve o'clock loud reports of gunfire came from the island. I ran to the window and raised the shades. Shadows moved behind the curtains of the other apartments. Frightened tenants looked out of their windows and across the bay to the Harry Sam Motel which stood at the summit of his mountain. The sky above the motel blazed a bright red, lighting up the night as if it were day. The sign on the roof of the motel blinked on and off rapidly: EATS EATS EATS EATS EATS EATS EATS EATS EATS EATS. I hurried back to bed with both arms outstretched and hit the sheets with such a thud the planks nearly collapsed.

*People are walking on the deck of a ship. Seated in two chairs are Dick and Pat Nixon and their dog, Checkers. Dick is signing autographs for a group of maimed war veterans who stand before the family, some on stumps and some on crutches and walking canes. One mutilated G.I. is blind and he bumps into the deck chair jarring Pat Nixon who smiles and returns to her knitting. Two other men appear. They are dressed fancier than the others. One says, "It was much better in Egypt at the time of the two* cities, Matthew, The artists and dreamers lived in one and the slaves lived in the other." They walk to the rail and lean over looking below at the hundreds of hands holding paddles which stick from the portholes. One man removes a small bottle of acid from his pocket, unscrews the top and pours it on one of the hands. The flesh of the hand falls away and drops into the water. A piercing scream is heard below. The man's companion falls to the deck and banging his fists on the boards, dies laughing. Pat Nixon is not amused; she walks over to the rail and jots down their names. She then returns to her chair and sits down in a huff. An ol woman appears. Under her armpit she carries the Christmas issue of the Reader's Digest (stars, snow and reindeer on a blue cover). The lead article is "Should Dolphins Go Steady—33 Parents Reply." She stoops over and pretends to pat Checkers. The Nixons and the war veterans are charmed by the sweet ol soul. Suddenly the ol woman swoops Checkers into her arms and splits. The Nixons and the soldiers hobbling on their crutches and artificial limbs give chase shaking their fists and shouting.

In the stateroom there is an orchestra of men in white dinner jackets entertaining ol generals with songs from the "bad ol days." Songs such as "Faraway Places with Strange-Sounding Names" and strains of "Don't Fence Me In" are heard. Betty Grable appears through the curtains to thunderous applause. She bends a knee and holds her left hip with her left hand and with the other hand touches the back of her hair—which is arranged in an upsweep; the ol men put their fingers between their teeth and whistle. Others stamp their feet and say, "Hip, hip, hooray." A crash is heard outside the stateroom as a deck chair overturns. The ol woman appears at the entrance holding a yipping dog. She speeds across the room in her black sneakers knocking the ol generals from their tables. The stateroom empties as the ol men chase the widow executioner holding the cocker spaniel being chased by the Nixons followed by . . . or is it the war veterans chasing the generals who are chasing the Nixons? Anyway, the Nixons and the soldiers enter the stateroom. Betty Grable says, "They went thataway." The entire string section rises with their violin bows pointed to the direction of the other exit. The ol woman jumps to the top of the rail and holding her nose and the dog under her armpit dives into the drink and starts making it out to sea plowing the water with lusty breast strokes. Tricky Dick and the Mrs. followed by the soldiers are not far behind.

Betty Grable's chance for a comeback has been spoiled. She sits on the stage brooding, eating a Hershey bar and holding her jaw in her hand. Not to be outdone she gets up and says to the orchestra, "Come on, boys." The ol woman followed by the four men followed by the generals followed by the Nixons followed by the war veterans followed by Betty Grable followed by the orchestra swim toward the skyline in single file.

Dawn. Only a few volleys of gunfire are heard. I went to the window and raised the shades. An object appears at the mouth of one of the statues of the nineteenth President of the United States resting upon the imposing slope of Sam's Island. It is a white coffin which plunks into the bay. Another coffin appears. Then 4–5–10–14. The dingy cloud above the motel lifts. The sun shows through. At eleven A.M. there is a bulletin.

LATEST ATTEMPT TO JAM UP THE WORKS FOILED. ECLAIR PORKCHOP A HERO AS HE ACTS AS A HUMAN PUMP DISLODGING THE BANTAM ROOSTER FEATHERS CONSPIRATORS USED TO PLUG THE PIPES.

Things were returning to normal in the big not-to-be-believed nowhere. Walking through the projects to work I saw women trudging to the laundromats with baskets of dirty clothes. The men were stepping onto the chartered buses that would take them to the Harry Sam Ear Muffle Factory. Carrying brown bags full of sandwiches, they walked resignedly with their heads bowed. The children were merrily playing on the amusement truck; romping over the stainless steel gnomes, giraffes and jackals and little trickster figures with long noses and stocking caps on their heads.

When I reached the hospital I unlocked the door with my passkey and went into the lounge of the psychiatric unit which was used by the orderlies to change their clothes and relax on their coffee breaks. Two orderlies were conversing while another stared at the center page of a popular men's magazine which displayed a cadaver that was studying esoteric pharmacology at the N/School of Social Research.

"Yeah, it gone be a good break for somebody. Say the man come in lass night jessa screamin' and hollin'. Nurse Rosemary D Camp promises that the orderly chosen to take care of him will get a five-dollar raise. Sho hopes it bees me."

"Me too," said the other orderly, turning to me as I buttoned my short-sleeved white shirt. "Doopeyduk, you heah 'bout the man come in the hospital last night jessa screamin' and hollin'?"

"No," I answered coldly, not wishing to encourage fraternizing with the other orderlies from Soulsville whom I considered lowly ruttish lumpen.

"Say he come in lass night talkin' all out hee head. Nurse Rosemary D Camp say who evah takes care o him good gone get a five-dollar raise."

There was a rap at the door of the orderlies' lounge. The men hurriedly stamped out their cigarettes and pushed the fumes through the opened window. Nurse Rosemary D Camp peeked in and her singsong voice said, "Mr. Doopeyduk, will you please come into my office?

"Yes, Mrs. Nurse Rosemary D Camp," I replied nervously. "I'll be down as fast as I can."

When I entered the room she invited me to sit in a chair next to her desk. She was a fat woman with a round doll-like face with rouged cheeks. Her arms were thick as hams and showed small dents here and there from the shoulders to her fingers resting on the desk. Hanging from beneath her cap were long twisted pigtails; pinned to the blouse of her uniform she wore a purple orchid upside down.

"Mr. Doopeyduk," she began, "Mishaps are bound to happen in an operation such as the one in which we are engaged on Unit Five. So I think that we might have been a little harsh with you after your accident with the patient who was here a few weeks ago." She smiled at me while I squirmed in the chair. "Otherwise we've found that you've been conscientious in many other matters arising in the course of your duties. So we've decided, Mr. Doopeyduk, to give you a special assignment for this evening. Your performance on this assignment will indicate to us whether you're ready for larger responsibilities."

"Mrs. Nurse Rosemary D Camp," I said, "I will certainly do my best to warrant your confidence."

"Good, then," she replied. "This is your assignment. There was an old man admitted to the floor last night. I'm afraid he's delirious and raving. We want you to get samples so that we can analyze them. He has meningitis and typhoid complicated by double pneumonia. You will be given a surgeon's mask and we want you to give him lots of fluids and rub his back with powder. Then at the conclusion to your shift we want you to make out a report on him."

I jumped to my feet and started for the door.

"One minute, Mr. Doopeyduk, we have a little surprise for you." She opened the drawer and pulled out A GOLDEN BEDPAN WITH MY INITIALS ENGRAVED ON THE BOTTOM.

I was all choked up. "I don't know what to say, Mrs. Nurse Rosemary D Camp."

"That's all right, Mr. Doopeyduk," the nurse said. "We're sure that you will prove yourself worthy."

I opened the door, knocking over the three orderlies who had their ears fastened to the keyhole. Ignoring them I walked to the old man's room with my nose upturned and holding the bedpan engraved with my initials.

The old man had been placed in a secluded ward. He lay under an oxygen tent in the bed, next to which was a floor lamp exuding a soft violet glow. He wore a damp waist-length nightgown and his bony knees were propped up under his hamstrings by pillows. His wrists were bound to the side rail and his eyes were two black dots. A thin layer of skin stretched around the small skeletal outlines of his face. I read the chart which hung at the foot of his bed.

Man: White male gave his name as Roger Young Ist. About 89 years old. Admitted to the floor at 2:00 A.M. Only possession—a musty can of newsreel entitled Versailles zgig. He fought five orderlies for the can yelling, "Gimmie back my newsreel, I want my newsreel." Scratched and bit and spat on them until he was subdued with vesperin. Went to sleep about 5 A.M.

Diagnosis: Schizoid with paranoid tendencies. Keeps muttering, "The Huns raping the nuns."

I changed the man every five minutes until the corner of the room was filled with sticky wet sheets. I applied the powder and gave him a rubdown.

He finally went off to sleep. The room was quiet. I sat in a chair next to his bed leafing through a magazine. At about 6:30 P.M. he suddenly rose, lurched forward and pointed a long bent finger toward the open door of the room.

"Save me! They're in the door! The Free-Lance Pallbearers are in the door! Look, look! The long frock coats and shiny black boots, the black box! It's them! They're going to try to take ol Roger Ist away from here! Please save me, ooooo, save me, no! Get back! Get back! Arra! Ggggg! Grggrrrrgrrg! Rrgrgrgrrrrgrgrrrgrrrrrrr g . . . . . . . . . . r . . . . . . . . . . !"

I ran through the door of the room and into the nurses' quarters. "Mrs. Nurse Rosemary D Camp! Please hurry—the old man is hallucinating; he seems to be having an attack of some sort."

All the orderlies and doctors ran clomping down the hall toward the room. But it was too late. The old man had given up the ghost.

We washed him, wrapped him in a shroud and placed him in a basket. He was then rolled into the morgue and placed in an ice-cold tray. (One of the morgue attendants was to say later that upon making a routine inspection be found the corpse holding the can of newsreel in a death clutch.)

It was the end of my shift. I filled out the report on the deceased and gave it to the nurse. "Thank you, Mr. Doopeyduk," she said. "You made the poor ol man's last hours as comfortable as possible. We'll be calling on you in the future for more tasks like these."

One of the orderlies helped me with my coat. "I will do my best to justify your faith in me," I told the nurse. (I detected a snicker from the orderly who was helping me with the garment, but I ignored him, attributing it to jealousy on his part.) I walked out into the streets of Soulsville toward home. The crisis over, the convoys of plumbers in battleships headed from Harry Sam Island toward the pier. They leaned over the rails of the ships guffing down the hot dogs and beer.

In Soulsville banners hung over the street. WELCOME SOULSVILLE'S OWN ECLAIR PORKCHOP. Barricades had been set up and Screws linked bands holding back the crowd which had come out to greet the newly appointed bishop. They were not to be disappointed because the parade turned out to be quite a spectacle. I lined up with the crowd to get a better view of the goings-on.

The first car in the procession was a big sleek Rolls Royce. The body of the car was painted lavender and the hood was a frieze depicting the Nazarene apocalypse. It was painted in wild wiggy colors.

It showed HARRY SAM the dictator and former Polish used-car salesman sitting on the great commode. In his lap sat a businessman, a Nazarene apprentice and a black slum child. These figures represented the just. Standing on each side of the dictator were four washroom attendants. In their hands they had seven brushes, seven combs, seven towels, and seven bars of soap, a lock of Roy Rogers' hair and a Hershey bar. Above the figures float Lawrence Welk champagne bubbles. Below this scene tombstones have been rolled aside and the Nazarene faithful are seen rising in a mist with their hands reaching out to the figure sitting on the commode.

There were purple velvet curtains on the windows of the car. Through the drapes of the back window was a wrinkled yellow hand. On one of the fingers was a large sardonyx ring.

It was Nancy Spellman, Chief Nazarene Bishop. It was a crime punishable by death to look at him directly so the people bowed their heads and closed their eyes. Following the automobile on foot were the Nazarene Bishops. They wore Dobbs hats and double-breasted suits with ball-point pens sticking from their pockets. Carnations were pinned to their lapels.

Next came a black Pierce-Arrow. A chauffeur's velvet glove gripped the car wheel. He sat next to a bottle of Fleischmann's which was as large as his body from the waist up. A spindly old woman sat next to him waving a long cigarette holder and dangling her leg over the car door.

She was holding her hands together responding to the cheers of the crowd. In the rear half of the car, through the roof, some plastic antlers appeared. The woman wore a green satin dress under a black bolero jacket. She wore a diamond ring on every other finger of her hands. Sparkling green mascara was smeared to the edge of her plucked-out eyebrows. Her hair was tinted blue-silver and frizzed in a permanent wave. A white ermine stole with black tails was thrown across her neck and dripped down her back. A heavy beaded necklace hung to her stomach. It was my father-in-law's mother and the bitch was dressed to kill. The automobile pulled to a halt. The chauffeur climbed out and went to the rear of the car and opened the trunk. Children who were poking their noses through the spokes of the tires were shooed away.

He brought a case to the side of the car and gave her a bottle. She held up a bottle of the anti-hoodoo lotion. Suddenly da hoodooed leaped from alleys and jumped from the windows of fleabag hotels, and dropped their forks and Chicago caps (which had been pulled down over their eyes) into their bean soups in restaurants as they left trails of screaming waitresses who tossed check pads into the air and jumped on tables, and the beasts bent bars of jails and hurdled the lamps of police stations, and nurses shrieked disbelief as da hoodooed knocked over trays in hospitals where they were undergoing the hoodoo kick, and they loped from the beds and toppled confessional booths in churches where they were being expunged of the fever—causing the priests to fling themselves upon the coins which had spilled from falling collection baskets, and da hoodooed bolted through the doors of churches, hospitals, jails, collar apartments, jumped from rooftops, leaped out of alleyways, and jaunting to the forefront of the crowd, snatched bottles from her hand before she could deliver her pitch. The chauffeur held fistfuls of dollar bills they slapped into his hands as the old woman stood up in the seat of the Pierce-Arrow, rolled up her sleeves and ran down her game.

"Come and get your anti-hoodoo lotion! Get rid of those ugly fangs, that tired hair. Be a delight to the womenfolk."

While she went into her thing I walked to the rear of the car to examine the plastic antlers of my father-in-law. I pressed my nose against the window and saw my father-in-law dressed in a tuxedo and resting his hand upon an ebony cane. He was swinging the antlers from side to side while talking to some ladies in cotton dresses who remembered him as the head of the colored Elks in 1928.

"How you, Miss Lucy?" he drawled, giving one woman a limp handshake and exposing his gold teeth. "How's the youngins? Hopes they's fine."

"Father-in-law, father-in-law," I shouted. He turned to the rear window and momentarily flashed anger; but remembering the women standing next to the car, be spoke for their edification.

"Well, my goodness, if it ain't my son-in-law. What you wont, dear son-in-law?" The women smiled at this exhibition of family affection. He rolled the car window down and beckoned me to come closer. "Look, my man," he said out of the hearing range of his admirers. "Make it. It'll mess up what you might call our 'image' if we are seen in the company of an orderly." I fell back to the curb and shoved my hands into my orderly's uniform which was still soiled from the old man's juices.

All the merchandise sold, the old woman had returned to her place next to the chauffeur. She clapped her hands and the car moved on. The car was followed by a battalion of old men wearing derbys and aprons with mystic signs sewn on them. Others were wheeled along by nurses who held up the old men's arms occasionally so that they could respond to the good wishes of the festive crowd. They were part of that celebrated contingent who in glittering ceremony underneath the watchful eyes of the founders of the nation —who wore frills on their wrists and fake moles on their cheeks—stood in solemn silence as their leader, my father-in-law, knelt, unsheathed his sword and kissed Calvin Coolidge's ass. At that time a minor stir was created when a protocol officer ran up and pulled my father-in-law from the President. He said that the proper procedure was to pull aside one flap and kiss the President between the cheeks instead of smacking the Chief of State all over his bottom like some kind of madman. My father-in-law nearly went to blows with the protocol officer for embarrassing him before his following and all those "fine white peoples." But the President saved the day, pulling up his trousers and saying, "We Americans are known for our informality."

For saving my father-in-law from a humiliation that could have set back "the struggle" fifty years, *Ebony* magazine hailed Calvin Coolidge as the second emancipator.

The old men were roundly applauded by the onlookers. Suddenly a woman fell into the arms of a man standing behind her. Another woman swooned. People began dropping like flies. A rank stench filled the air and the spectators held handkerchiefs to their noses and puked on each other. Up ahead was a 1938 Oldsmobile flanked by a V-shaped entourage of Screws on motorcycles. The Screws wore gas masks. Standing in the back seat of the car and wearing damp peppermint-striped pajamas and a cone-shaped hat was none other than Eclair Porkchop, newly crowned Bishop of Soulsville, direct from his negotiations with Dictator HARRY SAM, former Polish used-car salesman. Those who could withstand the odor which filled the street like quicksand fumes bowed their heads or held up their babies to receive Eclair Porkchop's blessing. The Bishop lighted from the automobile and walked on a red carpet toward the door of the Church of the Holy Mouth. Some young men on the sidelines teased the Bishop by playfully pinching his buttocks. He spun away, sticking out his hand like a quarterback dodging tackles. He executed pirouettes, arabesques, grands jetes saying, "Stop, hee, hee, that tickles. Now stop, now, hee, hee."

Those who could take the stench followed him until he was swallowed by the door of the church. He was shadowed by those men HARRY SAM assigned to protect his bishopric. They wore pantaloons and brogans. They were stripped to the waist and peering through the terrifying eyeholes of their masks they beat back the crowd with their whips.

All at once a man elbowed his way through the crowd. The hem of a long vicuna coat reached his ankles. He paced up and down in front of the crowd with his hands behind his back. Once in a while be glanced at his watch. He had a heavy mustache and a cigar jutted aggressively from between his teeth. A dwarf hunchbacked Negro ran through the crowd and joined the man. The Negro wore a raccoon coat and a straw hat. He waved a pennant which read "Fisk 1950." Underneath his arm he carried a small black case. "Hurry up, hurry up," the first man said to the dwarf as the little fellow opened the case, pulled out a mouth organ and began to play the Protestant hymn "The Old Rugged Cross." It was the mad slum lord Irving Gooseman and his Negro dwarf assistant Slickhead Fopnick. Irving cupped his thick red trap and addressed the crowd.

"All you little pretties and swingers of Soulsville, this is your main man Irving Gooseman and Slickhead Fopnick telling you all the bargains at the USURA pawnshop. No cash down—all you have to have is a gig. Take as long as you wont, all you souls, little pretties and swingers, boppers and groovers. Come on over to the store and look at some fine jools, dig some blond coffee tables and some zebra-skin couches. Now as an introduction to USURA pawnbrokers, we offer you a record that no home should be without. It's historical. It's edjoocational. It's a credit to you people. A forty-five disc of the historic meeting between HARRY SAM and Soulsville's own Eclair Porkchop: "A Meeting of Titans." just so that you can get a sample of this dignified recording, we're going to play a little bit of it." With this he pulled a folding stand from beneath his overcoat, set it up and mounted a small victrola on the top. He put the needle on the record and soon the voices of the two leaders could be heard.

AWWWWW, DO IT TO ME. AWWWWWW BABY. DO IT TO ME. WHERE DID YOU GET THAT LONG THING? MY MY O LORD, DON'T STOP, DON'T STOP. HELP PLEASE DON'T STOP. DO IT THIS WAY. DO IT THAT WAY. OOOOOO MY MY MY YUM YUMMY OOOO....

The sleep-in maids, porters and redcaps, hustlers, junkies, and Nazarene apprentices threw nickels, dimes, and quarters into the basket. All at once two Screws appeared around the corner and spotting the mad slum lord and Slickhead gave chase. Irving and Fopnick got their gear together and jumped into a T-Model Ford which was parked behind the crowd. The car rattled and bustled so, a door fell from its hinges and into the street. Smoke and oil spouted furiously from its radiator cap.

The Ford sped toward the railroad tracks where the eight-thirty express of the B.&O. Railroad was bearing down on the crossroads like gangbusters. The Screws were hot on the pair's trail, speeding in a jeep. Some of them were standing on the runners firing BB pellets at the car wheels. The crowd watched as the train came nearer and nearer and nearer and nearer (drum rolls) until the old T-Model just slipped across the tracks almost running down an old woman in white who was dripping wet and holding a yelping mutt by the scruff of the neck as she dashed across the road on the other side of the tracks. The Screws were left jumping up and down in the jeep, throwing their helmets into the road shoulders, tearing out their hair and slapping their fists against their foreheads in frustration as a lot of dumb numbers on boxcars whizzed by at one hundred miles an hour.

FIELD MARSHAL Theda Doompussy Blackwell sat on a white crate in his office. The doorman's coat covered his long johns to about two inches below his knees. A wig lay lopsided on his shivering head and his dentures were on the floor next to a bucket of hot water in which his feet rested.

He was sobbing and listening to a recording of "Yankee Doodle Dandy" which came from a Victrola horn in the corner of the room. Besides the white crate it was almost the only other furnishing. Not quite. On a wall was the famous petrified moose head.

Pete the Peek, Congressman, professional voyeur and Theda's co-conspirator groucho marxed into the room, picked up Theda's dentures and pushed them into the black hollow of the soldier's mouth. He then fixed the wig which was about to fall from the Field Marshal's head, and with a white monogrammed handkerchief dabbed at the tears rolling down his cheeks.

Thanks honey I'm so cold I'd freeze if I picked them up myself.

Think nothing of it, the Congressman said squatting in the corner.

They both swung their heads in time to the music until the needle got stuck on macaroni macaroni macaroni macaroni . . .

Pete lifted the arm from the record and returned to his place in the corner. It was close to 12 A.M.

I just had enough time to take off my pajamas when I got your message Theda. Geez I was having dis nightmare about some Hoo-Doo nigger cowboy who took over a radio station and broadcast strange fixes, laying a trick on a Western town. I forget da name. Anyway it got so bad dey had to call in da Pope to straighten tings out. Da bad dream ended with pigs with scrap iron for teeth doing da re-cap. It really got into me. My lips were wet and was screaming, "Mama Mama Mom O Mom help your baby." It was a deep-trip Theda; it was as if I had to don a snorkel and rubber suit to go through da black pools of my shut-eye. I woke up on da floor in a heap of panties, bras, lipstick tubes strewed about my bedroom. See me and da guys had a caucus last night. After it was over I wuz stuck with dis real dog who remained when all da other guys got good lookin pancakes and left. I wuz about to stick da pig when I dozed off and dat's when I had da dream. I had to go into da kitchen and have da maid prepare me a late snack out of da frig Kentucky Bourbon chased with water.

Well what about me? Field Marshal Doompussy Blackwell said squirming on his white crate. Does this look like my outfit to you? And why do you think my wig is all nappy and only a few patches of powder cover my decrepit yellow face? I didn't even have time to place a mole on my cheek I rushed over in my carriage so fast. The doorman was doll enough to lend me his coat.

What's up, Theda, is Frenchy up to his old tricks again? Pete asked dipping into a snuff box and removing the funnel from his head.

You said it Peter. O they treat me so mean—do you know what that child did this time?

No Theda, what?

Appropriated 2500 dollars so's a couple of ruffians could go hunt mammoth's bones and various botanical specimens to add to his Americana collection at Monticello. Can you get to that? Here I am in charge of Defense and I have to go around in ragged sneakers and borrow the doorman's coat because to tell you the truth honey I was ashamed to wear my General's outfit. I don't even have enough money to take it to the cleaners. He said he didn't believe in standing armies and that a good revolution from time to time is good.

Did he say dat Theda?

Said it as sure as you're standing before my eyes. Why that's why he got his ass out of Virginia that time when the British invaded and he was Governor. Said he was too busy inventing a cyptographic device called a wheel cypher to be concerned with force of arms.

Yeah Theda, remember dat time he was almost busted when he was ambassador to France and he was recuperating from an ailment in Italy and was seen smuggling Po Valley rice so's he could compare it to da rice grown in Carolina?

Gossip has it that he spent most of his time learning the process by which parmesan cheese was made and learning how to make macaroni. And you know what else, Pete?

No, the Congressman answered, as Theda leaned over and whispered into his ear.

Likes niggers a whole lot.

You don't mean it.

I kid thee not. When he was Gov of Virginia he tried to have a law passed against slavery and then later on wanted to banish slavery in the territories.

And he spends a lot of his time womanizing.

And remember what he did to the old man John Quincy Adams, Pete? I won't forgive him for that as long as I live. This impudent obscene underground pamphleteer accused the old man of giving all the baboons the original red ass and when the old man retaliated against all of those liberals, anarchists, beatniks and what have you by getting through the Alien and Sedition Acts, high and mighty couldn't even be a loyal Vice President—he pushed through his Kentucky resolution which declared the President's act illegal. Took it upon himself.

Well whaddya expect, Theda, look at all of dem far-out amendments he got pushed through da Constitution. He looks down his nose at us Congressmen, I see him, just because he can do fol de rol, calculate an eclipse, tie an artery, plan an edifice, break a horse, do a mean minuet and play da fiddle, he ain't so smart, why look.

O Peter you don't have to be so graphic.

Look at dis, Peter said, bringing out 24 cards. Credit cards to da finest stores in Boston and New York. He ain't so smart.

He has nothing but contempt for you Peter, you and your kind, why he called politics the hated occupation.

Well he can't think much of me because I'm politics from foot to head.

He said he didn't want to go the way of the French to Bonaparte.

Well if you ask me Theda my opinion, I tink some of dees protestors need a little Bonaparte right up side da fucking mop baby, pow dat's what dey need.

Now you're cooking with gas Pete my compatriot and dear friend. I've been thinking about it Peter and you know what would happen if the British start acting up, or them nigger pirates in Barbary start screwing around with our ships. Do we want to look like faggots?

He's stripped the Navy and uses the boats for those old nasty women he's always fooling around with, takes pleasure boat rides with those goddamn anarchists and those pseudo intellectual professors. Why just this morning he took off again. Papers piled high on his desk. Just went away. Too La Doo. Said he was nothing but a lowly dirt farmer, waved to us and said he'd see us around. Always using slang like that I can't keep up with him or understand a single thing he says half the time. Said he wanted to catch an eclipse tonight through his telescope. Last time he went to his farm he remained 3 whole months.

Geez dat's a shame Theda. If we had a ballsy leader da whole shebang would be one big goof off from coast to coast, everything would be boss.

Theda looked at himself through a hand mirror and busied the mole on his cheek.

There are plenty of talented men around. Yourself Pete?

O I'm just a poor simple Congressman. I just got da job because my uncle's an undertaker.

Then what about me, Pete? Theda hopped from the crate and clutching the lapels of the Congressman's coat pressed Peter against the wall.

Aw not me, baby, I'm not getting mixed up in no plots.

But your name will become a holiday Peter, just think.

I'd rather bar-be-cue a holiday dan be one Theda. No tanks. You saw what happened to da Aaron Burr conspiracy, dey busted da poor guy all da way down to da floor—he's ruined.

Aw Burr was a lemon. I've been secretly planning here in my little hole in the wall. Maps have been made, an invasion route laid out. Royal Flush Gooseman is extending credit for supplies in exchange for me sub-leasing Florida to him, plus I have an intelligence officer on the biggest cattleman's household staff to boot.

Gee Theda da way you run it down so clear and fresh as spring water you make it zap my mind.

Of course Peter, dear friend. Why just this evening our Indian scout out on the range sent a message via electronic horsey that he was coding Yellow Back Radio when all of a sudden it went off the beam. He suggests that it might not be long before I took my sword and led a cavalry charge on that part of the country full of black diamonds, black gold, abundant streams of trout and swarming with healthy steer beef.

Look Theda suppose we just bumped da guy off? I'll let da boys back home know dere's a contract and while's he's out looking for rare butterflies bingo poof and my man is in doornail country.

O Peter you're so sweet but sometimes I forget you're the Congressman from New Jersey. Assassinations were crude techniques of the Middle Ages.

Perish the thought that civilized men like ourselves would be forced to such tactics in this the century of American Enlightenment.

Wipe the mustard off your tie Pete.

O excuse me Theda I didn't notice.

No I have a better plan. If indeed Yellow Back Radio wilting feathers are preparing to take a dive into History why don't we take over the Western section of the country and then declare a civil war? Why with the plentiful resources and cheap labor out there our logistics will be unbeatable and we'd get rid of this crowd once and for all, Hamilton, Paine and Jefferson, the whole civilian crew. Phooey. What do they know. Why I'll be Emperor and Pete . . . well Pete you can park all the stagecoaches. By the way Pete how are things in Congress these days?

O Field Marshal I tink sooner or later we'll get da bakery bilt on da floor of the House. We're wasting money allatime sending out for pies.

I'm just a poor ol snoljer Pete. I mean far be it from me to interfere with the separation of powers but don't you think the fellows ought to put a little hoi-polloi into the proceedings? People are beginning to lose confidence; they'll decide they don't need us and we'll have free stores free money free land—what will happen to our little ego games if anarchy comes about?

A page walked in.

Hey chums there's some redskin out here sez he's got a message for you. He's out in the lobby with his valet and tailor.

Thank you page, Theda answered, but in the future please address us by our rightful titles . . . we're a young country and all but . . .

Up yours, the page replied bringing the forefinger of his right hand up with a sharp thrust. The page slammed the door.

Dear, dear, Theda sobbed as Pete screwed on his enormous red nose. Did you see that, they won't even appropriate enough money for me to get a first rate office staff.

Why do you think da injun's allowed a valet and tailor Theda?

O he's the last surviving injun in Yellow Back Radio Drag Gibson keeps him around in case the Pope wants to visit or something.

Chief Showcase, representative of red pow wow, was escorted into the room. The Field Marshal looked around for a chair.

Don't bother gents I'll just sit here on the floor. I know things are rough for you Field Marshal, having a freaky bopper peacenik for President and all who has no respect for the military.

I was on the way back from gay Paree where I bought this fine Pierre Cardin jacket with fur in the hood and I wanted to stop off to tell the Field

Marshal that signs point to an early invasion of Yellow Back Radio. Have a smoke.

O thanks Showcase, here try one Peter dear, the soldier said handing one to the Congressman.

Cough! Cough! Cough!

The conspirator's mouths became smokestacks as fumes filled the room.

You know Chief we always regretted the way those rude Western white trash, that human offal wiped out your people like that. It was really too bad.

Well Theda if we had had about 50 more troops at Big Horn I'd be the one sitting on that crate and you'd be going around the world reading militant poetry, that is if your ass wasn't on display in some museum.

Yeah, funny da way tings turn out ain't it, Pete said fidgeting his huge red thumbs and drawing on a cigarette with two free fingers.

Both Theda and Pete began to be wracked by spasms.

Easy easy gentlemen, Showcase said slapping them on the back to ease their agony. You must inhale them slowly.

When the two men were finished coughing and spitting blood Showcase returned to his seat on the floor in the corner of the room.

Now as I was preparing to report . . . Drag Gibson and the ranch hands were talking about you like a dog. They said they weren't troubled at all about your demand that they join the Union because they knew you didn't have enough troops to make it stick. It was so bad the way they were running you down I cried all the way to Paris.

O isn't that sweet of you, you fine sugar-pappa with the candy between your lucious red thighs. IT be your little old buffalo calf anytime you want.

Thanks Field Marshal and I'm here to tell you that you and Pete have nothing to fear. Theda something uncanny is happening on the ranch these days. At this very moment some nigger wampus is giving them a run for their money indeed. Cattle are wasting away emitting pitiful moomoos of mayhem, the fish die on shores and appear in bedrooms in strange flapping monster dances. The darkie even ran the Marshal out of town after a tremendous display of bullwhacking—popped the man with fiery whiplashes and played songs all over the Marshal's butt so good with his lash that a moose galloped towards a lake and almost drowned, the poor animal was laughing so. And if that wasn't enough the nigger put a hex on John Wesley Hardin and left John Wesley Hardin demented, only fit for tending the hogs.

You mean da famous gunslinger I've read about in da lurid sensational yellow kivered books?

That's the one Pete, the man do nots play—do nots stand for no chump issues. See, he got ringy cause Drag Gibson the cattleman ordered his waddies to burn down a circus troupe the Loop Garoo Kid was hooked up to.

Fact is, gentlemen, Drag is sick now—I don't think he's going to pull through. The local jack-leg squaw on the talk show who gives out the produce market reports and dabbles in astrology shut down her scene. The Kid put some cross on her, had some kind of gris gris dolls placed in her transmitter and the Woman had to sign off and get out of town.

Drag even went and got a mail order bride a week before the Loop Garoo Kid had her running through the mountains in the nude, had done offed, with her mind and she was screaming foul nasty things like "make that mojo trigger my snatch one mo time and mumbling some bad nigger words—you know how they move up and down the line like hard magic beads out riffing all the language in the syntax.

O Red man!! O Red man!! Talk that talk, the Field Marshal said twisting on a crate thrilled to his socks, what jive talking dada you bring us.

Think nothing of it Field Marshal, just hate to see some good cats get a wrong deal. When you going to give me the three colonies?

Soon Showcase soon, if you bring me some more good news like this I'll be polishing my sword and preparing my Army. Sounds like the West is really vulnerable at this point. By the way Injun, from now on call me Theda, Blackwell said, doll circles of pink appearing on the yellow of his jaundiced face.

It's a deal Field Marshal, said the injun rising from the floor and pulling his cashmere blanket about his shoulders, taking a few puffs from his diamond hookah with a beaver rimmed mouth piece. Tipping over to the Field Marshal the savage gave Theda a few taps on the thin layer of skin covering his coccyx.

By da way Injun if Drag hired John Wesley Hardin da great Western ghost chaser to get rid of da Kid and Hardin failed how did Drag have da compassion to keep him on? I thought Drag had da heart of Two-Pawed Bitch Wolf Of da Plains.

O Drag is still his old name Pete, Showcase responded, his hand on the doorknob and looking over his shoulder. Got a sign above John Wesley Hardin's pigpen chores—sez for two bits see John Wesley Hardin pay heavy dues.

O I see, Pete the Peek said as the door was closing behind Chief Showcase.

One more thing O noble Red man. How will we know when to move our forces on Yellow Back Radio?

I'll wire you Theda.

Well be sure to wire collect, Pete the Peek said.

No matter Gentlemen I'll pay for it, anything to help out. In fact Theda here's some money, why don't you go out and get some new duds? Don't want you to come to your new Palatinate looking like a bum. Show the cow-pokes you got class.

O no I can't take your Indian Bureau check Chief Showcase.

Never you mind, Theda, you deserve it, the abuse that a great military mind like yours has to take.

Well if you insist Chief. When Peter and I take over that territory you'll be set for life. Why you can have your little happy hunting ground right now here on earth.

I know you'll keep your word you fine white gentlemen, the Indian said as he walked out of the Field Marshal's office.

Field Marshal I don't want to dispute what da redman said, but don't you tink we ought to get a clean white man in here to give us da facts from da point of view of Science?

O what were you saying Peter? a blushing Theda Blackwell asked.

O drat it Theda can't you keep your mind on da affairs of State? With him lost in agrarian reveries and with my problems (catching flies!), one of us has to keep our heads.

Your problems Peter?

I've become a very complex freak, Theda baby, Peter said pulling his pockets inside out. Why I can grope grok frink—you name it. On da way over here I even learned to geek. So now I can geek as well as peek.

O Peter with such a crisis mounting don't fun me now please be serious. Peter threw up his hands.

Well I guess I have to show you—you asked for it.

Peter went to the control and pressed a button. The page walked in, a clothespin fastened to his nose. He carried a chicken by the neck. A real live chicken.

The Page threw the chicken at Pete the Peek who expertly plucked the chicken's feathers and then devoured the fowl-feathers, coxcomb, gristle, feet disappearing into his mouth.

Theda looked around for a lavender sink. He was sleepy, see, and thought he was still at home. He ran to the window and released his insides on passing tourists.

Hey what's going on up dere, buddy, and, you a wise guy? and other choice Americana expletives rose from the sidewalk below.

Pete approached Theda with a wishbone.

So you see Theda my problems are very serious and thought out.

Theda looked around and pulled the larger half of the bone.

To da conspiracy Theda!!

To the conspiracy Peter!!

A noise was heard at the window. Pete hurriedly put the wishbone into his coat pocket. Harold Rateater, Government Scientist, opened the window and stepped into the room. In one hand he carried a jar filled with smoke and dying insects. He was dressed in a plaid tight-fitting suit and wore a loud bowtie, his hair pasted with staycomb and parted down the middle. He did a mummy-walks-again stride across the room until he stood before Pete and Theda.

My goodness will you please knock next time Harry?

Don't have to Pete, I'm such a smart operator dat I defy da laws of nature. I walk in and out of windows instead of doors. Besides, understand you want to Peep through my long glass at dat Loop Garoo Thingamubob unidentified flying phenomenon what's been zooming around.

Please sir! the Field Marshal said, please break it down so that the laity might understand.

In otha words dis is some bad noos for Yellow Back Radio—the Prez ought to be informed at once—but I got da long glass so whats in it for me? he said gripping the telescope.

Pete was furious. What do you mean what's in it for you? We just appropriated a whole row of iron men so's Dr. Coult could study a rifle dat wouldn't leak gas and get jammed chambers. What more do you guys want?

Theda removed a mallet from his satchel and hit Pete on the head with it. A large lump rose and its peak was immediately occupied by a grey sparrow that flew in through the window.

Ouch! Field Marshal Theda whattaya have to go glunk me on da bean like dat for? the statesman complained.

Forgive Peter, Harold Rateater Government Scientist, he doesn't know any better. Having come up through the ranks he hasn't developed the respect for SCIENCE that a military man like myself has.

Dat's more like it chum, Harold Rateater said, counting the wad of green backs the Field Marshal forked over. Well who wants to look first?

Theda walked over, bent down and looked through the telescope which stuck out of the window.

Field Marshal Theda Blackwell could see into the Cattle Baron's bedroom. He saw the straws in cups of orange juice, the pills, the heavy breathing of Drag Gibson, and his Doctor friend listlessly staring through the window.

O this is too much, Theda said rubbing his frail thin hands together.

Come let me look too dere Theda, I'm da professional voyeur who's suppose to advise and consent like in da constitootion.

Pete the Peek gazed through and it was cookies. Plain cookies.

Yellow Back Radio was indeed falling apart, its batteries were going on the bum, and soon the whole kit and kaboodle would blow a fuse.

> The sheep are happier of themselves,
> than under the care of wolves.
>
> —THOMAS JEFFERSON

Meanwhile back at the ranch Chief Showcase entered Drag's sick room. The old fat and ignorant cattle rancher lay in bed, his chest rapidly rising and falling. The Dr. was seated next to the window, his head in his hands as he did vigil for his old friend. Whispering, he saluted the Indian.

O Chief Showcase how loyal of you to come see Drag. Why just a few minutes ago we found some horrible material stuffed in his pillow. It was made up of putrid matter I analyzed to be: a one-eyed toad, wings of a bat, cat's eyes and some strange powder. Things look grave indeed.

Chief Showcase gently sat on Drag's bed and put a hand on the Cattleman's forehead. Drag's eyebrows fluttered. The room was spinning as his eyes opened.

O Chief Showcase, he said weakly, good of you to come and visit me before I ride off into the eternal sunset.

Think nothing of it Drag, I was on my way back from Paris and I stopped off at that makeshift acreage they call the Capitol.

Even in his dying spasms Drag laughed as did the Doc, who beamed at the Indian for bringing a little humor into the room.

I overheard them talking about you Drag and it surprised me seeing as how any fool could tell that you are in charge, the top dog and the one who is really number 1.

O thanks sweet Redman, Drag said clasping the Indian's hand, but looks like Drag is about to enter the Great Corral in the Sky.

That's what they were saying Drag. They said they might raise a cavalry and investigate those mysterious wife deaths. They said you might fill up boot hill quicker than you think. They said you called them corny dudes and all but at least back East they either kills niggers or prizes them to death. Here sign this autograph.

Drag obliged, scratching a feeble signature on a scrap of paper provided by the Indian.

Well they ain't no threat, even in my dying breath I know that Unification it'll never happen. Why I understand that the largest bank in the country is out in this territory now.

The door opened. A messenger ran into the room and handed Drag a note. Drag's eyes popped. He sat up in bed and slapped his hand against his forehead.

Now I get it. Of course. Too much. That's it. Me getting sick and the cattle dying like that. Yeah of course. Now it makes sense. Hot diggity joe joe— won't be long now—

The Indian and the Doctor were amazed at this rapid recovery by one who only a few moments before had taken out a passport for the beyond. Whatever the contents of this note—it provided a powerful curative.

What's wrong Drag, what happened, they asked him eagerly.

A note from the Pope. It won't be long now. Everybody take off his hat. Imagine that—I am nothing but a lowly cattleman, ugly fat and ignorant, why I use to slop hogs and ride drag, that's why they call me Drag, because my first job was taking care of back tracking and sick cattle. But now a royal visit!

Drag leaped out of bed and in his nightgown and cap ran past the Indian and into the hall. Below the men were making bets on his hour of departure. They scooped up their money when they saw the boss at the top of the stairs . . .

Men, things are really going to change now—tomorrow all the way from Rome the Pope is arriving to straighten out this inner sanctum mystery once and for all. Hang out some confetti, get the fiddler, round up all the hurdy gurdy girls from the Rabid Black Cougar—a big huzza huzza time.

Everybody made eager preparations for the visit. Banners were hung over the street, ikons strategically placed, the whole town was incensed. And everyone was engaged in furious preparations for the Pope's visit. Everyone, that is, but Chief Showcase, who was sneaking towards the Hotel to send off a telegram.

*Woooooooo wee!! Um ma um ma um ma ha hall Su ha su ha su hall*
*Soo-kee o soo-kee soo-kee. Lallalalalalalalalala. My my my my goodness.*
*O get it. Get it*
*GET IT GET IT OOOOOOOOOOooooooooooooooooooooo*
*oooo oooo*
*o o Mewwwwooooooooooow.*

Your charm certainly works. Your strong black hands just seem to make my bones jump and shout for joy. Please ask the owner for my car keys. You can come to my apartment and take anything you want. Take my credit cards, take my status, it doesn't mean anything just do it to me more often, you know how you do things so fine and sweet. You the finest pipe fitter I've ever known, O I just wish I could do more to reward you for your thrilling expertise.

The Field Marshal nestled his head next to the black masseur's thighs as he lay in semi-consciousness on the table of an underground rub down Palace in the basement of the Army's headquarters.

Think nothing of it boss-man Theda, the masseur said, you know I'll do my bit to help relax you in these troubled times. The ship of state needs strong arms at its oars now don't it.

O you're so beautiful and understanding. Theda's eyes became moist as he closed in on the black man and started to purr like a kitten.

Mee-yow, mee-yow, he purred while the masseur softly stroked his back. O I think I'll just go out of my mind if you start sucking my toes like you did last week, Theda said.

The pink mist of the room was heavily perfumed and across the area on other tables, high ranking members of the Army were babbling softly out of their minds while big black masseurs in turbans and baggy pants were running their jazzy hands across their bodies.

You know, sweet and ample black man, I tried to get that provision in the Declaration of Independence, a forthright resolution, but nothing happened. The Southern planters were dead set against it and we needed their support.

I know, Theda, I read the broadsides, I know you did all you could. Me and my wife have a picture of you on our wall. Each morning we light candles fo it and pray fo you and Mr. Thomas Jefferson. He's a good man too.

Tom's all right, Theda said, but he's such a rake, nothing but a dirt farmer and anarchist. Hangs out with Jacobins like that Paine fellow. I've even seen him out with women from time to time. And he doesn't know how to keep his britches on at all. Some man in Conn. is suing him for adultery right now and he reads French books and plays electric fiddle with some rock group called the Green Mountain Boys. O he's disgusting sometimes.

Well suh, the masseur said, his hands pressing against Theda's neck, causing him to wiggle, what about Benjamin Franklin?

O he's just as bad, he and that Westerner Henry Clay, they carry on— Franklin draws cartoons—he invented balloon speech you know. And that

Clay always brawling. Me and the fellows tried to get Randolph of Virginia to
head the Convention but he was overruled. Some delegate with a squirrel cap
and a filthy backwoods buckskin jacket on spread the word that Randolph
was second rate at what jackasses could do infinitely better—o democracy
sometimes. Phew.

Big Woogie?

Yes Theda?

What about this Hoo . . . this religion the Hoo-Doo that your people practice?

Big Woogie stepped back. Some of the other black attendants started to
roll their eyes and drop their towels. Confusion broke out as the members of
the Army asked their attendants to continue massaging their tired bones.
Snapping his fingers, Big Woogie gave them the signal to return to their
work.

O it's nothing Theda, nothing to get upset about. Just some kind of superstition that our people brought from Africa. People believe in hants and such
things, that's all.

O I see, the Field Marshal said.

The page, now wearing his Hoover's cap and knickerbockers, walked into
the room.

Hey fuck-face Doompussy, whatever your name is.

Theda jumped from the table.

Well I never. Who gave you this address? I told them to never give out this
phone number—why this is one of the few luxuries I have in this life. . . .

Aw be quiet, the page said. I just came to give you this telegram that just
arrived.

Theda went into one of the phone booths for privacy, his bathrobe still
wrapped about him. He slapped his knees and gave a great hoot when he
read the telegram's contents.

> Drag is about to tip away.
> The whole thing belongs to you baby.
> Come on in your Highness.

Showcase

[2] WITH THE astonishing rapidity of Booker T. Washington's Grapevine Telegraph Jes Grew spreads through America following a strange course. Pine Bluff and Magnolia Arkansas are hit; Natchez, Meridian and Greenwood Mississippi report cases. Sporadic outbreaks occur in Nashville and Knoxville Tennessee as well as St. Louis where the bumping and grinding cause the Gov to call up the Guard. A mighty influence, Jes Grew infects all that it touches.

[3] *Europe has once more attempted to recover the Holy Grail and the Teutonic Knights, Gibbon's "troops of careless temper," have again fumbled the Cup. Instead of raiding the Temples of Heathens they enact their blood; in the pagan myth of the Valkyrie they fight continually; are mortally wounded, but revived only to fight again, taking time out to gorge themselves on swine and mead. But the Wallflower Order had no choice. The only other Knight order had been disgraced years before. Sometimes the Wallflower Order was urged to summon them. Only they could defend the cherished traditions of the West against Jes Grew. They would be able to man the Jes Grew Observation Stations. But the trial which banished their order from the West's service and the Atonist Path had been conclusive. They were condemned as "devouring wolves and polluters of the mind."*

The Jes Grew crisis was becoming acute. Compounding it, Black Yellow and Red Mu'tafikah* were looting the museums shipping the plunder back to where it came from. America, Europe's last hope, the protector of the archives of "mankind's" achievements had come down with a bad case of Jes Grew and Mu'tafikah too. Europe can no longer guard the "fetishes" of civilizations which were placed in the various Centers of Art Detention, located in New York City. Bootlegging Houses financed by Robber Barons, Copper Kings, Oil Magnets, Tycoons and Gentlemen Planters. Dungeons for the treasures from Africa, South America and Asia.

The army devoted to guarding this booty is larger than those of most countries. Justifiably so, because if these treasures got into the "wrong hands" (the countries from which they were stolen) there would be renewed enthusiasms for the Ikons of the aesthetically victimized civilizations.

## CHAPTER 4

[4] 1920. Charlie Parker, the houngan (a word derived from *n'gana gana*) for whom there was no master adept enough to award him the Asson, is born. 1920–1930. That 1 decade which doesn't seem so much a part of American history as the hidden After-Hours of America struggling to jam. To get through.

Jes Grew carriers came to America because of cotton. Why cotton? American Indians often supplied all of their needs from one animal: the buffalo. Food, shelter, clothing, even fuel. Eskimos, the whale. Ancient Egyptians were able to nourish themselves from the olive tree and use it as a source of light; but Americans wanted to grow cotton. They could have raised soybeans, cattle, hogs or the feed for these animals. There was no excuse. Cotton. Was it some unusual thrill at seeing the black hands come in contact with the white crop?

According to the astrologer Evangeline Adams, America is born at 3:03 on the 4th of July, Gemini Rising. It is to be mercurial, restless, violent. It looks to the Philippines and calls gluttony the New Frontier. It looks to South America and intervenes in the internal affairs of its nations; piracy is termed "bringing about stability." If the British prose style is Churchillian, America is the tobacco auctioneer, the barker; Runyon, Lardner, W.W., the traveling salesman who can sell the world the Brooklyn Bridge every day, can put any-

---

* Mu'tafikah—According to The Koran, inhabitants of the Ruined Cities where Lot's people had lived. I call the "art-nappers" Mu'taflkah because just as the inhabitants of Sodom and Gomorrah were the bohemians of their day, Berbelang and his gang are the bohemians of the 1920s Manhattan.

thing over on you and convince you that tomatoes grow at the South Pole. If in the 1920s the British say "The Sun Never Sets on the British Empire," the American motto is "There's a Sucker Born Every Minute." America is the smart aleck adolescent who's "been around" and has his own hot rod. They attend, these upstarts, a disarmament conference in Washington and play diplomatic chicken with the British, advising them to scrap 4 hoods including the pride of the British Navy: H.M.S. *King George the 5th*. Bulldog-faced British Admiral Beatty leaves the room in a huff.

[5]   The Wallflower order attempts to meet the psychic plague by installing an anti-Jes Grew President, Warren Harding. He wins on the platform "Let's be done with Wiggle and Wobble,"* indicating that he will not tolerate this spreading infection. All sympathizers will be dealt with; all carriers isolated and disinfected, Immumo-Therapy will begin once he takes office.

Unbeknown to him he is being watched by a spy from the Wallflower Order. A man who is to become his Attorney General. (He is also surrounded by the curious circle known by historians as "The Ohio Gang.")

The 2nd Stage of the plan is to groom a Talking Android who will work within the Negro, who seems to be its classical host; to drive it out, categorize it analyze it expell it slay it, blot Jes Grew. A speaking scull they can use any way they want, a rapping antibiotic who will abort it from the American womb to which it clings like a stubborn fetus.

In other words this Talking Android will be engaged to cut-it-up, break down this Germ, keep it from behind the counter. To begin the campaign, NO DANCING posters are ordered by the 100s.

All agree something must be done.

"Jes Grew is the boll weevil eating away at the fabric of our forms our technique our aesthetic integrity," says a Southern congressman. "I must ponder the effect of Jew Grew upon 2,000 years of civilization," Calvinist editorial writers wonder aloud.

[6]   New Orleans is a mess. People sweep the clutter from the streets. The city's head is once more calm. Normal. It sleeps after the night of howling, speaking-in-tongues, dancing to drums; watching strange lights streak across

* *The Harding Era*—Robert K. Murray.

the sky. The streets are littered with bodies where its victims lie until the next burgeoning. 1 doesn't know when it will hit again. The next 5 minutes? 3 days from now? 20 years? But if the Jes Grew which shot up a trial balloon in the 1890s was then endemic, it is now epidemic, crossing state lines and heading for Chicago.

Men who resemble the shadows sleuths threw against the walls of 1930s detective films have somehow managed to slip into the Mayor's private hospital room. They have set up a table before his bed. A man wearing a mask that reveals only his eyes and mouth calls the meeting to order.

This is an inquiry, it seems, and the man officiating wants to get to the bottom of why the Mayor, a Mason, allowed his Vital Resistance to wear down before Jes Grew's Communicability. This augurs badly, for if Jes Grew is immune to the old remedies, the saving Virus in the blood of Europe, mankind is lost. No word of this must get out. The Mayor even volunteers to accept the short bronze dagger and "get it over with." All for the Atonist Path. The visitors await his final groan, and when the limp hand falls to the side of the bed and begins to swing, they leave as quickly as they came.

This was no ordinary commission. When an extraordinary antipathy challenges the Wallflower Order, their usual front men, politicians, scholars and businessmen, step aside. Someone once said that beneath or behind all political and cultural warfare lies a struggle between secret societies. Another author suggested that the Nursery Rhyme and the book of Science Fiction might be more revolutionary than any number of tracts, pamphlets, manifestoes of the political realm.

[7]   New York is accustomed to gang warfare. White gangs: the Plug Uglies, the Blood Tubs of Baltimore, the Schuylkill Rangers from Philadelphia, the Dead Rabbits from the Bowery, the Roaches Guard and the Cow Bay Gangs terrorize the city, loot, raid and regularly fight the bulls to a standoff.

A gang war has broken out over Buddy Jackson, noted for his snappy florid-designed multicolored shoes and his grand way of living. There are legends about him. He went into the police station and knocked the captain cold when he didn't come forward with policy protection. Later, while orators and those affected with "tongues and lungs" were rapping as usual, he sent a convoy into Peekskill and rescued "Paul from the Crackers."

Schlitz, "the Sarge of Yorktown," a Beer Baron, has a lucrative numbers and Speak operation in Harlem. His stores are identified by the box of Dutch Masters in the window.

1 day, collection day, 3 Packards roll up to a store, 1 of the fronts belonging to the Sarge. The street, located in Harlem, is unusually quiet. The only sounds heard are the Sarge's patent leather shoes coming in contact with the pavement. Where are the salesmen, the New Negroes, the "ham heavers," "pot rasslers" and "kitchen mechanics" on their way to work? Where are the sugar daddies and their hookers, the peddlers, the traffic cops, the reefer salesmen who usually stand on the corners openly peddling their merchandise? (Legal then.) There are no revelers and no chippies. The streets are deserted . . . .

Schlitz looks into the window of his 1st store. What? No Rembrandt Dutch Masters but the picture of Prince Hall founder of African Lodge #1 of the Black Masons stares out at Schlitz, "the Sarge of Yorktown."

The mobster moves on, the 3 Packards following his course. The next store, the same story. The portrait of Prince Hall dressed in the formal Colonial outfit of his day, the frilled white blouse and collar showing beneath the frock coat and vest. The short white wig.

The painting is so realistic that you can see his auras. In his right hand he holds the charter the Black Freemasons have received from England. Schlitz shrugs his shoulders, puts a cigar in his mouth and walks over to the curb to speak to the driver of 1 of the Packards. He feels something cold at the back of his neck. He turns to see Buddy Jackson standing behind him, aiming a Thompson Automatic at him. The gun which has acquired the name of "The Bootlegger's Special."

Packing their heat, the hoods begin to open the car doors to assist their Boss. But they are pinned in. Up on the roofs, firing, are Buddy Jackson's Garders. Exaggerated lapels. Bell-bottoms. Hats at rakish angles. The Sarge's men sit tight. The bullet pellets zing across the front of the automobiles and graze the top and trunk. Buddy Jacksons exhorts the Sarge to leave Harlem and "Never darken the portals of our abode again." He marches the Sarge down to the subway, followed by many people coming from the hallways and apartments and alleys, bars, professional offices, beauty parlors, from where they've watched the whole scene. Most people read the newspaper to tell them what're the coming attractions. In the 1920s folks in Harlem used the Grapevine Telegraph. Booker T. Washington observed its technology. Booker T. Washington the man who "bewitched" 1000s at the Cotton States Exposition, Atlanta, September 18, 1895.

[8]    Picture the 1920s as a drag race whose entries are ages vying for the
Champion gros-ben-age of the times, that aura that remains after the flesh of
the age has dropped away. The shimmering Etheric Double of the 1920s. The
thing that gives it its summary. Candidates line up like chimeras.

The Age of Harding pulls up, the strict upper-lip chrome. The somber,
swallow-tailed body, the formal top-hatted hood, the overall stay-put exterior
but inside the tell-tale poker cards, the expensive bootlegged bottle of liquor,
and in the back seat the whiff of scandal. The Age of Prohibition: Speaks,
cabarets, a hearse with the rear-window curtains drawn over its illegal contents destined perhaps for a funeral at sea.

Now imagine this Age Race occurring before a crowd of society idlers
you would find at 1 of those blue-ribbon dog shows. The owners inspecting
their Pekinese, collies, bulldogs, german shepherds, and then observe these
indignant spectators as a hound mongrel of a struggle-buggy pulls up and
with no prior warning outdistances its opponents with its blare of the trumpet, its crooning saxophone, its wild inelegant Grizzly Bear steps.

For if the Jazz Age is year for year the Essences and Symptoms of the
times, then Jes Grew is the germ making it rise yeast-like across the American
plain.

An entry in the table of contents of a 205 book tells the story.


### The United States, When Harding Became President

A Period of Frazzled Nerves, Caused by the End of War-time Strain; of Disunity
Caused by the End of the More or Less Artificially Built-up Unity of the War
Period; of Strikes Caused by Continuation of War-time's High Cost of Living; of
Business Depression Which Came when War-time Prices Began to Fall; and of
Other Disturbances Due in Part to Economic Dislocations Brought by the War
and Its Aftermath. From All of Which Arose Emotions of Insecurity and Fear,
Which Expressed Themselves in Turbulence and Strife. The Boston Police Strike,
the Steel Strike, the "Buyers' Strike" and the "Rent Strike." The "Red Scare." The
Bomb Plots. A Dynamite Explosion in the New York Financial District. Deportation
of Radicals. Demand for Reduction of Immigration. The I. W. W. and the "One Big
Union." Sacco and Vanzetti. Race, Riots Between Whites and Negroes. The Whole
Reflecting an Unhappy Country when Harding Became Its President.

*Our Times*, vol. 6, *The Twenties*—Mark Sullivan.

[9]   Wall Street is tense. An incident has occurred which threatens to flapperize those yet uncommitted youngsters who adamantly refuse to eschew Jes Grew, last heard flying toward Chicago with 18,000 cases in Arkansas, 60,000 in Tennessee, 98,000 in Mississippi and cases showing up even in Wyoming, It would take a few months before a woman would be arrested for walking down a New Jersey street singing "Everybody's Doing It Now."* A week before, 16 people have been fired from their jobs for manifesting a symptom of Jes Grew. Performing the Turkey Trot on their lunch hour. Girls in peekaboo hats and straw-hat-wearing young men have threatened reprisals against the broker who dismissed them.

The kids want to dance belly to belly and cheek to cheek while their elders are supporting legislation that would prohibit them from dancing closer than 9 inches. The kids want to Funky Butt and Black Bottom while their elders prefer the Waltz as a suitable vaccine for what is now merely a rash. Limbering is the way the youngsters recreate themselves while their elders declaim they cease and desist from this lascivious "sinful" Bunny-Hugging, this suggestive bumping and grinding, this wild abandoned spooning.

## VOODOO GENERAL SURROUNDS
## MARINES AT PORT-AU-PRINCE

... only adds to the crisis. A corpulent, silkily mustached Robber Baron for whom a seal has been sacrificed to provide his hunk of toxic wastes with a covering notices this headline in the New York Sun and avers gruffly: The only thing they have in Haiti are mangoes and coffee. With prohibition there's no need for coffee, and mangoes appeal only to a few people. A glamour item. Haiti is mere repast after a heavy meal of meat and potatoes. It doesn't have any culture either. I didn't see a single cannon or cathedral while I was there. Look at this!

The Robber Baron removes a wood sculpture from his pocket. Look at this ugly carving my wife gave me. She bought it from 1 of those leather-necks in the black market... Have you ever seen such an ugly thing. The obtuse snout; the sausage lips? It was really clever of Wilson to send Southern Marines down there. Those doughboys will really be able to end this thing and quick! VooDoo generals. Absurd.

Why do you think he sent them there in the 1st place? says his companion,

* Castles in the Air—Irene Castle.

who carries a black umbrella and wears a bowler hat, grey suit and black shoes, a copy of a Wall Street newspaper under his arm.

I have figured it out. Word has it that the old man was feeble and his wife was running the government. Maybe it was an expedition for some new fashions for the old girl. Can't you see her walking across the White House lawn with a basket on her head above a torniquet? Wouldn't that be rich?

As the 2 men approach the intersection of Broad and Market a Black man opens the door for Buddy Jackson who struts alongside a high-yellow girl. They head toward the entrance of the bank where they plan to deposit the take from the previous night's cabaret business. Jackson is carrying a large sack. The broker is about to comment about Jackson's date, a "hotsy totsy," when a loud pop occurs. The picket line of young flappers disperses. People fly about the streets until they land dazed and bloodied. 3 Packards reach the intersection far from the scene and turn the corner on 2 wheels.

Flappers, ginnys, swell-eggs, brokers, stenographers, carriages, automobiles, bicycles are scattered about the streets. The broker and his friend, a few moments before engaged in a penetrating analysis of the economic implications of the Haitian occupation, lie dead, bubbles forming on the broker's lips. ½ his companion's torso lies next to him.

[10] Some say his ancestor is the long Ju Ju of Arno in eastern Nigeria, the man who would oracle, sitting in the mouth of a cave, as his clients stood below in shallow water.

Another story is that he is the reincarnation of the famed Moor of Summerland himself, the Black gypsy who according to Sufi Lit. sicked the Witches on Europe. Whoever his progenitor, whatever his lineage, his grandfather it is known was brought to America on a slave ship mixed in with other workers who were responsible for bringing African religion to the Americas where it survives to this day.

A cruel young planter purchased his grandfather and was found hanging shortly afterward. A succession of slavemasters met a similar fate: insanity, drunkenness, disease and retarded children. A drunken White man called him a foul name and did not live much longer afterward to give utterance to his squalid mind.

His father ran a successful mail-order Root business in New Orleans. Then it is no surprise that Papa LaBas carries Jes Grew in him like most other folk carry genes.

A little boy kicked his Newfoundland HooDoo 3 Cents and spent a night squirming and gnashing his teeth. A warehouse burned after it refused to deliver a special variety of herbs to his brownstone headquarters and mind haberdashery where he Sized up his clients to fit their souls. His headquarters are derisively called Mumbo Jumbo Kathedral by his critics. Many are healed and helped in this factory which deals in jewelry, Black astrology charts, herbs, potions, candles, talismans.

People trust his powers. They've seen him knock a glass from a table by staring in its direction; and fill a room with the sound of forest animals: the panther's *ki-ki-ki,* the elephant's trumpet. He moves about town in his Loco-mobile, the name of which amused many of his critics including Hank Rollings, an Oxford-educated Guianese art critic who referred to him as an "evangelist" and said he looked forward to the day when Papa LaBas "got well." To some if you owned your own mind you were indeed sick but when you possessed an Atonist mind you were healthy. A mind which sought to interpret the world by using a single loa. Somewhat like filling a milk bottle with an ocean.

He is a familiar sight in Harlem, wearing his frock coat, opera hat, smoked glasses and carrying a cane. Right now he is making a delivery of garlic, sage, thyme, geranium water, dry basil, parsley, saltpeter, bay rum, verbena essence and jack honeysuckle to the 2nd floor of Mumbo Jumbo Kathedral. They are for an old sister who has annoying nightly visitations.

The sign on the door reads

### PAPA LABAS
### MUMBO JUMBO KATHEDRAL
### FITS FOR YOUR HEAD

When he climbs to the 2nd floor of Mumbo Jumbo Kathedral. The office is about to close for the day. Earline, his assistant Therapist, is putting her desk in order. She is attired in a white blouse and short skirt. Her feet are bare. Her hair is let down. Papa LaBas places The Work on her desk.

Please give these to Mother Brown. She must bathe in this and it will place the vaporous evil Ka hovering above her sleep under arrest and cause it to disperse.

Earline nods her head. She sits down at her desk and begins to munch on some fig cookies which lie in an open box.

Papa LaBas glances up at the oil portrait hanging on the wall. It is a picture of the original Mumbo Jumbo Kathedral taken a few weeks ago: Berbelang, his enigmatic smile, the thick black mustache, the derby and snappy bowtie, his mysterious ring bearing the initials E.F., his eyes of black rock, 2 mysterious bodies emitting radio energy from deep in space, set in the narrow face; Earline in the characteristic black skirt, the white blouse with the ruffled shoulders, the violet stone around her neck; Charlotte, a French trainee he has hired to fill in for Berbelang, wears a similar costume to Earline's and smokes a cigarette. In the painting, completed 2 weeks before Berbelang left the group, she stands next to Earline.

Earline, now sitting at her desk, is smoking. 1 hand supports her head as she checks an order for new herbs and incense.

Daughter?

She looks up, distantly.

Jes Grew which began in New Orleans has reached Chicago. They are calling it a plague when in fact it is an anti-plague. I know what it's after; it has no definite route yet but the configuration it is forming indicates it will settle in New York. It won't stop until it cohabits with what it's after. Then it will be a pandemic and you will really see something. And then *they* will be finished.

Earline slams the papers down on her desk.

What's wrong, daughter?

There you go jabbering again. That's why Berbelang left. Your conspiratorial hypothesis about some secret society molding the consciousness of the West. You know you don't have any empirical evidence for it that; you can't prove....

Evidence? Woman, I dream about it, I feel it, I use my 2 heads. My Knockings.* Don't you children have your Knockings, or have you New Negroes lost your other senses, the senses we came over here with? Why your Knockings are so accurate they can chart the course of a hammerhead shark in an ocean 1000s of miles away. Daughter, standing here, I can open the basket of a cobra in an Indian marketplace and charm the animal to sleep. What's wrong with you, have you forgotten your Knockings? Why, when the seasons change on Mars, I sympathize with them.

O pop, that's ridiculous. Xenophobic. Why must you mix poetry with concrete events? This is a new day, pop. We need scientists and engineers, we need lawyers.

All that's all right, what you speak of, but that ain't all. There's more. And I'll bet that before this century is out men will turn once more to mystery, to

---

* B. Fuller terms this phenomenon "ultra high frequency electromagnetic wave propagation."

wonderment; they will explore the vast reaches of space within instead of more measuring more "progress" more of this and more of that. More Increase, Growth Inflation, and they don't know what to do when Jes Grew comes along like the Dow Jones snake and rises quicker than the G.N.P.; these scientists, there's a lot they don't know. And as for secret societies? The Communist party originated among some German workers in Paris. They called themselves the Workers Outlaw League. Marx came along and removed what was called the ritualistic paraphernalia so that the masses could participate instead of the few. Daughter, the man down on 125th St. and Lenox Ave. on the stand speaking might be mouthing ideas which arose at a cocktail party or from a transcontinental telephone call or —

Earline puts her head on the desk and begins to sob. Papa LaBas comforts her.

O there I go, getting you upset....

She confesses to him. O it isn't you, pop, it isn't you, it's ....

Berbelang?

O pop, he thinks you're a failure, he felt that you were limiting your techniques. He thought you should have added Inca, Taoism and other systems. He felt that you were becoming all wrapped up in Jes Grew and that it's a passing fad. He isn't the old Berbelang, pop; his eyes are red. He seems to have a missionary zeal about whatever he's mixed up in. I get so lonely, I would like to go out; tonight for instance. I'm invited to a Chitterling Switch.

A Chitterling Switch? What's that, Earline?

She shows him the card.

FOOD! GAMES! DRINK!

## A CHITTERLING SWITCH

sponsored by

*Madame Leware*

for

**anti-lynching campaign**

108 West 136th Street

THURSDAY, OCT. 22, FROM 9 TILL?

let's get our brothers off the limb

by chipping in a barrel of fins

**(surprise appearance by Mystery Blood!)**

We're attempting to raise money for anti-lynching legislation; James Weldon Johnson is supposed to speak...It's like a Rent Party, you know?

You and T use so much slang these days I can hardly communicate with you, but your Chitterling Switch sounds interesting. Do you mind if an old man comes along?

O pop, 50 is not old these days.

You flatter me; just wait until I lock the office.

And I must change, pop. I'll be right with you.

Papa LaBas glances into another office toward the main room of Mumbo Jumbo Kathedral.

Where's Charlotte?

Earline has entered the ladies room.

You know pop, she's been acting strangely these days. She's listless and cross. She had an argument with a client this morning and began to swear at him in French; isn't that a sign?

He pauses for a moment.

I must speak to her. Perhaps she's upset about Berbelang leaving as he did. You know, they were fond of each other. My activist side really charms the women; I suppose this is how he was able to woo such a beautiful thing as yourself.

O cut it out, pop!

Earline looks at her features in the mirror. Something has come over her. She finds it necessary to go through the most elaborate toilet ritual these days, using some very expensive imported soaps, embroidered towels, and she has taken a fancy to buying cakes even though she never before possessed a sweet tooth. She glances at the sign above the marble sink.


### REMEMBER TO FEED THE LOAS


O, that reminds her. She hasn't replenished the loa's tray #21. On a long table in the Mango Room are 22 trays which were built as a tribute to the Haitian loas that LaBas claimed was an influence on his version of The Work. This was 1 of LaBas' quirks. He still clung to some of the ways of the old school. Berbelang had laughed at him 1 night for feeding a loa. This had been I of the reasons for their break. Of course she didn't comprehend their esoteric discussions. Papa LaBas hadn't required that the technicians learn The Work.

The drummers, too, were clinical; their job was that of sidemen to Papa LaBas' majordomo. They didn't know Papa LaBas' techniques and therapy. Didn't have to know it. As long as they knew the score LaBas wasn't interested in proselytizing. But feeding, she thought, was merely 1 of his minor precautions. It seemed such a small thing. She would attend to it tomorrow or the next day.

I'll be with you in a moment, she shouts through the door to LaBas.

We have plenty of time, no rush, Papa LaBas answers her. He is inspecting the trays. He stops at the 12th tray, then returns to join Earline who is ready to go.

The pair moves down the steps. Outside T Malice is talking to a young woman who has her hands clasped behind her back and is swaying coquettishly. When he sees Papa and Earline he pulls down the brim of his chauffeur's cap and looks straight ahead. They tease him and of course being a good sport he can take it.


[11]   Every' time Woodrow Wilson Jefferson chases the dogs, chickens, hogs and sheep, the animals recoup and follow him. W.W. turns on his pursuers.

Go on now. Heah. Go on before I chucks you good with a stick. I told you to go on back to the farm before daddy comes back from the deacons' council and finds you gone, Woodrow Wilson Jefferson threatens his 4-footed friends. His head resembles that of a crocodile wearing granny glasses.

Woodrow Wilson Jefferson has decided to quit the farm and hit the Big City. He is ready. His grandfather had accompanied his slavemaster to New York in the 1850s and had returned with articles and editorials written by 2 gentlemen: Karl Marx and Friedrich Engels. The old issues of the New-York Tribune edited by Horace Greeley had been in the attic all these years. He liked the style. Objective, scientific, the use of the collective We, Our. Therefore there were no illusions and unforeseen events like these country folks in Ré-mote Mississippi, believing in haints and things; and spirits and 2-headed men; mermaids and witches. He would abandon this darkness for the clearing. Make something out of himself. The local people had said that he would be a doctor or even a preacher, but what did they know, backward, lagging behind.

He feels some feathery object brush against his heel and turns again.

Now get out of here, damnit. Where's my stick?

Jefferson goes over to a bush to make a switch. He commences to cut off a branch and whittles the stick so it would leave welts and draw blood. The animals get the message and begin to scamper toward the farmhouse, on the hill, in the background.

He continues on down the road apiece until he reaches the train depot. His bag is stuffed with the newspaper articles (487 to be exact. Wilson didn't always understand the issues but he certainly appreciated the style). When he reaches the train depot, he comes upon 2 men sitting on the station's porch, playing checkers. Behind them were ads for Doctor Pepper, hex signs, Chesterfield Cigarettes and Bull Durham tobacco.

Well if it ain't Rev. Jefferson's boy. Where you going with your hair all spruced down with butter? Where you on your way to?

Jefferson stands there at the Ré-mote train depot. He would ignore these men, lazy, shiftless, not ready. He would do something with his life. Not become just another hayseed whose only recreation is catching junebugs and chirping along with the crickets.

I'm gon on way from this damned town. Well ex-cuuuuuuuuuuuuuuu..s..e me! the man answers, mimicking. His companion spits some tobacco against the station house wall.

The train is in sight. The train that would take him to Jackson Mississippi. Then on to NewYork.

[12]  The party is held at a Townhouse in Harlem. It was lent to the revelers by a wealthy patron. It isn't an authentic Chitterling Switch but an imitation 1. It is what some of the New Negroes would imagine to be a Rent Party given, to meet the 1st of the month, by newly arrived immigrants from the South. In fact there is nowhere in evidence a delegate from the "brother-on-the-street." A man is pounding out some blues on the piano. Once in a while he sips from a cup of King Kong Korn that someone has placed on its top. People are moving from room to room; some of them are passing drinks. Ladies are wearing richly colored dresses, earrings, bracelets, brooches and beads and are well-plumed in a style that neuter-living Protestants would call "garish." 1 woman dressed in an exotic high-gypsy is taking in cash at the door, cash used to supply funds to anti-lynching campaigns.

61 lynchings occurred in 1920 alone. In 1921, 62, some of the victims, soldiers returning from the Great War who after fighting and winning

significant victories—just as they had fought in the Revolutionary and Civil wars and the wars against the Indians—thought that America would repay them for the generosity of putting their lives on the line, for aiding in salvaging their hides from the Kaiser who had been tagged "enemy" this time. Instead, a Protestant country ignorant even of Western mysteries executes soldiers after a manner of punishments dealt to witches in the "Middle Ages." Europe and the Catholic Church are horrified but not surprised at this "tough guy" across the waters whose horrendous murders in Salem led Europe to reform its "witch laws." Until Marcus Garvey came along to rescue the American Negro he was basking in his lethargy like a crocodile sleeping in the sun.

The man the Guianese art critic is directing his comments to mutters something about "ringtail" or "monkey chaser"; LaBas and Earline move on to avoid the ensuing conflict this exchange usually brings.

They see Berbelang and a well-dressed young blond White man whom they recognize from the society pages as Thor Wintergreen, the son of a famous tycoon.

O hello . . . Berbelang greets Papa LaBas and Earline.

Berbelang, what are you doing here?

No time to explain. We're leaving. I'll be home later on.

Berbelang and his friend move toward the door.

But . . . but what *time* are you going to be home?

I'll call you, Berbelang says, edging toward the exit.

Come up to the Kathedral sometime, Berbelang; I'd like to talk to you, LaBas calls after Berbelang.

He and his companion are putting on their coats which have been handed to them by the Hostess.

Yes I will . . . maybe 1 day next week. I'd like to talk to you too.

You see, pop? He doesn't seem to have any time for me at all.

This unhappy plea from Earline is a contrast to the gay laughter, the couples dancing, and the sound of glasses touching in the many rooms.

I think I'm going to leave, Papa.

But we just got here, Earline. It looks interesting.

'You stay. I'm going to go home to wait for him. Maybe we can have a talk.

Papa LaBas helps Earline with her coat. No sooner does she have it on than she rushes from the house, almost tearfully.

Shaking his head, LaBas turns around. *Nothing like an affair of the heart,* LaBas thinks, remembering the bittersweet days of his youth. *They'll work it out. They're beautiful young people,* LaBas thinks to himself as he moves through the halls and among the guests and into 1 of the back rooms inhabited only by 2 men and a Kathedral radio resting on a table, where 1 of them is playing cards. Papa LaBas recognizes him immediately as Black Herman the noted occultist who after a triumphant engagement in Chicago is visiting New York. He sits at the table: the famous batwinged eyebrows, goatee, and narrow mustache which travels from the bridge of his nose to the top of his upper lip. He wears a tuxedo over a white vest and about his neck he is wearing an amulet made in the shape of a triangle. He looks like his picture on his book jacket in which he sits on a globe, 1 booted foot atop a stack of 3 books, the top 1 entitled *The Missing Key* and subtitled *Key to Success*. In the photo his body is framed by designs of an arabesque nature.

A ribbon of black and red travels from his left shoulder to his waist. He sits quietly at a table, sipping from a cup and playing cards. Solitaire. Against the wall Abdul Hamid, the noted magazine editor, stands, his arms folded. He stares in the direction of the merrymakers in the other room. There seems to be a permanently fixed scowl on his face. They are listening to the Situation Report which comes from the 8-tubed Radio.

S.R.: JES GREW ONFLYING GIVING AMERICA A RISE IN THE TOWN OF
MUNCIE INDIANA WHERE IT IS ENGENDERING MORE EXCITEMENT
THAN THE LAST DENTAL INSPECTION. 800 CASES REPORTED SINCE
LAST NIGHT WHICH WERE IMMEDIATELY ISOLATED IN HASTILY
BUILT Y.M.C.A. BARRACKS. A HEAVY TOLL OF STRUT GALS AND
O YOU KIDS . . . SIMILAR OUTBREAKS REPORTED IN ST. PAUL
MINNESOTA AND WHEELERSBURG PENNSYLVANIA . . . POTENTIAL
VICTIMS GATHER ABOUT THE ALREADY INFECTED REJOICING
CHANTING GIVE ME FEVER GIVE ME FEVER . . . .

As the news report dies down the radio begins to blare the song "When The Pussy Willow Whispers To The Catnip."

Turn off that ofay music, Abdul almost snarls. He walks over to the radio and turns it off himself and then returns to the wall where he has been standing watching the other people dance. He wears a bright red fez and a black pinstriped suit and a black tie emblazoned with the crescent moon symbol.

Black Herman raises his head from the cards and sees LaBas standing in the doorway.

Why Papa LaBas, you old jug-blower you! I haven't seen you since the last Black Numerology convention. How have you been?

Papa LaBas walks into the room; Abdul stares sneeringly at his shoes. Then his face.

I didn't want to interrupt you, how have you been? I hear you're packing them in at Liberty Hall.

That's right. 4000 per night; as big as Garvey.

The man stood, a rare and elegantly limbed tree springing from the soil in time-capsule film.

That's a beautiful medal you're wearing.

Yes, Black Herman answers, shaking hands with LaBas. It was awarded to me by a foreign Potentate for my ability to perform the trick of the Human Seed. Lying buried underground for 8 days. Looks as if the prophecy you made at the Black Numerology convention is all around us, LaBas. This Jes Grew thing. How did you predict that? Mundane astrology?

No. Knockings.

Knockings, huh? You're quite good at that. What do you think that this Jes Grew is up to?

It's up to its Text. For some, it's a disease, a plague, but in fact it is an anti-plague. You will recall, Black Herman, that in the past there were germs that avoided words.

| S | A | T | A | N |
|---|---|---|---|---|
| A | D | A | M | A |
| T | A | B | A | T |
| A | M | A | D | A |
| N | A | T | A | S * |

was used to charm a germ in the old days. Being an anti-plague I figure that it's yearning for The Work of its Word or else it will peter out as in the 1890s, when it wasn't ready and had no idea where to search. It must find its Speaking or strangle upon its own ineloquence.

Interesting theory.

I don't quite agree with it, in fact I think it's a whole lot of Bull.

Black Herman and Papa LaBas direct their attention to the man standing against the wall. Gradually, Abdul came from the wall.

You both are filling people's heads with a lot of Bull. Do you think that Harlem will always be as it is now? Poorer people are traveling north and the

* The Conquest of Epidemic Disease—Charles Edward Amory

signs are already showing of its deterioration. The people will have to shape up or they won't survive. Cut out this dancing and carrying on, fulfilling base carnal appetites. We need factories, schools, guns. We need dollars.

But surely, Abdul my friend, you don't believe that the Epidemic is a hoax. It is taking the country by storm; affecting everything in its path, Papa LaBas challenges.

O that's just a lot of people twisting they butts and getting happy. Old, primitive, superstitious jungle ways. Allah is the way. Allah be praised.

The door is filling with others who've been attracted to the discussion. Abdul, seeing them, begins to turn up the decibels.

It's you 2 and these other niggers imbibing spirits and doing the Slow Drag who's holding back our progress.

We've been dancing for 1000s of years, Abdul, LaBas answers.

It's part of our heritage.

Why would you want to prohibit something so deep in the race soul? Herman asks.

That's right, LaBas joins Black Herman. When you reviewed my last work in your Journal of Black Case Histories, that magazine whose contents resemble the scrawls the patients compose with their excreta on the walls of those Atonist "hospitals," you accused me of having a French woman on my staff. I guess your teachings haven't made you realize your bad manners. The people who support your magazine are no longer available since some of your vitriolic remarks about them, and now you have turned against us. A new phenomenon is occurring. The Black Liberal; a new mark extorted in the manner of your former victims who became fed up with it and have withdrawn funds for your support. You are no different from the Christians you imitate. Atonists Christians and Muslims don't tolerate those who refuse to accept their modes.

Some of the people who were listening have decided that it's 1 of those discussions and have drifted away.

Christianity? What has that to do with me?

They are very similar, 1 having derived from the other. Muhammed seems to have wanted to impress Christian critics with his knowledge of the Bible, LaBas continues. They agree on the ultimate wickedness of woman, even using feminine genders to describe disasters that beset mankind. Terming women cattle, un-clean. The Koran was revealed to Muhammed by Gabriel the angel of the Christian apocalypse. Prophets in the Koran: Abraham Isaac and Moses were Christian prophets; each condemns the Jewish people for abandoning the faith; realizing that there has always been a pantheistic contingent among the "chosen people" not reluctant to revere other gods. The Virgin Mary figures in the Koran as well as in the Bible. In fact, 1 night you were reading a poem to the Black woman. It occurred to me that though your imagery was with the sister, the heart of your work was with the Virgin.

You'd better be careful with your critique Papa LaBas, Abdul replies. Remember "He that worships other gods besides Allah shall be forbidden to Paradise and shall be cast into the fires of Hell."

Precisely, Black Herman replies. Intolerant just as the Christians are.

Yes, LaBas joins in, where does that leave the ancient Vodun aesthetic: pantheistic, becoming, 1 which bountifully permits 1000s of spirits, as many as the imagination can hold. Infinite Spirits and Gods. So many that it would take a book larger than the Koran and the Bible, the Tibetan Book of the Dead and all of the holy books in the world to list, and still room would have to be made for more.

And I resent you accusing us of taking advantage of the people, Black Herman joins in. Why have you established yourself as an arbiter for the people's tastes? Granted that there are as many charlatans in our fields as in yours. Some sell snake oils, others propose the establishment of separate states and countries while at the same time accepting all of the benefits of this 1. I think that what bothers me most is your review of my dreambook in which you call me "crazy."

Abdul smiles. The smile of sheer mockery that makes you want to pulverize.

Strange, Herman says, for isn't the Koran accused of lacking chronological order, and hasn't your prophet Muhammed been accused of being prolix contradictory and unclear by critics? Accused of inaccuracy because he confuses Miriam, Moses' sister, with Mary.

Besides, "crazy" is a strange description for a man to be using who canewhipped those flappers outside the Cotton Club just because they wore their dresses short, LaBas accuses.

I didn't do it, but they had it coming. This time a cunning smile sweeps Abdul's face.

The girls pointed you out at the lineup, why do you deny it, Abdul?

Because I didn't do it, but they still deserved what they got, wearing their dresses like that. Tricks. Sluts. Swinging their asses nasty.

Maybe they felt that they should decide themselves what was best for them to wear, Abdul. It wasn't any of your business. And if you weren't the person who meted out those beatings of the high-yellow chorus girls, why were you suspiciously loitering about the Cotton Club?

None of your business, gris-gris man, Abdul utters with contempt.

Sounds as if you've picked up the old Plymouth Rock bug and are calling it Mecca. In the ancient Egyptian religions the emblems used in ritual were so bold that foreign countries burned their temples of worship and accused the participants of "obscenity" and "pornography."

Abdul sees that the doorway is empty. Deprived of an audience, he changes his demeanor. He suddenly becomes polite affable patient reasonable.

O.K. LaBas, Herman. You got me. Johnny James Chicago South Side. Are you satisfied? I wasn't born with a caul on my face, Papa LaBas. Nor was my coming predicted by a soothsayer as yours was, Black Herman, the old woman who predicted that you would be "the marvel of your age." I haven't developed a Hoo Doo psychiatry as you have, Papa LaBas, nor can I talk to animals or spend 1 dollar twice as you've done, Herman. You see, while you are cloistered protected by your followers and patrons and clients I'm out here on the street watching what was once a beautiful community become a slave hole. People are beginning to trickle in here from down home and I'll bet that sooner or later there will be an exodus rivaling the 1 of the Good Book. Who is going to help them? Happy Dust is here now. What strange enslaving drugs will be here later? Where are these people going to work and who is going to feed them? Are they going to eat incense, candles? Maybe what you say is true about the nature of religions which occurred 1000s of years ago, but how are we going to survive if they have no discipline? Look. I spent 9 long years in prison for stabbing a man who wanted to evict my mother because she wouldn't fuck him. I walked into the house 1 day and there he was, her clothes nearly off and his grubby fat fingers plying her flesh. 9 years I was in the clink and 2 of them in solitary confinement. It was then that I began to read omnivorously. I always wondered why the teachers just threw the knowledge at us when we were in school, why they didn't care whether we learned or not. I found that the knowledge which they had made into a cabala, stripped of its terms and the private codes, its slang, you could learn in a few weeks. It didn't take 4 years, and the 4 years of university were set up so that they could have a process by which they would remove the rebels and the dissidents. By their studies and the ritual of academics the Man has made sure that they are people who will serve him. Not 1 of them has equaled the monumental work of J. A. Rogers, a 1-time Pullman porter. Some of these people with degrees going around here shouting that they are

New Negroes are really serving the Man who awarded them their degrees, who has initiated them into his slang and found them "qualified," which means loyal. I applied myself. I went through biochemistry philosophy math, I learned languages, I even learned the transliteration and translation of hieroglyphics, a skill which has come in handy recently. I had no systematic way of learning but proceeded like a quilt maker, a patch of knowledge here a patch there but lovingly knitted. I would hungrily devour the intellectual scraps and leftovers of the learned. Every day I would learn a new character and learn how to mark it. It occurred to me that I was borrowing from all of these systems: Religion, Philosophy, Music, Science and even Painting, and building 1 of my own composed of their elements. It was like a Griffin. I had patched something together out of my own procedure and the way I taught myself became my style, my art, my process. Look, LaBas, Herman. I believe that you 2 have something. Something that is basic, something that has been tested and something that all of our people have, it lies submerged in their talk and in their music and you are trying to bring it back but you will fail. It's the 1920s, not 8000 B.C. These are modern times. These are the last days of your roots and your conjure and your gris-gris and your healing potions and love powder. I am building something that people will understand. This country is eclectic. The architecture the people the music the writing. The thing that works here will have a little bit of jive talk and a little bit of North Africa, a fez-wearing mulatto in a pinstriped suit. A man who can say give me some skin as well as Asalamilakum. Haven't you heard? This is the country where something is successful in direct proportion to how it's put over; how it's gamed. Look at the Mormons. Did they recruit 1000s of whites to their cause by conjuring the Druids? No, they used material the people were familiar with and added their own. The most fundamental book of the Mormon Church, the Book of Mormon, is a fraud. If we Blacks came up with something as corny as the Angel of Moroni, something as trite and phony as their story that the book is the record of ancient Americans who came here in 600 B.C. and perished by A.D. 400, they would deride us with pejorative adjectival phrases like "so-called'" and "would-be." They would refuse to exempt our priests from the draft, a privilege extended to every White hayseed's fruit stand which calls itself a Church. But regardless of the put-on, the hype, the Mormons got Utah, didn't they? Perhaps I will come up with something that will have a building shaped like a mosque, the interior furnishings Victorian, the priests dressed in Catholic garb, and soul food as offerings. What of it as long as it has popular appeal? This is the reason for Garvey's success with the people. O yes, he may look outlandish, loud to you, but the people respect him because they know that he is using his own head and is master of his own art. No, gentlemen, I don't think I would be so smug if I were you. The authorities are already talking about outlawing VooDoo in Harlem. These are your last great days, Herman, packing them in for 60 nights as you do your prestidigitation. A new generation is coming on the scene. They will use terms like "nitty gritty," "for real," "where it's at," and use words like "basic" and "really" with telling emphasis. They will extend the letter and the meaning of the word "bad." They won't use your knowledge and they will call you "sick" and "way-out" and that will be a sad day, but we must prepare for it. For on that day they will have abandoned the other world they came here with and will have become mundanists pragmatists and concretists. They will shout loudly about soul because they will have lost it. And their protests will be a shriek. A panic sound. That's just the way it goes, brothers. You will be just a couple of eccentric characters obsolete out-of-date unused as the appendix. Funny looking like the Australian zoo. But me and my Griffin politics, my chimerical art will survive. Maybe I won't be around but someone is coming. I feel it stirring. He might even have the red hair of a conjure man but he won't be 1. No, he will get it across. And he will be known as the man who "got it across." And people like you will live in seclusion and your circle will be limited and the people who read you will pride themselves on their culture and their selectiveness and their identification with the avant garde.

Well, Abdul says, looking at his watch, I have to get back to the office. I have an anthology that's really going to shake them up when I get done translating it.

What language is it in? LaBas asks.

Hieroglyphics. Abdul starts to shake hands with Herman and LaBas but seeing a couple arriving at the doorway his friendly face becomes a scowl and he withdraws his hand.

He wags his finger in their face. And if I ever see you characters hanging around my mosque I will have my men take care of you, Abdul says, his back turned to the 2 people. He winks at LaBas and Herman and then nearly knocks over the 2 people on the way out of the room; standing in the doorway are a high-yellow woman and her bespectacled light-skinned unsteady harassed-looking male escort.

Watch out with your old short Black ugly self, she scornfully shouts as Abdul flies by the 2 and out the door.

Julius? Why don't you do something, Julius? When these niggers manhandle me like that?

Yes dear my lovely Nubian queen, the man says meekly as he and the woman turn about and head for the other rooms. (Julius was a well-known Black doorman for a quality Gentlemen's club, hired to bounce the literary bad niggers who might become rowdy. He was W. E. B. Du Bois' Boswell, but Du Bois was always in conference to him.)

Papa LaBas and Black Herman move from the room and down the hall of the Townhouse now filled with people.

You know, maybe he's got something, Herman.

Maybe so but I don't think that he should experiment in public this way. He's doing a lot of damage, building his structure on his feet like this. That bigoted edge of it resembles fascism. An actor.... We'll see.

Papa LaBas reflects. Do you think we're out of date as he said?

I know that the politicians of this era will be remembered more than me but I would like to believe that we work for principles and not for self. "We serve the loas," as they say. Charismatic leaders will become as outdated as the solo because people will realize that when the Headman dies the movement dies instead of becoming a permanent entity, perispirit, a protective covering for its essence. Yes, Abdul will become surrounded by people who will yield inches of their lives to him at a time; become the satellites rotating about the body which gives them light; but that's ephemeral, the fading clipping from the newspaper in comparison to a Ju Ju Mask a 1000 years old. No, LaBas, the New York police will wipe out VooDoo just as they did in New Orleans, but it will find a home in a band on the Apollo stage, in the storefronts; and there will always be those who will risk the uninformed amusement of their contemporaries by resurrecting what we stood for.

The 2 men, Papa LaBas and his guide Black Herman, walk into the 1920s parlor of the Townhouse. People are standing about a light-skinned-appearing man.

Well I'll be damned, Black Herman says. It's the President Elect, Warren Harding.

They move into the center of the room where Harding stands beneath some white chandeliers. He is on the tail end of some remarks he is making to the gathering. The Hostess stands off to the side, next to a society interviewer from the Race press. Her party is made: an unannounced visit of the next President.

As you know, Mr. James Weldon Johnson visited me in Muncie and gave me information concerning the nasty war taking place in Haiti the administration was attempting to conceal.

The guests move in as Harding reaches into his hip pocket and removes a plug of tobacco.

I think we made a good shot with the Haitian material and the administration was put on the defensive. They were hard pressed to explain why a horrid war with Marines committing so many atrocities was allowed to continue. I promised Mr. Johnson that on the way to Washington I would drop by and see him and it was he who suggested that if I attended your little party I could hear some of that good music. The sounds Mr. Daugherty my Attorney General and Florence my wife keep hidden from me. So if you don't mind a gate crasher I think I'll just go and dip my fork into some of those chitterlings and pigs' feet I know you're cooking down in the basement kitchen.

The President Elect followed by 2 of his aides walks down the steps leading to the basement as titters fly through the room.

Well I have to go, LaBas says to Herman.

Wait, I'll walk you down the stairs.

Herman puts on his black top formal hat and black cape. They walk down the Townhouse steps. Black Herman and LaBas shake hands when they reach the sidewalk.

Keep in touch, Papa; there are some people in the harbor who want to meet you.

Good. Call me. LaBas walks toward his car. T Malice has the night off. He turns to Black Herman, the other man approaching the end of the block.

Herman, can I give you a ride?

The man turns around. No that's O.K. I'll walk.

Herman?

Yes?

These young kids these days know how to give a party, don't they?

You can say that again, Herman agrees before vanishing around the corner.

Biff Musclewhite has reduced his status from Police Commissioner to Consultant to the Metropolitan Police in the precinct in Yorktown in order to take a job as Curator of the Center of Art Detention. (More pay.) He is sitting with 1 of his old colleagues, Schlitz "the Sarge of Yorktown," nicknamed affectionately by the police station he so often visited over the years.

They are sitting at the table of the Plantation House located in the Milky

Way of Manhattan, the area of theaters and night clubs. The Southern Belle chorus line is promenading on the stage (the background of which is a riverboat) in their multipetticoated skirts, carrying parasols and wearing bonnets. Banjos strumming. Black waiters stand against the wall dressed as if they were in some 18th-century French court. White powdered wigs, frilled cuffs and shirts. The deep, blue lighting fills the club.

Gonna miss ya, Biff, remember the bags I use to bring to ya, ya got real rich outta that; the only guy retiring at $3000 per as a millionaire. I'll bet you have 1,000,000s in stocks and bonds inside your shoeboxes.

Yes, I've come a long way, hobnobbing with the rich out on Long Island... Curator of a museum... a long way from that punk kid you use to cover, down in the Tenderloin. Musclewhite laughs.

Yeah, remember when you went off to war and the whole gang turned out to say goodbye and sing "Over There." You really gave it to them Huns, Biff. We were proud of you.

... You know, Sarge, some would think that this was a plot for a Cagney movie. You and I brothers, you become a gangster and I become a cop.

Only you didn't go straight. I was always dumb but you were smart, taking more money from us than I would ever make in policy or bootlegging liquor, and now Curator of the Center of Art Detention which is kind of Big Cheese for us crooks. There you are taking bigger than me and getting away clean; how did you swing it?

Some of my friends over at the Plutocrat Club said there was an opening. I asked them how I could get the job if my only experience was as police commissioner. They said I had to learn the art of making a simple oil portrait resemble a window dressing in heaven. They said it was the gab that was the art. How you promoted it... So I've been learning these art terms from reading the New York *Sun*. And you know, I'm getting good at it.

Similar to my business. That's what I mean, Biff, you've always had a head on your shoulders. Your silver hair, the expensive clothing, hanging out with all the swanks. A good cover. You got it made, pal. The pressures I have... Buddy Jackson is muscling in on my operation in Harlem; we tried to get him the other day but the nigger seems to have 9 lives. My man hurled a bomb at him and a dame.

[*The curtain opens, revealing Charlotte's Pick, who is about 4' 1". He is in what appears to be a slave cabin and the stage foliage indicates that the cabin is in a forest. There are roots lying on a wooden table and an old tattered book.*

*We can see by the way Peter is mixing things, the greenish-yellow candles, the black cats walking about, and a black bird looking sinisterly down upon the whole affair, that Peter is* impersonating *a cnjah man. He removes a tattered book and begins to mumble words from it. The slave master's wife Charlotte materializes; she tantalizingly removes her hoop skirt and petticoats until she is down to a brief flapper's skirt. Bloodhounds approaching in the background. The audience begins to chuckle as Doctor Peter Pick goes through the motions of putting her down. Charlotte makes even bolder more suggestive overtures to him. The closer the noise of the bloodhounds comes to his cabin the more the audience laughs at the Pick's Predicament. The bankers, publishers, visiting Knights of Pythias and Knights of the White Camelia, theatrical people, gangsters and city officials who frequent the club are getting a big kick out of this.*

*An angel in a Green Pastures getup passes by. Pick invites him in and asks him to read the words. Nothing happens as Charlotte now begins to remove her blouse. The angel leaves the cabin, puffing on his cigar and tipping his black felt derby with ribbon band. The bloodhounds are closing in on the cabin as Peter Pick makes more attempts to send her back from where he conjured her. A local demon passes by and Peter Pick yanks its tail and pulls it into the cabin. It too reads from the magic book, the* grimoire, *and nothing happens. Charlotte is removing her brassiere and has unpinned her hair. The bloodhounds are heard crossing the swamps and some can he heard coming up on the ground a few yards from the Picks' cabin. Well, in desperation Pick passes the book to the planter's wife and asks her to read from it. She reads. Pick disappears!]* The curtains close upon thunderous applause and laughter.

*So this was the Charlotte his friends, Masons in the know, at the Caucasian lodge talked about. Her apartment where one was initiated into certain rites. They were calling it the Temple of Isis. The rites, it suggested, were of a sexual nature,* Muses Biff Musclewhite, who resembled the white-mustached Esquire symbol. Wellheeled. Dirty old man.

Some act huh!

Yes, Musclewhite distantly replies to Schlitz the Sarge; *the beauty, the enchanting body of this woman,* Musclewhite thinks. A . . . why don't we order.

The "Sergeant" snaps his fingers.

Hey Pompey! Cato! come over here, he calls to the 2 Black waiters standing against the wall of the Plantation House.

They respond smartly, approaching Biff Musclewhite and Schlitz the

Sarge's table, bedazzling in their resplendent uniforms. The Police Commissioner now Curator of the Center of Art Detention is examining the menu.

Schlitz the Sarge, about to give an order, raises his head when he gets it shattered.

The 2 men put the guns back inside their vests and hop some tables until they disappear through the door. The patrons scream. Faint. Panic. Screaming.

Shocked!! Musclewhite rises from the table and pursues the waiters. His friend's leaning back in the chair. Eyes staring straight ahead, about 1/3 of his head from the brow up scattered into the neighboring diners' dinner plates and on their clothes.

Outside the club the 2 men are nowhere to be seen. Only white powdered wigs lying on the sidewalk.

## CHAPTER 34

T FEELER, tensed up and high strung, his "good hair" waving under his beret, fled Harry's and ran to his bicycle parked in the parking lot. He began pedaling up University Avenue, turned left at Oxford, right at Hearst, and left at Euclid. He traveled up Euclid until he came to Keith, where he turned right to the Yellings' home. He jumped off the bicycle, ran up the path and through the door out of breath.

"What's wrong with you, you ol sissified nigger, come in here mess up my flo?" Nanny stood with a mop in her hand, a hand on her hip; she was doing the hall.

"I must see Minnie, quick."

Minnie, hearing T Feeler's voice, rushed out from the rear apartment behind whose doors much commotion was going on.

"It's O.K., Nanny," Minnie said.

"Well, he should knock next time. He trying so hard to be cute he don't even think about knocking. He ain't as cute as he think he is." Pouting and flashing T a murderous grin, Nanny went upstairs.

"Minnie, they're after you."

"Who's after me, T?" she said, showing him to one of the living room sofas.

"LaBas and some woman. They were having a drink at Harry's. They didn't know I was in the next booth. Anyway, they were talking about you. She told him that a stranger in the sky and out of your past would take care of you, and that this stranger would want to even an old score in which you acted hoggish. I didn't get much of the conversation, but it seemed they were discussing your father."

"You came all the way up here to tell me this?"

"But, Minnie...."

"I'm not worried about LaBas any more. Maxwell Kasavubu obtained a lawyer for me. Since Wolf died, they believe they have a good case for giving me the plant. Solid Gumbo Works will be mine, and I'll make it go public. I'll put those Workers out, and LaBas will be thrown out too. He's probably engaged in some last-ditch negotiations to keep me from getting the place."

"But, Minnie, be has some powers. They say that LaBas and his Workers are nothing to fool with."

"Quacks. They're quacks. We found out what they were making down there. Quack industry. Mumbo Jumbo. Now if you'll excuse me, T, I have to go back and help on the pamphlets we are putting out for the rally on behalf of Kingfish and Andy Brown—the brothers were unjustly busted in the home of one of LaBas' Workers. The corrupt bushwa is some kind of double agent because he called the police on his own brothers."

"Do you need a hand, Minnie?" T volunteered.

"Sure, T, why don't you take care of Big Sally's thirteen children? Then the sister upstairs who're minding them can come help us with the work."

"Yes, Minnie. Anything you say. You're the boss." T Feeler walked behind Minnie like a frail sad puppy.

## CHAPTER 35

Morning. LaBas had reached an impasse in the case. Whenever this occurred, he would take up another project. Usually, when he took his attention off of a case, he'd divert it to something quite different. He had decided to give his temporary living quarters a thorough housecleaning in the old-fashioned way. Marie LaVeau had written a book in which she talked about a Business housecleaning. This housecleaning not only got into the nook and crannies of the living space but the spiritual space as well. He was looking up names under "Domestics" in the yellow pages. *Domestic!!* LaBas called Nanny. He wanted to ask her some questions.

## CHAPTER 36

He was a blonde. He lay in the bed, tossing and turning. His room. What was that odor? The pungent odor of middle-class perfume making the air misty. He didn't feel right. His hair. What on earth was the matter with his hair? It was long and was covering the pillow. The pillows? They had a flower print and were pink. Pink? He rose in his bed and his breasts jiggled. BREASTS? THE BREASTS?? He looked back into the mirror next to the bed and his mouth made a black hollow hole of horror. "O MY GOD. MY GOD." He was a woman. You know what he said next, don't you, reader? He's from New York and so . . . . you guessed it! "Kafka. Pure Kafka," he said. A feeling crept over him. Tingly. What could he do? He felt like screaming, but he couldn't scream. Was that someone coming down the hall? He ran and jumped back into the bed, pulled the covers up to his neck and pretended to be asleep. Someone *was* coming down the hall. They stood for a moment outside in the hall. And then the knob slowly turned. Someone was now in the room; a dark foreboding shadow crept to the foot of the bed. A giant colored man— an Olmec-headed giant wearing a chauffeur's cap. Max started to really scream this time.

"Please, Ms. Dalton, you will wake the whole house," the figure says. *Look at that white bitch laying there. Sloppy drunk. Probably wants some peter too. That's all they think about anyway. Ill fuck her into a cunt energy crisis she mess with me. That's probably what she wont. Been hittin on me all night Probably pretending to be drunk. Wonts to see how far I go. I know Ian ain't gettin any. One simple dude. Tried to give me that old PROGRESSIVE LABOR line. Who don't know that? Who don't know that old simple ass mutherfuckin bullshit? Them mens was working at the Ford plant. Had some good jobs too. Then here come this Progressive Labor bullshit and them niggers lost they job after it was over. Ha! When is this bitch going to go to sleep? I wont to take that dark blue Buick with steel spoke wheels over to the South Side. Man, will them mo'fugs be mad when they see. Think I'm a pimp. Then I'll go up to the counter and roll out my 75 dollars. Man, they think I'm one of them pimps. Then I go get me some rangs. Lots of them. Have them all shining on my fingers. Shining. Justa shining. Gee. Bet I could have me plenty ol stankin bitches. Commisstee. That shit ain't nothin but some bunk. Roosia. Shhhhhhit Started to bust that mo'fug Ian right in the mouf. Must be a sissy. . . .* The door opens and in comes a woman tapping a cane. *Ahhhhshitt. Here come that other old crazy white woman down the hall. Look like Ms. Mary trying to say something. I better do something quick.*

Max finally realized the situation. He made a futile effort to move his lips. "Bigggg. Bigggggg." Meanwhile the cane tapping comes closer to the door. Bigger picks up the pillow and starts towards Mary Dalton when—

Max wakes up from the nightmare.

There was some bamming at the door real rough. Bam! Bam! Bam! Bam! Bam, Bam! Max leaped out of his dream and rushed to the door. Who could this be bamming at his door this time of night? The woman, trembling, rushed into the room.

"What do you want? I told you to never come here."

She wriggled out of her raincoat, then nervously wrung out a match after lighting a cigarette. She plopped down in a chair and drew her breath. It was Lisa, stripped of her Nanny's rags; sharp, voluptuous.

"It's LaBas. He called. He wants to talk about Ed's killing. Suppose he starts to ask me a lot of questions? You know I can't stand up under a lot of questions."

"You fool. You come here for that? I told you never to contact me here on this assignment."

"Look, you've only been here for a few years. I've been here more than ten, ever since his wife Ruby left. I've worked on that household and put my conjure all over the place. Then they sent you in to begin this organization to add to Ed's problems, just as I had worked hard to prepare Minnie to do that. We've done enough damage to that family. When will it end?"

"It will end when Solid Gumbo Works has folded."

"I can't wait any longer. Since Wolf was killed, she's brought those Moochers into the household. I have to shuffle about like Hattie McDaniel to take care of their needs. They write slogans all over the walls and sleep on stained mattresses. They leave rings in the bathtub. They've been up all night with the mimeograph machine, trying to free Kingfish and Andy."

"Yes, I know," Max said. "I wrote the copy."

"I have to fix breakfast and clean up their mess. You know how Moochers are, never clean up after themselves, always expect someone else to do their cleaning for them. I told you not to draw the girl into that organization. I was doing O.K. All I needed was some more time."

"You were taking too long. Besides, the Moochers provided us with the numbers to wear down Solid Gumbo Works."

"Well, I still maintain that if it bad been left to me, I would have put her on, Ed. I never did go along with his killing."

"It was necessary. You know that. If we hadn't butchered him that night, he would have discovered the cure for heroin addiction. That was the industrial secret you passed on to me; the papers of his you Xeroxed. We had to do it. If he had found a legitimate cure, our quack operation would have shut down: the southern mailhouse empire we built would shut down. Heroin, jukeboxes, our black record company in the east, The House of Cocaine. Everybody would have been asking for Ed's Gumbo. Wasn't it enough that be found a cure for cancer?"

"You thought you'd gotten rid of that threat when you killed that Chinese acupuncturist, but Ed found different means."

"You always respected him a bit, didn't you?"

"He was a man. Ed was a hard-working man. Sometimes I wanted to tell him who I was, where I was from, and what was wrong with me. That I had been sent into his house to train his child to drive him crazy."

"You can't quit. I received orders from Louisiana Red that we have one more job. You think you have problems. Do you think I like posing as a visiting lecturer at the University of California at Berkeley? The way the women in the English Department office whisper about my lack of potency and sometimes refuse to file for my office post box.

"Do you think that I enjoy it when they refuse to mimeograph copies of lecture notes for my students? Why, this campus reminds me of the set of I Was a Teenage Werewolf. If Louisiana Red hadn't promised me this one-million-dollar retirement money, I never would have taken care of this assignment. I was doing all right with my New York industrial spy firm. But you, you have to stay until it's over. They have you where they want you."

"I'm leaving."

Max pulls out a sheet of paper from a desk drawer. "You know that Louisiana Red doesn't play. They will get to you through your police record. You are a fugitive from justice, you know, you bag woman. (Reads) 'Real name: The Hammerhead Shark!' The title you picked up in that caper when you hit a man on the head with a hammer, put a hex on a congressman, double-crossed Jack Johnson, stabbed Martin Luther King, brought charges against Father Divine, brought down Sam Cooke in a blaze of gunfire and bad-mouthed Joe Louis. They know your penchant for Coon-Can and about your scar too. Not only are the law enforcement bureaus after you, but you know the consequences of crossing the Louisiana Red Corporation."

"I'm not frightened any more. I've sent a message to the Red Rooster and told him that I want out, Max."

"I've thought about leaving myself."

"You have? Why, Max, we can leave together, go to Reno; why, I can get a job as a waitress, you can deal blackjack."

"But they'll follow us."

"Not if we move fast enough."

"Maybe we ought to. You know how I missed you during those long days. When you couldn't be with me in my arms. How we had to limit ourselves to meeting every other Thursday, your day off. There must be thousands of us all over the country, meeting like this out of public view.

"Yes, my dearest, the American underground of Desire, the name of the first American slaver; we know each other on the street and recognize each other's signals. How we pay subscriptions to our propaganda organs which convince the public that it's only the Jim Brown and Racquel Welch bedroom scene that's the problem. We rule America, all of it, my Nanny and me. The 'Every Other Thursday Society.' Yes, I want to leave, Lisa. My cover is getting to me."

"I don't understand."

"That book I'm doing, the one on Richard Wright's book." He rushes to the bar, makes a drink and gulps it down. Then he slams the empty GLASS on the bar. "It's getting to me. I'm having these dreams. Just before you knocked on the door, I had one. I was the murder victim and this big brute was coming towards me with a pillow. "

"That dream will come true if you won't move over to the wall."

The startled couple turned around to see the gunman standing in the doorway.

"Son of a bitch. So you were going to take it on the lam and leave me stranded now that the assignment has heated up."

"T, take it easy, have a drink."

"No thanks, I'm not thirsty. Here I have been playing the fool for these past years, helping you set up Ed Yellings, and now you are going to drop me. Years of swallowing my pride and acting like a kookie rookie when all along you two were carrying on. I'm finished with this assignment. I feel sick about what has happened to Minnie. She wants more power now than Marie LaVeau, and you two did it to her. I'm going to call the Director of Louisiana Red Corporation, the Red Rooster, and tell him everything I know about you two. You see, it's all over. That's what I came up here to tell you about."

"What's all over?" Lisa says. "You don't make sense."

"About an hour ago Minnie busted George Kingfish Stevens and Andy Brown out of jail and then commandeered an airplane after miraculously evading San Francisco security, which was as tight as a drum. You don't have anything else to use against Solid Gumbo Works because Minnie has been shot."

"Shot," both Lisa and Max exclaim.

"Yes, she was shot by a passenger. The poor child was rushed to a New York hospital. It sickens me, my part in this whole thing."

He walks over to the telephone and dials.

"Hello operator, give me Louisiana Red Corporation in New Orleans, person to person to the Red Rooster, the number is area code 504—" but before be could say anything Max lunged for him and with incredible strength wrestled him to the floor. The gun went off, killing T Feeler.

"Max, let's get out of here. We really must go now."

Max slowly looked up from where he knelt over the corpse. "Who you callin Max, bitch? I'll whip you into bad health."

"Max, what's the matter with you? Why are you talking that way?"

"I'm gone fix you good. Killing you won't count. Not even the best critics will notice it. I'm going to kill you." He walks towards her. She screams.

"Max! Stop!"

"Max? Who Max? I'm Bigger," Max growls.

## CHAPTER 37

Chorus received the good news that morning. Yes, he had been ejected from a recital hall but he was still in demand. Another had called the day after his dismissal. His agent wanted him to fly to New York to check out its dimensions, its acoustics. His voice had been stifled so much over the years through bad distribution, poor and often hostile salesmen, indifference from those at the top that be insisted a clause be added to his contract giving him the right to satisfactory acoustics.

Chorus fed the cats, cleaned his apartment and was soon packing his white tuxedos. He drove to the San Francisco Airport and before long was airborne.

About ten minutes out, the stewardess asked him if be wanted to have a cocktail. He sipped his Bloody Mary and gazed out over some dry-looking mountains. He read a magazine. He napped for about a half-hour. He got up and walked down the aisle towards the bilingual toilet. He noticed a woman and two companions. He recognized her from her picture that had appeared in the *Berkeley Barb* and *the San Francisco Chronicle*. He recalled she made Herb Caen's column regarding some Moochers' benefit in which she shared the platform with Rev. Rookie.

He returned to his seat and read some more.

One of the woman's companions rose and went towards the cockpit. Sky-jack! The man addressed the passengers tellin them that no one would be hurt.

The two men, now wearing terrorist masks which looked like big woolen socks with two slits for eyes, walked down the aisle, putting the passengers' valuables into some sacks while the skinny woman with them, quite fashionably dressed, began making some kind of speech to the passengers. She went on and on, and the more she talked, the more Chorus became enraged.

Chorus went along with it, though. He didn't want any hassle. When they came to him, he would gladly give them whatever cash he had.

Fish came to Chorus and spoke sarcastically through his mouth opening.

"Well, what do we have here? Mr. Superstar. Big Nigger. I seen your picture in *Jet*. Some kind of actor you is."

Chorus fumed.

"Sell-out, oreo niggers like you—I can't stand. Fork over some of that money, you minstrel." He laughed. "Hey, Andy, look what we have here. A minstrel all decked out in a white tuxedo."

After taking Chorus' money, they moved on, robbing some of the other passengers.

Minnie moved down the aisle as the men kept an eye on the passengers. She caught Chorus' eye. She paused in front of him. She said she had seen his last performance. She said that she didn't think it was it relevant. She started calling him obscene names, standing in the aisle with her hands on her hips. She went on and on, and every time he tried to get a word in edgewise, she would scream, "YOU LISTEN TO ME, NIGGER. YOU LISTEN TO ME. LET ME FINISH. LET ME FINISH!"

Chorus knew what be had to do because he'd be damned if be was going through this scene again.

CHAPTER 38

They are dining at Spenger's Seafood Restaurant. Ernest Hemingway dined here and after talking to Frank Spenger went on to write *The Old Man and the*

*Sea.* Frank Spenger remembered a time when there were so many crabs in the Bay they made a nuisance of themselves.

LaBas is glum; he is eating a prawn. Ms. Better Weather is sobbing; she hasn't touched her food.

"That poor child."

"Will you control yourself, Better Weather, and continue with the report."

"After she busted Kingfish and Andy out of jail, they commandeered a car and somehow evaded the security at the San Francisco Airport."

"Amazing!"

"Anyway, they sky-jacked the plane, but then something happened. She was talking to one of the passengers; he jumped her and holding her with a gun to her back he was able to disarm Andy and Kingfish. He screamed, 'I'm sick of YOU cutting into my lines, bitch.' The captain rushed in upon the situation and mistaking the stranger for one of the sky-jackers killed him, but be got... he got—"

"O Better Weather, brace yourself. Tell me the rest."

"They took her to the hospital, and that was the last I heard from New York. As soon as I heard, I came right down. They told me you were eating here. What are you going to do?"

"What can I do? There's nothing they would do to reverse what has happened. The Board of Directors has made the decision. I have no vote."

"But you just told me she couldn't help herself. Isn't that what you said?"

"Better Weather, you know how the Corporation works. It is an individual with its own laws, an uncharacterized character like the Greek Chorus, a fictitious person. Once it moves, it moves by its own by-laws. Did you tell Sister?"

"I called her, but she had been told already. I think we ought to go up and see how she's doing."

"That's a good idea." LaBas paid the check, and he and Ms. Better Weather left.

## FLIGHT TO CANADA

Dear Massa Swille:
What it was?
I have done my Liza Leap
& am safe in the arms
of Canada, so
Ain't no use your Slave
Catchers waitin on me
At Trailways
I won't be there

I flew in non-stop
Jumbo jet this A.M. Had
Champagne
Compliments of the Cap'n
Who announced that a
Runaway Negro was on the
Plane. Passengers came up
And shook my hand
& within 10 min. I had
Signed up for 3 anti-slavery
Lectures. Remind me to get an
Agent

Traveling in style
Beats craning your neck after
The North Star and hiding in
Bushes anytime, Massa
Besides, your Negro dogs
Of Hays & Allen stock can't
Fly

By now I s'pose that
Yellow Judas Cato done tole
You that I have snuck back to
The plantation 3 maybe 4 times
Since I left the first time

Last visit I slept in
Your bed and sampled your
Cellar. Had your prime
Quadroon give me
She-Bear. Yes, yes

You was away at a
Slave auction at Ryan's Mart
In Charleston & so I knowed
You wouldn't mind
Did you have a nice trip, Massa?

I borrowed your cotton money
to pay for my ticket & to get
Me started in this place called
Saskatchewan Brrrrrrr!
It's cold up here but least
Nobody is collaring bobbling gagging
Handcuffing yoking chaining & thumbscrewing
You like you is they hobby horse

The Mistress Ms. Lady
Gived me the combination
To your safe, don't blame

The feeble old soul, Cap'n
I told her you needed some
More money to shop with &
You sent me from Charleston
To get it. Don't worry
Your employees won't miss
It & I accept it as a
Down payment on my back
Wages

    I must close now
Massa, by the time you gets
This letter old Sam will have
Probably took you to the
Deep Six
That was rat poison I left
In your Old Crow

Your boy
Quickskill

## CHAPTER 4

There's a knock at the door. It's Moe, the white house slave—Mingy Moe, as the mammies in the kitchen call him. He looks like an albino: tiny pink pupils, white Afro.

"Sorry to disturb you, Master Swille, but Abe Lincoln, the President of the so-called Union, is outside in the parlor waiting to see you. He's fiddling around and telling corny jokes, shucking the shud and husking the hud. I told him that you were scheduled to helicopter up to Richmond to shake your butt at the Magnolia Baths tonight, but he persists. Says, 'The very survival of the Union is at stake.' "

"Hand me my jacket, Uncle Robin," Swille says as be stands in the middle of the room.

"Which one do you wont, suh—the one with the spangly fritters formal one or the silvery-squilly festooned street jacket?"

"Give me the spangly one." Turning to Moe, Swille says, "Now, Moe, you tell this Lincoln gentleman that he won't be able to stay long. Before I fly up to Richmond, I have to check on my investments all over the world."

"Yessir, Mr. Swille."

Momentarily, Lincoln, Gary Cooper-awkward, fidgeting with his stovepipe hat, humble-looking, imperfect—a wart here and there—craw and skuttlecoat, shawl, enters the room. "Mr. Swille, it's a pleasure," he says, extending his hand to Swille, who sits behind a desk rumored to have been owned by Napoleon III. "I'm a small-time lawyer and now I find myself in the room of the mighty, why—"

"Cut the yokel-dokel, Lincoln, I don't have all day. What's on your mind?" Swille rejects Lincoln's hand, at which Lincoln stares, hurt.

"Yokel-dokel? Why, I don't get you, Mr. Swille."

"Oh, you know—log-cabin origin. That's old and played out. Why don't you get some new speech writers? Anyway, you're the last man I expected to see down here. Aren't you supposed to be involved in some kind of war? Virginia's off limits to your side, isn't it? Aren't you frightened, man?"

"No, Mr. Swille. We're not frightened because we have a true cause. We have a great, a noble cause. Truth is on our side, marching to the clarion call. We are in the cause of the people. It is a people's cause. This is a great, noble and people period in the history of our great Republic. We call our war the Civil War, but some of the fellows think we ought to call it the War Between the States. You own fifty million dollars' worth of art, Mr. Swille. What do you think we ought to call it?"

"I don't feel like naming it, Lanky—and cut the poppycock."

"Lincoln, sir."

"Oh yes, Lincoln. Well, look, Lincoln, I don't want that war to come up here because, to tell you the truth, I'm not the least bit interested in that war. I hate contemporary politics and probably will always be a Tory. Bring back King George. Why would a multinational like myself become involved in these queer crises? Why, just last week I took a trip abroad and was appallingly and disturbingly upset and monumentally offended by the way the Emperor of France was scoffing at this . . . this nation, as you call it. They were snickering about your general unkempt, hirsute and bungling appearance—bumping into things and carrying on. And your speeches. What kind of gibberish are they? Where were you educated, in the rutabaga patch? Why don't you put a little pizazz in your act, Lanky? Like Davis . . . Now that Davis is as nit as a spit with his satin-embroidered dressing case, his gold tweezers and Rogers & Sons strap. He's just bananas about Wagner and can converse in German, French and even that bloody Mexican patois. Kindly toward the 'weak' races, as he referred to them in that superb speech he made before the Senate criticizing Secretary of State Seward and other celebrities for financing that, that... maniac, John Brown. And when he brought in that savage, Black Hawk, on the steamboat *Winnebago*, he treated the primitive overlord with the respect due an ethnic celebrity. You can imagine the Americans taunting this heathen all decked out in white deerskins. Davis' slaves are the only ones I know of who take mineral baths, and when hooped skirts became popular he gave some to the slave women, and when this made it awkward for them to move through the rows of cotton, he widened the rows."

"That's quite impressive, Mr. Swille. I have a worthy adversary."

Swille, smirking and squinting, flicks the ashes from a cigar given him by the King of Belgium. "An intellectual. What an intellectual. Loggerhead turtles? Oysters? Hogarth? Optics? Anything you want to know, Davis's got the answer. And his beautiful wife. More brilliant than most men. As aristocratic as Eugénie, wife of my good friend Imperial Majesty Napoleon Bonaparte III. I was having dinner with her just a few weeks ago. You know, she's the daughter of the Count of Montijo and the Duke of Peneranda. Men who like nothing but the best. I call her Gennie, since we move in the same circles. Why, I'm thinking about refurbishing the Morocco Club in New York—just no place for the royal ones to go any more. We were eating, and she turned to me and asked why Du Chaillur searched for the primitive missing link in Africa when one had shambled into the Capitol from the jungles of the Midwest."

Lincoln looks puzzled. "I don't get it, Mr. Swille."

"She was talking about you, silly. They're calling you the Illinois Ape. Eugénie's a brilliant conversationalist. But Varina Davis has it over her. Those glittering supper parties at the Montgomery White House—and did you see the carriage she bought Jeff? Imported it from New Orleans. Yes indeed, from New Orleans. Almost as good as mine. Upholstered in watered blue silk. Can't you see those two representing the... the Imperial Empire of the Confederate States of Europe in London? They might even make him a knight— Sir Jefferson Davis. I can see it all now. And then upon their return, a ticker-tape parade down Broadway, with clerks leaning out of office windows shouting, Long Live Jeff. Long Live Varina. Long Live Jeff. Long Live Varina. The Duke and Duchess of Alabama. What a man. What a man. A prince.

One of my friends recently visited this six-plus-foot tall specimen and said he just felt like stripping and permitting this eagle-eyed, bladenosed, creamy Adonis to abuse him and ... [pant, pant] humiliate him."

"Come again, Mr. Swille?"

"Oh, Abe, you're so green. Green as jade in a cocaine vision."

"Mr. Swille, mind if we change the subject?"

"We have a delightful life down here, Abe. A land as Tennyson says 'In which it all seemed always afternoon. All round the coast the languid air did swoon. Here are cool mosses deep, and thro the stream the long-leaved flowers weep, and from the craggy ledge the poppy hang in sleep.' Ah. Ah. 'And sweet it is to dream of Fatherland. Of child, and wife and slave. Delight our souls with talk of Knightly deeds.' Walking about the gardens and the halls! And, Abe, a man like you can have a soft easy hustle down here. You could be walking around and wallowing in these balmy gardens and these halls. The good life. Breakfast in a dress coat. Exotic footbaths. Massages three times a day. And what we call down here a 'siesta.' Niggers fanning you. A fresh bouquet of flowers and a potent julep delivered to your room. Roses. Red roses. Yellow roses. White roses. We can bring back the 'days that were.' Just fancy yourself the Earl of Lincoln, or Count Abe. Or Marquis Lincoln. Marquis Lincoln of Springfield. You could have this life, Lincoln." He goes to the window and draws back the curtains. There is a view of the hills of Virginia. "It's all bare now, Lincoln. But we will build that city. From here to as far as the eye can see will be great castles with spires and turrets. We can build one for you, Lincoln. Sir Lincoln."

"I'm afraid I wouldn't like it down here, Mr. Swille. I'm just a mudfish. I don't yen for no fancy flies."

"Think about it, Lincoln. You can take an hour and a half putting on your clothes down here. Why ... why ... I'm thinking about taking up Meditative Transcendentalism. I've sent to India for a Swami. You know, you may not be so lucky in the next election year. If it hadn't been for those Hoosiers and Suckers and other rags and patches who packed the Wigwam, you'd be back in your law office in Springfield. Their conduct was disgraceful. Why, I had to tell the networks not to carry it. They hollered you the nomination. Steam whistles. Hotel gongs. Comanches! Liquor flowing like Babylon. Not even top-shelf, but Whiskey Skin, Jersey Lightning and Brandy Smash."

"The boys were just cuttin up, Mr. Swille, just jerking the goose bone."

"And then bribing the delegates with Hoboken cigars and passes to quiz shows. Washington, Jefferson and Monroe must be bowling in their chains.

And that lunatic wife of yours. Must she dress like that? She looks like a Houston and Bowery streetwalker who eats hero sandwiches and chews bubble gum. Why does she wear that brunette bouffant and those silver high-heel boots? She looks like a laundromat attendant. Old frowzy dough-faced thing. Queens accent. Ever think about taking her to the Spa? And why does she send those midnight telegrams to the Herald Tribune after drinking God knows what? And there's another thing I've been meaning to ask you, Mr. Lincoln."

"What is that, Mr. Swille?"

"Do you think it appropriate for the President of the United States to tell such lewd jokes to the boys in the telegraph room? The one about the cow and the farmer. The traveling salesmen and the milkmaid. The whole scabrous repertoire."

"How did you know that, Mr. Swille?"

"Never you mind. And you think it's befitting your exalted office to go about mouthing the sayings of that hunchback Aesop? No wonder the Confederate cartoonists are beginning to depict you as a nigger. They're calling you a Black Republican down here, and I've heard some weird talk from the planters. Some strange ugly talk. I want you to read that book they're all reading down here. Uncle Robin! Give Lanky that book they're all reading down here."

Robin goes to the shelf. "Idylls of the King, Mr. Swille?"

"Yes, that's the one."

Robin removes the book from the shelf and gives it to Lincoln.

"This book tells you about aristocratic rule, Lincoln. How to deal with inferiors. How to handle the help. How the chief of the tribes is supposed to carry himself. You're not the steadiest man for the job; you'd better come on and get this Camelot if you know what's good for you. You, too, can have a wife who is jaundiced and prematurely buried. Skin and bones. Got her down to seventy-five pounds. She's a good sufferer but not as good as Vivian, she..." Swille gazes toward the oil portrait of his sister.

"What.....Anything wrong?" Lincoln says, beginning to rise from his chair. Robin starts toward Swille.

"No, nothing. Where was I, Robin?"

"You were telling Mr. Lincoln about Camelot, sir."

"Look, Lincoln, if you don't want to be a duke, it's up to you. I need a man like you up in my Canadian mills. You can be a big man up there. We treat the Canadians like coons. I know you used to chop wood. You can be a powerful man up there. A powerful man. Why, you can be Abe of the Yukon.

Why don't you resign and call it quits, Lincoln? You won't have to sneak into the Capitol disguised any more. What ya say, pal?"

"Look, Mr. Swille, maybe I ought to tell you why I came down here. Then we can cut this as short and sweet as an old woman's dance."

"All right, Abe. But before you tell me, look, Abe, I don't want to get into politics, but, well, why did you up and join such a grotesque institution as that party that..."

"We call ourselves the Republican party, Mr. Swille but don't look at me. I didn't name it."

"A far-out institution if there ever was one. Free Soilers, whacky money people, Abolitionists. Can't you persuade some of those people to wear a tie? Transcendentalists, Free Lovers, Free Farmers, Whigs, Know-Nothings, and those awful Whitmanites always running about hugging things."

"Look, Mr. Swille," Lincoln says in his high-pitched voice, "I didn't come here to discuss my party, I came to discuss how we could win this war, Mr. Swille; end this conflict," he says, pounding the table. "We are in a position to give the South its death-knell blow."

"'Death-knell blow.' There you go again with that cornpone speech, Lincoln. 'Death-knell blow.' Why don't you shave off that beard and stop putting your fingers in your lapels like that. You ought to at least try to polish yourself, man. Go to the theatre. Get some culture. If you don't, I'll have to contact my general; you know, there's always one of our people keeping an eye on things in your...your cabinets. Why, under the Crown...."

"Now you look here, Mr. Swille. I won't take your threats. I knew it was a mistake to come down here, you...you slave-flogging pea-picker."

Arthur Swille, startled, removes his cigar from his mouth.

"Yes, I know what you think of me. I never went to none of that fancy Harvard and don't lounge around Cafe Society quaffing white wine until three in the afternoon, and maybe my speeches don't contain a lot of Latin, and maybe my anecdotes aren't understated and maybe I ain't none of that cologned rake sojourning over shrimp cocktails or sitting around in lavender knee britches, like a randy shank or a dandy rake.

"I know you make fun of our nation, our war and our party, Mr. Swille. I know that you hold it against us because our shirts stick out of our britches and we can't write long sentences without losing our way, but you wouldn't be sitting up here in this...this Castle if it weren't for the people. The public people. And the Republic people in this great people period, and that ain't no pipple papple pablum either, pal."

A train whistle is heard.

"Mr. Swille, listen to your train. That great locomotive that will soon be stretching across America, bumping cows, pursued by Indians, linking our Eastern cities with the West Coast. Who built your trains, Mr. Swille? The people did, Mr. Swille. Who made you what you are today, Mr. Swille? A swell titanic titan of ten continents, Mr. Swille. Who worked and sweated and tilled and toiled and travailed so that you could have your oil, your industry, Mr. Swille? Why, we did, Mr. Swille. Who toted and tarried and travestied themselves so that you could have your many homes, your ships and your buildings reaching the azure skies? We did, Mr. Swille. Yes, I know I'm a cornbread and a catfish-eatin curmudgeon known to sup some scuppernong wine once in a while, but I will speak my mind, Mr. Swille. Plain Abe. Honest Abe. And I don't care how much power you have in Congress, it won't stop me speaking my mind, and if you say another word about my wife, Mr. Swille, I'm going to haul off and go you one right upside your fat head. Don't forget I used to split rails." Lincoln turns around. "I'm leaving."

Uncle Robin, blinking back tears, applauds Lincoln until Swille gives him a stern look.

"Hey, wait a minute, come back, Mr. Lincoln, Mr. President."

Lincoln, stunned, stops and slowly turns around.

"You know, I like your style. You're really demanding, aren't you?" Swille takes the old keys from his right hip and fastens them to his left. "How's about a drink of Old Crow?"

"Well, I'll stay for a few more minutes, but I warn you, Mr. Swille, if you so much as whisper some calumny and perfidy about my wife, I'm going to belt you one."

"Sure, Mr. President. Sure," Swille says as Lincoln returns to his seat in front of Swille's desk. Swille is at the liquor cabinet reaching for the Old Crow, when, zing! a bullet comes from the direction of the window and shatters the bottle. The contents spill to the floor.

"Why, I'll be . . ." Swille says, staring at the pieces of glass on the floor. Lincoln and Uncle Robin are under the desk. Moe, the white house slave, rushes in. "Massa Swille, Massa Swille, the Confederates are outside whooping it up and breaking Mr. Lincoln's carriage. We hid Mr. Lincoln's party down in the wine cellar until the episode passed, and do you know what, Mr. Swille? Somebody has drunk up all the wine."

"Somebody has drunk up all the wine!" Swille and Uncle Robin say.

"Uncle Robin, give me the telephone. I want to call Lee."

Uncle Robin obliges, tiptoeing across the room, grinning

"I don't want any of that grey trash snooping about my door," Swille says, frowning.

Outside, rebel yells can be heard.

"Hello? Give me that Lee.... Well, I don't care if he is at the front, tell him to bring his ass away from the front. This is Arthur Swille speaking..." To Lincoln, Moe and Uncle Robin, "That got em."

"Hello, Lee? What's the big idea of your men come busting up to my place and annoying my guests? I told your boss, Jeff Davis, to keep that war off of my property ... Why, you impertinent scoundrel." Hand over the phone, he mimics Lee to the trio in the room, "Says extraordinary emergency supersedes the right to privacy enjoyed by the individual no matter what station in life the individual may hold.... Look, You little runt, if you don't get those men off my property, I'll, I'll... My father's dead, I'm running this thing now. I don't care how long you've known the family—my brothers and Ms. Anne and me are running things now ...

"Who's up here? Why, the nerve. For your information, Mr. Abraham Lincoln is up here,"

Lincoln tries to shush Swille, but Swille signals him that it doesn't matter.

"You'll do no such thing." Hand over the phone, to Lincoln, "Says he's coming up here to arrest you ....

"Look, Lee, if you don't get those men off my property I'm going to create an energy crisis and take back my railroads, and on top of that I'll see that the foreign countries don't recognize you. And if that's not all, I'll take back my gold. Don't forget; I control the interest rates ...

"Now that's more like it... Now you're whistling 'Dixie'.... No, I won't tell Davis... Forget it.... That's fine." Turns to Lincoln, "Says he's going to send an escort up here to see to it that your men return safely to your yacht, *The River Queen*. Lee said be was preparing to blow it up but will call it off in deference to your comfort..."

Turning back to the phone, "What's that?... Oh, you don't have to come up here and play nigger for three days for punishment; anyway, who will run your side of the war? Look, Lee, I got to go now." Hangs up. To trio, "Boy, when you say gold, they jump. And speaking of gold, Mr. President, I'm going to give you some."

"Why, Mr. Swille, now that you mention it," Lincoln says, fidgeting and pushing his feet, "I didn't come all the way through Confederate lines just to pass the time of day. We need some revenue bad. Why, we're as broke as a skeeter's peeter. I'm leaning toward the peace plan originally proposed by Horace Greeley of the New York paper . . . . it's called . . . Well, the plan is called . . ." Lincoln reaches into his coat pocket for a piece of paper. "Ah, Mr. Swille, I didn't bring my glasses, would you read it?" Lincoln hands the piece of paper to Swille.

"And cut the formalities, Mr. Swille. You can call me Abe." Lincoln, once again, reaches out for a handshake, but Swille is too busy reading to notice. Lincoln, embarrassed, puts his hand in his pocket.

Swille takes the paper and examines it. "I . . . well, your writing, your aide's writing, is nearly illegible. Here, Uncle Robin, can you make this out?"

Robin looks at it. "Compensatory Emancipation it says, Massa Swille."

"Compensatory Emancipation, that's it! Sure enough is, Mr. Swille. It goes like this. We buy the war and the slaves are over. No, like this. We buy the slaves. That's it. We buy the slaves or the bondsmen and then they pay the South seven and a half percent interest. No, dog bite it. How did it go? My aides have been going over it with me ever since we started out from *The River Queen*. I got it! We buy up all the slaves and then tell them to go off somewhere. Some place like New Mexico, where nobody's hardly seen a cloud and when they do show up it looks like judgment day, and where the cactus grows as big as eucalyptus trees, where you have to walk two miles to go to the outhouse and then freeze your can off in the cold desert until it's your turn and then the outhouse is so dark you sit on a rattlesnake. Other times I think that maybe they ought to go to the tropics where God made them. You know, I've been reading about this African tribe that lived in the tropics so long they trained mosquitoes to fight their enemies. Fascinating, don't you think? I need that gold bad, Mr. Swille. Whatever I decide, it'll come in handy."

"Sure, sure, Lincoln, I know. You'll decide what's best. I know that the war is even-steven right now, and this gold will help out. I'll take a chance on your little Union. The nerve of that guy Lee. I'm going to take back that necklace I gave Mrs. Jefferson Davis. Why, they can't do that to me. Just for that . . ." Swille goes to his safe, removes some bags of gold and places them on his desk. "That ought to do it, Mr. President, and if you're in need of some more, I'll open up Fort Knox and all that you guys wheelbarrow out in an hour you can have."

"Why, thank you, Mr. Swille. You're a patriotic man. But all of this gold, really, I . . ."

"Take it. Take it. A long-term loan, Lincoln. I'll fix these confederates. That Lee. Sits on his horse as if he was Caesar or somebody."

"The Confederates are innocent, Mr. Swille. The other day one of them was tipping his hat and curtsying, and one of my snipers plugged him. And in the Chattanooga campaign, Grant tells me that once he was ascending Lookout Mountain and the Confederate soldiers saluted him. 'Salute to the Commanding General,' they were saying."

The men share a chuckle on this one.

"My generals may look like bums, with their blouses unbuttoned and their excessive drinking and their general ragged appearances, but they know how to fight. Why, that Grant gets sick at the sight of the blood and gets mad when you bring up even the subject of war, and he's never read a military treatise — but he can fight. His only notion of warfare is, 'Go where the enemy is and beat hell out of him.' Crude though it may sound, it seems to work."

"You know, Mr. President, I'm beginning to like you. Here, have a Havana. I have three homes there. Ought to come down some time, Mr. President, play some golf, do some sailing on my yacht. Get away from the Capitol."

"Well, I don't know, Mr. Swille. I'd better not leave town with a war going on and all."

"Where did they get the idea that you were some kind of brooding mystic, tragic and gaunt, a Midwest Messiah with hollow cheeks? I was saying to myself, 'How can a smart corporation lawyer like this Lincoln be so way-out.'"

"I keep my mouth shut, Mr. Swille. And when I can't think quick enough I walk over to the window, put my fingers into my lapels, throw my head back and gaze toward the Washington Monument, assuming a somber, grave and sulfurous countenance. It impresses them, and the myths fly."

"You know, Mr. Lincoln, I wish you'd do something about that fugitive-slave law you promised to enforce during the campaign. There are three of my cocoas at large. I'd like to bring them back here. Teach them a lesson for running away. They're giving the rest of the cocoas around here ideas. They're always caucusing, not admitting any of my white slaves or the white staff— they pass codes to one another, and some of them have taken to writing.

"They're in contact, so it seems, with slaves in the rest of the country, through some kind of intricate grapevine, so Cato my graffado tells me. Sometimes be gets blackened-up with them so's they won't know who he's working for. He's slow but faithful. So faithful that he volunteered for slavery, and so dedicated he is to slavery, the slaves voted him all-Slavery. Sent him to General Howard's Civilizing School. You should have heard my son, who was an authority on sables. He said they're so trusting and kindhearted. I sent him to the Congo to check for some possible energy resources, though he told them he was looking for the source of the Nile. They're so trusting.

"He was majoring in some kind of thing called anthropology in one of those experimental colleges. You know the young. First I wanted him to go to Yale, like me. Then I saw that the little stinker had an angle. What a cover. Anthropologists. We used to send priests, but they were too obvious."

"You must be very proud of him, Mr. Swille."

"He was doing well until ... until these Congo savages captured him and ... and ... well."

"Oh, I'm sorry, was he ..."

"You might say that he was killed. But, Mr. President, we all have our trials. An unpleasant subject. A smart one he was, like your Todd. Very inquisitive. It's upon my son's advice that I don't permit any of the employees to use the telephone. I permit Uncle Robin to use it because he's such a simple creature he wouldn't have the thought powers for using it deviously. He's been in the house for so long that he's lost his thirst for pagan ways and is as good a gentleman as you or me."

Lincoln nods, approvingly.

"Why, thank you, Cap'n Swille."

"Don't mention it, Robin. I don't know what I'd do without you. He brings me two gallons of slave women's milk each morning. It keeps me going. He travels all over the South in an airplane, buying supplies for the estate. He's become quite a bargainer and knows about all of the sales ...

"Of course, I still buy the ... well, the help. Just got back from Ryan's Mart in Charleston with a boy named Pompey. Does the work of ten niggers. I got him working in the house here. He doesn't say much but is really fast. The boy can serve dinner before it's cooked, beats himself getting up in the morning so that when he goes to the bathroom to shave he has to push his shadow out of the way, and zips about the house like a toy train. I'm really proud of this bargain. Why, on his days off he stands outside of the door, protecting me, like a piece of wood. He can stand there for hours without even blinking an eye. Says he would die if something happens to me. Isn't that right, Uncle Robin? Though he's asp-tongued and speaks in this nasal tone, Pompey is a saint. He doesn't come down to the races, nor does he Camptown; doesn't smoke, drink, cuss or wench, stays up in his room when he's not working, probably contemplating the Scriptures. They don't make them like that any more, Mr. Lincoln. I have a shrewd eye for good property, don't you think, Abe?"

"Well, Mr. Swille, if you've read my campaign literature, you'd know that my position is very clear. What a man does with his property is his business. Of course, I can't help but agree with one of my distinguished predecessors, George Washington, who said, 'There are numbers who would rather facilitate the escape of slaves than apprehend them as runaways! That law is hard to enforce, Mr. Swille."

Swille rises. "Look, Lincoln, one of them kinks, 40s, wiped me out when he left here. That venerable mahogany took all my guns, slaughtered my livestock and shot the overseer right between the eyes. And the worst betrayal of all was Raven Quickskill, my trusted bookkeeper. Fooled around with my books, so that every time I'd buy a new slave he'd destroy the invoices and I'd have no record of purchase; he was also writing passes and forging freedom papers. We gave him Literacy, the most powerful thing in the pre-technological pre-post-rational age—and what does he do with it? Uses it like that old Voodoo—that old stuff the slaves mumble about. Fetishism and grisly rites, only he doesn't need anything but a pen he had shaped out of cock feathers and chicken claws. Oh, they are bad sables, Mr. Lincoln. They are bad, bad sables. Not one of them with the charm and good breeding of Ms. Phyllis Wheatly, who wrote a poem for the beloved founder of this country, George Washington." He begins to recite with feeling:

> Thy ev'ry action let the Goddess guide.
> A crown, a mansion, and a throne that shine,
> With gold unfading, Washington! We thine.

"And then that glistening rust-black Stray Leechfield. We saw him as nothing but a low-down molasses-slurper and a mutton thief, but do you know what he did? He was stealing chickens—methodically, not like the old days when they'd steal one or two and try to duck the BBs. He had taken so many over a period of time that he was over in the other county, big as you please, dressed up like a gentleman, smoking a seegar and driving a carriage which featured factory climate-control air conditioning, vinyl top, AM/FM stereo radio, full leather interior, power-lock doors, six-way power seat, power windows, white-wall wheels, door-edge guards, bumper impact strips, Tear defroster and soft-ray glass.

"It was full of beautiful women fanning themselves and filling the rose-tinted air with their gay laughter. He had set up his own poultry business, was underselling everybody in eggs, gizzards, gristles, livers—and had a reputa-

tion far and wide for his succulent drumsticks. Had a white slave fronting for
him for ten percent. Well, when my man finally discovered him after finding
he'd built a dummy to look like him so we'd think he was still in the fields, do
you know what he did, Mr. Lincoln? He stabbed the man. Stabbed him and
fled on a white horse, his cape furling in the wind. It was very dramatic.

"You defend Negro ruffians like that, Mr. Lincoln? You yourself, Mr. President, said that you were never in favor of bringing about social and political
equality with them. You don't want them to vote, either. I mean, I read that
in the newspaper. They're not like us, Mr. Lincoln. You said yourself that
there are physical differences. Now you know you said it, Mr. Lincoln. When
General Fremont got brash and freed the slaves in the Western territory, you
overruled his proclamation, and now the military man tells me that you have
some sort of wild proclamation on your desk you're about to sign, if this
compensatory thing doesn't work."

"I haven't made up my mind yet, Mr. Swille. I guess I'm a little wishy-
washy on the subject still. But ... well, sometimes I just think that one man
enslaving another man is wrong. Is wrong. Is very wrong." Lincoln pounds
the table.

"Well, I won't try to influence your decision, Mr. President. Would you
like Uncle Robin to help you with one of those sacks?"

"Thank you, Mr. Swille."

Uncle Robin goes over and helps Lincoln with two of the heavy gold bags.

"And before you leave, Mr. President, go down to the kitchen and have Barracuda the Mammy fix you a nice snack. She'll be so thrilled. All she talks
about is Massa Lincoln, Massa Lincoln. Maybe you can sign a few autographs."

Swille rises and walks over to Lincoln, who is now standing, his hands
heavy with sacks of gold. "And think before you sign that proclamation, Mr.
President. The slaves like it here. Look at this childish race. Uncle Robin,
don't you like it here?"

"Why, yessuh, Mr. Swille! I loves it here. Good something to eat when you
wonts it. Color TV. Milk pail fulla toddy. Some whiskey and a little nookie
from time to time. We gets whipped with a velvet whip, and there's free dental care and always a fiddler case your feets get restless."

"You see, Mr. President. They need someone to guide them through this
world of woe or they'll hurt themselves."

"I'll certainly consider your views when I make my decision, Mr. Swille.
Well, I have to go now. And thanks for contributing to the war chest, Mr.
Swille."

"Sure, Lincoln, anything you say." Swille goes to the window. "Hey, I think the escort Lee sent up has arrived. Look, Lincoln, I'm throwing a little shindig for Mr. and Mrs. Jefferson Davis. Why don't you come down? I'd like to get you two together for one day. Take time off from the war."

"You can arrange that, Mr. Swille?"

"I can arrange anything. They called my father God's God, Mr. President. Davis may hate your flag and you, but everybody salutes our flag. Gold, energy and power: that's our flag. Now, you have to leave, Abe, and don't knock over any of the objets d'art in the hall. I don't think your United States Treasury [chuckle] can replace them."

"I'll be careful," Lincoln says. "I'm glad you could spend some time with me, Mr. Swille."

"Not at all, Lincoln. Have a good journey back to your yacht, and, Robin, help Mr. Lincoln with his bags of gold."

Lincoln and Swille shake hands. Lincoln and Robin begin to exit with the gold. Barracuda comes in, eying both of them suspiciously.

"Massa Swille, there's some poor-white trash down in the kitchen walking on my kitchen flo. I told them to get out my kitchen and smacked one of them on the ear with my broom."

"That's Mr. Lincoln's party, Mammy Barracuda. I want you to meet the President of the United States, Mr. Abraham Lincoln."

"Oh, Mr. Linclum! Mr. Linclum! I admires you so. Now you come on down to the kitchen and let me make you and your party a nice cup of coffee."

"But I have very important business to do on *The River Queen,* the tide of battle...."

"Shush your mouth and come on down here get some of this coffee. Steaming hot. What's wrong with you, man, you gone pass up some of this good old Southern hospitality?"

Lincoln shrugs his shoulders. "Well," he says, smiling, "I guess one little cup won't hurt." She waltzes around with Abe Lincoln, who follows awkwardly. She sings, "Hello, Abbbbbe. Well, hello, Abbbbbe. It's so nice to have you here where you belong."

The President blushes; be finds it hard to keep in a giggle. Swille and Robin join in, clapping their bands: "You're looking swell, Abbbeee. I can tell, Abbeeee. You're still growin', you're still goin...."

Barracuda and Lincoln waltz out of the room. Uncle Robin follows with the bag of gold, doing his own little step. Delighted, Swille chuckles from deep in his belly.

## CHAPTER 5

Inside the kitchen of the main house of Swille's plantation, Uncle Robin sits on a high stool reading some figures over the phone which have been scribbled on a sheet. He is, at the same time, munching some white-frosted Betty Crocker glossy cake and drinking coffee that Aunt Judy, his wife, has prepared for him. Next to his hand is a copy of *60 Families*.

" . . . and slave quarters number 3 wants to Put 259, 344, and 544 in the box . . . . What you mean? Chicago, it's an hour behind in your time, it ain't too late." He hears footsteps approaching. "Hey, somebody's coming. I got to go." Uncle Robin takes a sip of coffee, looks innocent and begins to hum a spiritual. It's Moe, the white house slave.

"Uncle Robin, are you abusing your phone privileges? I don't know why the Master lets you use it. He doesn't let any . . ."

"Oh, Mr. Moe, I was just ringing in the supplies for the week. I didn't mean no harm."

"I don't know why he trusts you, Uncle Robin He thinks you're docile, but sometimes it seems to me that you're the cleverest of them all, though I can't prove it."

Uncle Robin stares blankly at him.

"Well, I guess you are pretty simple. I don't know what gives me the notion that you're more complex than you seem."

Moe goes to the kitchen table. Uncle Robin rises, fetches a cup of coffee and places it in front of Moe.

"What did you think of President Lincoln's visit?"

"What you say, Mr. Moe?"

"That visit. You were right there in the room."

"Oh, that. I don't understand what they be saying. I never did understand good Anglish—it takes me even an effort to read the Bible good."

"You are impoverished, aren't you? No wonder they call you an Uncle Tom."

Uncle Robin ignores this, eating another slice of cake. "I don't know, Mr. Moe, suh. Sometimes it seems to me that we are all Uncle Toms. Take yourself, for example. You are a white man but still you a slave. You may not look like a slave, and you dress better than slaves do, but all day you have to run around saying Yessuh, Mr. Swille, and Nossuh, Mr. Swille, and when Mitchell was a child, Maybe so, li'l Swille. Why, he can fire you anytime he wants for no reason."

"What! What did you say? How dare you talk to a white man like that!"

"Well, sometimes I just be reflectin, suh. Ain't no harm in that."

"Well, you can just stop your reflectin and if I hear you talkin like that again, I'm going to report to Massa Swille of your insolence, do you hear? Now you behave yourself and don't you ever let me hear you making such statements."

But before Uncle Robin can issue some apologies, saying that the devil must have gotten ahold of his tongue or that he will promise not to express such notions again, the red light above the kitchen door begins to blink, which means that Massa Swille wants Moe to come into his office. Moe wipes his mouth with a napkin, gulps the coffee down so quickly it stains his junior executive's shirt.

"Oh, dammit, now what will I do?"

"Hold on Mr. Moe." Uncle Robin rushes to the cabinet, takes out some spot remover and dabs it on Moe's shirt. The button-down collar's stain disappears. Moe rushes out of the kitchen.

## CHAPTER 6

Lincoln salutes the Confederate soldiers Lee has sent up to escort him and his party back to *The River Queen*. He climbs into the carriage and sits next to an aide.

"Did you sell him some bonds?" the aide asks.

"Yeah," Lincoln says, leaning back in his carriage, removing his stovepipe hat and boots; he takes off his white gloves last.

"Gilded Age ding-dong if there ever was. Hands like a woman's. I feel like a minstrel...."

"But you did sell him some bonds?"

"Yes. First I gave him the yokel-dokel—he saw through that. And then he went on about my lack of culture and poked fun at my clothes. Talked about my shiny suitcoat and pants. Then he said some nasty things about Mary. Well, I know that she's . . . she's odd. Well, you know, I couldn't stand there and listen to that, so I blew my top."

"And he still gave you the gold?"

"Yeah. You know, if we lost this war we wouldn't be able to repay Swille. We're sticking our necks out, but with the cost of things these days, we have to turn to him. Why, we still owe a bill for that Scotch plaid cap and cloak I bought so I could enter the Capitol in disguise. The Confederates thought I was frightened, but that wasn't it at all. I was trying to duck the bill collectors who were holding me responsible for the debts owed by the last administration. Buchanan said there'd be days like this. No wonder he was trembling when he shook my hand at the inaugural ceremony, and when I was sworn in —whiz—took off down the platform steps. Said he had to catch a train. Said 'Good luck, Hoosier!' Now I know what be meant."

"It was a close call, when the Confederates came up to the house just now. You should have seen the secret service men in the next carriage scramble from the Queen Mary. I don't think they know what in the hell they're doing. And I think one of them, that fat one, is a little off into the bottle. Mr. President, you ought to fire that one."

"I don't plan to fire that one. Just put him on detail at insignificant events. The theatre. I might need Swille's support some more and so I'm going to start doing more for culture. Tidy up my performance. I want you to get me and Mary Todd some tickets to a theatre from time to time and invite Ulysses."

"Look, sir."

On the side of the road some of the colored contraband were appearing. They started waving their handkerchiefs at the President. The President waved back. One man ran up to the carriage; Lincoln stuck his hand out to shake the slave's hand but instead of shaking the President's hand the man began kissing it until he dropped back behind the carriage. He stood in the road waving.

"They love you, sir."

"Curious tribe. There's something, something very human about them, something innocent and . . . Yet I keep having the suspicion that they have another mind. A mind kept hidden from us. They had this old mammy up there. She began singing and dancing me around. The first time in these years I took my mind off the war. I felt like crawling into her lap and going to sleep. Just sucking my thumb and rolling my hair up into pickaninny knots. I never even gave spooks much thought, but now that they've become a subplot in this war, I can't get these shines off my mind. My dreams . . . . She must do Swille a lot of good."

"She didn't treat us very well; told us to abandon her kitchen."

Lincoln laughs. "You know, I can't help thinking sometimes that the rich are retarded. That Swille couldn't go to the bathroom, I'll bet, without an escort or someone showing him the way. And do you know what he subsists on?"

"What, sir?"

"Slave mothers' milk."

"It's supposed to reverse the aging process. Said he got the idea from some fellow named Tennyson. Sir Baron Lord Tennyson. Sounds like one of those fellows we used to beat up and take lunch money from back in Springfield. Anyway, Swille says he got the solution from the hormone of a reptile, and that this Tennyson fellow wrote a poem about it. One depressing work, if you'd ask my opinion. All about immortality and ennui. These people down here don't seem to do nothin but despair. This Tennyson guy was talking about flowers a lot. Do you know of him? Is he all right? And who is this ennui feller?"

"Ennui means . . . well . . . it's like a languor, a general discontent concerning the contemporary milieu. Tennyson, he's an aesthete, Mr. President."

"Well, I'll be as dull as a Kansas moon. You say he's what?"

"An aesthete. He knows about flowers, reads poetry aloud lying on French Impressionist picnic grass. Visits the lofts of painters. Attends all of the openings. Is charming and fascinating with the women."

"Well, I don't think that this Swille fellow's got all of his potatoes. He said something about a town named Camelot. Where is this town, aide? How far away is this town Camelot? Is it a train stop? Is it in Virginia?"

"Camelot is the mythical city of the Arthurian legend, Mr. Lincoln."

"Well, I'll be a flying fish on a worm tree. This Swille kept talking about the place and about how a king was going to rule America. I think he was trying to buy me off. That's my last dealings with him. His kind make you feel like . . . what's the name of the character in Mrs. Stowe's novel?"

"Uncle Tom, sir?"

"That's it. They have you tommy to them. The man started to talk strange, a lot of scimble-skamble, about knighthood and the 'days that were' . . . Hey, what the hell's going on down here, anyway? Did you hear all that screaming back there? Nobody even noticed. I didn't say nothin cause I figured if nobody noticed it, then I must be hearing things. Did you notice it, aide, all that screaming going on back there?"

Lincoln rested his head against the window and looked out into the Virginia night, the blackest night in the South. There was an old folk art cemetery with leaning tombstones behind an ornate black wrought-iron fence. A woman in white floated across the cemetery. A wolf howled. Bats flew into the dark red sun.

"Aide, did you see that?"

"I can't see anything for the fog, sir. But I think I did hear some screaming. As soon as we entered Virginia we heard the screaming. First a little screaming and then a whole lot. As soon as the sun goes up out here you hear the screaming until the moon goes down, I hear tell, Mr. Lincoln."

"Like hell."

"What's that, Mr President?"

"The screaming, it reminds you of hell. This man Swille was talking about whips and said something about people being humiliated. Is that some kind of code?"

"Grant said it was decadent down here, Mr. Lincoln. Said it was ignoble. Others call it 'immoral.' William Wells Brown, the brown writer, called it that."

"Grant said ignoble?" Lincoln laughs. "Swille offered me a barony. What's that all about?"

"I heard talk, Mr. President. The proceedings from the Montgomery Convention where the slaveholders met to map the Confederacy have never been released, but there are rumors that somebody offered Napoleon III the Confederate Crown, and he said he'd think about it. It was in *The New York Times*, August—"

"The Crown!"

"But Nappy Three said that slavery was an anachronism."

"Hey!" Lincoln said, snapping his fingers. "I got it! Of course."

"What's that Mr. President?"

"Look, it's common sense. Why, I'll be a jitterbug in a hogcreek. Aide, when we return to Washington, I want you to return Swille's gold. We don't need it."

"But, Mr. President, we just risked our lives coming through Confederate lines to get the gold. Now you don't want it? I don't understand."

"We change the issues, don't you see? Instead of making this some kind of oratorical minuet about States' Rights versus the Union, what we do is make it so that you can't be for the South without being for slavery! I want you to get that portrait painter feller Denis Carter to come into the office, where he'll show me signing the . . . the Emancipation Proclamation. That's it. The Emancipation Proclamation. Call in the press. Get the Capitol calligrapher who's good at letterin to come in and draw this Proclamation. Phone the networks. We'll put an end to this Fairy Kingdom nonsense. Guenevere, Lancelot, Arthur and the whole dang-blasted genteel crew."

"A brilliant idea, Mr. President. A brilliant idea."

"And I want you to clear the White House of those office seekers and others pestering me all day. Wanting to shake my hand. Do you know what some bird asked me the other day?"

"What, Mr. President?"

"The jackass called me long distance collect when the rates are at their peak and wanted me to do something about a cow he'd bought that had been pumped full of water so's to make it look like the critter weighed more than it did. Well, I called the fellow he bought it from and the fellow said that if the farmer produced a bill of sale he'd return the money. Well I called the farmer and told him what the other fellow said and then the farmer said he couldn't find the bill of sale and wanted me to take the first train out of Washington to help him look for it. Said he needed someone to watch the cow, who was some high-strung critter. Well, I don't think we can tie up the federal machinery on business like that, aide. And another thing, Swille seems to know more about the government's business than I do. I want you to investigate the leaks. Did you send Major Corbett away?"

"We put Major Corbett on active duty, Mr. President."

"Good. Invite Mrs. Corbett to review the troops with me and General Hooker tomorrow. Tell her afterwards we'll take tea. Give my boots a little lick of grease and go to the drugstore and get me some of that Golden Fluid hair slick."

"But what will I do about Mrs. Lincoln, Mr. President? The press will be there. Suppose they take a picture?"

"Oh, tell Mother . . . tell her that I was detained. I don't know which one's going to be the death of me, Mother or the niggers."

"How much gold did Mr. Swille give you, Mr. President?"

Lincoln counts. "He was supposed to give me five, but I only count four."

"What could have happened, sir? The nigger?"

"I doubt it. Poor submissive creature. You should have seen him shuffle about the place. Yessirring and nosirring. Maybe he didn't intend to give me but four. I'm tired. Can't you make this thing go faster?"

"Yessir," the aide says. "Right away, sir."

He leans out of the window and instructs the coachman to go faster. Lincoln opens his purse and examines the five dollar Confederate bill. Bookie odds favored the Union, but you could never tell when you might need carfare.

CHAPTER 21

ZUMWALT, Jack Frost, and Zumwalt's bodyguards, the Floorwalkers, sit in S.C.'s old suite. They have plenty of ice. Jack Frost is drinking whiskey and getting meaner by the minute. The TV picture comes on. There are thousands of people in Times Square, curious about what S.C. is going to lay down. A big cheer goes up. They switched to the studio. "What's that, Sandour . . . ?" Realizing that she was on camera, the woman started to speak.

*This is billed as a major speech. By Santa Claus. He's now climbing the steps and is approaching his seat on the platform, acknowledging the cheers of the crowd. He is followed by a little black bellboy from the hotel, who is carrying his bags. The Mayor is here to introduce him. This is a very fine moment for the Mayor. Yesterday he rode beside S.C. as he greeted him as he arrived from "Spain," the hacienda owned by a department store magnate. Santa is approaching the speaker's stand.*

*There's a motley crowd here. Chickens and hustlers from Times Square. Jook Sing gangs from Chinatown, El Barrio, and Harlem. For some reason, this Santa has been able to attract much of the city's hoodlum element. Low riders, Joe Boys, Yangs, Fugis, and a number of blue- and purple-haired young women who have gotten themselves up in lavender mascara and rouge, some of them are wearing Mohawk haircuts, and there seems to be a lot of gum-chewing going on. The governor is already on the stand. And now, ladies and gentlemen, the introduction of Santa for his Times Square speech which officially gets the Christmas season going. Usually this speech is made by Oswald Zumwalt, but this year, for some reason, Santa is making the speech himself, no longer confined to Ho Ho Ho. Santa Claus is the only major public figure who doesn't have to sneak around the country like a thief. As anarchist groups grow in the United States, attacks on public officials have increased. And now, the Mayor of New York, Kevin Grouch.*

"Ladies and gentlemen, I consider it an esteemed honor and a great privilege to introduce to you a man who brings good cheer to us all during this Christmas season. A man who can have the key to this city any time he wants, the key to our hearts, and isn't it appropriate that the ceremonies occur here because this is St. Nick's town, the Knickerbocker town. He has requested this time to make an important speech to us all. Ladies and gentlemen, our own. Santa Claus." S.C. rises and starts towards the microphone as a great human cheer goes up. Doves are set flying. A huge dirigible floats above carrying the words "Merry Christmas." Balloons rise.

"Thank you, ladies and gentlemen. I consider it a pleasure to be here with all of you New Yorkers, from the Bronx, from Queens, from Brooklyn, and from good old Manhattan. I wish I could delight all of you with candy canes, and fill your stockings; I'd like to soar above your roofs."

Watching the ceremony on TV, Zumwalt cracks his knuckles. He is beginning to sweat. Jack Frost shoots up from his seat and looks to Zumwalt, and to the Floorwalkers, for an explanation.

"I think it's time to have a grown-up Christmas, children of all ages. A Christmas where we can get to the bottom of things. Get to the bottom of what's troubling this country so. This is no time for animal crackers and gingerbread." Jack Frost shakes his fist at the set.

"What's wrong with him? What is he saying? Should we plug him?"

"Let him go," Zumwalt says. "I'll explain later."

Warming to his subject, Santa begins to pace up and down the platform, his hands clasped behind his back. He tugs at his beard and a tongue-in-cheek grin comes over his face. Nobody stirs in the crowd. All you can hear is an occasional police horse's hoof clop against the sidewalk. The motor of a small plane buzzes overhead. Times Square stands still as in one of those last-day films, the city frozen, people clogging up the exits from the city in an attempt to escape the monster.

He continues slowly, tentatively. "On the way over here I was thinking of an appropriate metaphor with which to describe this cold famine of the spirit which is afflicting those of us who reside in this wonderful Northern Hemisphere, these cold winters, and what has been described as the cold, mean mood of the country. I've thought about what made us what we are today, a nation of Scrooges. And I thought back to the beginning of these cold, blue winters, that long winter of 1980 which began America's long Christmas blues. Every year, as you have seen, the season gets colder and more heart-less, and whole families perish in tenement fires. Every year the American dead wander about a little more restless, and the days grow short. They wander about in the day as well as the night, all those brave people who spoke out, emerging from the cemeteries: The lynched, the shot, the martyred.

"I look at France, weeping to melancholy violins, England getting tanner each summer, Berlin a permanent beige, Amsterdam butterscotch, and of course the browning of Paris, Spain darker than usual, and I think of this nation of lonely people, of lonely alienated male assassins alone in their motel rooms , hamburger wrappings scattered about, empty ice cream cartons in with the rubbish, people alienated from the past, the future, nature, and one another. And how did we get that way, and what is wrong with us? We scream and kick and say no when we can't get our way. We say no to the sick, no to the destitute. We say no to the millions of refugees now crowding our cities, tired, jobless, hungry, using garbage-can lids for pillows. And the little children searching for discarded cans or bottles, wearing ragged sneakers in the snow, and I keep thinking of a two-year-old when I think of an appropriate metaphor with which to describe this sour, Scroogelike attitude which began with the Scrooge Christmas of '80. Ladies and gentlemen, boys and girls, The President, whose Secret Service code name was Rawhide, had been elected and a mood of grouchiness and bitchiness swept the land, as cold as the Arctic winds, but it wasn't half as cruel as what was to come.

"Two years old, that's what we are, emotionally—America, always wanting someone to hand us some ice cream, always complaining, Santa didn't bring me this and why didn't Santa bring me that." People in the crowd chuckle. "Nobody can reason with us. Nobody can tell us anything. Millions of people are staggering about and passing out in the snow and we say that's tough. We say too bad to the children who don't have milk. I weep as I read these letters the poor children send to me at my temporary home in Alaska.

"And where are the eggs, and the apples, and the oranges? Where is the milk? I'll tell you where they are, rotting in warehouses and on lake embankments. Rotting. The grain is rotting unused." Santa pauses to look over his shoulder at the politicians who sit on the platform.

The Governor is frowning like a distempered bear. The Mayor is trying to laugh the whole thing off, but he is getting nervous too. His Tartar blood is rising and he is more than a little mad. Santa Claus continues. "Look at all of the people homeless, wandering the streets. Suppose one of them was Jesus

Christ. Would you say no to Jesus Christ? Would you lock the door of the church and freeze the Lord out?"

Santa turns to the murmuring dignitaries who are sharing the speaker's stand. He turned around and pointed to the Mayor. "Do you know what the Mayor would do if Jesus Christ came to Gracie Mansion and asked for some Christmas cheer? The Mayor would probably have the Lord deloused and thrown in the Tombs. The Mayor is eating. Look at him, a bald-head, fat as a rich ball of butter. Got a head like a bald-headed turtle. He had dinner with the Rockefellers last night up at Asia House. We got hold of the menu from one of the waiters inside. Let me read it to you." Santa put on his spectacles. The Mayor is livid. "Cold Gaspe salmon, roast fillet of beef with roast potatoes, and vanilla ring with black cherries."

The Mayor gets up and tries to wrest the menu from Santa Claus but Santa puts his hands on his hips and bumps the Mayor into the audience with his belly. The Mayor is carried to the street by the hoodlums, and when he comes up he is tattered, his jacket missing and one shoe off. He is rescued by some policemen. The Governor scrambles off the stand and is rushed from the scene by a speeding limousine, leaving the other dignitaries to fend for themselves. Some police are trying to get to Santa, but the crowd blocks their way, and other mounted policemen begin to move into the crowd; screaming begins. "I know what they're going to say," Santa shouts, "they're going to say that Santa is crazy. Do you think Santa is crazy?" The crowd yells no. "They're going to say that Santa is out of his mind. Do you think that Santa is out of his mind?" The crowd yells "No!" "I say they're the ones who are crazy. There is now a nuclear bomb for every man, woman, and child in the country; in other words, ladies and gentlemen, boys and girls, each person has a personal nuclear weapon, and this situation exists after what happened in South Carolina. When will they learn? I say we fight the people who destroyed the Adirondack lakes, the New Jersey shore, and Niagara Falls. I say it's time to fight the people who rob us in the supermarket and give our children slow, agonizing leukemia death. I say it's about time to fight the people who gave us acid rain, fight the people who destroyed the ozone belt, and the carbon dioxide excreters whose wastes will soon cause the oceans to rise twenty feet. Do you know who owns Christmas as well as just about every other holiday in this country? The oil men. Not only do they own the department stores, but they're buying up all the copper, lead, and zinc as well. How many of you can live the life that the rich of this country lead? How many of you have dined with Brooke Astor? How many of you have gone skiing at Aspen, Sun

Valley, Klosters, Zermatt, Gstaad? How many of you can buy your clothes at
Adolfo's or Oscar de la Renta's, or how many of you have had brunch at the
Four Seasons or have eaten chopped liver and strawberry cheesecake at Mel
Krupin's, or have had your hair done by Monsieur Marc, your face done by
Manzoni? I say it's time to pull these naughty people off their high chairs and
get them to clean up their own shit. Let's hit them where it hurts, ladies and
gentlemen. In their pockets. Let's stop buying their war toys, their teddy
bears, their dolls, tractors, wagons, their video games, their trees. Trees
belong in the forest." Before Santa can continue, a huge cheer goes up and
people start chanting, "Boycott! Boycott! Boycott!" and some of the gang
members help him down before the police can stop his speech. Fist fights
break out between supporters of Santa and his opponents in the audience.
The gangs are battling the police with their chains and blackjacks. The police
are cracking heads left and right. The whole area before the speaker's stand
begins to take on the appearance of a hockey game.

## CHAPTER 22

A string quartet from the Marine Band was playing some sad music, the kind
the Germans call *Traurig*. The spruce tree burned, sending sparks into the
black Washington sky. In the park across the street from the White House,
the President stood, watching the old tree go down. He'd knocked down
quite a few and stood there, reeling in the snow. He wore an overcoat over his
pajamas. He needed a shave and he hadn't bathed for awhile or looked at
himself in the mirror. After the tree had become ashes, the President dismissed the string quartet and headed back to the White House, and the room
where his wife lay in state. She had been so badly burned that they had to
keep the coffin closed. The civil service employees and the White House staff
and children had watched in horror as the First Lady fried and sizzled down
to fat. They were helpless to do anything about it. "God! God!" the President
cried, shaking his fist towards the falling snow. "Who will do all the hand-
shaking? Who will see to it that my socks are packed? Who will listen to the
drafts of my speeches and rub my back until I fall asleep? Who will see to it
that the Rose Garden is trimmed and that there are three hundred places set
for a state dinner? Who will take charge of the Easter Egg hunt? And suppose

I have to make a decision affecting the future course of human generations to come? Who will make it for me?"

He sat in the room in which the coffin had been placed, sobbing and drinking the refills his faithful White House butler John kept bringing. The room began to move. The President's head began to whirl. He thought he heard the tinkle of a little bell; it was delicate, almost inaudible, still he thought he heard it. There, standing before him, was a black-bearded ascetic appearing man. He was elderly and his narrow face had an olive complexion. He was wearing a gown, a long cloak covered with equilateral crosses, sandals, and a long Bishop's hat. He walked with the support of a staff. On his chest he wore the Star of David. The man had a nervous habit. He held three tiny gold balls in his fist, and he was constantly squeezing them.

## CHAPTER 23

He had that wet look all right. Reverend Clement Jones was as greased as a pig and was wearing a suit that must have cost about eight hundred dollars. Admiral Lionel Matthews sat, tight-lipped, formal, banging his hand slowly against a table. He couldn't conceal his rage as he watched different television sets, set up in the Oval Office, broadcasting reaction to Santa's speech. The young hoodlums who were devoted to Santa Claus could be seen running through the streets, setting fires and overturning cars, not only in the United States but elsewhere in the world. They wore their faces painted in a manner that used to be acceptable only in the National Geographic, confirming for Lionel Matthews, Reverend Jones, and the King of Beer, Robert Reynolds, that these indeed were the last days of the West, unless true patriots put their feet down. Mobs roamed the area about the Holiday Inn, and some placed flowers at the entrance to the hotel where Santa was staying. Some of the dreads had the crowd swaying as they played their haunting renditions of "Santa Claus Is Coming to Town."

Bob Krantz was on the phone obtaining information about the situation as Reverend Jones, the Admiral, and the King of Beer Robert Reynolds were discussing the scene that the networks and cable were broadcasting. "It's all the wimmin's fault," said Reverend Jones. "They refused to yield their wombs to the Lord's plans during the sixties and the seventies. They refused to remain home nesting, but took leave of their God ordained role and went out there to try to mix it up with men. And now their chirren are upon us in the 1990s. Chirren they abandoned as they sought to 'find themselves.' St. John warned us about Santa Claus, he warns against the Nicolaites, chapter two, verse six, the Book of Revelations."

"That's all very interesting," the Admiral said, "but I think they ought to let me handle this Santa Claus business. Bible quoting and TV preaching doesn't seem to be affecting the matter, if you ask me."

"Maybe we ought to have Bob ring the Governor of New York and advise him on how to handle this Santa Claus business. Have him send in the guard. The local New York police can't seem to handle it," the King of Beer Robert Reynolds said.

"He won't do anything about it. He's one of the leaders of the forces of the Antichrist," Reverend Jones said. "Wish the Rock were here. He'd know what to do. Never will forget the day we got the news from Attica. I was in the middle of a sermon when one of the deacons told me. I felt proud of being an American that day."

"Me too," said the Admiral. "That Rock. What a way to go, too, huh," the Admiral said, nudging and winking at his companions. "Said he was so wrapped up in those two women that the emergency squad had to take a crowbar to pry them loose, and the black gal, she—"

"Was it true that he brought the bloody and brain-smeared clothing from the prison up to his estate at Pocantico Hills, placed them in a seldom-used Japanese bedroom, stripped and wallowed about in them?" asked the King of Beer. Bob Krantz put down the telephone receiver before anybody could answer. The men trained their eyes on him.

"Goddamnit, the interest rates have shot so high that you need binoculars to see them. Three department store executives have jumped from their windows and millions of youngsters have put pressure on their parents to follow the Christmas boycott that Santa requested. If it weren't enough that we have these world crises heating up, Santa Claus has to go and blow his stack. Some of the protestors are lying down in front of Christmas tree shipments. I've ordered that future shipments be sent with an armed guard escort," Krantz announced.

"Why don't you arrest him?" the Admiral demanded.

"Arrest who?" Krantz asked, wearily placing his glasses on the desk.

"Arrest Santa Claus," the King of Beer said.

"Be serious, gentlemen."

"Now look here, Krantz," Reverend Jones said. "We put you in power, and don't forget how the Lord gave me the power to lift that car off you. We demand that you do something about Santa Claus."

"I'm sorry," Krantz said. "I haven't gotten much sleep. I'll try to figure something out."

"You ought to let me have one of those nuclear submarines," the Admiral said. "I'd surround the Holiday Inn and make Santa Claus come out and surrender."

"That's not a good idea," the King of Beer said. "The last time you manned a nuclear submarine you were eighty years old and you rammed it into the West Coast. Remember? There are some members of Congress who'd crow our ears off if they knew that you were up here in the Oval Office giving advice. Besides, you'd have to bring the sub into New York Harbor before you could surround the Holiday Inn with it."

The Admiral stared at his shoes.

"Gentlemen, don't worry. Kevin Grouch, the Mayor of New York, says that he has the whole thing under control."

"Are you sure that you can trust him, Krantz?" Reverend Jones asked. "He and his Yid buddies might be behind the whole thing if you ask me. I mean, which race of people would rejoice the most if Christmas was ruined?"

"Good point," the King of Beer said.

"I'm always impressed by your scholarship, Reverend," the Admiral said.

"Incidentally, Krantz, what's the status of Operation Two Birds?" the King of Beer asked.

"The countdown begins tomorrow," Krantz answered. "Next week will advise the top-rate vitals to leave the target cities."

"I have to get back to Colorado," the King of Beer said.

"How's the fight with the Injuns coming?" Reverend Jones asked.

"My family has been making beer since they came through the Cumberland Pass with Dan Boone. They shot Injuns alongside Mordecai Lincoln and joined old Andy Jackson in his war against the Seminoles. Injuns come and Injuns go, but Regal Beer is here for an eternity." The King of Beer picked up his stetson, shook hands with the other three, and, spurs jangling, left the Oval Office. The Admiral and Reverend Jones and Krantz rose. The Admiral put on his Napoleon hat, and Reverend Jones, his coat.

"How's business?" the Admiral asked the Reverend.

"Pretty good," the Reverend responded. "Opened a few more mail-order colleges last week. Prayed for the sick, and warned the wicked. Krantz, you're doing a good job," Reverend Jones said. The Admiral nodded.

"I owe it all to you. You, the Admiral, and the King of Beer. I guess I'd still be working for Babylonian television were it not for your intervention, Reverend Jones."

"That wasn't me, that was the Lord, son. The Lord's advice is worth more than ours. Never forget that, son."

"I don't," said Bob Krantz. "I speak to the Lord day and night."

"Good boy," the Admiral said. "Stay on your knees. That's the best position for running the state." The two men pumped his hands and left. Relieved, Bob Krantz leaned back into his chair and lit a cigarette. Cigarettes were his only remaining vice.

He'd stopped drinking and snorting coke a few years before, but whenever those three dropped by the White House—they always "just happened to be in the neighborhood"—he couldn't conduct the business of state without them sitting around, offering ridiculous advice on anything that came to mind. The Reverend went about each day warning of the Second Coming; the Admiral sometimes wandered through Washington streets without the slightest idea of where he was; the King of Beer was a bore with his strange obsessions and his "injun"-hating.

Just as he had asked the press to begin building up resentment against a strange and foreign power, here comes Santa Claus to foul things up by removing the war hysteria from page one. What had come over Santa Claus? All he had uttered in the past was ho ho ho, but now he was given to inflammatory, polemical rhetoric, ranting diatribes, and stale invective.

Krantz put on his coat and began to head from the Oval Office to his apartment in the Watergate complex. What had really frightened him was the Attorney General's conclusion that he didn't have enough manpower to quell the disturbances taking place in New York. But soon New York's agony would be over, and if Santa happened to remain behind after Christmas Day, there would be no more him, either. He wondered was he doing the right thing. Would Christ do what he was doing were Christ in his place? He turned out the light, and walked down the hall.

*I know it's going to hurt people but we must think of future generations in this country. Though I wouldn't want anybody confusing my views with those of Reverend Jones, he's right in a way. The Gussack race has been pushed around. Why, if we hadn't escaped across the land barrier connecting Africa to Europe there wouldn't even be any of us. The ice age saved us. And then look at all of the things we've given to the world. Christianity, music and art—and now they're surrounding us. What would anybody do? Christ would want us to do the right thing. What would happen* to his religion if we weren't taking this step? Yes, dear Savior, I'm doing the right thing, Krantz thought.

So overcome by the spirit, Bob Krantz dropped to his knees. He removed his glasses. "Heavenly Father, I come before you with a great burden. Thou came to me when Reverend Jones lifted the wheels from my body. Thou helped me during the long months of convalescence, and I vowed that I would be Thy humble servant. It was Thee who told me that I should take the job as Dean Clift's presidential aide after the Colorado gang offered it to me. It was Thee who told me to push through Operation Two Birds, a plan to save all of Thy Christian work from being overrun by the forces of the AntiChrist, Thou sayest, sweet Jesus.

"They congratulated me on Operation Two Birds, Lord, because they didn't know that it was Thy plan, and that Thou had brought it to me, as the instrument for Thy desires. Lord, I'm beginning to have doubts about this plan, I mean, won't a lot of people get hurt, Lord? I'm asking you to relieve me of my doubts, sweet Jesus. I am asking Thee to send me a sign that Operation Two Birds is the right thing to do." He rose. The long hall was dark. He heard some heavy breathing down at the other end. He began to sweat and slowly trot towards the exit. He heard some growling. He looked behind him and some hairy, red-eyed thing was galloping towards him on all fours. He ran until he was safely outside the White House and underneath the moonlight. He looked back. Nothing was there.

## CHAPTER 24

Vixen hadn't stopped crying since she heard Santa's speech. She knew now why she'd always go into flushes when the former soap-opera star was behind her at the water cooler, or passed her in the hall. He had been beaten by Bob Krantz, beaten by Zumwalt, and his bodyguards, and seemed to have an overall Hegelian victim thing with people, but now she'd discovered the real man underneath all the paint and white dye. She had been through eight or so American men, and they'd all turned out to be mama's boys. Competitors for the Great Teat whose conversations revolved around themselves. Bully the blacks, bully the women. Macho tots. Santa had shown himself to be different from the other self-centered knaves who pulled her pigtails in grammar school, went too far in the back seat of the car in high school, and leaned on her in every relationship. And Sam. The biggest disappointment of them all. From the day her marriage broke up to the present, she'd gone through some relationships only because she was too embarrassed to go into a store to buy a dildo or vibrator. New England, she guessed. She tried a "sexual preference" relationship, but all her partner talked about was how awful men were. She talked about it so often one could conclude that what she really wanted was a man, but that can't be true because Freud was a patriarch. There was no answer as to why her "sexual preference" roommate always talked about men.

But now that she knew that she loved Santa, she was ready for a meaningful relationship. She wasn't political but she had always envied her mother for coming to maturity in the sixties when the Celtic-African visionaries walked the land, M.L.K., J.F.K., and R.F.K. Days of thunder and days of drums. Brave hearts exploding like tropical flowers. "The Impossible Dream" and "Bridge Over Troubled Water." And then the blue seventies and the cold eighties. Santa, of all people. The only voice that hadn't become as jaded as Ann Sheridan in *Juke Girl* (1942) in which a young actor named Ronald Reagan organized the lettuce workers against the bosses. The only compassionate voice in a Scroogelike country, the kissing cousin of South Africa. She always thought that her mother was a dizzy hippie with that silly Billie Holiday gardenia over her ear, and the Dorothy Lamour sarong. But now, Santa had won *her*! She knew that she could do something to help people. She knew where her place was: near Santa Claus. Her heart was thumping rapidly with excitement; her palms were sweating. How had he put it? The Terrible Twos. The right metaphor for this affliction. She always complained about not having enough. She always felt she needed more. She knew that for families in South America, her four bedrooms, two baths, and huge living room and parlor would seem like a villa. She knew that under the Dutch, in what the Dutch called South Africa, whole black families lived in one room.

And now Santa had spoken out. Spoken out against the consumption and greed. She wanted somebody like Santa. He had what the Japanese called *Yamato Damashi*. He was thoughtful and reflective, unlike some of the men she knew who were always standing before a pinball machine, or shooting bears. That's all Alaskan men seemed to enjoy doing. That reminded her. She would get rid of her black bear coat. She would sell her three thousand dollars' worth of dresses. She would get rid of her Lincoln. She would shove herself from her high chair and stop behaving like a daddy's girl. She would help Santa fight the powerful people his speech would surely offend. She finished packing her luggage. Now she had to confirm her plane reservations. She'd scribble a note to Flinch Savvage, or Sav-vage as he pronounced it. He was sweet. If only he didn't have a drinking problem. She removed some pink, scented stationery from her desk and began to hurriedly scribble. She was interrupted by Blitz, Santa's helper who was now on loan to her.

"Sorry to disturb you, Madame, but Master Savvage is here. "

"Tell him I'm busy, Blitz."

"Yes, Madame." But as Blitz turned to the door, Flinch Savvage forced his way in. "Why haven't you answered my calls, I knew you were home." He staggered about the room. He knocked over a lamp.

"I'll take care of this," she said, dismissing Blitz.

"I bought a couple of tickets to the Ice Capades, thought we could have dinner and then—"

"You're drunk."

"I've only had about two beers."

"You know that you can't drink. It makes you crazy."

"Gimmie a kiss." He stumbled towards her, she sidestepped, and he fell against the dresser.

"Look, you may as well know, I'm leaving for New York. I'm going to join Santa Claus." She was adjusting an earring.

"You what?"

"I told you that I'm going to join Santa Claus. He needs me." He grabbed her arm.

"Stop, you're hurting me."

"I won't let you go."

"You haven't the power to stop me. I'm in love with him."

"You love him. When's the last time you looked at his waistline?"

"That's all you think about. Your body. Your education. The right kind of aftershave lotion. What good is it? They use you against your own people. Besides, you're a lousy lover. So inhibited. Afraid to experiment. Afraid to do what I want."

"That's not what you were saying the other night." He grabbed her roughly to him.

"Let me go," she screamed. Blitz rushed in. Savvage picked up Blitz's mangled and distorted body and threw it against the wall. She was hysterical. "Now you've proven that you're a man." She laughed, scornfully.

"Vixen, I—"

"Get out."

Savvage started for the door. He looked to her and then to Blitz, whom she was helping to his feet. Savvage left.

## CHAPTER 25

The colonial-style table was covered with bottles of tranquilizers and whiskey. While the President's physical self sat in a dark blue bathrobe monogrammed with the Presidential seal, his spirit-plasm flew hand in hand with St. Nicholas, out the window, and soaring above the Treasury Department building, the Taft Monument, the Washington Monument, the J. Edgar Hoover Memorial Building. The President lost consciousness and came to, riding with St. Nicholas in an elevator. Its walls and floor were painted white. He didn't know what to make of it. Noticing his confusion, St. Nicholas said, "We're on the way to the American hell, so hold on, it's quite a place. You know that the hell of Dante, and the hell of the Bible are uncomfortable, but you ain't seen nothing yet," he said, as they flew into Kentucky's Mammoth Cave. "The American hell is a hell of roving duppies, Hopi two hearts, witches, warlocks, Bruhas, and all manner of evil spirits which can change shape as much as they wish."

"Why the elevator?" Clift asked, as they approached an elevator located inside the Cave surrounded by the rock.

"Because it was the elevator that made the United States, at one time, the most powerful capitalistic country in the world, because without elevators you couldn't have skyscrapers. And so in the elevator we go from world to world, an elevator that never gets stuck between worlds. In the American hell there are ten worlds." The elevator stopped. "This is the first world," St. Nicholas said. The elevator opened on what seemed to be a hospital floor, but the rooms had bars on the windows. Out of his peripheral vision, the President was sure he saw an animal in a white smock dash by. He appeared to be a wolf or a coyote, and he ran swiftly through the corridor.

"Don't worry about them. Don't let them get you. They won't strike unless you strike first," the Saint said. They walked into the waiting room and there, leafing through a 1940s issue of Life magazine, was a man he recognized from his shining army black shoes and his beige pants and the jacket he made famous. When the figure spoke, he sounded as if he were speaking under water or choking on bubbles. He noticed the President and then the

Saint, got up, and approached him excitedly. "At last you came, you came."
The President turned to Saint Nicholas, who merely smiled and rolled the
three gold balls nervously about in his hands.

"I tried to get Sherman to come," the figure said. "Sherman used to be my
right hand. I'm lost without him. He'd take care of things while I went out to
play golf with Freeman Gosden and Charles Correll. Those fellows used to
keep me in stitches. Sherman would look after all of the details but Sherman
seems to be only interested in maple syrup and zucchini marmalade where
he is up in New Hampshire. Can't say I blame him. But what's important is
that you came to see about Harry.

"Harry's behind that wall there," the figure said, pointing. "Those doctors
who come and give him his pills say they're doctors, but they look like coyotes to me, and those pills, every time he takes those pills he seems to get
worse." A black dog entered the room, red-eyed, baring its teeth. The figure
put its hand at its sides as straight as arrows. The dog sniffed the figure's
trousers, turned around and trotted out of the room.

"He's one of the guards," the figure said. "Here, come see about Harry."
Nicholas and Dean Clift followed the figure to a barred window through
which he could see a short man wearing a straw hat, double-breasted suit,
bow tie, and white loafers. He was walking briskly up and down the room
using a cane for support.

"He walks up and down because he doesn't want to go to sleep. He says
that when he tries to sleep he dreams of Japanese faces, burnt, twisted, and
peeling, with no eyeballs. It was the generals and scientists who made him do
it. Harry never thought much of himself, that's why he swore all the time. He
was intimidated by scientists and generals just as I was always impressed by
the top-rate vitals of big business, and so when they told him that they
wanted him to drop little man and big man on those Japanese cities he gave
his ok. What did he know about physics? How did he know that the people
who were wounded would carry that white flash in their genes and that
dozens of deformed generations would be born? It was just supposed to be a
war, not judgment. That was no military act, that was an insult to nature and
to God. Harry Truman is the most tormented and alienated person down
here. The nightmare followed him beyond the grave."

Dean Clift couldn't believe what the General told him. Harry Truman?
That gutsy spunky haberdasher from Missouri? The populist? The one who
stood up to General Douglas MacArthur? What was harder to understand

was why the General was there. The World War II General who had become such a grandfather image to America of the 1950s. What was he doing here? Where did he go wrong?

St. Nicholas put his fingers to his lips.

The General pulled a Camel from a pack of cigarettes.

"I know what you're thinking. What am I doing here? Why aren't I on another floor? Me. Who is the father even to Walter Cronkite. Doug MacArthur told me that I could have been the second messiah. He was on his knees saying Ike, Ike, you could be the second messiah. He wanted me to put a nuclear field in the Yalu River, he said. Up on Morningside Heights. I was president of Columbia then, and they didn't have much for me to do, and so I used to invite all of the old war buddies over and we'd swap war stories. But I know that you're still wondering why I'm here. Come over here." They followed the old man to a window in the land of Diddie Wah Diddie, sometimes cold, sometimes hot, depends upon the floor you go to, sometimes city, sometimes desert with the coyotes flying above the cactus and the rattlesnakes.

Coyotes with the wings of long-extinct reptiles.

The Saint stood behind them in the shadows which were the color of blue they use on Spanish television horror movies. Dwight Eisenhower was standing at the window looking down at the Congo jungle scene that had materialized below. A primitive rural road was nearly hidden by large clumps of bush. Dean Clift was watching, watching the pitiful, weary old spirit as he sadly kept his attention riveted to the road, and while studying the General he thought of Chuck Berry, the Coasters, Fats Domino, Arthur Godfrey, Debbie Reynolds, and Eddie Fisher, 3-D movies, and the Kefauver committee. Suddenly, a black Citroen pulled up and a body was shoved out. It owned a bloody, contorted, intellectual-looking face, scholarly mustache and goatee, and a poet's eyes underneath a startling black pompadour. The ghost from Abilene, Texas, began to wail and grieve.

"If it hadn't been for Dulles," he cried. "That man had so much Bible and brimstone inside of him. The whole family—everybody but Allen was like him. They even had a fidgety woman preacher in the family. Dulles became haunted by that young black man. Said that when the young man, then a new leader of the Congo, visited Washington he sassed Dillon and the others. Swore up and down that Lumumba would bring the Communists to the Congo. Said that the Communism was the bitch of Babylon. Kept it up. Kept it up so much that I started smoking again, though I had sworn off the habit.

And so one day, I was anxious to get out and play a couple of rounds of golf at Burning Tree and they'd been pestering me all day about this Patrice Lumumba fellow, and so I stamped my foot and said, a guy like that ought to take a hike. I should have known when they started shaking hands and congratulating each other that something was up. I didn't mean for them to go and kill the man.

"I always wondered how it would have turned out if I hadn't relied so much on the people around me. I said to myself, Ike, you got it made. You rose from an obscure soldier to the pinnacle of military power. I didn't want to blow it all by being President. I didn't want to rock the boat during those eight years. So I delegated responsibility. Maybe I could have become the second messiah as Douglas said. But, I guess I can't really complain. This place is a country club in comparison to the people down in the tenth world. I hear they have spirit-eating cannibals down there who are on the prowl for fresh ghost meat."

The laughter could be heard coming from inside the Citroen. The corpse of the Congo leader, its hands tied behind its back, lay face down in the dirt. The Saint informed Dean Clift, who was close to tears, that they had to leave.

"Got to go?" the old soldier said. "Well, it's pretty decent of you young fellows to come down and see about Harry and me. And that part about not losing a night's sleep over the damage done by little man and big man. Don't believe a word of it. Harry cried in justice Douglas's arms. And you know what happened to the young man who flew the B-52 plane? He went crazy, you know." He started to wave as Nicholas and Dean Clift left for the elevator. "Hold on a minute." They turned to see the General trying to catch up with them.

"That Atlas nose cone. You know the one they put up into space? They made a tape of my voice and put it inside the nose cone. Is that Atlas still flying around the globe?" Saint Nicholas assured the spirit that indeed the Atlas was still flying and that he had passed it flying to Washington.

The old soldier paused again before vanishing into the mist. "You know," he said, "I don't know what I miss more, Mamie or the quail hash she used to make. She never complained. The perfect Army wife. You know, we moved twenty-seven times. That's what I remember about that woman—hanging up and taking down drapes. She got so that she could fill out a change-of-address card in ten seconds flat."

## CHAPTER 26

Before she boarded the plane, she had sent her resignation to the North Pole Development Corporation by telegram. It was hard to say who was in charge. The company was left in a state of chaos after the strange turn of events in New York. Santa's speech had had a devastating impact upon the stock market, frankincense and myrrh were taking one hell of a beating. Conflict had broken out between Santa's supporters, mostly young, and Santa's detractors, mostly old.

After the flight from the West Coast to La Guardia, Vixen had successfully hailed a cab for the trip downtown to the Holiday Inn.

"Why all the traffic, driver?"

"You must not have heard the news, ma'am."

"I just got in from Alaska, we don't get much from the outside world where I'm living, and there is only one TV channel, something about mountain interference with the signals."

"Santa Claus and some of the young toughs who've taken up with him, some really tough schoolboys, had some kind of ceremony in Flushing. There were motorcycles and cars everywhere. There's a church up there that's supposed to have the hair and a piece of skull from the original Saint Nicholas. I'm telling you, Christmas isn't the same since I was a kid. It's become real complicated. I mean I'm all for free enterprise and against Communism, and so I didn't oppose it when this fellow, Oswald Zumwalt, bought the rights to Santa Claus, but this season they've taken it too far. Why, some of these juveniles were arrested for taking their family jewels and money to Santa Claus at the Holiday Inn. They had baskets and bags of loot for him. And the students have taken up outside the hotel. Roughing up passersby who say something bad about Santa Claus. And that speech he made. Out-and-out socialism. Now I understand why he wears red."

Vixen crossed her legs and the cab driver glanced at her knees through the rearview mirror. He studied her. No, it couldn't be. She looked at him through the mirror. "Anything wrong, driver?" she asked. She frowned. She looked at the picture and name on his license.

"Sam?"

"Vixen? Vixen, I thought I'd never see you again. All I had was your note. It's been years."

"I live in Alaska now."

"Yes, I remember. You've been in the newspaper, you work for the company that's marketing Santa Claus."

"Yes. What are you doing with yourself?"

"O, married. I have two kids. We live in Hoboken, across the river. "

"Still painting?"

"Not as much as I used to. Just don't have any more time. I teach classes at Pratt and drive the car at night. It's really expensive supporting a family and teaching. You have any kids?"

"No, I never married, Sam. I just didn't think that childrearing and a career mixed."

"I know what you mean. We have this two-year-old. She always wants to eat daddy's drumstick and sit in daddy's chair. I let her have her way but it's pretty tough, you know; I was the one who always had the drumstick and now I fight with a two-year-old over it. You know how two-year-olds are. Their plates will be full but they'll have their eyes on everybody else's plates, or they'll have a cookie in their hand and yet ask for another cookie, or the whole bag of cookies."

"You look very good, Sam."

"I try to take care of myself. Had a heart attack a couple of years ago, but now I'm watching the old waistline."

"What happened to Romeo?"

Sam studied her in the mirror. Their eyes met for a moment. "O, he's doing fine. He's running an ad firm in Los Angeles and has bought a condominium." The car reached the Holiday Inn. The scene was bedlam. Crowds had gathered in front of the hotel to catch a glimpse of Santa. Youth gang members, some wearing white berets, scanned the crowd; some stood on rooftops.

CHAPTER 27

James Providence and Luke Charity, two Indians who worked in the mail-order room of the Big North, were drinking some kind of Canadian ale, relaxing in a bar many of the employees of Big North frequented. They were wearing plaid shirts, denims, and boots. They were staring at the scene at the bar from the table where they sat.

"I never did like him. What is he doing in this bar anyway, drinking with us?"

"What do you think it's all about?" said Luke.

"Who knows. Everything is uncertain. I hear that the Japanese bank has had to give Big North a loan so that they can meet the payroll." The headlines on the newspaper that lay next to James's elbow read, "Santa No Longer Jolly." The caption under Santa's picture, taken during the Times Square Rally, read, "Says No More Ho Hos."

"When I went home last night and the wife said that Santa had made that speech, I was nearly knocked on the seat of my pants. That guy, I thought. The meekest, most pushed-around guy you'd ever want to meet."

"Well, he certainly did turn the tables on them. I'd love to see that Oswald Zumwalt's face."

"What do you suppose it all means?"

"Beats me. There's talk of a strike. I've even heard that Big North is going to be sold. The lobby was full of creditors this morning. Nobody has been able to reach Zumwalt. It's OK with me. My kid said this morning that he didn't want anything for Christmas. The wife too. They heard Santa's speech and agreed with him."

"I got the same thing over at my house. The kids said they were going to stick with Santa. That these bad men he was talking about ought to get the rod for being naughty." The men laughed. Suddenly, there was the sound of broken glass. The men looked up. Flinch Savvage was leaning over the bar. He started quarreling with the bartender, demanding more drink.

"How long do you think they're going to let him stay in here, carrying on that way?"

"The bartender can't do anything. Flinch has pull with the company." Luke leaned over and whispered to James. "I hear he's diddling that Gussuck girl, Vixen."

"How do you know that Flinch is getting it?"

"My sister works up at the ski lodge. She says that Flinch and the woman are there quite often." Flinch tried to punch a man standing next to him. He missed and landed on the floor. He got up, brushed himself off, and returned to his drink.

"Jesus, do you think he's going to be able to find his way home?"

"Who cares. He never cared for us Indians. Remember how he used to be such a goody-two-shoes. Sucking up to the nuns."

"I never did like him."

"You shouldn't be so hard. He used to go hunting with us. Was a good shot. Used to bag a lot of deer. Then he went away to the white man's college. He changed."

"Maybe you're right. He did try to save the old chief from jail."

"Yeah, but they jailed him anyway. He died there, but then the tree got even. The tree picked a life to make up for the chief's. That was a mean old tree with a nasty temper. It didn't want to be disturbed. No ravens would go near it." There was a crash. Some of the other Indians lifted Savvage to his feet. He staggered, and shoved the Indians away from him. He said something like "Goddamn Indians."

"Boy, anybody else would have been thrown out of here an hour ago."

"They're afraid of that Vixen. She's right up there next to Zumwalt. Arctic woman. You remember Manny? She fired Manny because she was walking through the hall one day and she thought she heard him mumble 'that bitch.' Manny had three kids to support. She made it so that he couldn't find another job in town."

Flinch Savvage finally left the tavern. He staggered down the deserted, sleet-covered streets toward his car. It was teethchattering cold. He was humming a chorus from "Rudolph, the Red-Nosed Reindeer," about one of the famous antlered animals introduced to Alaska by Sheldon Jackson, the missionary who brought them from Siberia. "Serves the bitch right. She and her fat bastard deserve each other. She'll come back after she finds out that he was drunk when he made that speech. That's probably what happened. He was drunk, why, everybody knows about his drinking problem. Zumwalt will fire him for that speech and then he won't be wobbling about so high and mighty." Flinch drank some whiskey from a wax cup he'd brought out of the bar. He slipped on some ice, went up into the air, and came down crashing on a hip. There was a sharp pain in his side. A car pulled up. Blitz was in the front seat. He was with three little men who worked with Big North's boiling, churning chocolate vats. Blitz helped him into the car. "Boy, Blitz," Savvage said, "am I glad to see you." Blitz didn't say anything.

## CHAPTER 18

OPENING NIGHT. The play was going splendidly. The ninety-nine people were sitting on top of one another, and must have been uncomfortable, but they were paying close attention to the developments onstage. Tremonisha had supervised every detail: costumes, lighting, props, sets, et cetera. But where was Tre? He'd called her house, but there hadn't been an answer for a week or so. Nobody had seen her since their encounter in the office where her blowup with Becky had taken place. Becky had brought in another director who merely supervised the details of mounting the play that Tre had created. Becky insisted that Tre's version of the play not be tampered with. They waited a half hour after the scheduled opening time for her to show up, but when she didn't they decided to begin. She'd worked out every detail with such professionalism that there was really no need for her now. Ian's respect for her had certainly increased, and he hoped that she'd never learn what he and the fellas said about her behind her back, all of the scurrilous, unprintable things. They talked about Clotel the mulatto and Coreatha the black woman, and how they and their native-American, Asian, and Hispanic sisters had had babies by every conceivable European man from the tip of Argentina to the Arctic—how they'd performed the hemispheric sixty-nine with Frenchmen, Dutchmen, Spaniards, Portuguese, Russians, British, Scots, Irishmen, and God knows what other kind of European white eyes.

Act I was a tremendous hit, with some of the audience breaking into applause after particularly dramatic lines and speeches. The only male member of the cast was the skeleton of Ham Hill, which they'd borrowed from one of the local medical schools. The play opened with the female judge, who wore her hair in a dignified bun, Cora Mae, her lawyer, Ham Hill's lawyer, played by an excellent black actress, though on the plump side—but the casting director had said that they'd lose one-third of the white male audience if they didn't include "a ham," as this type of actress was called—the female jury, and female bailiff. Even the two gravediggers were female. They all stood around the grave as the coffin of Ham Hill was raised. Ball had included some telling eye exchanges in this scene. Ham Hill's defense lawyer, who was wearing a black pin-striped suit, white silk blouse, and huge black bow tie, her hair straightened and glossy, was glaring with contempt at the plaintiff, Cora Mae, now a radical feminist lesbian, part owner of a bookstore, and her lover, a woman with short hair, a round face, and wearing glasses. The two embraced and sobbed as the coffin lid was raised. Cora Mae's lawyer, who was dressed like one of the female executives one sees in Ms. magazine—attache case, business suit—remained expressionless during the entire scene, which ended with the skeleton of Ham Hill being removed from the coffin and placed into a patrol car—offstage—for the trip to the courthouse, accompanied by thunder, lightning, and great applause. Though one drunken black male first-nighter was ejected from the theater for standing and shouting—"Looks like a case of dig the nigger up and kill him again."

The second act took place inside the courtroom and was highlighted by Ham Hill's defense attorney demolishing the testimony of Cora Mae. She showed the jury photos of Cora as she appeared twenty years before, in the sixties, with heavy makeup, miniskirt, eye shadow, rouge, blond hair with black roots: a sleaze and a tease. Over the objection of Cora's defense lawyer, Ham Hill's attorney said that there was no difference between Cora Mae and the man who opens his coat and displays his genitals to females in public places. Her description of Cora Mae as a flasher brought an eruption of discussion from the courtroom, whereupon the judge banged the gavel for order. Cora Mae, the defense attorney claimed, craved attention from men and only complained about Ham Hill when she noticed that Ham Hill wasn't staring at her in the fateful encounter outside the supermarket where Ham Hill worked as a packer. At that moment the skeleton, with a sardonic grin, began to slide to the floor; the bailiff propped it up. This gesture by the corpse, as if done to make a point, was applauded wildly by the audience. The judge overruled the objections of Cora Mae's lawyer, stating that Ms. Mae's reputation in the sixties was certainly relevant to the case. The second act ended with Cora Mae's lover—both of them were dressed in men's clothes and looked as though they'd just climbed from beneath a manhole—jumping to her feet and complaining about Cora's treatment and the judge citing the woman for contempt and ejecting her from the courtroom. It took five strong women to accomplish this deed.

During the intermission Ball went out into the lobby. Average everyday normal middle class people were congratulating him and patting him on the back, while the white feminists stared at him stonily. He could tell that their black feminist friends had really enjoyed the performance of Ham Hill's defense attorney, but wouldn't let on before their white sisters; one came up to him later and told him so. The fellas had said that a lot of feminists were okay when you had a one-on-one relationship with them, but when they were around the sisters they'd get all fired up. The academic black Marxist-Leninists were in one corner sneering, and the black avant-garde members of the audience segregated themselves from the rest of the people in the lobby. They were standing near the wall, sulking.

Drat them, Ball thought. He figured that he had it made. The third act would begin with Cora Mae back on the stand. Under questioning, Cora Mae would reveal that it took her twenty years to bring charges against Ham Hill, the lynch mob victim, because she'd been converted from a rock and roll sex kitten to a radical feminist and was only now capable of assessing the heinousness of Ham Hill's crime. That she felt it was important to clear her name. That if there was no trial, there'd always be the suspicion that she was trying to lure Ham Hill, the supermarket packer, who'd been lynched by her husband and his friends. That sex with her husband was no good after the incident and that he'd spent many nights during their married life pacing the floor and sitting on the porch, staring at the stars. She would testify that her social life had been ruined until she took up with her lover and opened the radical lesbian bookstore. The audience would hiss and catcall at this explanation, Ball was sure. Confident, Ball decided to leave the workshop performance of his play and head upstairs to the Lord Mountbatten, where "the important play" was taking place. As he walked up the aisle well-wishers touched his elbows or shook his hands.

## CHAPTER 19

They had the Lord Mountbatten set up like a German cabaret of the 1930s. The audience was seated at tables, and was being served liquor and sandwiches.

The actress playing Eva Braun sat on a dressing room bench before a large mirror. It was supposed to be her bedroom inside the Fuhrerbunker. She was adjusting a bridal headdress and powdering her face. She wore a frilly pink slip and was speaking her lines to the audience through the mirror. A tiny orchestra of tuba, trombone, two violins, saxophone, bass, and drums was positioned behind the mirror. On one flat board that represented the bedroom's wall was a photo of Klara Hitler, Hitler's mother, who looked like the dictator. Ms. Braun must have just made some kind of pungent point because as Ball entered, the audience of mostly women was applauding loudly. He sat down at one of the tables and the two women who were occupying the other chairs frowned. During the scene the sound person had simulated the noise of airplanes and bombing taking place in the background.

"Now he's going to marry me. Now that the enemy is closing in, he wants to tie the knot. Well, I have news for him." (The audience applauds wildly and Becky French, seated with her party of feminist celebrities at the front table, beams out over the audience. She notices Ball. Ball waves at her, but she ignores him.) "All these nights he kept me locked up in this Romanesque cemetery with its stone walls and security guards while he was gallivanting all over Europe. I knew what he was doing. Don't think that I'm not aware of the other women. All of them, Goebbels, Goring with his big bovine bitch of a wife, and his cream-colored uniforms. Don't think that little Eva doesn't know what's going on."

(Audience applauds madly.)

"As for Der Fuhrer, as he calls himself, he nearly screwed his little niece Geli to death because he couldn't deal with an older, more mature woman. They said that Geli committed suicide, but I know. He killed her because she got pregnant by a Jew. A woman that would come between him and Klara his mother. Look at that bitch." (She points to the photo of Klara Hitler hanging on the wall.) "Boy, was she a nudge." She walks up and down the floor with her hands on her hips, occasionally making sweeping gestures with one hand. She's constantly smoking a cigarette. "'Adolf, why do you want to go to Vienna to study art? Adolf, why don't you try to settle into a legitimate business?' 'Yes, mama.' Boy, was he devoted to her. Even spared the Jewish doctor who took care of her. As for his thing about the Jews—well, everybody knows why he does that. They talk about him behind his back. Those insane speeches he makes when he's had all of that cocaine and heroin. The Jewish problem. The only Jewish problem Germany has is him." (Applause.) "God, that woman has been dead these many years, but she still controls him.

Sometimes when he's making love to me, if you want to call it that, he calls out her name. Klara. Oh, Klara. It's disgusting. And if you knew what I know about him in bed, then you'd understand why he's trying to conquer all of these countries and be such a big man." (The actor playing Hitler emerges from where he's been seated in the audience and joins Eva, the spotlight following him. There's a chorus of boos from the women in the audience. The trombone makes a clownish sound, and there's a clash of cymbals from the drummer.) "Eva. Eva. The allies are bickering among themselves, according to the shortwave. There's hope yet. Are you ready? The preacher will be here soon." (He rushes back into the audience, the spotlight following·him. Eva turns to the audience.) "That's that cocaine and heroin talking. There's no way he's going to get out of this place alive. That's his problem," she says, lighting a cigarette. (A black woman in the audience says, "Tell it, honey." Other women join in. "Tell it, honey," followed by titters. The two women at Ball's table smile at him. He turns his eyes away.) "Well, I'm not going to be like those other women." (Wild applause.) "Eva's got some sense. (More applause. Hitler emerges from the audience again, this time with a priest in priestly garb carrying a Bible.)

"Eva. Are you ready, my sweet?"(Eva, to audience: "Watch this.")

"Ready for what?" (She turns toward the two men. The priest gets a load of her thighs where the slip line ends. She crosses her legs. His eyes grow large and he almost drops his Bible.)

"Ready for the wedding, Eva. Eva. You're not even dressed." (Eva rises.)

"Look, you little shrimp. I'm not going to stand for this dreckscheisse any longer." (Both the priest and the Fuhrer are horrified. The audience laughs and applauds.)

"Eva, what's come over you? Father, she doesn't know what she's saying."

"I do know what I'm saying. Boy, did you have me fooled. All that sweet talk about destiny and how you were going to get me a job as a Hollywood film editor. I should have known."

"Eva, what are you talking about?" Hitler says.

"While you were away getting yours I was here getting mine, or as the American song says, you should have been concerned about who was making love to your old lady while you were out making love." (This line brings the house down.)

"Eva, you've been listening to those nigger records. I'm going to take them away from you." (A huge, blond, blue-eyed chauffeur approaches the front from the audience. Eva turns to him.)

"Are you ready, Otto?" (Otto nods.)

Hitler says, "Eva, what is the meaning of this?" (Stunned, Hitler turns to the priest, who shrugs his shoulders.) "I'm going to get married all right, but not to you. I'm marrying Otto," Eva says, closing her eyes and bobbing her leg in defiance. The priest sneaks a glance at her legs.)

"You and him!!" To Otto: "Otto, you're a loyal German, I need you."

"He's not German, he's Jewish." (The audience goes wild.) "A better man than you will ever be." The priest says, "But he has blue eyes, and an Aryan nose."

"Many Jews have such features," Eva says. "Besides, I decided, why should I have a half-breed when I can have the real thing." (Eva removes a revolver from the dressing table drawer. Hitler and the priest do a double take and take a few steps backward.) "My own private, intimate gun, where—what are you doing?" Hitler says.

"I went through your coat pocket. That's where I found the names and telephone numbers of Christian women you've been screwing all over Europe. Now you two get on your knees. Get their guns, Otto." (Delighted, the audience applauds. Otto goes over and takes Hitler's gun.)

"Please don't shoot. Why, I'm the savior of the German nation, the German nation is like . . . well . . . a bride to me."

"And so you treated her like your other women. Destroyed her because she couldn't measure up to your mother." (Otto grins.) She fires shots into Hitler, after each one reciting a specific crime. "This is for tortured France. This is for ravished Poland. This is for maimed Czechoslovakia. This is for Mother Russia. This is for all of the women you've ruined . . . my sisters." (The audience is on its feet applauding, hooting, cheering, and the two women sharing a table with Ball stare at Ball, menacingly. Come to think of it, he's the only man in attendance.)

"Please don't shoot me," the priest says. "It was his fault. He made me do it. He made all of us follow him. He swayed us with his brilliant oratory and mesmerized us with pageants and fireworks, he somehow managed to tap into our collective un—" (Eva kills the priest with one shot.)

"Go warm up the car, Otto, I'll be right with you." (Otto exits. Eva walks over to where a fur coat is hanging and removes it. She puts the coat over her slip and picks up a packed suitcase. She pauses. She puts it down. She places the gun in the hand of Hitler's corpse. She goes to the dresser and picks up a lighter. She pours some of the fluid on Hitler's body. She throws a match and flames begin to cover his body. She walks over and removes Hitler's mother

Klara's picture from the wall, and throws it to the floor where it crashes. She calmly walks offstage as the audience goes nuts.)

## CHAPTER 20

Ball decided to get out before the crush. He walked down the deserted halls until he came to Becky's office. The door was open. He decided to sit down at Ickey's desk until it was time to return to the basement workshop. What? On top of Ickey's desk was a newsletter called Lilith's Gang, "a publication for feminists in the culture industry." On the first page was THE SEX LIST! Next to each male writer's name was a column that included the offense he'd committed. There were names of black as well as white male writers. He recognized some of the names. Floyd Salas. "Author of a poem entitled 'Pussy Pussy Everywhere,' in which he proposes that women lure men using furtive means." John A. Williams. "Author of book entitled, *! Click Song*, Tremonisha says that this book glorifies mixed marriages. Our people in subsidiary rights assure us that this book will never reach paperback." Cecil Brown. "Said in an article that 'there are as many female Hitlers as male Hitlers, and probably even more.' If he ever returns to the States we'll keep an eye on him." Next to Randy Shank and Jake Brashford's names was written "incorrigible." "Shank we understand is having hard times, but it will take time to reduce Brashford's reputation since he is supported by many aging white males of the modernist persuasion. They still have power, but within ten years most of them will be dead." He scanned the list for his name. Ian Ball. "Has shown improvement after that terribly sexist Suzanna. He's also a southerner and is not as bitter and as paranoid about women as some of his northern soul brothers. With this issue we're removing him from the sex list mainly as a result of Tremonisha's recommendation." Ball almost leaped out of Ickey's chair, he was so happy. If he had been close to Tremonisha at that moment he would have hugged and kissed her.

He heard voices coming down the hall. "Eva's Honeymoon" must have been almost over. He opened the door to Becky's office part of the way, to see who was approaching. The old lady was being helped down the hall by her chauffeur. If the two had looked toward Becky's office they would have seen a lone gray eye staring at them.

"I hope, madame, that this will be your last exercise in folly," the chauffeur said.

"Oh, don't be angry with me, Otto," she said, patting the arm that was aiding her. "I've always wanted the world to know. To know my side. What really happened."

"But—"

"Don't worry, they can't trace it to me."

"It's just dangerous, madame, don't you think?"

"We've been together for forty years now. You can trust me. I know that you couldn't trust the others, but you can trust me. Trust me, Otto. This will be the last of my creative efforts. I promise. I just couldn't resist the temptation to dance on the grave of that son of a bitch. It's been forty years." They walked past where Ball was standing behind the door. When the coast was clear he headed down the stairs toward the basement where his workshop was probably ending. He stood outside the door, and heard Ham Hill's defense lawyer summing up the defense for the jury.

"Something is wrong with Cora Mae. You see, white people can't own you anymore, so they try to own you with their eyes. They can't punch you anymore without getting harmed, so they try to punch you with their eyes. They try to control you. Nigger, what are you doing here, we don't want you here, they are saying to you with their eyes. Years ago it was the lynch rope. Now it's the rude stare. They look at you in airports, in restaurants. They stare at you like they're not used to anything." He could see some of the black women on the jury following Ball's directions ("as she is saying this the black jury members nod their approval"). "They've been accusing the blacks and Jews of owning the evil eye when they are the ones with the evil in their eyes. So here is this young boy, Ham Hill, minding his own business when this this . . . vixen intrudes upon his space, glares at him with lust in her eyes, and when he pays no attention accuses him of reckless eyeballing, causing her husband and his friends to lynch the lad until he is dead." He could hear Cora Mae yell out, "No. It's not true."

"And twenty years after this child has been murdered, she comes along and says that what he did to her was similar to what her husband and that lynch mob did to Ham Hill. Now I ask you, ladies and gentlemen, isn't that the most air-headed thing you ever heard of?" Cora's attorney says, "I object, your honor." While the audience laughed, Ball walked away from the door and got a drink from the bartender, who was dressed in white jacket, black bow tie. He asked for a gin and tonic.

Who knows, he might luck up tonight, he thought. The bartender mixed his drink. "Looks like a hit, Mr. Ball. Congratulations." Ball smiled and sat at the stool of the bar, which had been set up in the lobby. He slowly imbibed. He could tell by the loud cheers and screams that the lawyer's speech was over. God, he was getting nervous. He went outside and walked around the block. When he returned he went back to the workshop space and listened in at the door. Cora Mae's lawyer was making her closing statement to the judge and jury.

"And when she felt his hot and dirty eyes on her she felt as though the scum of the world was taking an X-ray of her body. The men in this country think that all of the women are available to them, and so they use their eyes to scout in the same way that a predator stalks its prey. And though my distinguished opponent argues that Mr. Hill's only crime was that of having his eyes in the wrong place at the wrong time, I disagree. This man knew what his eyes were doing. He was raping her, in a manner of speaking, ladies and gentlemen. No, he didn't struggle with her or molest her with his hands; he did it with his eyes. He undressed her with his eyes. He accosted her with his eyes, he penetrated her with his eyes. He eye-raped her, ladies and gentlemen. For him, all she was was a cunt." Ball walked over to the bar and had another drink. He sat there for about ten minutes. Suddenly, there was wild applause mixed with a few boos. The people began to pour from the theater. They began to collect in the lobby and almost immediately the well-wishers came up and shook his hand, the ordinary black and white everyday people, that is. They had obviously enjoyed themselves. Even some feminists he'd seen on the art scene from time to time, including a few who'd given him problems in some of these little fly-by-night drama magazines, were congratulating him. The New York black avant-garde was leaning against the wall, grumbling, their jaws all tight. The men were dressed in an unorthodox way, anything to be different, and the women were wearing bizarre attire. There was this tall one who looked like she always wanted to fight and was always writing articles cussing white folks out, and would go up to Harlem and denounce the brothers who were with Anne—the American white woman— but next night she'd be in one of the downtown lesbian clubs dancing with Anne. The fellas said that this must have meant that she wanted to have all of the white women for herself. A bunch of backbiters and verbal scorpions, still back there with Malcolm X and John Coltrane when everybody knew that the greatest black militant they'd produced was Koffee Martin, who was from the South. Anyway, if they really wanted to embrace some politically far out position, let them go and mix it up with Pol Pot or the cynical and mean regime that runs Ethiopia.

This snit, who in his books was always dusting this politically incorrect person or that backslider and traitor, came toward Ball, leaving his group against the wall sulking. He rudely pushed through the crowd of well-wishers, and when he got to where Ball was standing he said: "White women elected Ronald Reagan, twice." Ball stamped his foot. The little fellow scampered back to his friends, to the amusement of the people who were gathered about Ball. A feminist came up and elbowed her way through the people who were telling him how great he was.

"Mr. Ball. I have an apology to make," she said.

"What apology, Ms.?"

"I was chairperson of women's studies at a small obscure university in Cincinnati and . . ." She broke down; it took a few seconds for her to regain her composure. "One of my students wanted to write a dissertation on your plays and I—I . . . ."

"Go on," Ball said.

"I turned her down. I said that you were a notorious sexist even though I hadn't seen any of your work." Ball smiled and put his arm around her. She began crying on his chest.

"I understand," he said. "Sometimes we feel that our goals are so righteous, so necessary for the benefit of personkind, that we in our haste make mistakes that we later regret. Don't give it a second thought." The people gathered around murmured their approval. A woman whose shape revealed her to be a lover of animal fat and starches stepped forward.

"Me too, me too," she said. Ball and his admirers turned to her. "Do you remember a few years ago when you tried to get a one-acter staged at the theater I ran, and you got turned down? It was my fault. Now that I've seen *Reckless Eyeballing*, I feel so . . . so . . . I feel so bad." She too broke down and began sobbing like an infant. Ball had his arms about each in his attempt to console the two women. Suddenly a loud challenge came from the top of the stairs leading to the restrooms. "Ian. You ain't nothin' but a gangster and a con artist." It was Brashford; Ball and the people with him were shocked as Brashford began to descend the stairs. Uh oh, Ball thought. Brashford was going to imitate James Mason's drunken entrance in *A Star Is Born*. This classic beauty, a woman some would describe as "olive skinned," started up the stairs toward him and grabbed his arm. She was dressed in a black silk dress and wore some fine jewelry. She could not deter Brashford, who kept walking down the stairs and behaving like a Cossack in a succoth, as Isaac Babel would say.

"Tricking these people. You ain't nothin' but a trickologist with your fuzzy quick lines. You mischievous malicious bastard."

"Come on, dear," the woman said. He yanked his elbow from her grip and waved her away. "Ain't no way in the world for a jury to bring in a verdict of guilty against that corpse. In the version you gave me he's acquitted, after a confession from Cora Mae that she realized that she and the boy were in the same boat. Fellow sufferers. They made you change it. These vain, conniving bitches made you do it." The two feminists that Ball had been comforting glared at Brashford, and some of the patrons who remained to congratulate Ball looked at Brashford with utter disgust. The woman with Brashford said, "Dear."

"You keep out of it," he said. He wore a light blue suit that must have cost a grand and one of those Mike Hammer hats, which slid about his head as he came down the stairs. He also wore one of those British coats that intellectuals of the fifties favored. It was kind of like part of the existentialist's uniform. Camus wore one like it. It had shoulder straps, pockets, belts, and other features of little discernible use. A couple of Brashford's old-time liberal buddies, now neo-conservatives, who'd written little and had fallen hook, line, and sinker for the major intellectual, political and cultural trends of Europe only to be disillusioned time and again, started up the stairs to try to restrain their friend, the only colored in their club.

He punched the two, who already seemed out on their feet, and they fell down the stairs. The effort had placed Brashford off balance also, and he came tumbling down. Their friends helped them up, and Brashford sat up on the bottom stair, pulled a flask from his suit pocket, and took a long swig of something. He made a grunt, offending some of the firstnighters.

"I'm your literary father, you shit. And look at what you've done to me. A pitiful old man who has only one play to his name. But you wait. I'll show you. Wait until my masterpiece about the Armenians is staged. Lengthy Struggle Toward the Borders of Darkness. It's about this alcoholic father, see, with these two sons, who are real losers, and the mother, well she's a hophead and injects herself offstage and . . . and . . ." Some of the people started to leave. Others shook their heads in sadness.

"These bitches had better not touch my play. Fucking twat. They hate the black man worst of all because they're sleeping with these other guys and are afraid to take a shot at them. Shit. Hey, that's not bad. I'm beginning to miss the old days when you were just hated because you were black." He began to laugh at his own joke. Others began to leave. He shouted after them.

"Hey. Where you going? Would you like to see a little ham bone?" He pulled up his trench coat and began to slap his thighs rhythmically. He began to sing some lewd choruses of the song "Mama Don't Allow," offending people with every dirty stanza. He finally reached the chorus: "Mama don't allow no Playboy reading in here / Mama don't allow no Playboy reading in here / We don't care what the Mama don't allow we going to read our Playboy anyhow," whereupon a few grimfaced feminists had stood all they were going to stand, and stormed out. A security guard finally came and told Brashford to leave. Brashford got up and tried to take a swing at the security guard, but the guard caught his arm, and brought it behind his back. The Mike Hammer hat fell to the floor. Somebody picked it up and followed the security guard and Brashford out of the theater. The people who had remained turned to Ball.

"This should be a night of victory, of triumph for me, but instead my heart is heavy. You all know how much I love Brashford. He befriended me after I wrote a long panegyric about him in the Downtown Mandarin in which I expressed my thanks to Brashford that the younger generation had such a fabulously endowed genius such as Jake to serve as our role model. That one play that he wrote, The Man Who Was an Enigma, though badly structured and containing some clumsy surrealistic passages and perhaps the most blatant example of author intrusion on record since the protagonist's life pretty much paralleled that of Jake's and in which the female characters are simply sexist and, well, I must have counted about forty mixed metaphors, served as a beacon for aspiring playwrights. But don't be so hard on Brashford for his behavior tonight. Remember him at his best as well as at his worst. Remember the good times as well as the bad. And don't be so hard on his generation. Those old men. All of their gods have failed, in a manner of speaking. As for what he said about me. Look, I've found that in this business people are going to say things and if I have raised antagonism, so be it, for that's what one gets when one tells the truth as one sees it." The two feminists who had wrongly attempted to censor his work cried even harder. They were embracing each other. From others came shouts of "hear, hear." There were congratulations all around. People were commenting on his magnanimity as they exited from the theater. He decided to take a little stroll backstage to see if the actors and actresses had left. There was one woman left. She had played Cora Mae's lawyer. She was undressing, and she had one foot up on a bench; she was removing her stockings and shoes.

"Oh, excuse me," he said.

"Oh, that's all right." She began pulling a dress over her slip. He had a chance to examine her hips, which didn't have any excess, and her legs—her beautiful legs. If she was a piano she'd probably be a Baldwin. A piano that his hands and fingers could, well, play beautiful music upon. She removed the judge's pompadour wig. She hung up the black robe. She slipped into another dress. It was expensive and showed good taste. She turned to him and smiled when she saw him standing there, fascinated. They let their eyes do all of the talking and maybe later other parts of their anatomy would be communicating, that is, if he was lucky. The gin made him feel lucky. She finally said, "Aren't you going to the party?" The way she said it gave him a hard-on.

"I don't feel like partying. Just maybe going home and sacking out. Why don't you come over for a quick drink?" Sometimes they answer something that hurts your feelings, or they tell you that they had something else to do, but this was his night.

"Why not," she said. She had eyes like Judy Collins.

He took her home and fucked her until she was sore. Gin always affected him that way.

## CHAPTER 21

Lieutenant Brown slammed on the brakes and the police cars came to a screeching halt. "Loathesome" jumped from the car and ran up to Becky's apartment building. She was standing outside. She was in a white bathrobe and was wearing a towel about her head. She was still holding the gun. He took the gun from her and tried to talk to her and to calm her down.

"I think I hit him," she said. She pointed in the direction of Fifth Avenue. "Loathesome" headed in that direction. He saw drops of blood traveling in the same direction. He reached Fifth Avenue and turned the corner. A man in a beret and coat was leaning against the wall of a building; he was holding his side. He seemed to be in agony. O'Reedy gave chase. The man ran about a block and turned into an alley. It was about 3:00 A.M. and nobody was on the street. *Middle man, huh. Sean ought to see what I have to deal with. Creeps. Maniacs. Guys like this hair freak. I keep these freaks out of the public's hair. And do I get thanks. No. My own son . . .* He entered the dark alley. He slid against the wall, holding his gun. *Nancy. Somebody hit him in the face.* He felt something hard in his mouth. His teeth. His attacker wore a leather jacket, a leather beret, and a black mask. O'Reedy had the height and weight advantage over the man. He recovered in time to duck another blow. He licked some blood. The man was all over him, pummeling him. O'Reedy fell to the ground. All he could think of was that Tremonisha had gotten the Flower Phantom's description wrong. He was shorter. O'Reedy was taking quite a beating and was about to pass out when he heard his gun fall to the pavement. He became alert. The Flower Phantom grabbed the gun. He stood over O'Reedy. The three Spanish guys were at his side. They were folding their arms. They had big smiles. They were wearing some suits that had broad pointy shoulders, and pants that draped about their ankles. One wore a hat with a wide brim. Another was sporting a goatee. They wore shirts with exaggerated collars. They weren't wearing ties. The S.O.B.s weren't wearing ties! They moved to see O'Reedy looking down the barrel of Nancy. The Flower Phantom pulled the trigger. It didn't work. The Flower Phantom kept pulling the trigger; the same thing happened. In frustration, he threw the gun down. O'Reedy grabbed it and fired. The bullet missed the flower Phantom's head by about two inches. The Flower Phantom started to run toward the other end of the alley. But he didn't get far. He was hit by a bullet that put a big hole in him, you could see through the hole to the wall across the street from the other entrance to the alley. He went up into the air and then slammed against the wall. O'Reedy could hear his ribs crack. He looked toward the direction of the gunfire. The jogger was standing—no, it was Lieutenant Brown. He was holding a shotgun.

"Everything okay, sir?"

## CHAPTER 22

He got up and went into the kitchen. The actress he'd brought home was still there. She was drinking some coffee. On the counter were two shopping bags with the name of the gourmet shop located around the corner from the hotel. Ball's postcoital manners were bad. He'd like whoever he'd balled the night before to clear out before dawn.

She looked good and probably went through tormenting exercises to remain that way. She looked to be about thirty-five. All of that gin. Her box was snug and fit him tight, and he kept saying O Jesus, and he wasn't even a religious man. She had sweet eyes set in a sweet face. She pushed a copy of *Hurry*, the weekly news magazine, across the table. He yawned. He looked at the picture on the cover. A man with long, black hair, the sort of forehead cut favored by writers Tom Wolfe and Frederick Douglass, and a frankfurter nose. He had a head like a California condor's. He resembled a young Charles Laughton—a young Charles Laughton in drag. He was standing next to a camera. The story read: CEZANNE OF THE CINEMA, and underneath in small letters was his quote: "Wrong-Headed Man Made Me Weep." She smiled as he looked over the cover.

"Towers Bradshaw, my husband," she said.

"The producer of Wrong-Headed Man?"

"Yeah," she said, sighing. "Only for him it's not just a movie. It has become a way of life. The Jews have their book, the Germans have their cathedral at Koln, the Egyptians their sphinx, he has his Wrong-Headed Man." She was smart. He now liked that in women. Tremonisha had really changed him. He turned to the magazine inside where the story began. It showed another photo of him. She was standing behind him, of course. They were standing in front of a twenty-five-room Bel Air mansion, and five or six big cars were in the background. Wrong-Headed Man was getting to him all right. His eyes were glassy and he had about five days' growth on his chin. He appeared as though he hadn't gotten a good night's sleep in some time.

"The picture was taken on the day that I decided to leave him." In the photo she looked as though she'd already left. "He'd been up for a week reading Wrong-Headed Man. He'd wake me in the middle of the night, he'd be sweating and panting and he'd want me to read some lurid and sick passage from the book. During the session with the photographer he went into one of those crazy fits, you know, kind of like Jerry Lewis, and they had to call his mother to calm him down." He looked over at the basket on the kitchen table. It held what looked like French rolls. He walked over to the table, and yawned again. He hadn't bothered to put on a shirt. He wore only a pair of jeans and sneakers. No socks, and no underpants. She stared at him for a moment. "I like your body," she said. "How do you keep in such good shape?"

"I used to play soccer back home. I keep in shape over at the Y. I swim." He sat down to a plate of different kinds of cold cuts, some preserves, cheese, and coffee. There was something curled up on the plate. He didn't like its looks.

"What's that?" he asked.

"Schmalz." It looked disgusting.

"This is a German breakfast, kind of like the kind we have back at home in Freiburg," she said. So she was German. He wondered why she kept saying what sounded like kommen, bitte, kommen, bitte, all night long. She told him that she was from Freiburg, a university town, and that in her twenties she went to Berlin, where she hung out with filmmakers in Kreuzburg, the Turkish section. She'd met Wrong-Head's producer at the Munich Film Festival where he'd come to be honored for his first film, Little Green Men. She came to the States with him. They were married. Since she left him she'd been getting small parts in the New York theater. Before that she'd appeared in her husband's films. She was always getting mutilated or decapitated. In one, she was dismembered by a chainsaw.

"I still don't know what he saw in the film. It was so unlike him to take on a project like that." He did science fiction plots that were so embellished with special effects that you forgot the weak story lines and the bad acting. "I mean, I agreed with the main character's point of view, I think, but I thought that some of the situations were, well, morbid. She doesn't seem to offer any alternative to fucking men, and that lesbian business seemed to be really a tease. But, of course, I'm white." She was dark and Mediterranean looking, probably from Bavaria, he thought. A G.I. had told him that he'd seen Italians with black faces and kinky hair in Frankfurt, and in the German south the people looked like mulattoes.

"What do you think of Wrong-Headed Man?" she asked.

"In my opinion, a woman who puts urine and spit into her guests' drinks deserves what happens to her." They laughed.

"Do you want some more coffee?" She started for the counter where the sterling silver coffeemaker—a gift from his mom—stood. When she came by him he pulled her to him. She sat on his lap. She was wearing a thin dress and he could feel her in his lap. She kissed him for a long time. He put his hand inside her dress and felt her ass. She pulled away and headed toward the counter for the coffee.

"He and Tremonisha have had a falling out, I hear," she said.

"First she dragged this actress in to play the missionary who had no acting ability at all, but Tremonisha insisted. She got the role over all of the other talented black actresses." He looked at the schmalz. He decided that he wasn't going to have any of it. He could see the stuff lying all fat and sluggish in his arteries.

"Do you know the actress?" she asked. No, he didn't know her, but the fellas had said that to compare her with Butterfly McQueen would be an insult to Ms. McQueen.

"Then he threw out her script."

"Yeah, I heard about that," he said.

"She threatened him with a lawsuit."

"What did he do?" She came back and set the coffee next to his plate. She walked back to her chair at the other end of the small table. She sat down and cut a roll in two and spread some jam on one half. He looked up at his poster of Bugs Bunny, his favorite Disney character.

"He owned the film and so he cut off all contact with her. He forgot that Tremonisha even wrote it. Kept calling it his play. His film. He's been working on it for a year now. He'll never finish it." The magazine called the film his greatest challenge. "I hear that when he's not working on it he dresses up in that adventurer's suit and makes believe that he's Joe Beowulf. He spends the day tooting up his nose and playing computer games," she said. Joe Beowulf was a swashbuckling white man that he'd created. He went about the world slapping women left and right and bringing Third World people to their knees. He remembered the ad carried in the newspapers. It showed Joe Beowulf in a camouflage suit and a machine gun in hand. Lurking in the background were the illustrator's version of black muggers. The illustrator thought that blacks still wore Afros. "Fighting the Grendels of this World," said the copy that accompanied the photo.

"Guy sounds like he has a lot of problems. Why did you marry him?"

She paused, and shifted her weight before saying, "Guilty, I guess."

"Let's go down to MacDonald's," he said.

"But you just—"

"Yeah. I like your German breakfast, but I lost a lot of protein last night, I need some food."

"Let me get my coat." She went into the bedroom. He finished his cup of coffee. German coffee tasted like Maxwell House. He turned to the article again. The one about the filming of *Wrong-Headed Man*. The magazine said that the film had something to do with "incest, sexual brutality, and Sapphic love." He looked up the word, Sapphic. The dictionary said that it had something to do with dykes.

After breakfast, he went back to his apartment to read the newspaper. He was still a little woozy from the gin and exhausted from fucking all night.

The morning's headline hit him in the face like Boom Boom Mancini. "FLOWER PHANTOM SLAIN." He scanned the column, trying to focus upon the important details. A was slain a few blocks from the apartment of Becky French, after the suspect attempted to enter her apartment from a fire escape, located next to her window. The man was identified as Randy Shank, a black playwright who had achieved some notoriety in the 1960s. Detective Lawrence O'Reedy pursued the man through the East Village and foiled his attempt to make good on his threat to "get" Becky French for her support of Tremonisha Smarts' stand on castration for perpetrators of rape. Ms. Smarts, whose play *Wrong-Headed Man* received international recognition, was Shank's first victim. At the time, the suspect told Ms. Smarts that he was patterning his actions after those of the French Resistance who shaved the heads of women who collaborated with the Nazis. Experts claimed that Mr. Shank, who became known as the Flower Phantom for his bizarre habit of leaving a chrysanthemum with his victims, was suffering from a paranoid fantasy and that instead of being the political hero he desired to be was actually a hair fetishist. This was shocking to Ball. He had to regain his composure. The phone rang. It was Becky French. He asked her was she all right. She said her only regret was that she'd used a .22 instead of a .44. She said that if she'd used a .44 they'd still be cleaning up his intestines. Ball cleared his throat.

"The reason I called is because I have some good news. We're taking your play to Broadway. Several producers have expressed interest. We have to see which one will give us the best deal. Perhaps you realize now why it was important to change the play so that Cora Mae's viewpoint condemned both Ham and his lynchers. That one can be murdered by reckless eyeballing just as easily as with a weapon. It's the same thing. Congratulations, Ian. I never told you this, but after Jim came up missing I wasn't even going to give you a workshop, but Tremonisha argued on your behalf. You owe her one, Ball. You'll be pleased to know that now you'll be able to work anywhere in this town." Ball jumped up from the table where he was having breakfast. Broadway. People in mink coats arriving from the suburbs. Chartered buses in front of the theater. Interviews. Women. Gol-lee, he said to himself. He was becoming "bankable." Producers would be lining up. Three-hour lunches. Talk shows. *People* magazine. Parties. If only Chester Himes and Jake Brashford were less controversial, more amiable, more toned down. If only they had cooled it. They could have had all of this too.

He dialed Brashford's number. He wanted to tell him the good news. He was sure that Brashford had gotten over his hangover by now. He identified himself to the speaker on the other end. A woman.

"Oh, yes. I saw you last night. I was with my husband." So the woman with what James Fenimore Cooper called "tartar cheeks" was Brashford's wife. "He's really sorry for the way he behaved. He said that he will make it up to you somehow. He was really not himself. The lawyers have gone down to bail him out of jail."

"Jail?"

"Yes. After the security guard took him outside, Jake managed to get free. He knocked the security guard cold with one punch. Then the police arrived. He got into a slugging match with the officers. I've never seen him like that. It all started at dinner. He went through three bottles of wine. The reason we were only able to catch the last act of your play is because he spilled the wine on his pants in the restaurant and then had to go home and change. When he got to his studio he started to drink again and went into some anti-Semitic tirade, which is what always happens when he's drunk or feeling sorry himself. It's crazy because I'm Jewish and he has a Jewish son. I think it's the play that's making him this way. He's trying to write a play of universal values, but everywhere he turns, he runs into ethnicity. For twenty years he's been hopping from group to group. He must have tons of discarded drafts in his closet. For the last year it's been the Armenians, now he's talking about doing the Jews. He's so depressed these days, Ian. He's so lonely. He's like the trumpet player in that movie *Young Man with a Horn* who was seeking the ultimate high note. For Brashford that high note is universality. It keeps eluding him. The blacks of his generation avoid him and the younger generation has never heard of him." I'm hip to that, Ball thought.

"Of course, Ms. Brashford—"

"You can call me Delilah."

"And you can call me Ian, Ms. Brashford. Don't you worry about my abandoning Jake. Why, he's my Immamu, my guide, my shaman, and my guru. Ms. Brashford, Jake is, well, like a father to me. Everything I know, I learned from him. He taught me how to survive in this city, me, a poor country boy. I'll always be grateful, and Delilah, where I come from the saying goes you love your friends and you hate your enemies."

"That's so sweet of you, Ian. Jake always told me that you were his best friend. "

"Did he say that, Delilah?"

"He says it all the time. He'll probably talk to you when he returns from abroad, Ian. We're leaving as soon as he's out of jail. I think that we need a vacation. We both agree that he needs a change of scenery. He says that on some days he just feels like taking his four volumes of Malraux, his Duke Ellington records, his Motherwells, and his *Complete Plays of O'Neill* and going to live in a coal bin."

"Where do you plan to go?"

"We're leaving tomorrow for Tel Aviv."

It had been a dense morning for Ian.

Jim, Randy Shank, and now Brashford. Jim thought that the whole country was like New York and as soon as he left Manhattan he wandered into an obeah zone. The wrong neighborhood. Lost in the night. Randy Shank, appropriate that his ending came as it did. Sometimes he was the son of a gun, a loud, belligerent, talking hot dog, but his real bullet was a flower, as evidenced in his early poetry, lyrical, tender. Driven from Europe by Tremonisha and Johnnie Kranshaw's badmouthing, marked as a man who would go to any lengths for sex. Brashford, isolated, yammering about the theft of black culture by the Jews, condemned to wander from ethnicity to ethnicity until he was left with the very group he roiled against. Maybe these city guys were right about him, Ball thought. Maybe he was acceptable because he was from the South and therefore viewed as a genteel and "slow-to anger" person. Those northern blacks had reputations all over the hemisphere as those who would stand for no gunk, but no one was listening to them anymore. The people in the United States were tired of hearing about their apartheid and so imported the apartheid from abroad. They sent relief money to Africa without so much as a glance at the thirty million or so who went to bed at night hungry in the U.S. So audiences applauded *Master Harold and the Boys* because this was about somebody else's apartheid and they could laugh and attend matinees because nobody was pointing the finger at them. Maybe he was just another insouciant import. Maybe they felt that as a southerner he would look back to the old days when the darkies articulated their words very slowly and carefully. How did that ad for Jamaica put it: "Come back to the way things used to be," uttered by an old black man, beckoning. It didn't bother Ball what reasons were given for pushing him, he just wanted success, as his second-sighted mother used to say, "Boy, your eyes are bigger than your belly." And what about Tre, and the rest of America's black sisters? He could understand their bitterness, and their hurt. Extras in a land where Anne—the American white woman—had the leading role, her smiling face on the products, the covers of magazines, the ubiquitous face (it was the 1980s and the demand for black models was now on the decrease, while that for Swedish types was on the increase). It was miraculous that so many were able to maintain their poise and their sanity and not go off the deep end like Toni Case Bambara's Velma, who had to "undergo a riding." Velma, who got so fed up with the boy-men in her life that she growled. The black women were objects of scorn and desire, like Toni Morrison's Sula, who wanted to be free as any man, in a time when a woman who smoked cigarettes or sat in bars was regarded as a witch. If sometimes the fellas viewed some of them as hostile, perhaps their hostility was merely a defense mechanism.

He could understand Clotel, getting it from both sides, neither black nor white but Anne and Coretha in one. And what about Anne? What if women were harming themselves, mutilating themselves, and risking bad health to look like you? The black ones, ninety percent of whom risked baldness by straightening their hair? The Asian ones having the slants removed from their eyes by plastic surgery, and the doctors rearranging the bones of the Jewish women's noses with mallets. No wonder Becky was so haughty, so demanding, and so full of herself. People were undergoing torture in order to look like her. He could understand the women, Ball could, and Tre had taught him to communicate to a woman without having to devise tedious strategies for getting them into bed. Tre had taught him that there was more to a woman than a cunt. Much more.

But on the other hand, suppose Cecil Brown was right when he said that there are probably more female Hitlers than male. That got Ball to thinking. Weren't women the ones who were always interested in what was going on in their neighbors' intimate existence, like the Mouth Almighties in *Their Eyes Were Watching God*? Weren't they the ones who rummaged their children's possessions, and went through their husband's pockets? Weren't they the gossips? Hadn't some of the feminists said that what went on in your house was also political? Suppose they gain power. Would they send people into your house to see what you were doing in there? Go through your pockets, spy on your children? Were women more fascistic than men? Was this why men wanted to get away, like a prisoner escaping from some domestic Devil's Island? The North, Ball decided, was one hell of a complicated mess. That's why it fascinated him so; his mother complained that he was trying to become more northern than the northerners, with his video cassettes, comic books, Coca Cola, rock and roll records, baseball. Ball called the airlines to reconfirm his reservation that afternoon. He would pick up the reviews in the airport. He couldn't wait to get South.

## CHAPTER 21

IT DIDN'T take long for Beechiko to establish herself in Longsfellow's Greenwich Village four-story brownstone. She supervised the housecleaning, which was done by Samantha and Teddy Crawford, a black couple from Saint Albans. She nearly drove them crazy. Pointing out dust under the bed, and on the living room furniture they'd missed. Demanding that they clean the stove every week. Insisting that they do windows. Sometimes she would entertain Mr. Longsfellow's guests after they'd had their brandy and conversation, usually dealing with the lowering of cultural standards in the United States, or as one of their intellectual heroes said, the descent into the primeval slime. She would sing ancient songs accompanying herself on the koto, and for very special occasions she would entertain Mr. Longsfellow's gentlemen friends with Shirabyoshi dances which dated to the reign of the Emperor Toba (1107–1123). The men would applaud politely and Beechiko would serve the white men tea. She was happy serving Mr. Longsfellow and writing, in the evening, her second book about the treatment of Japanese women in the novels of Japanese men. Having indicted most of the Japanese male writers in history, she was completing her last chapter on sexism. Her first book was receiving good reviews. The publisher had hailed it as a New Year's Eve for Japanese-American women, and the Japanese men who criticized the book were dismissed as misogynists.

Mr. Longsfellow enjoyed her too. They spent until the early mornings discussing John Updike's theology, and V. S. Naipaul's trenchant comments about the Third World. She was having the time of her life except for two things. Her appearance. She'd tried to do something about her eyes, you know, well, to make them more modern. She hated what for her was an ugly Japanese face. But that didn't bother her as much as the fact that she wasn't a blond. Another famous editor she'd had a crush on had already run away with a big old blond. Mr. Longsfellow had married a blond shiksa too. His first wife gazed down at her from an oil portrait that hung on the wall above the staircase. She hated her features. Sometimes she'd cry herself to sleep, wishing that she was a blond. Her second problem was the Crawfords. They were insolent. Always muttering under their breaths.

One day they had it out. It was late morning, and Mr. Longsfellow had been up all night with some friends, discussing Great Books, and the Crawfords were preparing breakfast. Beechiko was already upset. She had an early morning conference with her editor, and had returned to the Village on the subway. There was a handsome couple sitting across from her. The man looked like Martin Sheen; the woman resembled Christie Brinkley; the child was the most beautiful kid you'd ever want to see, and she started playing with the child. The couple wouldn't give her the time of day. Wouldn't even look in her direction. She had been so hurt.

"I told you that Mr. Longsfellow wouldn't be eating that sort of breakfast anymore."

"Don't tell me, Beechiko, or whatever your name is. Mr. Longsfellow has been drinking coffee for thirty years. He loves bacon and eggs. Everything was fine till you come here, you old two-dollar whore," Samantha said, slamming the utensils on the table.

"You ain't doing nothing but gettin' in the way. I have a good mind to take my fist and jam it in your jaw," her husband threatened.

"That's it. Resort to violence. I've read a lot of books about your type. Besides, I'm looking after Mr. Longsfellow's welfare. He is a man who, as you know, has very high standards. You call this breakfast?" She picked up the bacon and held it close to her face. "Look at this grease." She turned up her nose.

Mizuni took the plate and started to dump the eggs, hash browns, ham, and bacon into the trash can. Crawford grabbed her while Samantha took over the plate. Beechiko flipped Crawford's 230 pounds over her shoulder and then, using the bacon, began a pulling contest with Samantha. That's how Longsfellow found them, yelling and screaming at the top of their lungs. He was dressed in a kimono that she'd bought for him. He wore fur-lined slippers whose exquisite leather bore a brilliant sheen. How handsome he looks, Beechiko thought.

"Here, here what's the matter?" Mr. Longsfellow said, looking from one to the other.

"She come in here giving orders. Samantha and I have been serving you for thirty years now, Mr. Longsfellow. We served your wife. I sho do miss her," Crawford said. Mr. Longsfellow lowered his head.

"Me too," Samantha said. "Sweet as she could be. Long blonde hair," Samantha said, looking toward Beechiko with an evil grin.

"She whatun nothin' like this old yellow bitch. Who ever named her Beechiko named her right, cause she ain't nothin' but a bitch, old skinny evil thing."

"That's not called for, Samantha. Crawford. We'll be civil in my house, and I don't want to ever hear you call Beechiko that name again, do you hear?" Beechiko folded her arms and smiled.

"Yes, Mr. Longsfellow," the Crawfords said, unanimously.

"Now my bedroom needs straightening up. Get to it."

"Yes, Mr. Longsfellow." The Crawfords exited, glancing over their shoulders at Beechiko, who was enjoying herself. Longsfellow lowered his white-haired head again and hobbled toward the breakfast table. He sat down, and Beechiko began serving him tea.

"I'm just looking out for your welfare, Mr. Longsfellow. The bacon is full of sodium nitrite."

"Thanks for all you've done for me, Beechiko; what is this?" he said, staring at a bowl that Beechiko placed before him containing miso soup.

"This is your new breakfast, Mr. Longsfellow."

"What would I do without you," Mr. Longsfellow said. He held her hand for a long while. She winked to herself.

With Mr. Longsfellow's vote of confidence, Beechiko ruled the roost. She made the Crawfords' lives miserable, being constantly on their case, prying into their cleaning schedule, going after them for every particle of dust they overlooked, for every faint ring in the bathtub. She personally supervised Mr. Longsfellow's meals, and the laundering of his clothes.

Soon, however, her glory would end. Mr. Longsfellow had warned her not to enter the room that had been shut ever since his wife's death. She couldn't resist, and in the course of prying through his wife's belongings came upon her blonde chemotherapy wigs. She was sitting in front of a mirror trying one on when she saw the reflection of her adversary. Samantha was standing in the doorway, leaning against one of its sides, her arms folded and that wicked glint in her eye.

"UUUUUU. Immon tell. Immon tell, Mr. Longsfellow, he gave orders to everybody not to enter this room, and here you is in here trying on Mrs. Longsfellow's blonde wig. Only me, and Mrs. Longsfellow knew about those wigs. You robbing the secrets from Mrs. Longsfellow's grave." Before Beechiko could say anything, Samantha snapped a photo with her Polaroid.

Samantha turned and headed toward Mr. Longsfellow's study where he had fallen asleep on top of some Great Book. He'd left the television set on. Beechiko started after her.

"Please, please don't tell. I'll do anything. Please don't."

"You'll do anything?" Samantha asked.

"Anything, I don't want Mr. Longsfellow to know."

Samantha let go with a grin. She pointed to a closet at the end of the hall. "Go get that vacuum cleaner and follow me."

The Crawfords supervised her now. They made her do all of their chores, and sometimes they wouldn't even come to work and she'd have to cover for them. It got so that they'd show up only for meals that she had to serve them, in between going to the matinees or the track. One weekend while Mr. Longsfellow attended a conference upstate about the wasteland of American culture, they invited all of their friends over, and made her do all of the cooking, and when they finished eating they made her entertain them on the koto, and ridiculed and laughed at her.

She'd bought the mystical hokiness promoted by black feminist writers which held that black women were sort of like Christ figures who were abused by black men, Herods, Satans, and even the best among them, Pontius Pilates, but in the humiliating scene that she'd just endured, the women laughed louder than the men, and had no sense of the sisterhood that bonded her with them. They were different from the black women she met in publishing circles and at literary parties. Elegant matrons. They were drinking up all of Mr. Longsfellow's scotch, and they said motherfucker more than the men. She was in bed now, and she could hear the refrains from the tune "Honkey Tonk," made popular by Bill Doggett. She hated its bass line. Da doom Da doom Da doom Da doom Da. The low-down chicken-pecking vulgar solo made her feel strange in her viscera. She felt a presence in the room. Yes. There before her stood a small figure. The figure began to glow. She recognized him from the newspapers. His face was appearing in all of the Xmas ads. Black Peter. (Black Peter had transformed himself into the image of the post-yuppie Black Peter that the toy makers had designed.)

"I could feel your distress, far away," he said.

"What, I," she wanted to scream, but she couldn't.

"I'm going to grant you the wish that you desire."

"But."

"It may relieve your torment, or it may bring additional problems," he said. Before she could say anything, he disappeared.

## CHAPTER 22

Tommy awoke, springing up on his pillow. He'd had the same dream. That President Jesse Hatch was wringing his father's neck and his father was protesting by flapping about and jumping up and down on one leg. "What's the matter, Tommy," his aunt said, coming into his room and turning on the lights. She sat down on his bed and embraced him. He cried on her peacock's breast.

"It was that dream again, Auntie. The President, Jesse Hatch, was wringing my father's neck, and then, then a man, he all covered with blood, and my father was hopping about and his neck was gone, and blood was spurting out of his wound, Auntie, it was awful."

"You don't have to talk about it," his aunt said. She was peering over her glasses. "Your father's death was very cruel." First his mother and then his father, and now he was living with his aunt who was a widow. Her husband was killed because he was too busy preening. Tommy got up and had some seeds for breakfast. He cleaned himself and prepared to go to school. The breakfast made him feel better, and he waved to his aunt as he gathered his notebooks, crayons, pencils, and backpack.

School was not a pleasant experience for him. The other kids always razzed him. They made fun of his looks, especially. They felt that they were the best-looking creatures in the world. They were always strutting about, preening, and craning their necks. They wouldn't talk to him nor would they play with him and at lunchtime nobody would eat with him. His teacher led the young peacocks in ridiculing turkeys, after which the peacocks would turn to him and laugh or tease him with gobbling sounds. All they taught in school was about peacocks, and how they were the handsomest birds on earth. That their proto-ancestor was a cross between a phoenix and a nightingale and that their shit was like angel food. Turkeys and peacocks were cousins but you wouldn't know it from the way they treated him. It figures, though, if you think about it. Bears and dogs are cousins, too, but whenever you see a photo of them together the dogs are barking at the bears. Tommy Turkey wasn't doing well in school. Not only was he grieving about his father's death, the President and his family having had the tough old bird for dinner, but he was tired of hearing about peacocks. Reading books about ancient dead peacocks. Peacocks were beginning to think of themselves as too gorgeous for the supermarket freezer, in a time when California nurseries were cultivating flowers for adventurous tastes. Marigolds were being served with dinner in Japan. Peacocks could be next.

If it weren't for his aunt reassuring him and giving him confidence, Tommy would have run away to the wild turkeys in the woods. The peacocks wouldn't wander anywhere near them. One day the peacocks were strutting about as usual, being real pleased with themselves, their teacher telling them how great they were, when Black Peter entered. The peacocks cheered because they had seen Black Peter in all of the promotional ads for the department store. They thought that he was the impostor Peter. Some of them had bought Black Peter dolls. The teacher said something about his objecting to this intrusion, and Black Peter turned him into a plate of roasted peacock, commenced to sit down, tie a napkin to his neck, and dig in. Some of the peacocks threw up. Others fainted. One of them tried to run out of the classroom when Black Peter headed him off, and plucked out some of the peacock's feathers. The peacocks were scared. They started making those sounds of peacocks when they get scared. Black Peter stood at the front of the class, slapping his hand with his rod. "Tommy Turkey, would you come to the front of the class?" Tommy Turkey pointed to himself, he was so surprised.

"Yes, you, Tommy." Tommy walked to the front of the room.

"I don't blame you for what you've done to Tommy Turkey, kids, it's your teacher's fault, and the educational system's fault. You just don't know what it means to be a turkey, how turkeys have provided a food supply for the poor over and over again, but I'm sure, Tommy, that you'd prefer that for the Thanksgiving meal soybeans be substituted for turkey." Tommy smiled. Some of the other peacocks smiled. Black Peter opened a large book that he'd brought. The painting was by the black illustrator John James Audubon. It was a picture of a turkey. Not only was it beautiful, but Audubon had commented that the turkey was indigenous to North America. The peacocks had never seen a turkey who looked this beautiful, not in a gaudy way as they did, but understated and quiet. Turkeys subtly changed their colors to express their emotions, another fact that the peacocks had never learned.

"Also, did you know that Benjamin Franklin proposed that the turkey be made the symbol of this country? That *Meleagris gallopavo* is the Latin name for turkeys," the peacocks looked at each other, impressed, "and that turkeys have been given names in many other languages as well, including pavo, the name given to turkeys by Christopher Columbus's crew, and did you know that they were called *guanajo* by the Carib Indians, and *guajolote* by the Aztecs, and *chumpe* by the Mayans? Did you know that turkeys have great fight-back, and have survived regardless of their decimation by hunters, and with all of the nobility that the turkey is associated with you give Tommy here such a hard time." The peacocks lowered their heads. "Ridiculing him and calling him derisive names just because some ignorant people have begun to identify the name turkey with Broadway flops and bad craftsmanship. And most of all, though your teacher never told you this," the class looked over at their teacher, all of which was left were some bones on a plate. "Turkeys and pea-cocks are cousins. It's possible that you have a common ancestor. Finally, before you ridicule Tommy Turkey, think of this. If they weren't eating turkeys for Thanksgiving, they might start to eat peacocks. Don't ever think that you are too pretty for the freezer." The classroom was silent. Black Peter left the classroom. After a while the peacocks approached Tommy Turkey and offered him some of their corn and grain. Tommy smiled and from that day on Tommy never had any trouble at the school of peacocks.

## CHAPTER 23

Samantha came into her room the next morning. She held an ice pack to her head, and her eyes were bloodshot. She'd come to demand that Beechiko clean up the mess that her guests had made. Mr. Longsfellow would be arriving from upstate later in the morning. But Samantha took one look at her and grimaced, "I tole you not to be wearing any more of Mrs. Longsfellow's belongings." She went to the bed where Beechiko lay sleeping. All she saw was a heap of blonde hair sticking out from underneath the covers. She yanked at the hair and the sleeping person turned toward Samantha. Saman-tha sobered up real quick, and her hair stood straight up. "Samantha, who the hell do you think you're talking to? Have you lost your mind? Go brush your teeth. Your breath reeks of whiskey," the person said in a husky and hoarse voice. But Samantha didn't hear all of the reply. She almost ran through the door, trying to get out of the bedroom. Beechiko tried to call out to her, but all she heard was a lot of commotion downstairs, followed by the slamming of a door. When she got downstairs, the Crawfords' car was turning out of the driveway. She looked at them out of the window, and when Crawford saw her, his eyes bulged as though he were being strangled. He took another look. He rubbed his eyes. He took off toward Eighth Avenue doing about sixty. Beechiko turned to the mirror that stood in the living room. Her heart almost stopped. She threw her hand up to her face in horror. Just then she heard the key in the door. She tried to run upstairs. She tried to scream. Her thoughts couldn't come together. Her body wouldn't do what her brain wanted. She could not control what she said. She was imprisoned in another's body. Mr. Longsfellow didn't see her at first. He was shocked by the scene in his living room. Liquor bottles all over the place. Dirty plates with half-eaten food on the dining room tables. Cigarette butts and roaches everywhere. The downstairs toilet was stopped up. Longsfellow removed his overcoat and put down his copy of Salmagundi magazine. He brushed off the snow and hung his overcoat in the closet. "Crawford, Samantha, and Beechiko, what is the meaning of this?" he shouted upstairs.

And then he saw her. He just stood there for a minute, his eyes not blinking. Beechiko tried to say something, but somebody else's voice came out.

"Wadsworth."

"Grace. My God. Grace. What—" and then Longsfellow thought. For Wadsworth Longsfellow, there was always a rational explanation for everything. He had read that grieving spouses sometimes, after losing a loved one, had a supernatural experience in which they actually saw their dead husband or wife.

"Wadsworth, aren't you glad to see me?"

He thought for a moment. "Frankly, no. Things around here couldn't be better. For the first time in my life, I'm happy. I've met someone who not only knows how to treat a man, but shares my interests."

"Wadsworth. What are you saying? All of the years we spent together, I thought you were happy," Beechiko found herself saying.

"You never bothered to ask. You were always complaining. Always whining, and I won't forget that last vacation we had together. As soon as we got off the plane in San Juan, you started to complain about the weather, about the hotel, about the room service, and you called the bellhop a dirty Mexican."

"Wadsworth, you little schlemiel, don't you talk that way—"

"I'll talk any way I want, and . . . and here's something that you can roll over in the grave about. I'm going to ask Beechiko for her hand. She's Japanese. She also likes characters who come alive and breathe. She despises postmodernism. One-dimensional trash." Beechiko wanted to run into his arms, but she couldn't, she was paralyzed.

"But, but, she's not blonde," his dead wife said.

"I don't care about that."

"Ha. You who used to burn candles for Marilyn Monroe. You had to go into therapy over that."

"That was the fifties. These are the nineties."

"But what about her . . . her . . . . eyes?"—and when she said that pulled back the corners of her eyes. "Stop it. Stop," Mr. Longsfellow said, and she found the body in which she was imprisoned laughing. She wanted to shake the body. She wanted to—and then she awoke. It was quiet downstairs. She dressed and went down. Mr. Longsfellow was seated at his desk. The downstairs was in a mess from where the Crawfords had left it. He rose and walked over to her.

"Where are Crawford and Samantha?" she asked.

"I got rid of them."

"You what?"

"I came back early and they were playing some terrible music. Some bum who had passed out said it was called 'Nighttrain.' It just had this insufferable saxophone solo. It sounded like a tomcat in heat. It assaulted my sensibilities. I fired them, of course; I gave them severance pay." He showed her the photo of her with his wife's wig on. She was embarrassed.

"You don't have to be a blonde, Beechiko. I love you the way you are. I like your hair. I like the texture of your skin. Your eyes . . . so inscrutable." Beechiko smiled shyly. Mr. Longsfellow embraced her for a long time. She looked out of the window, and there winking at her was Black Peter. They winked at each other. He had given her the best Xmas she ever had.

## CHAPTER 24

Black Peter, the impostor, awoke. He must have blacked out. His last memory was that of him and his cronies trying to top each other in a liquor-imbibing contest. His friends must have left because he couldn't find his wallet. His eighteen year-old Minnesota Viking was sleeping next to him. Her blond hair covered a teddy bear. Her hand clutched a halfeaten Mars bar. The ashtray was full of roaches. He'd have to somehow get out of bed, throw cold water on his face, and prepare for another appearance. He had to do everything that Jack Frost told him. He was about to ring for breakfast when Jack Frost burst into the room. His hands were full of newspapers.

"Pete, why didn't you tell us you were doing this stuff? It's terrific. Look at all the great publicity we're getting."

"Huh," Black Peter said. Jack laid the newspapers out on the table. Black Peter rubbed his eyes and examined the press. His chest got tight. He took a second look, and a third.

"Boy is Elder Marse going to be happy when he sees this. Why you and I are liable to get a bonus." On the society pages of the *New York Exegesis* was the announcement of the wedding of Beechiko Mizuni to Wadsworth Longsfellow, former editor of *Organic Society*. They told the press that they were grateful to Black Peter. On another page there was a photo of peacocks with their arms around a turkey. The caption read: Black Peter brings understanding between Peacocks and Turkeys.

"Good picture of you, Pete," Jack said. On the entertainment page there was an announcement that Fryer Moog was opening at some of the Village nightclubs. He'd gotten back his chops and reassembled his quartet from the old days after spending what he called many wasted years in Hollywood. He had gained back some of his weight and jogged every day. You couldn't keep the guy away from juice bars and vegetarian food. He too thanked Black Peter, and there were others. A woman who needed a liver transplant for her child said that Black Peter showed up and contributed the check. A farmer whose family farm was about to be foreclosed said that Black Peter had arrived in the nick of time to rescue him. "Even though I'm a white man, if he were running for President I'd vote for him," the farmer said. And so the stories went.

"And to think, we all thought you were pissing your life away at Xmas parties all over town, and here you were, flying all over the country, rescuing people. The department stores are mobbed. How did you manage to do it, O, tell me sometime about it, Black Peter—" Before Black Peter could say anything, Jack Frost exited the room.

Black Peter poured himself a glass of strong whiskey. He looked outside the window, and he saw people on crutches, as well as with other disabilities, and Third World women desiring blonde hair, blonde women desiring Afros, black men requesting that Peter bless their superman capes, white men begging Peter to teach them how to say hey dude, hey bro, hey home and to do the moon walk, but Black Peter was faced with some heavy "existentialist" questions as a New York Intellectual would say. If he were he, who was *he?* Or, who was doing him while he was doing *him?* His life was becoming like a riddle popularized by Abbott and Costello.

## CHAPTER 25

Meanwhile, in his apartment in the Netherlands, a cold metaphysical place, somewhere in the Arctic, where the favorite musician is Rudy Vallee, Nick was preparing for his annual visit for the Xmas season; Nick was pacing up and down, his hands held tightly behind his back. It was December fifth. He was furious, and earlier that morning had fired two elves who'd been assisting him for so many seasons, the other elves had forgotten when they joined the team. His favorite assistant, Destar D'Nooza, was shining his black boots. Mr. D'Nooza had the sad, drooping eyes of a basset hound, and an outstanding nose. In a former life he had served Lord Mountbatten when Mountbatten was the Viceroy of India, an experience for which he had always been grateful and told stories about it to the other elves, who hated him.

"Boss, you zeem so...so nervous. What bother you, boss?"

"'What bothers me,' he asks," Nick said. "You see these headlines that Black Peter is getting?" "Black Peter Cured My Gallstones" read the headline of the *International Herald Tribune,* a newspaper that Nick read every morning.

"O, boss, why should you worry about dat? It's just a Turd World trick to embarrass you. You still on top, boss. The happiest part of my life is bringing a brilliant gloss to your boots."

"You really think so, Destar?"

"Tink so. I knows so, boss. Why dat Black Peter is impostor anyway. We check it out. He speak English very bad, loss. Very bad. He say, we bees, as in, we bees going. He don't know how to conjugate verbs, boss, like I do. I went to school in London—"

"Yes, yes, you've told me a number of times, Destar. But I think you're wrong, I knew about the impostor four years ago when I... when I—"

"Boss, don't worry about dat. Don't you worry. You choose wrong man. Dis Dean Clift have no credibility, and so when you make your appearance, though you change him, nobody believe, boss. Wasn't your fault. You have a better idea this time. It will really alter the course of history. You so great, boss, you so—" Destar began sobbing.

"What's wrong, Destar?" Nick said.

"I just tink, boss. I'm so happy to be of service to you. A . . . bug like me, able to do my part for Western civilization."

"You're a loyal elf, Destar, and if you continue such devotion I'll see to it that you get that English country manor you were never able to obtain during your earthly stay."

"O, tank you, boss, tank you, would you like a little lamb dish with some curry before we prepare for our annual journey?"

Nick nodded.

## CHAPTER 26

Bob Krantz bunked in Nance Saturday's apartment for the night. He was up all night going to the bathroom and occasionally his trips stirred Nance. Krantz woke up screaming several times. He had a bad night. At breakfast the next morning, Krantz told Nance the whole story. Nance sat there, stunned. Reverend Jones and his pretend friends. The possible murder of Admiral Matthews. And most shocking of all, Operation Two Birds. During the Iran-Contra Investigation in the 1980s, it had been revealed that Oliver North was part of a plan to round up all of the black leaders and put them in camps. But those plans sounded mild in comparison to Two Birds, which called for low-yield nuclear attacks on cities with surp populations, poor blacks, Hispanics, Asians, no longer the model minority, and the millions of whites who were as useless, nonvital and up to no good like the rest. Nance was shocked. He knew that a lot of people in power were crazy, but not that crazy. A preacher in the White House talking to ghosts. Operation Two Birds. A computerized superhero robot on loan from Hollywood. The murder of the Secretary of Defense.

"Look, Virginia Saturday is my wife. My ex-wife. You could go on her show. Tell the world about it."

"Who would believe it? Look what they did to Dean Clift after he made those claims. They'd do the same thing to me." Nance thought about it. He stroked his heavy mustache. It was so heavy it must have weighed about two pounds.

"Maybe you have a point."

"Besides, I'm still indebted to Reverend Jones. He saved my life."

"But now he's trying to get rid of you. What kind of loyalty is that?"

"Reverend Jones is the only man in America who can stop our country's sinking into the abyss."

"You talking about niggers?"

"No, why get so sensitive. We're not against blacks. There are blacks who are high in the government. The man who now runs Reverend Jones's evangelical empire, Reverend John the Conqueror, is black. He does all of the preaching while Jones advises Jesse Hatch on how to run the government." Krantz looked at his watch. He walked over to the TV set and turned it on.

"Damn, all you do is watch the news all day."

"Maybe there'll be something about—"

Jesse Hatch was answering questions from reporters.

Q: "Mr. President, are you telling us that Robert Krantz developed this whole scheme, that nobody in the White House knew about it?"

A: "That's right, he was going to explode neutron bombs on Miami, New York, and other cities with large concentrations of surps, and blame it on our ally, Nigeria, and then destroy some nuclear generators in Nigeria." Nance looked at Krantz. "It's not true, he's lying," Krantz said. Krantz and Saturday kept their eyes trained on the set.

Q: "Bob Krantz was brought into the White House by Reverend Clement Jones. Has Reverend Jones been informed of this development?"

A: "Reverend Jones is really disturbed about the news, ladies and gentlemen, and he's shocked that Krantz has usurped the power of the Oval Office."

"That can't be so, Jones was in on the plan from the beginning," Krantz pleaded. The camera switched to Reverend Jones. He seemed to be near tears as he told the reporters how Krantz had been like a son to him, and how he was so disappointed that Krantz had gotten involved in such a nutty scheme. Krantz turned off the television set. He sat in a chair, gazing out the window. Nance went over and placed a hand on his shoulder. There was a knock at the door. Nance answered. It was a man. He and Nance talked for a minute, as Krantz sat in the living room of the two-bedroom apartment. Nance and the man disappeared into a room that Nance referred to as his "office." There was a procession of people into the apartment all morning. Men and women. Women with children and babies. This went on until about twelve noon, when Nance said he had to start making his runs to La Guardia.

CHAPTER 27

Nola Payne, Supreme Court Justice, wasn't able to finish her address before the National Association for the Advancement of Feminists. She was heckled and treated rudely by those who had fought to make her the second female justice on the Supreme Court, having become disillusioned with the first one, among whose first decisions was one holding that President Nixon was above the law. Nola was accused, by the feminists, of voting on the side of the patriarchy ninety-nine percent of the time and having abandoned those who had made her.

A questioner had asked Nola about her statement in an op-ed printed in the *New York Exegesis* that women had been crippled by their former oppression and that now was time for a new feminist responsibility and a mature feminism. That the feminists hadn't proven that they had gone beyond the phase of rage and storm. That their problems weren't being imposed from the outside.

She said that they could no longer blame their problems on sexism, but now had to look to themselves, to their own self-destructive behavioral patterns for an explanation for their failure. That the society had become gender blind. She said that they had to change their culture, give up their clinging to men, their Cinderella fixation, their addiction to dependency so that men would accept them. She said that if men discriminated against them—maybe it was their fault.

A woman got up and called her a middle-class bourgeois bitch. When she said something good about her male colleagues on the court they called her a traitor and started to boo her. Somebody asked her about the court's scheduled review of the 13th, 14th, and 15th amendments, the Emancipation Proclamation, and the Dred Scott Decision. She said that the court just wanted to take another look at them, and when someone quoted Reverend Jones's speech quoting Genesis:9 that slavery was a good thing, and that it solved the unemployment problem, and that he needed some hands around his house to help his wife with her watercolors, she said that Reverend Jones didn't have a racist or sexist bone in his body, and that blacks, gays, Asians, and other surps were not carrying their weight, and that this was the reason for the West's decline. Tumult erupted and Nola Payne had to leave by the back entrance. As her chauffeur drove her home she took more than a few swigs from a flask of bourbon she carried around. By the time she reached home, her blood alcohol content was way above that of the legal limit. He had to help her up the steps of her lavish Georgian home, and her maid had to undress her and help her into her nightgown.

Her face was puffy and red. Her blue-tinted hair was becoming unglued. Her round, soft stomach felt like Beirut, Lebanon. The feminists, her former allies, had especially given her a hard time when she announced her support for the Conversion Bill; she said that those who did not pledge allegiance to Reverend Jones's brand of Christianity should be deported.

Why did women hate her so? Why couldn't they understand that the 90s demanded responsible feminism? One that had serious issues to deal with, one that had gone beyond bra burning, sexual preference, and abortion on demand. She had to show that she could take it like a man. Could support tradition and values. That it wasn't like the old days when they were in the Village. Times were more complicated. And what was wrong with a Christian country? Reverend Jones's ideas were a little bit bizarre, but somebody had to stand up against the excesses of the last thirty years.

The maid peeked into the bedroom where Nola lay stretched out on her big bed. Sometimes the maid would find fifteen or sixteen whiskey bottles underneath her bed, or in the closet.

"Your Honor," the maid said.

"Yes, what is it, Maria?"

"Would you like something before I go, Señora?"

"No, Maria, I think that I'll just get some sleep."

"Those women treated you awful, Madame. I saw it on television. All of that pushing and shoving. It's amazing that you were not hurt, Madame."

"Thanks, Maria." The woman started out the door. "You have plans for this evening?" Nola asked.

"We're having a Xmas party, just members of my family."

"That must be nice."

"Yes, Senora. I must go now. Merry Xmas, Señora.

"Merry Xmas, Maria."

She went to sleep. It began to rain. Shango hammered the sky. She awoke about one a.m. and put her hand on the table. Someone was calling her name. Nooolllaaa. Nooolllaaa. The French doors to the bedroom swung open. She could see the lights of Washington in the distance. She sat up. She went to close the French doors. She hated being all alone in the house. At fifty she was still young, and some men found her attractive when she was sober, but there was no time for dates. She was all work. She drove her law clerks seven days a week, and since she had become Chief Justice, she worked even harder. She was in her bed alright, but it seemed to be suspended. She wasn't alone in the room. "Who's there," she called. She could make out a man in black robes. His back was turned to her. She could make out some of the words he was saying. "Yet fear, still more, the still fearful doom / That takes the richest of heaven's slighted gifts / And leaves thy body and thy soul in darkness / To roam the earth a senseless corpse, or gives thee Before thy time, to the tormenting fiends / Such was my crime—with life, health, reason blest / And heart with rapture glowing, I looked round / Such was my punishment; the beam from heaven / That pours its light into the mind of man / Was suddenly extinguished, and a shroud / Darker, than that of death, enveloped all / Within me and around me. In this gloom / Peopled with specters, filled with scenes terrific / How long I lived-of the dread agony / Could life be called—I know not. To the dead / and the condemned. Time measures not his steps / And every moment seems eternity. "

The poor man turned to her. She started to scream but the specter seemed harmless. It was shimmering in a pale green light. She could identify his face, wrinkled, gaunt and crawling with maggots. There was a huge hickey located above his eye. He wore a wig which had become the home for many insects. It was judge Taney, the man who had been a Supreme Court justice when Dred Scott came before the court, in 1857. The case of Sullivan vs. Scott where a slave sued his master for freedom after the master transported him into a free territory.

"I could have had that beam of light, Nola Payne," Taney said. "I had the education: Greek, Latin, standards, tradition were all mine. I was in the right social class and had all of the breaks, but I met my match when Dred Scott came before me; he had something that I didn't have. A slave as lowly as he was. I had such a contempt for the African. I said that he had no rights that a white man was bound to respect, and when he came into the courtroom, I couldn't take my eyes off him. What dignity.

"O, if only they had had black studies in my time. If only I had become acquainted with Ivan Van Sertima, if only I could have spent some time at the feet of James Spady instead of in those schools where I was taught that the white man was the center of the universe and that women and blacks were put here to be their slaves. Scott had courage, but I made the wrong decision. A decision etched forever in the annals of law, and I am condemned to wander around the American hell discarded by history like the Spruce Goose, my name spoken with disgust. Bewarrreee, Nola Payne. Beewarreee. This Reverend Jones is a dangerous man, and the Conversion Bill is bad news. Why, if the Jews and blacks are thrown out of the country, it will become dull and phlegmatic, like Canada. And so I'm condemned to wander eternity, reciting my brother-in-law Francis Scott Key's awful poetry. Would you like to hear the choruses that were omitted from 'The Star-Spangled Banner'?"

"That won't be necessary, Chief Justice Taney." Nola turned to the voice that was standing at the threshold of the garden. There attired in priestly clothes was Nick.

"Who are you?" she asked.

"Nicholas of Bara," Nick said. "Chief Justice Taney is giving you good advice."

"But they all said that Clift was making it up."

"They were wrong."

"It is you, isn't it?" Nola said, now sitting up in her bed.

"It's me. Clift was right. He did the right thing. You do the right thing, or you, too, will become like Taney. A man brought to disgrace by vanity." Nola Payne began to sob. And when she awoke the next morning, the sun was so bright that it burnt through her eyes, and it was only eight a.m. It would be a beautiful Xmas day. She called the justices into special session. She rose and went into the bathroom and removed the pills from their cabinets and watched as they went down the toilet. She went into the library and took all of the whiskey out and poured it down the sink. She took a bath and thought for a long time. She knew what she had to do, after Roger Taney's pitiful narration of his infamous role in the Dred Scott decision. She prepared her own breakfast and ate in the garden. She walked down the stairs and got into her limousine. Her chauffeur was shocked. This was the first time in five years that he didn't have to help her down the stairs, as she was recovering from a drunken stupor. She arranged for a special session of the Court. She went to the Court and cast votes that would shake Jesse Hatch's administration to its foundation. She wrote the majority opinions for the vote against the Conversion Bill and for overruling a lower court by handing the reins of power to Dean Clift, who had been wrongfully removed from office by the Hatch administration.

## CHAPTER TWENTY-TWO

ANOTHER beautiful California day. Sunny. A temperature that was just right. A fall breeze that lightly massaged your skin. The birds were doing a jam session. He threw a bran muffin into the toaster and cut up some fruit. He began his bath. He poured himself a cup of the dark French roast mix. The drink had mitigated some of his anger. He had a big headache, but he felt better. John Coltrane had put some fight into his craw. Would he leave? Hell no. Being denied tenure usually meant that the institution to which you were attached wanted you to shove off. But he liked the weather. The Thai, Haitian and Gumbo restaurants. DeLauer's Newsstand. Lake Merritt.

He hadn't felt angry in twenty years. It felt good. During the long night he had gotten his old Black Panther beret out of the trunk. It still fit. The first paper that he always read was the Tribune. JACK LONDON BAILOUT DENIED. Just as he had warned, Robert Bass of Caesar Synthetics had pulled his money out over the threatened suspension of his son, and his friends had followed suit. No relief could be expected from the state, either. They owned the governor, whose name in Armenian meant "the servant" (the servant to corporate interests). The governor's every speech indicated that he hated education. But a new buyer had stepped in. He couldn't believe what he read. A one-hundred-million endowment. A mysterious Japanese group had put up the money? When he arrived at school to find out whether he'd been rehired by African-American Studies, he found little groups gathered, discussing the deal. Charles Obi was coming toward him like one of those fast walkers, hips moving.

"Dr. Obi," he said, "you still haven't said whether I'll be teaching this semester. The semester opens in two weeks." He was almost pleading.

"Can't talk now, Puttbutt. Got to go to a meeting." Obi buzzed on by and disappeared into President Stool's house. Puttbutt went to the African-American Studies department. The secretary, Effie Singleton, was at the Xerox machine. He never noticed before, but she was very attractive. He wasn't supposed to notice, but he couldn't help his eyes. They were straying over her hefty bosom and down to those hips that spread out. The weather was warm for fall and he could tell that she didn't have much on underneath her light cotton dress. For a moment a sweet sensation swelled up within him.

"What's up?"

"They're worried about their jobs. Matata has been switching up and down the hall all morning and Ms. Giddy went into her office. I peeped into her room and she had her head on the table and was crying."

"I don't understand." She pressed the stop button on the Xerox machine. She whispered.

"Rumor has it that the Japanese went to make some changes around here. You know what they think of black people. Everybody knows how they treat their minorities, the Koreans and the Pakistanis. The Okinawans." Then, changing the subject, she said, "How was your annual trip to Europe?"

"Lovely. Wined and dined in Rome. Standing room only in Geneva." He went into the mailroom. Some secretaries were standing there, drinking coffee. When he entered they got real quiet. Then they broke into laughter. He figured that he knew what they were laughing at. Him. He ignored them.

He looked at his mail. Protest Japanese Invasion. The flyer said that a meeting would be held at the Sea Wolf Lounge that evening. It was signed by—by Robert Hurt! The academic post-hippie. One of these radicals with tenure!

## CHAPTER TWENTY-THREE

He went to Hurt's office. Hurt was listening to the FM radio. Some composer was talking.... "The piece might be called minimal because it's simple, repetitive, yet aggressive." Sounded like somebody pushing a new type of wine cooler.

"Hi, Bob."

"Yeah, hi," he said, looking up only fleetingly. Puttbutt wasn't his type of Negro. Hurt liked his blacks raw and ungenteel.

"This letter signed by you. I just wanted to see if it were true. I mean, you're one of the few humanists around here. I never expected to see your name on this blatantly racist document. You're always putting me down for my reactionary stances. And here you are. Signing this chauvinist document."

"When it's war, it's all hands on deck."

"What do you mean?"

"It's just going too fast. A few months ago we were debating about whether our admissions policy was unfair to Asians. Now the Japanese have bought the school. If they want white men to be fair, then they have to give us a little time to catch our breath. What's going to happen to white men? And not only that, they're buying think tanks, politicians. I mean, in a few years people in this country will be speaking Japanese." I'm way ahead of you, Puttbutt thought. "There won't be a place for us. They're already the biggest investors in California. California is going to become a suburb of Tokyo. What are they going to do with us. First they buy Radio City Music Hall, the Empire State Building. Next thing you know, they'll be leasing the White House to the president. When is it going to end. Hell, this is nothing about multiculturalism versus high art or Afrocentricity versus Eurocentricity. This is about civilization against barbarism."

"But I thought that you were against Eurocentrism. You were the one who helped the students get through their global requirement courses. I was opposed to it."

"This is different."

"But what about your suspension of the Bass kid. That's what caused the financial crisis in the first place. The university lost Robert Bass, Sr., and the alumni's support."

"A mistake. Look, the kids and I have our differences, but the things that join us are far stronger than those that separate us. I mean, you didn't get mad. Why should I get mad. Why should I stick out my neck for you. In fact, his group is going to serve as bodyguards at the meeting tonight. You know, I had them all wrong. Those SS uniforms and swastikas they parade around in? Kid's stuff. Just a style. They call it nazi chic. Besides, what are you worrying about this innocuous nazi paraphernalia. Haven't you heard? Nazism is dead. Germany is reunified now. Anyway, the Nazis killed the Jews. Not the blacks." That wasn't exactly true. Allied troops found blacks imprisoned at Buchenwald. "I'm beginning to doubt whether the holocaust took place. I never voiced such opinions before, but now that I'm reunited with my brothers, I can say what I please."

"But, but you were the one who wrote that piece in the *Berkeley Espresso* saying that the left was riddled by anti-Semitism. Now you're sounding like that Frenchman, what's his name."

"La Pen. He has some good points. Besides, how do we know that the Jews haven't encouraged the Japanese to buy this school. To my way of thinking, the international Zionist bankers and the Japs have gotten together. They want to split up the West's institutions among them. Jack London goes to the Japs, the way I see it."

"I don't get it. You were going to suspend Bass Jr. on the basis of principles, now you're talking about joining those people."

"Are you coming tonight? We have a place for a black man like you. You know I attacked you in the campus paper about your book, *Blacks, America's Misfortune*. But now I think that you've raised some issues worthy of discussion. Like all of these single black women on welfare, for example. Fucking anything with pants on. Look, our group is color-blind. We could use somebody like you. An individual."

"I don't think so," Puttbutt said. He started out but then wheeled around. "I know that you're not like the rest of these fellows. Keeping everything in secret. Why was I turned down for tenure?"

"You'll get it eventually. I can tell you that the majority of those voting were on your side, but one of the speakers opposed your receiving the honor. Something you wrote," he said without looking up.

"Something I wrote?"

"Yeah. The old guard, the Miltonians, led by Professor Crabtree were bitterly opposed to it."

"Racists."

"Racists. Don't be paranoid. Professor Forrest died last year, leaving the department with one less Miltonian, and they want a Miltonian to take his place. You know that they're in a war with the deconstructionists, the feminists and the New Historicists." Did Puttbutt know. As a lone New Critic in the department he felt about as secure as a Gypsy in Czechoslovakia. The Miltonian bias against French theory and multiculturalism had been shaped by Milton. The prescient Milton warned about the seduction of the American critical fraternity by French theorists when he said, "Nor shall we then need the monsieurs of Paris to take our hopeful youth into their slight and prodigal custodies, and send them over back again transformed into mimics, apes, and kickshaws." Their feud with the multiculturalists was also Miltonic. For Milton, the leader of multiculturalism was Satan. "Besides, you're the one who wrote in the *New York Exegesis* that race was of declining significance, and that we were now in a color-blind society. Make up your mind, Puttbutt."

"Paranoid, huh. Well what about Marsha Marx. She told me that they weren't going to bring April Jokujoku out here, and I get an invitation to a party for April Jokujoku." Hurt sighed and leaned back in his chair.

"You black guys are always obsessing behind black feminists. Paranoid misogynists. April Jokujoku is just a better writer than you and all of those other black writers trying to threaten white males. Now if you'll excuse me, I have to make some calls. We have to get the press out tonight. Tell the word to the country. The invasion has begun."

"The Japanese couldn't be any worse than the people who are running things now," Chappie muttered.

"What did you say, Chappie?"

"Nothing." He had to keep his opinions to himself. It was a humiliation, but it was better than nothing. Hurt might tell the other racists on campus what he said. That after being doublecrossed by white racists who played him like a violin, using him to front their side of the argument concerning affirmative action, minority enrollment, etc. that he was willing to try some new kind of racism, yellow racism.

Chappie went home and slept for the rest of the afternoon. He always handled stress like that. When the 7.2 struck, he slept for three days. The earthquake had left many Californians stressed out, One thing good had happened though. Dr. Yamato had canceled the Japanese lessons until further notice. Totemo Yokatta Desu, Puttbutt thought. He felt great. He wanted to continue the lessons but he needed a rest. They were in the middle of te verbs and nai verbs and you had to memorize the ones ending in consonants and vowels in order to know which endings they would take. He had been thinking about giving up. He never thought he'd appreciate English so much.

## CHAPTER TWENTY-FOUR

For a week before the beginning of the fall semester, rumors flew across the campus. Everybody was talking about the quiet Japanese scholar who had moved into the president's home and who was running things until a permanent president could be found. The Japanese were minding their business, running the university, their public appearances as rare as those of Bigfoot. Even Effie, who knew everything, didn't know who he was. The African-American Studies department hadn't advised him as to whether he would be teaching. What would he do? This was the agony of the year-to-year appointment. Both departments pretended that his appointment was automatic, but he'd always have to go through the old runaround before getting his year-to-year papers signed. If he spoke to one of the good old boys and the GOB didn't answer, or answered him curtly, he took this as a sign that he'd been fired. If Obi or Ms. Marsha Marx didn't give him so much as a smile, he would worry for days. Obi was torturing him by holding up his contract. He couldn't report him to the union for fear of being against the brothers and sisters. Besides, the union was more interested in international left-wing issues than in the rights of the employees it was supposed to be representing. Hell, he'd heard that Daniel Ortega lived in one of the most expensive houses in Managua and owned a three-thousand-dollar watch. He couldn't understand why the Berserkley left were always supporting these Marxists who were doing better than they.

The English department and the African-American department were similar. They had a habit of weeding out dissidents. You just weren't rehired. They were both paralyzed by theory, too. A famous black feminist reflected the thinking in her remark that she was more interested in representations than in reality. (While thousands of black families were living out in the streets, the black intelligentsia at the *New York Exegesis* were obsessed with the questions of identity.) But nobody complained about these attitudes for fear of playing into the hands of the enemy (white people). Before his tenure denial he would have opposed such thinking. But now, he wasn't sure. He was beginning to see himself caught between the struggle between black and white nationalists, though the white ones didn't see themselves as such. Though black nationalism was seen as the only nationalism around, bitterly excoriated in the mass media, whites bonded with whites all the time. When a white was murdered or raped the story was played up by the victim's fellow whites in the press. Whites looked out for each other in business, politics and culture. Whites were even praised by white critics for "evolving" forms that blacks invented like the blues, rock and roll and jazz. The white government that begrudged every dime that was seen to go for the aid of blacks readily supported their fellow whites in Europe with a multibillion-dollar Marshall

Plan. They sent relief to the Kurds after they had "won" the war against Saddam Hussein. Many blacks thought it was because, in the words of Lesley Stahl, some of the Kurds had blond hair and blue eyes. They were even considering sending billions of dollars to the whites in Russia, who had been their enemies for many years, even threatening them with annihilation. Blacks weren't the only ones who saw the new Russian-United States cooperation as an example of two Caucasian countries getting it together. Shintaro Ishihara said the same thing in *The Japan That Can Say NO*.

When Chappie wrote articles denouncing black nationalism the white nationalists who controlled the publications he wrote for happily published them. He could write about the humiliating experience he had working in a department dominated by black nationalists, Afrocentrics, and accuse them of thought control and the like. Before his tenure denial he wouldn't have hesitated. But now he didn't want to be seen as favoring one group of nationalists over the other. He thought that any kind of nationalism was for the birds, and usually led to struggles with groups different from the favored group and led to anti-Semitism since the Jews, being considered cosmopolitan and rootless, were seen as a threat to nationalists.

It was usually the whites and the blacks who were seeking separation from each other, though any examination of American culture would show that they couldn't do without each other and that the blacks had become a sort of Schmoo of American culture, Al Capp's creature, who was an all-purpose thing. You could hate it, love it, exploit it, despise it, enjoy it, eat it, wear it, wash with it, kick it around, feel it up, pat it down, and it would still be there for your use. Chappie wasn't for any group. He was for Chappie, which is what he meant when he was always referring to himself as an existentialist the hip philosophy for the individualist. One day, after he became tired of waiting for Charles Obi to come to his office so that he could find out whether he'd be teaching, he decided to check out his mail in the Department of Humanity. There was a note instructing him to report to the president's house as soon as possible. Why would anybody be inviting him, a thirty-thousand-dollar-a-year lecturer, to the president's house? Maybe they were going to fire him. With trepidation and apprehension he started toward the end of the campus where the president's two-million-dollar house stood on a slope. In the distance he could see the Golden Gate Bridge. Behind the house one could see the beautiful Oakland Hills, where mansions stood and lavish homes of the cream of Oakland society.

He had heard about the art collection that was on exhibit at the president's office. Van Goghs, Gauguins, Monets and Renoirs, but when he entered the house he discovered that all of this had been removed. Japanese paintings hung where these modern paintings used to hang. Dominating the wall was a painting divided by five lines. It was done in dark and light greens, reds and oranges. Hundreds of soldiers, adorned in the armament that feudal Japan dressed in for war, some of it so beautiful that it wasn't meant to be used in battle (the Edo style), are engaged in battle. They fight in between trees and in the foreground of mountains. He read the name of the painting. "The Battle of Sekigahara, 1600." He gave the receptionist, a Japanese woman, his note. She picked up a phone and the man on the other end said that he would see him. He went inside of the office that he was directed to enter and saw the man sitting behind the desk. He rose. It was Dr. Yamato! His Japanese teacher!

"Puttbutt-san, O-genki desu ka," the doctor said, bowing. The president's desk had been replaced and what appeared to be an ancient hand-carved Japanese desk was in its place. Some paintings from the Kano and the Tosa school hung on the wall. One was by the great flower painter, Hanabusa. Hana was the Japanese name for flower.

"Genki, desu," Puttbutt said, surprised. Staggering from surprise. I'm sorry, he said. Dr. Yamato looked at him and said, "Hai." Dr. Yamato smiled. He couldn't believe it. He'd never seen Dr. Yamato smile. It was like seeing the Ayatollah Khomeini smile.

"Where is the president?"

"He's retired to the Ozarks," Dr. Yamato said. In that halting but steady manner of his.

"What? The president went without a fight?"

"He's like these other greedy American executives. He wanted us to give him a golden parachute. But there was a matter of this two-million-dollar home, and the unauthorized purchase of cars for some of the big wheels in the administration. Seems that he brought his ugly arbitraging methods into the university." Dr. Yamato, wearing that same old black woolen suit, walked to the window.

"You Amerikans pay your executives too much money, that's part of the problem here. Waste. You're over your heads in credit. Each American should be limited to two credit cards, and you should take rapid transit and stop consuming so much energy. BART de Ikimasu. The school is suffering from budget cuts and this man was being chauffeured around in a limousine. Needless to say, he went quietly. Your vice president, Whitherspoon, has been forced into retirement too. Allowed these various factions of ruffians to run this school. The FF and the skinheads. They've taken control of the place. We're going to take this campus back. There are going to be many changes around here." Dr. Yamato had a glint in his eye. "I'm going to need your help."

"My help? But I'm just a lowly lecturer. Why would you need my help?"

"I need somebody with whom I can communicate. Somebody that I can trust." When he said that, Puttbutt knew that the $245.00 he paid to learn Japanese by Spring had been worth it.

## CHAPTER TWENTY-FIVE

Yes. The reason that the Americans are so backward is because of what they call their core curriculum. Changes are in order. We will help them. Try to civilize them. Show them that there are some things that all educated people must know in order to be culturally literate. Get them to realize that there's more to life than Captain Video. Your president, how do you suppose he was spending his time. Chotto Matte Kudasai." Dr. Yamato rose and went into an adjoining room. Puttbutt wondered would Yamato ever change those frumpy clothes of his. The black suit. The hat. The beat-up briefcase. He'd probably abandon the limousine that had been made available to him. Yamato would probably still take BART and remain in his office during lunch hours, eating bowl after bowl of noodles.

On the wall was a print of a shishi by Yoshitoshi. Blood was pouring from the shishi's wounds but he stoically ate his rice cake. Just before Dr. Yamato reentered the room carrying a box, Chappie glanced at a newspaper clipping that lay on his desk. It showed a photo of Kazumi Tajiri, who was identified as a subchief of a small right-wing political group. He was a suspect in the shooting of the mayor of Nagasaki, Hiroshi Motoshima. The mayor had criticized Emperor Hirohito for being responsible for World War II. Yamato opened some of the boxes. Racing magazines. Playgirl centerfolds. It was full of whiskey bottles. Jack Daniel's. There was another huge stack of *National Enquirers* and *Star*. A newspaper bore the headlines about an ailing JFK, from the secret place he had been kept since he was wounded in Dallas, commenting about the direction the family's morality was taking and denying his liaison with Marilyn Monroe. Dr. Yamato shook his head in disgust.

"He was little more than a cash cow for the Bass group, hired to lure funds to the school. We also discovered that he was using funds from government research grants to buy first-class theater tickets, flowers for his women and for entertainment."

"What kind of changes are you going to make, Doctor."

"Many of your colleagues will not be coming back."

"I don't follow, Dr. Yamato."

"We're going to close down the Department of Humanity and move it into Ethnic Studies. You have African Studies, Chicano Studies, Asian-American Studies, Native-American Studies and African-American Studies. We will have a new department, European Studies, with the same size budget and faculty as the rest. My backers would like to eliminate all of these courses which allow for so much foolishness, but they also want to show to the faculty and students how conciliatory we are. We will allow for these frills. Are they really necessary? All they accomplish for these people is to glorify some mythic past and to promote such dubious claims that Europe is the birthplace of science, religion, technology and philosophy. I've been reading this so-called philosopher, Plato. All about such foolishness as to whether the soul has immortality. What nonsense. Hegel and the rest are full of such nonsense also. This ignorant man maintained that the Chinese had no philosophy. What rubbish. No wonder the Americans can't make a decent automobile. Their intellectuals spend all of their time on these fuzzy and useless Greeks and German idealists. If one were to apply the empirical razor to all of these so-called theories, the entire history of Western philosophy could be covered in one week. Also, I am considering dropping the inordinate number of courses devoted to the work of John Milton. My staff has checked this character's background. He spent some time in jail, you know. We do not think it appropriate to include courses about an ex-convict in our catalog. That also goes for pederasts. We found out that his nickname at Cambridge was The Lady."

"I'll have to think about it, Dr. Yamato."

"Now, I want you to see your new office."

"My what?"

"Your new office." The Japanese woman showed him to a spacious office. There were other Japanese moving about the building; files were being taken out in boxes. He could see all the way down to San Mateo. He just sat there for a while. He picked up the right-wing student newspaper. Dean Hurt's picture was on the cover. He was speaking to a rally of faculty and students, mostly white, who were complaining about the undue pressure on the university that this mysterious Japanese money, as they called it, would pose.

Hurt was shaking his fist in the manner of Lenin in a poster he'd once seen. He went over to the literature division of the Department of Humanity to start packing the office that he shared with three other lecturers. On the way, he saw Professor Crabtree who tried to manage a weak smile. He smiled back. Professor Crabtree had always ignored him and now he was trying to be friends? What was that all about, Puttbutt thought.

## CHAPTER TWENTY-SIX

The Department of Humanity had gotten the word to clear out, though they didn't know where they were going to go. Dr. Yamato had recommended that they hold classes in some of the coffee shops located near the campus until some space could be found. The atmosphere was gloomy. He noticed among their boxes one entitled CONFIDENTIAL FILES. He went over and picked it up. One of the secretaries saw, and protested.

"Mr. Puttbutt, you can't touch those boxes." It was the Latino woman who worked in the office. She came on to the white men, affecting a Billy Burke type musicality in her voice when relating to them, cozying all up to them. She treated Puttbutt and even some of the Latino males on the staff shabbily. He picked it up anyway.

"But . . ." She tried to block him from leaving the department.

"It's all right," the chairperson said, sighing. "He's working in the president's house with Dr. Yamato." The chairperson, Dr. Milch, could hardly conceal his annoyance but tried to be pleasant.

"Thank you," Puttbutt said.

"Chappie, may I talk with you for a moment?" He put the box down and followed him into his former office. He glanced at the boxes full of books and papers. A family photo was sticking out of a box. Some back issues of the *New York Review of Books* were lying on his desk. Keys. A memo pad.

"I'm disappointed in you, Chappie. Consorting with this Yamato character, this creature. Besides, you're the second most powerful person on this campus. The first time that a black has achieved such status. The job should have gone to a black woman." He was raising his voice. Puttbutt hated for people to raise their voices. Perhaps it was because during his early years people were constantly barking at him. Shouting into his face like the character played by Lou Gossett, Jr., in *An Officer and a Gentleman*.

"What?" Puttbutt was surprised at Milch's fury. Milch began moving toward him from behind his desk. The guy was breathing heavily and stammering.

"You black guys had your chance. Wright and Baldwin were once the canon, but Zora overthrew them. Sent them hurling from the literary firmament. Cast them down. The fact that they would choose you, a black man, instead of a black woman shows how backward these Japanese are."

"Mr. Milch if you and your colleagues don't like Mr. Yamato then I'm sure that some other universities would be interested in your candidacy. Besides, the black and Chicano men are always complaining about your favoritism."

"I don't follow."

"They say that you encourage them to enter the master's program while you're always setting aside positions for the women in the Ph.D. program."

"Women have been held back. They need more encouragement. You black fellows are the worst offenders. Black women writers say that black men mistreat their wives and the wives throw them out."

"That's what I thought it was about. Well, if you're a feminist, then why can't I be a masculinist? Do you need for me to send some more boxes over or may I offer you some assistance in packing your things?" His pale face lit up like a fire. He left him that way. Glaring at him, angrily. He never thought he'd hear himself say those words. What was coming over him. His grandfather could be right. That you couldn't expect a fair deal with whites. As soon as Puttbutt got to his old office, a crummy ill-lit room which he shared with other lecturers, including two TAs, who received more respect than he, he opened the files. He removed his. He read the confidential report on his tenure. Apparently he had some support, but the Miltonians had been rallied by Crabtree who had fought against Puttbutt's candidacy citing the article he had written many years ago in which he said that Shakespeare's *Othello* was racist. He'd forgotten all about it. It was his master's thesis. Written when he was in his Black Power period. Nobody discussed racism anymore. Racism was something that blacks had made up in order to make whites feel guilty, so the line went. Puttbutt had learned the argument well. He used it. Published articles about how blacks couldn't seem to get it together. The *New York Exegesis* even considered him for a seat on its editorial board. All sorts of foundations offered him fellowships for using this line. He'd hoped nobody would ever find it, but apparently it had been shown to the members of the tenure committee. He didn't have anything to lose now. Dr. Yamato had sent them packing.

## CHAPTER TWENTY-SEVEN

His picture was on the cover of the *Sun Reporter.* Puttbutt named special assistant to the acting president of Jack London College, the story announced. People were lined up outside his office door. Matata Musomi, who said on some resumes that he had attended Oxford, and others that he'd attended Cambridge, was there; he looked up from the European newspaper at Puttbutt with sarcasm in his eyes. Charles Obi brought his greasy smile. He took Crabtree first. Crabtree gave him a watermelon grin.

If Crabtree had been a hat wearer, he would have been holding his hat gingerly in hand. The corners of his mouth pushed back into a huge smile, revealing some very expensive dental work. He looked around the office. He must have been impressed. The sleek Japanese furniture. Paintings on the wall. The view of the Pacific. The grand light shafting in.

"What can I do for you, Professor Crabtree?" Puttbutt said, leaning back in his chair, his hands supporting his head. He tried not to rub it in, considering the reversal of fates. Professor Crabtree paused for a moment before speaking. Finally, with a good deal of effort:

"I know you must be surprised that I came in today. After the rude way I've always treated you."

"You have been rude, Professor."

"I . . . I'm not the most pleasant person in the world, but once you get to know me, I play a good game of poker. You play poker?"

"Come to the point, Professor. Dr. Yamato has a great deal of work for me to do. He wants all of us to husband our time. He feels that Americans waste too much time."

"You heard about what happened over in the Department of Humanity. Seems to have been a big shake-up. I understand that the English and poetics departments have been moved to Ethnic Studies. Anglo-Saxon Studies. From Chaucer to the Beatles."

"That's right."

"A lot of my colleagues, including myself, are, well, you know, concerned about our status."

"I did hear something to that effect, Professor. What do you want me to do about it?"

"I . . . well, it seems that you have some pull with that Japanese chap."

"Dr. Yamato."

"Yes, that's his name."

"Dr. Yamato and I decided that it would be wasting money to keep people on the staff whose courses were drawing only a few students. Your Sir John Suckling seminar and the course in Old Norse. There are only three students attending. The Japanese don't like to waste money." The professor didn't say anything. "And, you haven't published a book or an article in fifteen years, and the articles that you have published show considerable borrowing."

"I...just haven't had the time. I ... "

"I know. Going to these Humanity conventions which provide you with an opportunity to meet women other than your wife, and to sample exotic cuisine. Why your professional organization's program included more infor-mation on the restaurants in Chinatown than on the topics when it met last year in San Francisco. I also found out, Professor, that it was you who was instrumental in getting my tenure denied."

"Who told you that? That's supposed to be a secret."

"I took the liberty of looking at my confidential files."

"But you're not supposed to look at those files! They're offlimits." He began to rise from his chair until it apparently occurred to him that he didn't have the clout he once had. "Your article on *Othello*, I felt, wasn't first-rate. Your thesis that race relations in this country haven't changed since Shake-speare's time. The play was written in sixteen-three. That's preposterous. And to call Shakespeare a racist is really overdoing it, don't you think? What claptrap!" Crabtree squirmed in his chair as he said "claptrap."

"I wrote it during my Black Power days."

"Cockamamie detritus."

"Oh, is it now?" Puttbutt didn't feel like defending a paper he had written years before, but he was irritated by the imperious tone now creeping into Crabtree's voice. He stood and leaned on the desk, staring right into Crab-tree's eyes. Crabtree recoiled.

"The only thing that has changed is that thick lips are in now. All of these white women desiring lip enhancement operations," Puttbutt said. Even say-ing that gave him relief.

"Come now, Professor Puttbutt." Crabtree smiled wryly.

"Shakespeare makes Othello into a primitive. He's warlike. His moods change rapidly. His anger is always on the surface, ready to burst. It arises from a 'hollow' hell. And the character, Othello, is always down on himself. He says in act 2, scene 3, 'I am black/And have not those soft parts of conver-sation/That chamberers have.' Why would a general, a man of war, espe-cially an African, be so down on himself. African warriors see themselves as the cock of the walk. They have these griots who follow them around like Bundini Brown, telling them how great they are. Shakespeare also promotes a common belief among white men that they can have any woman of any background, but when a black man and a woman of another race get together the motive has to be perverse. You white men can have all of the women you want, while anytime a black man and a white woman fall in love it's because, according to Shakespeare, she's enchanted by him. The black has put some kind of spell on her, or she is fascinated by his oppression. What incredible ego. Shakespeare believed that the only uncorrupted interracial relationship can be that between a white man and a colored woman."

"William Shakespeare didn't have a racist bone in his body. Surely you're projecting." Puttbutt rose and went to the window. He looked down. A white fraternity had set up a platform. Some of the pledges had painted their faces black. One large white boy had put on the mammy attire. Head rag. Red and white polka-dot dress. Huge pillows for breasts. The "slaves" were being auctioned off to the older brothers. This was the fraternity's Annual Slave Day. Despite Dr. Yamato's memo to all of the departments and to the students that racism would be punished severely, the overt racist acts were continuing with broad support from the media, who were insisting that these young bigots be allowed to "express themselves." It was the target of their abuse, the media and the corporate-financed think tanks were saying, who were the real oppressors. They were accused of insisting that everyone be politically correct.

"You blacks are always complaining about racism. Racism this and racism that. You use racism to explain away your failure. All of this talk about racism on the campus of Jack London. I've been teaching here for thirty years and have never found a single instance. Do you hear? A single instance. And now you have to reach back and drag Shakespeare into it. Is there no end to you people's paranoia? Now you have some sort of code that makes it an offense to call someone a nigger. Why that word doesn't bother me at all." While Crabtree was speaking, Puttbutt was thumbing through a copy of *Othello* that had been left behind in Whitherspoon's hurried attempt to clear his former office.

"Scene 3, Othello's speech, 'She loved me for the dangers I had pass'd, And I loved her that she did pity them.'

"Doesn't prove a thing."

"He paints Othello as a noble savage."

"Where? Where did you find evidence of that?"

" 'The Moor is of a free and open nature,/That thinks men honest that but seem to be so,/And will as tenderly be led by the nose/As asses are.' When's the last time you read the play, Professor?"

"I...I—"

"And if you don't think that Shakespeare's play can be applied to contemporary situations, what about the character of Emilia, a racist feminist?"

"Feminism in Shakespeare's time. You are stretching things, Puttbutt."

"Act 3, scene 4, Emilia says, speaking of men: 'Tis not a year or two shows us a man;/They are all but stomachs, and we all but food;/ They eat us hungerly, and when they are full/ They belch us.' Certainly some misandry reflected in that speech, Professor Crabtree. As for racism, in act 5 she calls Othello a 'black devil.' There are many feminists on Jack London's campus who could be Emilia."

"But I thought you were on their side."

"I'm on my side, Mr. Crabtree. My side." He studied Crabtree's face. He couldn't believe what he said. He was sounding like his father. Accepting his father's vision of the world. As a battleground between the strong and the weak. His countenance flagged for a moment before reassuming his supercilious demeanor. Like many Eurocentric professors, as they were being called in the newspapers, he regarded Shakespeare as little more than a cultural hammer to be used to intimidate the infidels. So busy counting iambic pentameter, they'd never taken Shakespeare at his word. They could read *The Merchant of Venice* and *Othello* without taking into account what some of the characters and the language meant to Jews and to blacks.

"You've been here thirty years, Crabtree. That counts for something. Maybe we can work something out. It's not like the old days when you only needed to know Greek, Latin, English and French. Dr. Yamato is requiring that every faculty member study Japanese." Crabtree turned from his usual chalk white to red. He wished that he could read his thoughts. He threw one of the copies of *Japanese by Spring* that lay in a stack on his desk at Crabtree. Crabtree caught it, examined it and then threw it to the floor.

"How about teaching a course in freshman composition."

"Composition. That's preposterous, a man of my rank."

"Suit yourself."

"You'd better respect your betters, young man. I was teaching the Milton seminar when you were in high school. Don't you forget." Puttbutt glanced at a sheet of paper on his desk. "Two students."

"What?"

"You had exactly two students enrolled in that course on Middle English. Dr. Yamato believes that such courses constitute Anglo-Saxon ethnic cheerleading and feelgoodism. It has to be freshman composition or nothing." Crabtree rose. He stood there staring at Puttbutt for a moment. The anger contorted his face. He finally spun around and left the room in a huff. Puttbutt shrugged his shoulders.

## CHAPTER TWENTY-EIGHT

The dark European was rubbernecking. This was a quiet California street, but he could imagine the local primitives staring out from behind their blinds like the invisible savages in a Hollywood movie, spying upon a caravan whose inhabitants were unaware of their presence. Herman Melville said that the true savages were not located in West Africa, but in the suburbs of upstate New York. That was becoming true of the American suburbs. Though Puttbutt pushed the media line that the inner cities were the Paradise Lost part of the American Dream, and that blacks needed to change, to become self-reliant, and to be more responsible, he knew from talking to his white students that drugs, alcoholism, incest, spousal abuse, child abuse, violence, fractured families were widespread in American society, extended beyond the city limits into Paradise Regained. One of the jobs of the media was to protect white America, its customers, from their devils. They must be seen as selfless stewards presiding over a society overrun by blacks, Latins and yellows, engaged in "a tangle of pathologies." Though 12 percent of those arrested for looting, including Santa Monica yuppies during the Great Los Angeles Uprising of 1992 were white, the pictures of whites were associated with cleaning the streets after the chaos.

The object of his neighbor's gaze was a white stretch limousine easing up in front of his house. Robert Bass got out, a middle-aged man, well tanned and fit. He was with his son, Robert Bass, Jr. Bass Jr. had gotten rid of his neonazi uniform and was wearing a blue blazer and white slacks and black hosiery. His hair was beginning to grow back. It was combed and neatly parted. They came up the steps. Knocked on his door. He could imagine the shocked neighbors. He opened the door.

"Yes." He pretended that he didn't know who Bass Sr. was, but he'd often seen his photo on the society page.

"Mr. Puttbutt?"

"That's right?"

"My name is Robert Bass." Puttbutt shook his hand warmly. "Of course, you know this asshole. My son." Robert Bass, Jr., stared at his shoes, shined to a black gloss. Then he looked up at Puttbutt. He was really hurting. Puttbutt could tell that the old man was sore with Bass Jr.

"I'm glad to meet you. Won't you come in." They followed him into the living room. His Japanese texts were lying on the table. He offered them tea in Japanese. He made some kocha (black tea) and poured it all around. The young Bass was very silent. Whenever Puttbutt would look his way, the young Bass's eyes would retreat.

"What can I do for you, Mr. Bass?"

"I just want to apologize for my son. He was mixed up with the wrong crowd, but we're hoping that it's a passing thing. Hell, I hadn't been following the little bastard. Found all kinds of nazi paraphernalia in his room. I gave him a beating he'll never forget. Just to think, we licked those bastards back in forty-five, and my own son, a kraut lover. As for his complaints about affirmative action, his high school grades were so low that it was only my influence that got the rascal into London anyway. He's been kicked out of every boarding school in the West. Thought he'd be an upstanding college man like me. Why I was captain of the Berkeley rowing team in '39. Used to participate in the races at Lake Merritt."

"I'm sorry, Mr. Puttbutt. How can I ever make it up to you?" the Bass boy said. Puttbutt almost fell out of his chair.

"I told him that we'll cut him out of his inheritance if he doesn't find some way to make amends." It was rumored that Bass Sr. was worth about ten million. "And I hope you don't have any hard feelings about my role in this matter, Mr. Puttbutt. If I had any idea of the racist hell that my son and his friends were putting you through, I would have sent his ass to military school. You know, we're not a very close family. I'm always in the Lear. Trying to bring the free-market ideas to the underprivileged areas of the world, I haven't had a chance to attend to my responsibilities as a parent. But I think we've come upon a solution."

"What is that, Mr. Bass?"

"We want him to wait on you hand and foot. Sort of like doing community service."

"I'm at your beck and call, Mr. Puttbutt. I'll do whatever it takes to make it up to you."

"We want to install a phone direct to your house and the little son of a bitch will have to be your servant. Now let's talk business. I know that you're in touch with some powerful Japanese people. What ya say you introduce me to some of them. Come over to the club." Robert Bass, Sr., was leaning toward Puttbutt now. Sort of man-to-man. This club had been in the news for years for not admitting blacks.

"That may be a good idea, Mr. Bass."

"Hell, I have to go with the flow in order to remain in business."

"That's the way it looks, huh Mr. Bass?"

"This Yamato chap. How do you know him?"

"He's my teacher."

"You study Japanese, Mr. Puttbutt?"

"Yes. It's like mental push-ups. In fact, I have a little reading material for you." Puttbutt reached into a box and handed Bass Sr. a copy of JBS. Bass Sr. accepted the book with a smile.

"Mind if I have one, Professor Puttbutt?" Puttbutt handed one to junior.

"I'll have my secretary call you next week, maybe your Japanese friends can meet us over to the club. I've reserved a private room there. They have a tennis court. Maybe your friend likes to play tennis. Sauna. Anything. You tell Dr. Yamato that Bass and Co. is at his service. My son is at your service." He frowned at his son.

"Professor Puttbutt..."

"Yes, Robert?" The three stood. Robert Bass Jr.'s voice was trembling. He broke down and began to cry. He put his arms around Puttbutt's neck and cried on his shoulder. Puttbutt kept his hands at his side as he'd been taught by his parents. Sort of at a parade rest position. He had been taught to be undemonstrative. Puttbutt was embarrassed. He tried to put himself in the kid's place. If he were about to lose on ten million dollars, he'd be crying too. The kid stepped back.

"I have a gift," he said. He placed a fancy package on the table. The company parted. The old nosey neighbor next door couldn't stand it. The sucker had moved outside and was pretending to trim the bushes. The Basses got into their white stretch limousine and eased on down the street. The neighbor's blond, blue-eyed wife was staring at Puttbutt. She was wearing her gardening shorts. She was, as the Nihon-jin would say, so-so. Her husband looked at her and then to Puttbutt; he began snapping at twigs angrily. Puttbutt went inside and opened the package. The gift from Bass Jr.; the very individual who had been making his life so hard. It was a beautiful sweater. Made in Bologna.

## CHAPTER TWENTY-NINE

The changes on Jack London campus were occurring quickly. He'd become adjusted to his new position as assistant to the acting president and was kept busy in his new office. A lot of people came to ask him for requests and advice. People who had formerly treated him like shit. He felt like Pirate Jenny in Kurt Weill's *Threepenny Opera*. He gave them all a copy of the text *Japanese by Spring*. Dr. Yamato permitted some of them to retire without problems, others protested. He was walking up the hill toward work when he saw some commotion going on in front of the campus entrance. It was Robert Hurt. He was haranguing some of the students. His listeners were mostly white, but there was also a sprinkling of some yellows, browns and blacks. Led by Hurt they had presented Dr. Yamato with their demands. He was in Dr. Y's office when he received them. Dr. Y had smiled contemptuously, balled the paper on which the list was written in his fist, and flung it into the wastepaper basket.

Hurt looked as though he hadn't slept in days and had taken a lot of drugs. His speech was incoherent and rambling. He was attacking the Japanese character and made other scurrilous remarks about Japanese culture and values. He spotted Puttbutt.

"And there he is now. Chappie Puttbutt. Not only is he a traitor to white people, but to blacks as well. Let's get him." Puttbutt began to trot toward his office at the end of the campus. Some of the students who were passing on their way to and from class paused to watch this strange sight. The third world nationalists were calling him a banana. Robert Bass Jr.'s former friends, who were providing some sort of protection for Hurt, were also in pursuit as well as some of Hurt's listeners. Just as one of them began to catch up with him, as he ran near the Student Union, which was built along the architectural lines of London's Klondike Cabin, he noticed a line of men dressed in black and assuming a martial arts position. Hurt and his followers halted. Assessed the situation, and retreated. Bass's ex-allies, however, stood their ground. They were daring the men who were dressed in quiet suits, ties and shoes. The leather-jacketed Amerikaners moved toward the men. Suddenly there were some swift movements. Legs flying. Hands chopping. A knife flashed. After a fierce and murderous melee that lasted less than sixty seconds, Bass's former allies were lying on the ground moaning. Wounded. Those who weren't began hightailing it from the campus. The arrogant yellow-haired youth who'd assisted Bass Jr. in making Puttbutt's life miserable was spitting out some teeth. His mouth was bloodied and he was bawling and screaming. These ruffians have finally received their comeuppance, Put-tbutt thought. He walked past the men, who were brushing off their clothes and straightening their ties. Some of them were Japanese, a few were black. They behaved as though nothing has happened. Domo Arigato, he said. The men bowed. Two of them followed him to his office and stationed them-selves outside his door. Were these the extra measures that Yamato had in mind when he said that he would bring order and stability to the campus? The phone rang. Effie Singleton told him that April was at the airport and there was nobody there to greet her. African American Studies were under-going a transition and considering Marsha Marx's new status, nobody had advised April that her services were no longer needed. Ms. Jokujoku was demanding a chauffeur-driven limousine and police escort to bring her to the university, after which she wanted Indian food and a massage. He told the secretary to tell Ms. Jokujoku to take the next plane back to New York. That there had been changes on campus and that he would have somebody write her a letter that would tell her what's what.

"Marsha Marx is out here in the lobby," Effie Singleton said. Marsha came into the office. He could tell that she was angry.

"What can I do for you?" he said.

"This is what you can do for me." She handed him the letter informing the Women's Studies department that they had to move their things into the new Ethnic Studies department, the Department of European Studies. She was leaning on his desk and stamping her feet.

"You're moving us over there with those patriarchal pigs?"

"I'll be frank about it, Marsha. The new owners of the university have decided to cut back on the budget. The Women's Studies department is merely a front for European Studies. You said so yourself." Puttbutt picked up a sheet of paper that was lying on his desk. "'Europe is the source of our law, our values, and our culture, yet little had been done to recognize the role of women, the establishment of this great civilization,'" he quoted from an MLA speech she'd made. "The way we see it, there's no significant difference between your aims and those of your patriarchal allies. You just wanted in. What we've decided to do in European Studies is to hire fifty percent men and fifty percent women. That should satisfy you."

"What?"

"Look, European Studies is just one of the many departments on this campus. Things have changed." Puttbutt was becoming impatient with his colleagues.

"The members of my department insist upon working in a male-free department," she said. She was furious.

"If you feel that way why don't you move your people to Mills? As long as this is a coed college we will not tolerate any separation between the sexes."

"But Chappie, I thought you were different from the rest. Sympathetic to the goals of women."

"I am. But my mother raised me not to take any flak from anybody, man or woman. She is an expert on the choke hold. I've always disagreed with her and my father. They told me that the world was a scumbag. They told me that every day would be war. But I didn't believe them. I always supported you but then I discovered from the confidential files that you assisted the Miltonians in getting my tenure denied. You wanted to bring April out here to get the tenure that I was denied, while all along assuring me that this wasn't your aim."

"But you understand, don't you? We just wanted one of our own. Besides..."

"Besides, what?"

"Our study group discovered that you once rented a porno movie."

"What?" He'd forgotten all about it. He had rented some combo films in connection with a study on fascism and pornography after reading that white male neonazis were fascinated by porno films that featured black and interracial sex. Really got off from these films.

According to Spy magazine, David Duke owns one of the prime collections. Wouldn't you know.

"You checked out my movie rentals. But you're the ones who are always insisting on the right to privacy."

"The private is the political. You men do all of your oppression in the dark. It is our right to shine a light upon your black deeds."

"Well what about women and pornography. Half the people who rent porno movies are women. Playgirl has six hundred thousand subscribers. What are you going to do with them?"

"Look, Chappie." Softer now, pleading. "We should be on the same side. United in our fight against white male patriarchy and its control and manipulation of modes of production. Both sexism and racism are equal contradictions."

"Oh yeah, then explain to me why black and brown women are worse off than white women. Why there are few women of color in the main feminist organizations and why the black and brown women are always accusing you of racism. One of the reasons you wanted to bring April in was to stifle the criticism that your department includes few women of color. Besides, you're looking out for yourself. I'm going to look out for me. And I'll tell you what. A lot of black men and white men are getting sick of your double-dealing opportunistic feminist bullshit. I'm also sick and tired of you comparing your situation with that of blacks. I'm sick of gays and the rest of them doing it too. Gays have more money and jobs as a group than black people ever will, yet all we hear about are these middleclass women and their eating disorders, when millions of women and children have nothing to eat. You don't jump on men of your background as much as you do the fellas. You lynched Clarence Thomas. You white gender-first feminists in the media and on the campuses have gone Clarence Thomas crazy. What do you want from the man?" He thought that he knew. "The only difference between you and the women in the Klan is that the women in the Klan dress better."

"Chappie. What happened to you? It was only last year that Women's Studies ranked you as among the ten male instructors on campus who were sensitive to women's needs. It must be the Japanese. How can you work for those men. The way they treat their women. They used the women in Korea as comfort girls during the war. And why aren't they among the other Ethnic Studies departments?"

"The Japanese feel that they've been at the civilizing business longer than the rest. They feel that all culture and knowledge emanates from their islands. And that's why they've created a new Department of Universal Studies. They feel that Japanese culture should be emulated by the world."

"But that's the most Asianocentric garbage. Married men with geishas. They're so homogeneous."

Homogeneous. Homogeneous. Puttbutt was having a humongous pain from this word. This word was making a real nuisance of itself. Showing up in studies and magazine articles. He hated the word as much as he hated hegemony. Paradigm. Discourse.

"You white people make me sick with your homogeneity. You're the ones who are into some kind of narrow-assed homogeneity. The Japanese language includes thirty-five hundred characters of Chinese language. Kanji. They have Korean components in their culture. They absorbed English during the occupation. They have a special Katakana set aside for English. They read books by Western writers. They trade with the world. And you call them homogeneous. You're the ones who are homogeneous. No matter how high a white may rise in this society's intellectual circles, with few exceptions they're still monolingual and culturally restricted crackers. You are the ones who want everybody to be like you, through your enforced assimilation. You—"

"Chappie, what's wrong with you? I've never heard you talk this way. Your white friends are beginning to worry about you these days. You sound so, so bitter. So angry. These windy incoherent diatribes. These Japanese chauvinists must be getting to you." He tossed her a copy of *Japanese by Spring*. She caught it. She had a surprised look.

Marsha's mouth ruled her face. Sometimes, it seemed as though it ruled her. It was like the hand in *The Beast with Five Fingers*. Like the maniac killer's limb in *Body Parts*, her mouth seemed as though it were independent of the face. It had a life of its own. Thought processes of its own. It was like the act he'd seen on the Ed Sullivan show. A Spanish ventriloquist shaped his hand into a mouth. The mouth was like a little human with its own eyes. Her twisting, flat red mouth slashed and burned men. Gates through which dry cutting words flew. He'd seen the mouth in action. Spewing language in rapid-fire bursts. Mowing down whatever man found himself unlucky enough to be in its way.

But jobs were hard to find these days. So dire was the job market that whites, some of whom had criticized multiculturalism formerly, were boning up on Native American literature and Latino literature and becoming experts on these disciplines so that they might find teaching jobs. Though Richard Bernstein, a *New York Times* critic, was writing yet another book—a book that was supported by a fellowship from the Freedom Forum—arguing that multiculturalism benefited African Americans, Asian Americans, Hispanics and Native Americans, only whites were the ones who were making the big dollars from this burgeoning industry. Though some were sincere and qualified, others were merely out to improve their incomes, during the era of George Herbert Hoover. The American Cultures program at Berkeley was inaugurated after student demands that the university become more multicultural. With the American Cultures program, the university was requiring that each student take at least one course in ethnic culture before graduating. This program was being ridiculed as a black giveaway program by D'Gun ga Dinza and other anti-diversity personalities in Eastern think tanks. Ishmael Reed attended a meeting of American Cultures Fellows at the University of California at Berkeley. After reading the Bernstein proposal, he thought that he'd find a room full of brothers and sisters. He and one other black man were the only "people of color" present. Those who were benefiting the most from multiculturalism, in this room, were white women. One white woman asked another, who was addressing the group, her advice about what to do if a "third world" student challenged her authority to teach a multicultural course without her having experienced oppression in her background. She was advised to tell her students that multicultural people weren't the only people who were oppressed. She said that an unwanted sibling had it just as bad as a "person of color." Hmmmmmmm, Ishmael Reed thought. Gerald Ford was an unwanted sibling and he became president of the United States.

The millions of dollars that were going to multiculturalism were being exploited by some whites in another way. He was told by a person in Berkeley's American Cultures office that some departments were taking the funds earmarked for multicultural courses and transferring these funds to the traditional-courses budget. This is the irony. While neoconservative Eastern intellectuals, fearful that reethnicity would reveal their having undergone an identity transplant (many of those who were writing angry op-eds about black culture had changed their names), were pushing back-to-basics and denouncing multiculturalism as an infidel movement, millions of multicultural dollars were being spent on traditional courses. How did Don King put it? Only in America.

Marsha Marx was mad. Her mouth looked as though it would leap from her face and give him a good mouth-smacking. His skin began to crawl. But the mouth held its place. Marsha wanted to keep her job and Chappie Puttbutt was doing the hiring and the firing. He remembered the expression that Colin Powell used during the Gulf War. About bringing all of the tools to the party. That's what he, Puttbutt, was doing. His parents were right. Life was war. And on this campus, he was second in command.

"If you're going to remain on this campus you'd better start to get down with some of these Japanese verbs."

Marsha was silent for a moment. "Chappie, do you know what you are, you're a reactionary asshole."

Puttbutt leaned back in his chair. "Ms. Marx, without the asshole, human life would cease to exist."

She left, slamming the door.

# ESSAYS

A PROFESSIONAL media organization recently gave an award to a magazine that endorsed the Simi Valley jury's acquittal of Rodney King's tormentors because, according to the organization, that took courage. Shelby Steele was congratulated in the *New York Times* for discussing matters that are "unspoken"—his unoriginal notion of blacks feeling guilty for receiving advancement as a result of affirmative action was borrowed from a mean-spirited editorial by Midge Decter, over five years before. Nevertheless, Steele's ideas appear and are promoted regularly by *Harper's,* the *New York Times Magazine,* the underwriters of PBS, and other powerful sections of neoconservative opinion.

The profitable literary scam nowadays is to pose as someone who airs unpleasant and frank facts about the black community, only to be condemned by the black community for doing so. This is the sure way to grants, awards, prizes, fellowships, and academic power.

A grants-giving agency sent me the confidential letter nominating a black conservative writer for a very generous grant. The nominator said nothing about the literary merit of the author's work but praised his ability to needle blacks. Currently, blacks are depicted as members of an uptight community, where thought control is rampant. They're "paranoid" and can't take criticism.

As someone who for years has aired the dirty laundry of the black, white, yellow, and the brown community, as well as that of men and women and a whole host of -isms, I can testify that among all of my targets, blacks are the least thin-skinned. Though I have had trouble with a minority of black people who want to exercise thought control over blacks, they amount to a sect. No black person has tried to drive me out of business as the feminists have. No black group has called for a boycott of my books as feminists at the University of Louisiana at Baton Rouge did (the boycott collapsed because none of them had read my books).

The true thought police are corporate sponsors and a minority of men who control American public opinion. They are the ones who decide which op-eds are printed or the kind of slant that's to be placed on news involving blacks. Though they pretend that criticism of blacks is prohibited by political correctness, their publications and news and commentaries carry a steady stream of criticism of black behavior.

Even when certain outlets, such as National Public Radio, pretend to solicit a variety of viewpoints in the name of free speech, those black, brown, and yellow writers who do not adhere to politically correct views of race are excluded from the public discussion. For example, a few years ago, the senior editor of a well-known men's magazine approached me about doing an opinion column. I sent a tongue-in-cheek piece that argued that if street drug dealers were to be executed for their crimes, then upperclass money launderers should receive the same punishment. Not only did the editor turn down the piece; he sent a note to my agent, suggesting that black behavior was responsible for the drug crisis and that I was merely trying to make whites feel guilty. A few months after the letter was sent, President Bush and then drug czar William Bennett, who certainly can't be accused of desiring to make whites feel guilty, made the same proposal. (In 1992, U.S. Attorney for New York Robert Morganthau said, when bringing indictments against BCCI that the 35,000 arrests of New York street dealers that year were not as important as breaking up money laundering banks like BCCI. Though television networks run footage of black small-time drug dealers all day, seldom do they carry stories about money laundering, presumably because the banks are some of the principal stockholders of the networks.) Not content with merely reprimanding me with a note, the editor hired a black writer to challenge, out of context, a line that I'd written in a *Life* magazine piece that being a black man in the United States was like being a spectator at your own lynching. The black writer said that black men were lynching themselves, and that their problems were crime, drugs, and sex. (This was printed in an issue that carried a full-page photo of a nude woman in chains; about six months later, a woman sued the publisher, successfully, for holding her as a sex slave.)

This black writer, and the editor who hired him, are laboring under a misconception if they believe that drug addiction is a black problem exclusively. While the media bombards the public with images of black women as irresponsible cocaine mothers, statistics indicate that the white suburban rate for cocaine pregnancies is about the same as that in the inner city. According to a *New York Times* survey, the typical crack addict is a forty-year-old white male professional, married, and suburban. Cocaine addiction is a sizable problem on Wall Street, but stories about this white collar crime are usually carried on the business shows and not reported as news.

I wasn't surprised at the revelation that social problems are occurring in the white suburbs. I've been reading the fiction of white students for twenty years, and they paint a picture of the American suburban life where drug addiction, alcoholism, and fatherless homes are widespread. In most of these stories the father is missing or is, as one student wrote in a poem, "a tourist" in his own home. The son of an investment banker told me that he and his friends rarely see their parents, and that they spend their lavish allowances on drugs and alcohol. Even though studies show that white teenagers are more prone to drug abuse than black teenagers, the image of drugs as a black problem prevails, not only in the media, and political circles where the war on drugs means a war against black neighborhoods, but in the country's leading intellectual publications. One would think that intellectuals would inject a tone of reason into this public discussion, but, in the United States, the intelligentsia often sell their intellects to the highest corporate bidder.

In the old days, muckrakers like Lincoln Steffens used their talents to fight big steel, big oil, and big meat; today's intellectual goes after welfare mothers, the homeless, and the hungry. They might write an op-ed article justifying the murder by a vigilante of an unarmed homeless man. They might write a lengthy article opposing the distribution of food stamps or argue that poverty is often a lifestyle choice. They might hire out their talents to places like the Heritage Foundation or the American Enterprise Institute, outfits with apparently unlimited access to the television networks.

This group of think-tankers, op-eders, television commentators form the chief impediment to black progress. In the words of Carl Rowan, they have brilliantly used the media to "outpropagandize" the group whom they perceive as the enemy. Lacking the access to the media, those whom they target have little recourse to combat this propaganda. They are like the Bosnians trapped in a conflict with the Serbs, who have the arms and the ability to engage in a steady debilitating war.

When a *New York Times* reporter recently congratulated a prominent black woman for having the courage to air the dirty laundry of the black community, as though such laundry was unaired, I was wondering whether that reporter reads her own paper. The *New York Times* regularly prints front-page stories accompanied by pictures, associating blacks with spousal abuse, drugs, child abandonment, and illegitimacy. This coverage reached its *National Enquirer* low with the front-page photo of a black baby who'd been murdered by his parents after having been abused with a toilet plunger. This was rivaled by another front-page story in April 1993 about a black man murdering a white woman during a domestic dispute. Pictures of the couple were printed on the front page; the story jumped to the inside where it took up an entire page of the newspaper. Though editors at the *Times, New York* magazine, and producers of the network news shows feel their goods to be superior to tabloid shows like "Hard Copy," "Inside Edition," "A Current Affair," "Unsolved Mysteries," and "America's Most Wanted," I believe that these programs have more dignity since they're not prone to blaming everything on blacks.

When the *Times* is not maligning black character in print—Sam Roberts's column is a virtual sniper's nest against blacks—they do the job with pictures and Willie Horton-style layouts. For example, in Anne Matthews's *New York Times Magazine* article "Crime Turns the Campus into an Armed Camp," the victims of crime were represented by photos of white women and the group causing the problems, alcoholism, robbery, were represented by photos of black males and one Asian male. With this layout the *Times* was suggesting that if black and Asian males weren't on American campuses, campus crime would vanish.

This conclusion runs counter to a study aired on CNN, which reported that the typical perpetrator of campus crime is a nineteen-year-old white male. College presidents were accused of remaining silent about the crime situation as a way of staving off bad publicity. This response is typical of the way the media and other institutions deal with white pathology. Silence.

In the print and electronic media, pictures of blacks are associated with social pathology, while whites are represented as society's stewards. They are shown counseling and assisting blacks who mess up in other ways, or speaking on their behalf.

The coverage of whites by the media is similar to the plot of the movie *Grand Canyon.* Whites were born to prevent blacks and Latinos from getting into trouble, and Asian Americans are depicted as the group that blacks and Latinos ought to be like.

But according to Bill Ong Hing, a professor of Immigration Law at Stanford University, among Asian Americans, the Vietnamese have the fastest growing dropout rate in California.

Asian American intellectuals like Peter Kwong (*The New Chinatown*) and Ronald Takaki (*Strangers from A Different Shore*) and journalist William Wong complain about what they regard as the "model minority" stereotype, but their opinions are ignored by the very media that praise their groups for their devotion to the work ethic. Gwen Kinkead (*Chinatown, A Portrait of a Closed Society*) writes about a crime-infested community quite different from the one portrayed in publications such as the *New Republic* and the *National Review*. Chinese American gangs control 60 percent of New York's heroin trade—a fact that doesn't attract the attention of conservative writers who always lecture blacks about drug-related crime. When it comes to criminal gangs, however, the media and the segregated American opinion industry seem incapable of seeing any color other than black.

(Ironically, in the 1890s, when the Japanese were feared and hated, San Francisco papers designated blacks as the model minority. "The negro always takes an interest in every crop that he cultivates and he is more easily managed than the Japanese," editorialized the *San Francisco Chronicle* in 1897.)

Just as whites speak for blacks, they also speak for Asian Americans, thereby protecting white Americans from the harsh criticism of American society made by militant Asian American intellectuals. No one seems to care about what veteran dissident Frank Chin or a new generation of Chinese Americans like Hoyt Sze feel about issues such as assimilation. When Andrew Hacker wrote a typical why-can't-you-blacks-be-like-Asians article, Frank Chin wrote a reply to the *New York Review of Books*, which went unpublished. I published it in my magazine, *Konch*. Chin answered Hacker's argument that the "real and deep racial dilemma remains," because "whites feel blacks and others should adapt to white ways," an indirect blessing of Asian Americans who have, in the eyes of Hacker, Jim Sleeper, and others, done exactly that. Chin wrote: "Just because we read, write and speak your language as well as you do, Mr. Hacker, does not mean we believe your rhetoric, agree with your racist cowardice.... The Asian or black or any non-white 'model minority' Shangri-la people is a fiction, a product of white racist self-serving wishful thinking, not reality."

Chin's *The Year of the Dragon*, a play that was broadcast on the PBS network in the '70s, had the same effect on audiences as Richard Wright's *Native Son*. It showed white audiences Chinese tour guides smiling at them during their tours of Chinatown and pouring out their resentment in private. The four horsemen of Asian American literature, Jeffery Paul Chan, Frank Chin, Lawson Fusao Inada, and Shawn Wong wrote in the *Big Aiiieeeee,* a magazine they edit, "We began another year angry! Another decade, and another Chinese American ventriloquizing the same old white Christian fantasy of little Chinese victims of 'the original sin of being born to a brutish, sadomasochistic culture of cruelty and victimization' fleeing to America in search of freedom from everything Chinese and seeking white acceptance, and of being victimized by stupid white racists and then being reborn in acculturation and honorary whiteness. Every Chinese American book ever published in the United States of America by a major publisher has been a Christian autobiography or autobiographical novel." This sort of social protest makes contemporary conservative writings by the media-ordained black critics and writers seem tame.

Asian American militant writing is not the only minority writing, however, that criticizes white American society in an incisive manner. In fact, compared to other minority writers, blacks, no matter how militant, are in the political center. No black writer has challenged the values of white society as trenchantly as Leslie Silko, a Native American writer. Her book, *The Almanac of the Dead,* one of the most powerful novels ever written by an American, prophesies an apocalyptic doom for American Civilization, because of its atrocious treatment of Native Americans. In the novel, white serial murderers are guided by the voices of dead Native Americans, craving revenge. The same voices urge suburban whites to suicide and "accidental" death. By comparison James Baldwin's and Eldridge Cleaver's indictments of white society amount to little more than gentle nudging.

While Asian Americans are promoted as a model minority by an establishment media, their tangle of pathologies being virtually ignored, Latinos are all but invisible to the media. To show that another community is beset by problems, which in some ways are more devastating than those suffered by millions of blacks, is to challenge the notion that all other colored minorities can make it except for blacks. Latinos, suffer from poverty, high school dropout rates, and other problems that the media portray as peculiarly black problems. Writer Brent Staples was correct to point out that though "Gang Violence is often thought of as a black problem...Latinos lead the country in gang killings, with Asians tending toward extortion and theft."

An example of how Latino culture is viewed as one of invisibility can be seen in an exchange between Martin Peretz, editor in chief of the *New Republic,* and writer Nicolas Kanelos. In the June 5, 1989, issue of the *New Republic,* Martin Peretz wrote: "Let's imagine a literature professor designing a course in keeping with the new ideological marching orders. She chooses some black authors and is eager to bone up on some Hispanic ones from the United States, *especially if someone will tell her who they are* [my italics]. She also doesn't know the work of many Hispanic writers. But, then, who does?" (German critics like Gunther Lenz and English critics like Bob Lee, who are acquainted with American multicultural literature, must chuckle at this kind of remark.) Nicolas Kanellos answered Mr. Peretz in the 1989 issue of *Before Columbus Review:* "It is obvious that Mr. Peretz did not take the time to research and evaluate the history and accomplishments of the non-white American ethnic people—traditionally the 'other' in official American Civilization. Had he done so, he would have found out, for instance, that Hispanic letters north of the Rio Grande date back to 1598, with an epic poem on the colonizing of New Mexico, and, since then, thousands of volumes have been written, mostly in Spanish, but also in English (since the nineteenth century)."

Just as the yellow underclasses are ignored by the media, so are a prodigious number of white poor. Proportionate coverage of white poverty in America would make the story of blacks in America a triumph instead of the failure that the media focus upon. But white poverty isn't the only pathology in the tangle of pathologies one finds in white America. Instead of discussing these the media rarely mentions them.

Much of my data is garnered from the very newspapers and television news shows where think-tank operatives discuss crime, drugs, illegitimacy, and welfare as predominantly black problems. Even when a reporter on a news show presents the facts regarding a particular social malady—for example, that two-thirds of American welfare recipients are white and two-thirds reside in the rural areas of the United States—the pictures accompanying the narrative usually depict blacks.

The *New York Times,* for instance, which used pictures of two black men to accompany a story about child abandonment, presented a different picture when citing a serious study about the issue. The study, conducted by Frank Furstenberg and Kathleen Mullan Harris of the University of Pennsylvania, involved a representative sample of the population according to race, geography, income, and education. It concluded that "Although it has long been common knowledge that many poor children, especially those whose parents never wed, had little contact with their fathers, . . . the phenomenon of the disappearing father is alarmingly widespread."

Two-thirds of American children will spend a period of their lives in a single-parent household. Secretary of Health Louis Sullivan, a black member of the Bush cabinet, put the number at 60 percent. Clearly this is not a problem peculiar to the black community. With the rise of single-parent households and the United States's soaring divorce rate, child abandonment is an issue that cuts across racial and class lines. According to the American Association of Retired Persons, one-third of the women who get divorced are left in poverty. (In fact, the next time a conservative brings up black child abandonment to me I'm going to ask him when he last saw his children.) The media seldom mention the millions of white women—many of them middle class—on the dole as a result of being abandoned by their husbands. While poor black men are scolded in op-eds and by think-tank infotainers for abandoning their families (often the reason is because a woman cannot receive financial aid if there is a man in the household), the fact that middle-class and upper-class white men leave their wives and children in poverty receives little editorial comment. In relation to the entire U.S. population the proportion of white single mothers (37.9 percent in 1990) who live in poverty exceeds that for the entire black population (29.3 percent).

In addition, those who assert that the two-parent household is the solution to black poverty can't explain the fact that 50 percent of the children who live in poverty, live in two-parent homes located in rural and suburban America. A study conducted by Mary Jo Bane and David Ellwood of Harvard's Kennedy School of Government, and printed in *Science,* finds that "Half of America's poor children live in two-parent homes, often in suburban and rural areas," and concludes that "the key to understanding poverty lies, beyond an exclusive focus on the ghetto poor." Though the media portrays the urban environment as violent and the white suburbs as quiescent, battery in the home is the leading cause of injury of American women, and child abuse, committed by both men and women, also occurs in the home. This happens in equal proportions in the suburbs, rural areas, and the urban areas. Feminists may have a point when they say that the two-parent household may be the most dangerous place for a woman to be. That also goes for children.

Contrary to feminist propaganda, men aren't the only perpetrators of domestic violence. A report issued by Sheriff Sheman Block, dealing with child abuse in Los Angeles County, revealed that in 1991, for the first time, "mothers represented the greatest perpetrators of child abuse with 41 percent of the cases linked to mothers." Though the proportion of black children killed by parents and caretakers dropped, "the proportion of white victims jumped from 20 percent to 31 percent."

Responding to one of Alice Walker's frequently venomous attacks on black men, this time printed on the op-ed pages of the *New York Times*, May 5, 1993, Elaine Brown said that violence is frequently learned from the mother ("Mammy's not-so-nurturing switch"). Feminists like Cornel West and Henry Louis Gates Jr., who believe that critics of Alice Walker are "misguided," seem to be restricted by feminist ideology, for they rarely, if ever, comment on violence meted out by matriarchy. They would be hard pressed to explain why two-thirds of the rapists in the California prisons were abused by their mothers, according to *Gender Monthly*. West and Gates air their views about black misogyny in the *New York Times* where no ethnic group of men has been maligned for misogyny as much as black men. I know for a fact that letters to the *Times* about, for example, Italian American misogyny go unpublished. This is typical.

Violence isn't the only suburban problem. Dr. Arnold Washton, director of a New York treatment center, said that there are more crack addicts among white middle-class people than any other segment of the population "despite all of the poor black crack addicts you see on TV and Page One."

A study conducted by National Rural Development Institute contradicts the claims of Mr. Walter Goodman and others that the black urban underclass is our "least tractable social problem." It concluded that the social and economic strains facing rural children are every bit as bad, perhaps worse, than those facing city youth. Predictably, Goodman, a neoconservative, raises the issue of young unwed black women, regularly, in his *Times* column. While the rate of unwed black mothers is on the decline, the fastest rising rate of "illegitimacy" is among white women (who also have the highest percentage of cocaine pregnancies). According to the Children's Defense Fund, "two-thirds of the teens who give birth each year are white, and two-thirds do not live in big cities." So why are Mr. Goodman and other neoconservatives so concerned about unwed black women yet shun the problem of unwed and poverty-stricken white mothers? Is it because he believes that these black women are soaking up the welfare budget? This myth and others like it were ably refuted by black women scholars and professionals in an issue of the Nation that was aptly entitled "Scapegoating the Black Family."

Moreover, Terry K. Adams and Greg J. Duncan, in their study "The Persistence of Urban Poverty and Its Demographic and Behavioral Correlates," say that "Media images of urban poverty often present households headed by young, never married black women.... [D]ata show that this image does not fit most or even a substantial minority of the persistently poor living in urban areas." To argue that the fractured family exists only in the inner city is to engage in the worst kind of racially based hypocrisy. Indeed, one of the first novels written by a black author, William Wells Brown, dealt with Thomas Jefferson's fractured family.

Many of the new poor are white mothers who are either divorced or separated from their husbands. (Only 44 percent of the fathers who are obligated to pay child support actually do so, according to USA Today.) National Displaced Homemakers, an organization devoted to improving the circumstances of these impoverished women, reports that "[o]ne in five are living with unrelated people in doubled up households. Three quarters of the displaced household members, which rose from 13 million in 1987 to 15 million in 1989, are white." According to the American Association of Retired Persons, one third of divorced women live in poverty. Sometimes it seems that the only difference between a poor man not marrying a woman and leaving her broke and a middle-class and upper-class man marrying a woman and then leaving her broke is that the poor get chastised more by neoconservative columnists who ignore the delinquency of white men, some of whom belong to their class. For them to see the fractured family, in a country where almost half of the marriages end in divorce, as a peculiarly black phenomenon sounds racist.

Often, it seems that the media are willing to promote a racial war in America in order to boost their ratings. A sensational piece of bilge carried on CNN, April 24, 1993 was entitled "Mounting Urban Violence." The program showed blacks with guns as perpetrators of crimes and whites at shooting ranges preparing to defend themselves. Even though white-on-white crime involving guns is pervasive, rarely are whites as a group portrayed as violent people—this in spite of the fact that a study printed in the New York Times concluded that whites, among racial groups, are the ones most likely to engage in violence against all other groups, Asian Americans, African Americans, Latinos, gays, lesbians, Jews, pro-choice advocates, etc. Still, violence and drugs are perceived as black problems.

Typical was a story about violence printed in the Parade section of the *Sunday Examiner & Chronicle* entitled "Tame the Beast Inside." Accompanying this story about dealing with managing one's own "fear and rage," written by former world champion boxer Jose Torres, was a photo of black youth rioting in Los Angeles after the first Rodney King verdict. (Here again, the white and Latino participation in the riots has been removed.) In a sidebar eight teenagers were asked, "Why Is There So Much Violence?" All eight teenagers were black. Black kids are constantly associated with violence in the media.

After years of front-page pictures about black violence in inner-city schools, the *New York Times,* on April 21, 1993, quoted a justice Department report of 1989, which found "surprisingly little difference between cities, suburbs, and non-metropolitan areas in a number of measures of school violence." Yet even when the media does report stories of white violence the participants are often provided with excuses. For instance, a rise in battery against women that occurred in Alaska was blamed on male depression about unemployment that resulted from the Exxon oil disaster. The murder of a Little League baseball player by a youngster on a rival team was blamed on violence in adult sports. But the network news shows illustrated this story with pictures of black athletes fighting instead of showing white athletes engaged in brawls.

By offering justifications or explanations for this violence instead of condemning it, the news media and the neoconservative policy wonks often seem to be condoning it in a manner similar to how some members of the German government blame violence against foreigners on the foreigners. When a black man was murdered by a white mob in the Howard Beach section of New York City, a *New York Times* writer said that it was because whites were afraid of the underclass. When a trigger-happy white Louisiana suburbanite killed a visiting Japanese student, Yoshihiro Hattori, who had mistakenly knocked on the wrong door, NBC News said that the Japanese ought to learn slang so that they will understand what is meant by freeze.

Attacks upon Asian Americans by white individuals and mobs is on the rise. Vincent Chin, a Chinese American, was beaten to death because two white men mistook him for a Japanese. They were acquitted. On August 25, 1992, Milton Fujii, Japanese American director of community affairs for the University of California at Berkeley, was attacked by a left-wing white mob that mistook him for the Chinese American Chancellor, Chang-lin Tien, with whom they had a dispute. A member of the mob yelled at him, "Lock up the

Japanese. Intern the Japanese." Echoing the 1990 study that concluded that members of the white group are those most likely to assault members of all other groups, a study released in May of 1993 by Northeastern University's Center for Applied Social Research concluded that 60 percent of those who commit urban hate crimes are young white males.

Hundreds of thousands of women are raped each year by white males, but unlike some black urban males who assault women, these suburban males are neither referred to as "a bizarre new form of human" life by white writers like Pete Hamill, nor accused of lacking values by people like Joe Klein.

White suburban women who are tackled and pummeled by their drunken husbands on Superbowl Sunday must be shocked to hear that all of the violence in the United States takes place in the inner city. They are encouraged and glamorized by firearms organizations and the media when they arm against the black male underclass, but statistically they are most likely to have these weapons used against them by their boyfriends and husbands. The media also ignore the fact that with such weapons in the home gunshot wounds are the third leading cause of death of American children, black and white, and that 75 percent of suicides among men over age sixty-five between 1979 and 1988, according to the American Society on Aging, were from such firearms.

Though violence is stereotyped as a black issue, whites commit, according to the *Wall Street Journal,* 54 percent of all violent crimes, and the sharp increase in violent crime over the past decade has been the same among blacks and whites alike. Reporting the same facts on August 29, 1992, the FBI said that the rise in crime not only occurred among poor youths in urban areas, but "in all races, social classes, and lifestyles." Yet when CNN network carried the story, they used pictures of blacks only and virtually ignored the white perpetrators of violent crime, another example of how the media and the think-tank wonks protect whites. And when the Centers for Disease Control issues a report that "white teenagers have the fastest growing death rate [from gunshot wounds], up 24 percent a year from 1988–1990," this gets completely ignored by writers from *the Atlantic Monthly, Harper's, New York* magazine, the *New Republic,* the *McLaughlin Report,* and other infotainment outlets.

Claims made by journalist Jim Sleeper in an issue of *Tikkun* that crime is "heavily black" and urban, an attitude endorsed by Michael Kaus *(The End of Equality),* is contrary to conclusions of a Senate committee chaired by Joseph Biden, Jr., which described the increase of violent crime in the rural areas of the United States as "astonishing." "Most rural states—those with 50 persons or fewer per square mile—had greater increases in violent crime over the past year than did New York City," the Biden committee reported. Another Senate committee, chaired by Senator Herb Kohl, concluded that racial disparities in the criminal justice system account for the large number of incarcerated black youth, who are four times more likely to be incarcerated than whites who commit the same crime. Mr. Kaus, of all people, should know that the inner cities are not the only places where social pathology occurs. He grew up in Beverly Hills.

Though black ethnic character has been discussed in a negative fashion frequently in the print and electronic media, journalists, like the *Times* reporter who congratulated a black woman for courageously airing the dirty laundry of the black community, have a habit of hailing every new black-pathology author for "breaking the silence" or saying the "unspoken" about the root of problems in the black community. Rarely do the commentators who are on the payroll of these magazines comment about the social distress among the ethnic groups to which they belong. One wonders when black-pathology thinkers like Lee Eisenberg, Norman Podhoretz, Ben Wattenberg, Roger Rosenblatt, and the Jewish American commentators who lined up behind Anita Hill are going to "break the silence" about the pathological violence among Jewish Americans, which, according to Barbara Harris, executive director of the Transition Center, a kosher shelter for battered women and children in Queens, New York, exists in over 10 percent of Jewish American homes.

"Nobody likes to talk about it because Jews as a group take a lot of pride in looking good," explains Julie Spitzer, associate rabbi at Baltimore Hebrew Congregational and author of *Spousal Abuse in Rabbinic and Contemporary Judaism* (1985). "We live with so many myths. Jewish families are not supposed to be dysfunctional, and Jewish husbands are supposed to be, by definition, nurturing," Sherry Berliner Dimarsky, executive director of SHALVA (Safe Homes Advice and Legal Aid for Victims of Abuse) was quoted as saying in the winter issue of *Lilith* magazine. Don't feminists at *Ms.* magazine, NPR, and the *Village Voice* who have made black misogyny into a fetish care about what happens to Jewish American women? Why doesn't Ted Koppel do an edition of "Nightline" about the subject? He could invite Mickey Kaus on to give his opinions. What about the *New Republic, Harper's, the New York Times Magazine*? Walter Goodman? Why haven't they addressed the problem of the Jewish American dysfunctional family?

Members of the Jewish American group are not the only ones who have a stake in looking good. Mary Sansome, of the Congress of Italian American Organizations, says that she has a difficult time obtaining funds for Italian Americans because the government and city agencies feel there's no need. When is the last time that black underclass theorist Ken Auletta commented on the Italian American underclass?

As long as some ethnic groups continue to hide their underclass for fear of looking bad, a true picture of the American underclass will never emerge, and blacks will continue to be scapegoated by opportunists out to make a quick buck, or to enhance some career move, or to hype ratings and newsstand sales.

Irish American writer Pete Hamill's scolding of black Americans in *Esquire* included only sixteen lines about the white underclass. Unlike many black-pathology writers, he at least admits that it exists but says that it's been contained. Contained? A study released in October 1992 by the Center on Budget and Policy Priorities disagrees with Hammill's throwaway line. While the increase among black and Latino poor rose 22 percent each between 1989 and 1991, whites accounted for 51 percent of the increase. "Half of the nation's 35.7 million poor people are non-Hispanic whites and recent poverty trends among this group have not been encouraging. Nevertheless, poverty among non-Hispanic whites has received scant attention in recent years. Many Americans think of the poor as being predominantly members of minority groups, and poverty debates in this country frequently become ensnared in controversies about race and ethnicity," the report concluded.

Organized crime, which includes Irish American, Italian American and Jewish American members, is expanding its influence in American society by taking over businesses, unions, and other legitimate segments, as well as continuing to participate in the kind of professional violence that amateurish black muggers and crackers don't have the sophistication or the equipment to create. Commented Rudolph W. Giuliani, United States attorney in Manhattan, "if we take back the labor unions, the legitimate businesses, eventually they become just another street gang. Spiritually, psychologically, they've always been just a street gang."

Not only does organized crime, a coalition of mostly white ethnics, earn tax-free revenue in the hundreds of billions of dollars; it also influences foreign policy. Yet, concluded Hamill in his *Esquire* article "Breaking The Silence" (March 1988), the black underclass is a greater threat to our national security than the Russians. What a preposterous conclusion. It's ironic that the same claim was made by Irish-pathology writers only two generations ago.

The claim that white ethnics made it to the suburbs from Ellis Island solely through legitimate hard work and traditional values is just a Reaganite, Fourth of July lie. In his book *The Rise and Fall of the Jewish Gangster in America*, Albert Fried wrote, "It is no secret that Jewish criminals did what others did before them and have continued to do, that they all have used crime as another way of moving upward and onward in the American manner. First the Irish . . . ; then the Jews and the Italians; and now, presumably, the Blacks and Hispanics and the Chinese too have successively climbed the same queer ladder."

One could argue, however, that blacks were never able to accumulate as much profit from the underground economy as the white underclass because of racism, even when it came to exploiting their own neighborhoods. The movie *The Cotton Club*, written by Irish American William Kennedy, is about the Irish and Jewish underclass fighting for domination over the multibillion dollar Harlem policy racket. Ted Robert Gurr, professor of political science at the University of Colorado, has written, "From the 1840s to the end of large-scale European immigration after 1918, each new wave of immigrants—Irish, Germans, Italians—added disproportionately to crime and mayhem in our cities." The fact that Hamill lectured the black underclass for its pathologies and devoted only sixteen lines to a far more lethal white underclass, and none to other nonwhite underclasses, could be considered racist. Yet Eisenberg, in his sensational flame-throwing and irresponsible introduction to Hamill's article, said that anybody who opposed Hamill's arguments is a racist ideologue.

Hamill's criticisms of the black underclass have been made about some Irish Americans, the group to which Hamill and William Buckley and Moynihan belong. Hamill, who apparently agrees with William Buckley that blacks are heavily into drugs and illegitimate children, ignored the fact that this is the same stereotypical charge made against the Irish, only in this case the drug is alcohol, which is responsible for many more pathologies—such as wife abuse and vehicular homicide—than drugs. As for illegitimacy, Bob Callahan, author of *The Big Book of the American Irish*, points to the stereotype that the typical Irish American was a person with thirty-five children that he couldn't support, all of whom were headed for the poor house. As for crime, Callahan remembers growing up in a New England in the 1930s and 1940s where the newspapers separated information about "American Crime" from "Hibernian Crime."

While some blacks may enter a career of street crime (just as some Irish American gangs like the Westies), Irish Americans are now more associated with white collar or government crime, particularly pertinent when you consider that the last presidential administration included Irish Americans in key posts and was one of the most scandal-laden in history. According to Callahan, all the pathologies on Moynihan and Hamill's list exist in the Irish American community.

In a recent PBS documentary series, "Crime, Inc.," "hundreds" of people, far more than those who are being murdered in Washington, D.C. and Los Angeles, were murdered in the streets of New York as "underclass" Irish American, Jewish American, and Italian American gangs fought over the spoils of the bootlegging racket. But white gang activity isn't merely a thing of the past. It exists today. Martin Sanchez Jankowski (*Islands in the Street: Gangs and American Urban Society*) discusses the existence of white gangs. Such gangs, however, rarely, if ever, show up in the discussions of social pathology by professional intellectuals. For example, the most violent gang of the last twenty years, according to the New York City police, was not a black or Hispanic gang but the Westies, an Irish American gang, whose activities are explored by T.J. English (*The Westies*). According to English, the Westies were "the most brutal men this violent nation has ever seen." I've never heard such Irish American critics of blacks as Charles Murray, William F. Buckley or Pete Hamill discuss the Westies or even acknowledge the fact that close to 100,000 illegal Irish immigrants reside in Northern California, some of whom are blackmailed by their employers into working for sub-minimum wages.

If Pete Hamill, author of *Letter to a Black Friend,* thinks it's a good idea for black middle-class people to return to the ghettos to aid their "underclass" brothers and sisters, then why isn't it a good idea for Mr. Hamill to relocate to South Boston or the Bronx to aid the Irish American "underclass"? Hamill went so far as to suggest that some kind of genetic mutation, a "bizarre new form of life" explained crime in the inner city. Yet when William A. Tatum was slated to become the editor of the racebaiting and inflammatory *New York Post,* Hamill compared Tatum's coverage of Jews with that of the Nazi magazine, *Die Sturmer's.* I thought that was ironic, since casting unpopular minorities as "animals" (Hamill's word for inner-city youth) and as members of a separate species was *Die Sturmer's* trademark.

Doesn't Hamill care about the suffering of millions of Irish Americans? Don't Ben Wattenberg, Nathan Glazer, and others care about the Jewish

American underclass? During David Dinkin's first political campaign for mayor, he said that 44,000 Jewish Americans live in poverty in New York City alone. Don't the people at the *New Republic* or the *New York Review of Books* consider the plight of impoverished Jewish American senior citizens in Florida to be worthy of some of the space it devotes to denouncing black culture and values? The attitudes of some white ethnic critics of black behavior could be considered hypocritical. I asked a young white critic and friend, who was accosting me at a Cambridge party about my misogyny, what he was doing to alleviate the suffering of thousands of women who belong to his particular ethnic group—Polish American women. He said that he didn't identify with them. Why don't the critics of black culture and behavior identify with the less fortunate members of their groups? Why doesn't William Buckley, Jr., do a special broadcast of "Firing Line" from Appalachia to highlight the suffering and impoverishment of thousands of Irish Americans who live there?

As I began to accumulate more material, I discovered that even I had succumbed to myths about the black community.

I grew up in petit bourgeois surroundings where people were not just devoted to the work ethic but were members of a virtual work cult. My late stepfather is regarded as a saint because he worked hard all of his life, rarely missing a day. He became a devoted patriot and church worker because American society had rewarded him, he believed, for his hard work. (But even with his capabilities, he wasn't offered the job of plant foreman at Chevrolet until a few years before his retirement. He blamed the fact that he had been passed over for the job on racism. When they approached him about the job, he told them, bitterly, to give it to his sons.) A childhood friend of mine who was recently killed in an automobile accident is regarded as a martyr because his death occurred when he fell asleep at the wheel, while driving to a second job. Among the people whom I grew up around, people who are seldom featured by the media, working with your hands was considered more difficult and honorable than working with your head. The moral exemplars in our community were those who put in a lot of overtime. Welfare cheaters and idlers were spoken of in less than endearing terms. I was influenced by these values, but upon closely examining the attitudes of my relatives and their friends and even myself toward those less fortunate, I realized that some of these attitudes were in fact based upon myths.

Shortly after my stepfather died an excruciating death—a man who was married to the same woman for thirty-seven years and who left a will assuring that she would live the rest of her days in comfort, a man who taught Sunday school for thirty years—I heard a black-pathology hustler whose career has been advanced by his loud and ugly denouncement of black leaders and black people talk about a "poverty of values" within the inner city. I thought of the millions of black people who, like my father, and my childhood friend, pay their dues, only to be smeared by show-boating media hotdogs out to make a quick buck as opinion makers. I think that if I had found myself face to face with this man, at that moment, I would have punched him out, even though I'm not a violent man. But this man, and others like him, have generous access to a media that shuts most blacks, Latinos, and other minorities out.

The lack of minority representation in the media for me was exemplified during an exchange between George Will and Sam Donaldson on an edition of "This Week with David Brinkley." Donaldson asked Will how the black community felt about a certain subject. If George Will is a spokesperson for blacks in the media, then black people are really in trouble. This is a man who described the racist reaction to the Goetz shooting of four unarmed black men as "healthy," and the shooting down of an unarmed Iranian airbus, deliberately, by American forces, as "ethical."

After I began to collect and examine material I began to notice that the media, even a place like National Public Radio, had accepted the corporate think tankers' "underclass" theory of America's social problems, that is, that a majority of America's social problems were related to the personal behavior of black people. NPR's Daniel Zwerdling's coverage of Africa, shuttling back and forth between Kenya and Liberia, consisted of dishing up the most sensational and ghoulish stories for the entertainment of his upscale audience. His negative report on Zambia, aired on May 9, 1993, was typical. Journalists should cover corruption in Kenya, but that's all we get from them. Lurid stories with hints of cannibalism. African journalists complain that the American media only cover the basket cases of the continent and never mention the role that the United States and the Soviet Union played in creating those basket cases. The civil wars, the arms race, and other problems that ravage the continent. Listening to NPR's Africa coverage, you wouldn't know that there are fifty countries in postcolonial Africa.

I began to tape news shows and commentaries. One particularly shocking to me was a commentary by Roger Rosenblatt, of the "MacNeil/Lehrer News Hour," during which the black youth involved in the Central Park rape of a young stockbroker were used to smear all black youth, whose activities were equated with Satanism.

After examining all of this evidence, which clearly showed that the media was scapegoating blacks, and occasionally Latinos, for America's problems, I talked about my frustration during a panel held by Bumbershoot, an annual Seattle Arts Festival. I casually mentioned that maybe there should be a boycott of television network news, as a way of highlighting the abuses of blacks and Latinos by network news. I was not prepared for the enthusiastic response. The summer before the Seattle festival, I had gathered some young black professionals to show them the Roger Rosenblatt tape, which, for me, was the last straw.

They were interested in organizing a boycott against network television news, but their interest didn't survive one meeting. After I returned from Seattle, I asked novelist Floyd Salas, president of PEN Oakland, whether he would appoint me to head a committee that would organize a one-month boycott against television network news. Salas not only agreed, but it was largely due to his efforts, along with Claire Otalda, and Gregory Nicosia, that, despite opposition from some members of PEN West, a resolution was finally passed at the PEN International conference, at Rio, in 1992.

I contacted writers, scholars, and artists and, with very little cash, PEN Oakland and the Before Columbus Foundation sponsored town meetings, panel sessions, and poetry and fiction readings, to deal with the lack of balance in images of blacks and Latinos. These meetings took place in ten cities. By coincidence, I was asked to write a piece for the op-ed page of the *New York Times*. I told the editor about the boycott and asked whether this would be a suitable subject for an op-ed. "Why Boycott TV Network News," in which I announced the PEN Oakland Boycott and the reasons for it, was published in the *New York Times*. The response to the article far exceeded my expectations.

The PEN Oakland post office box was flooded with mail. The boycott tapped into black, Latino, and even white anxiety about media coverage of blacks and Latinos. The *New York Times* critic Walter Goodman, who believes that dysfunctional families are the reason that blacks don't prosper (but can't seem to explain the material success of thousands of dysfunctional white families), accused us of "frightening network executives" in an April 14, 1991, column entitled "Drawbacks to a Boycott of TV Network News." I answered Mr. Goodman with "Blaming Everything on Blacks," an abbreviated version of which was published in the *Oakland Tribune*. Goodman accused me of desiring Affirmative Action quotas when I pointed out how pictures—such as those broadcast on the "MacNeil / Lehrer News Hour" to accompany the

Rosenblatt commentary—frame black people for social pathologies that are widespread in American society. But the tapes, and other data that I have accumulated, provide irrefutable evidence that such is the case.

Some of this may be due to the fact that some TV news film crew personnel, from my experience at least, are more to the Right than the reporters. For instance, after I was taped for an NBC News network show in 1989, the cameraman began to taunt me about crack, illegitimacy among young black women, and so on. When I informed him that the typical person involved in such behavior was white, a spirited discussion ensued that spilled out onto my front porch. The last thing I said to him was that his network, NBC, with CNN, is a major contributor to myths that all antisocial behavior is black. (Ironically, six months after PEN Oakland's first annual boycott of network news shows, a NBC network representative contacted me about sharing some of my documentation with them. Their representative seemed surprised that rural youth suffer more, using all of the indexes, than urban youth. NBC never reimbursed me for the cost of faxing my research to them.)

Mr. Goodman is one of a number of reporters and columnists at the *New York Times* who are disciples of Moynihanism. Like the religious fundamentalists who, incidentally, are also ridiculed and grossly caricatured in the *Times*, they refuse to entertain any facts that would dispute the dogma. If, as Sam Roberts claims, Daniel Moynihan showed "courage" when he predicted the rising proportion of single-parent households in the black community, did Moynihan's inability to predict the rapid rise in white illegitimate births show a lack of courage? Though underclass activities exist in yellow, white, and brown communities, the *Times* hasn't assigned a Sam Roberts to monitor those as much as blacks are monitored.

In his reply, Goodman also mentioned that the number of blacks engaged in these activities is disproportionate to their numbers in the population. I'm not so sure. Take crime for example. Some studies assert that whites commit crimes in the same proportion as blacks, but because of racist practices in the criminal justice system, blacks get arrested more. Sheriff Michael Hennessey blamed the fact that African Americans make up nearly half of the San Francisco County jail population on "institutional racism.... The lopsided numbers.... are an indictment of our society's priorities and its inability to create equal justice under the law," he said.

For our first boycott we were able to assemble a coalition unheard of in these days of division and polarization. Buddhists in Boulder, Colorado; blacks and whites; Latinos in Houston, Texas, and New York; gays and lesbians; integrationists in Berkeley, California, and nationalists in Atlanta, Georgia. Writers in Boston, Brooklyn, New Orleans, Washington, D.C., and Detroit. During some of the events, writers addressed the stereotypes of African Americans, Latinos, and Asian Americans that pour into the nation's living rooms each night; others concentrated on specific shows. Boycott Coordinator Professor Eugene Redmond's East St. Louis group responded to what African Americans of that city considered to be an unfair and biased portrait of East St. Louis that appeared on CBS's "Sixty Minutes."

Of the Oakland kickoff event, *Oakland Tribune* columnist Alix Christie noted that "two hours of poems, songs and appeals by Blacks, Whites, Latinos, and Asians" dealt with the "exclusion of a diversity of viewpoints from television news." She hailed it as "the truest town meeting I've seen."

The applause in Seattle that greeted my suggestion that a boycott take place was not the only surprise in store for me during my organizing activities: In a one-hour exchange with phone-in participants on Jay Marvin's WTKN radio show in Tampa, Florida, even the right-wing callers agreed that the picture of African Americans on television is not balanced.

Representatives of the networks who were asked by reporters to respond to PEN Oakland's complaints agreed that there is a problem, but their explanations for the problems were not, in my opinion, convincing. Answering the issues raised by PEN Oakland's boycott on National Public Radio, ABC's ombudsman said that ABC television news merely "reflected reality" because "crime, poverty, and violence are urban problems." When challenged by Washington drug policy experts, who'd been invited to appear on the show by Bill Drummond, of the University of California at Berkeley's School of Journalism, he had to back down. CNN's Ted Turner and Steve Haworth said that black faces go with drug stories on their network "because they rely upon local police forces when busts are going to be made, and don't get calls saying there's going to be a bust of a high school in a white neighborhood." Home Box Office did a feature called "Crack USA" and apparently had no difficulty in locating a number of white crack faces.

In September 1991, CNN aired a series called "Black Men in Crisis." Its simplistic conclusion was that black men in Atlanta commit crime out of "boredom" and "impulse." A psychiatrist was brought on to give the conclusion a predictable neoconservative sound bite. He said that all of their problems came not from unemployment, poverty, and racism but from "inside" of them. I've never seen any of the networks do a long-distance psychoanalysis of white and Asian ethnic criminals who commit far more profitable crimes.

Nor have I seen any of the white males, whose inside trading crimes threaten the foundation of the capitalistic society, brought onto the couch. The following year, Larry Woods, the commentator on "Black Men in Crisis," travelled to the Midwest to do a show that represented blonde, hard-working farmers as the salt of the earth.

Don Browne, executive director of NBC News, said finally, in response to the boycott, that the best way to avoid negative stereotypes is to hire more black journalists, editors, and producers. A move I would applaud. If, since that date, NBC has hired more minorities, it certainly doesn't seem to have affected their nightly news programming.

The most thorough response to our boycott was made by the San Francisco ABC affiliate. During a lengthy feature about the boycott, KGO-TV agreed that television news reports unfairly focus on blacks in drug stories and furnished statistics and graphs to show the lack of minority hiring by the news media. Now "ABC World News Tonight" might even show a white cocaine infant from time to time. But in a series called "The American Agenda," their use of disproportionately black images to go with "social pathologies" is no different from that of the other television networks. Toward the end of 1992, "The America Agenda" report on heroin addiction showed blacks, exclusively. This integrated staff should be informed that members of yellow and white ethnic groups are the ones who drive the heroin market, not blacks.

If I have a beef about newspaper coverage I can always write a letter. And the newspapers, to their credit, often publish stories that indicate that some of their emotional and sensational op-ed writers and columnists occasionally do push myths about minorities ("The Mythology of Black Violence in America," "Myths of the Black Underclass," "Negative Stereotypes About Welfare Recipients," and "Crack Is Not a Black Monopoly," are among the clippings that I possess.) And local television stations usually include community programs that are moderated by blacks, Latinos, and Asian Americans. Radio stations include call-in programs that are as close to participatory democracy as you're likely to get from the electronic news. The network news organizations, however, provide no opportunity for critics to challenge their news stories. With the elimination of the Fairness Doctrine, the networks are not even obligated to provide equal tinie to opposing viewpoints.

This arrogance is a danger for the future of democracy. The exclusion of a variety of viewpoints from the black, Latino, and Asian communities and the inability of members of those communities to respond to unbalanced images amounts to censorship. Moreover, health professionals are beginning to cite these images as contributing causes of the lack of self-esteem among minority youth. In the July 17,1989, *New York Times,* Dr. John T. Chissell said that this condition is partially brought on by the images of themselves that they see in the media.

I announced the second boycott in New York Newsday on August 31, 1992. In addition to the cities that were included in the first boycott, Philadelphia and New York were added for the second.

The networks responded to our first boycott by agreeing that some of our charges about the coverage of blacks and Latinos were true. We'd caught them by surprise. By October 1992, however, they were ready for us. They stonewalled. Replying to reporter Lynda Seaver, who confronted the networks with our charges, spokespersons for CBS, NBC, and CNN all stood behind their reporting. Roy Brunett, manager of communications for CBS News in New York, said: "We cover minority issues fairly and we take great pains to make sure we don't single out any one group." Ha! NBC was defended by Heather Allen, the West Coast bureau chief in Los Angeles. She said that NBC had created the Women in Minorities Task Force to monitor nightly newscasts and magazine shows aired by the network. The task force, which is made up of African and Asian Americans, Hispanics, gays, and lesbians, concluded, she said, that "there is a fair mix." But on May 30, 1993, the NBC network did yet another story about teenage pregnancy in which all of the pictures were of black women, promoting the canard that it is a black problem. The response to our second boycott indicates that the networks have decided to satisfy the growing and angry complaints about their coverage of blacks, Latinos, and others, by policing themselves. Even Walter Goodman said of the boycott that "there are not many other ways that viewers can express dissatisfaction with what shows up on the tube."

We live in a country where General Electric, which sponsors one of the chief outlets for anti-black propaganda, "NBC News," has been in trouble with the law more times than your average mugger. Gerry Spence, citing a Bureau of National Affairs estimate, writes in his book *With Justice for None: Destroying an American Myth* that "the cost of corporate crime in America is over ten times greater than the combined larcenies, robberies, burglaries, and auto-thefts committed by individuals. One in five of America's large corporations has been convicted of at least one major crime or has paid civil penalties for serious misbehavior." The reason that we hear less about the underclass behavior of corporate suite gangs who do more damage to the society than street gangs is because they provide the revenue that keeps big-business, television on the air. I suggested in the *Nation* that the way the Crips and the Bloods (Los Angeles gangs) could improve their image is by sponsoring television network news so that their underclass activities will never be mentioned.

Up to now, only the dirty laundry of the black community has been hung in public. The Crips and the Bloods side of the story. In order to free American society of its social secret—secrets which condemn millions to suffer in silence—it's time for us to let it all hang out. We also need to challenge the obsolete and unscientific blame-the-victim explanation of America's racial crisis. We need to encourage a new consensus that is not based upon fear, myth and hunger for ratings and profits, or upon some upscale opinion merchant's ambition, or the need to build the self-esteem of whites by promoting the disesteem of blacks and others, but a consensus that is built upon reason and probity.

PRESENT in the Shee Atika Hotel's Haida suite that night in March 1979 were Jack Barry of the *Portland Oregonian,* Nelson Frank, president of the Shee Atika Corporation, Loren Sanderson, executive director of the Haida Corporation, Tom Abel, director of the Craig Community Association, Bob Callahan, executive director of the Turtle Island Foundation, and me, a child of asphalt in Alaska. Frank, Sanderson, and Abel were Haida Indians. Abel, with his dark, handsome face, raven black hair which reached the nape of his neck, the top framed by a band, resembled the kind of Indian you see in the movies who tells Cochise that he's a fool for believing in the white man's treaty.

Shee Atika had been hit with a lawsuit by the Sierra Club, threatening to send Shee Atika into debt and its thriving multimillion dollar hotel into receivership. I couldn't believe my ears. Wasn't the Sierra Club those gentle folk who published arty nature books? I had read somewhere that the Club was "tough" and "mean," "an outfit that always goes for the groin," but dismissed these statements as complaints by enemies of the environment. Waterfalls. Fish jumping. Grass as green as that in a Salem cigarette ad. These were people who tramped about loaded down with backpacks, and were concerned about the whales.

If the Sitka Tlingits, the Alaska Indians who ran the Shee Atika Corporation, were in a battle with the Sierra Club, they had their work cut out for them. Its lobbyists displayed all the zeal of those people who push roses on you in airports. The Club had millions of dollars at its disposal; all the Sitkas had was borrowed money, borrowed time, and lots of heart.

At issue in the controversy was a magnificent piece of land within a 50-mile radius of Sitka, called Admiralty Island. The Sierra Club was upset and expressed its objection in a lawsuit against the government and Shee Atika, claiming that Admiralty Island held the largest population of brown bears in North America and the largest population of eagles in the world. They felt any development would harm the Island as an "ecosystem." During my early questioning of the Sierra Club spokespersons, it occurred to me that they were more concerned with the implications of the lawsuit for the animals than for the Indians.

The whole affair had a divisive effect on the Tlingit tribe. It had divided the Sitka Tlingits from the Angoon Tlingits. The Angoons had been promised that if they sided with the Sierra Club's position, they would be given subsistence and recreational rights to the Island.

Now the court battle had shifted to Congress. A bill written by Congressmen Morris Udall and Presidential candidate John Anderson and supported by the Sierra Club and the Carter Administration would preserve Admiralty Island as a national monument and prohibit development. A competing bill, the Breaux-Dingell-Huckaby bill, would open Admiralty Island to multiple land use and development as well as for recreation and subsistence. This bill was supported by the Sitkas. The House passed the Udall-Anderson bill in May, which the Sitkas blamed on environmentalist pressure. The Sierra Club, they claimed, had turned the debate into an environmentalist rally.

This was my third trip to Alaska and the second to Sitka. In between the trips to Sitka, I had traveled to Anchorage for a poetry reading. On the morning of my departure, I learned that a corporation I'd formed had been handed over to some squatters by a cowpoke, hanging Oakland judge who should have been retired to Orange County 20 years ago. This decision effectively killed the corporation since the officers the judge awarded it to were incapable of producing a product; the judge was fully aware of this when he made the decision. Meditating on the lakes and mountains, the hundreds of miles of ice below—17,000 square miles of Alaska is ice—dissolved my troubles, the way the blues do. When I did see a village, buried near the coast, the main streets were waterways. The land I'd come from had been "developed." The land below was as hostile to man as a puma.

Anchorage is what rock and roll would be like if it were a city, with jalopy airplanes rattling across the sky. It's a city of contradictions. A totem pole next to a hamburger stand . . . . a disco named Moby Dick . . . mountains tinted with amber. You leave a party at 11 P.M. and it looks like noon outside. I saw

Richard Pryor appear in "Silver Streak" while in Anchorage. When Pryor replied to the villainous art dealer, "Don't call me nigger," and shoved a gun in his face, the entire audience cheered. And I was the only black in the theater.

As we neared Sitka, finally, Jim Pepper, a jazz musician who was traveling with us, told some jokes. What happens to a polar bear who sits on the ice too long? He gets polaroids. Later, at the Shee Atika hotel, Pepper's drummer, whom they called the Tasmanian Devil, said that he was so hungry he could eat a whale's ass.

After dinner, I wanted to talk about Raven myths, but Andy Hope, who ran Shee Atika, wanted to talk about Cecil Taylor and Sonny Rollins. His interests were international and multicultural. Perhaps that's one of the reasons his corporation includes Eskimos, Athapascans, Aleuts, and Tlingits. But there was no compromise. So Hope went home to watch the Michigan State-Indiana State basketball game and Callahan and I went downstairs to the banquet hall to hear Pepper play some Ornette Coleman and John Coltrane. As a child, Jim Pepper traveled with Sophie Tucker, performing "Indian dances." He became interested in jazz after hearing Charlie Parker when Pepper was fifteen years old. He expounds on such subjects as the influence of Afro-American music upon Cree music. In the banquet room I observed the Tlingits watching the whites discoing in their dining room. But that's only part of this story.

Callahan and I went back to the Haida suite where the Tlingits and the Haidas had come to tell us their story. Callahan and the Haidas got into it quickly.

The last time the Irish and Haidas squared off, both were carrying rifles, Callahan explained. He later accused me of egging the Indians on. Afterwards, he told me jokingly that he was going to get a bunch of white people together and do to me what the Indians and I had done to him. All I had said was that with trillions of dollars in sales, the Fortune 500 corporations, all but one owned and managed by white men, were squatting up the resources of the United States, and that this prodigious gouging was causing blacks, whites, women, the middle class, and the lower class to war among themselves for the scraps, for squatters rights. I said that this powerful class of white men constituted a feudalistic Romanov class, and when they attempted to justify their control over vast resources they often used arguments which sounded similar to the Romanov's appeal to divine rights. The rest of us lacked "qualifications." We didn't meet their "standards."

Callahan argued that it was too simple to blame it on race and gender, that it was dangerous to view Europe as a monolith. He said that the same generals employed to fight the Indians in New England were first used to fight the Irish in Ireland, because the Irish were also a colonized people. Callahan said that the man who designed the first Indian reservation in New England had originally designed one for the English to hold the Irish in Ulster; he argued that the Irish came here because they were homeless and that the South got the idea of plantations from those the English had set up in Ireland.

I told Callahan that I didn't mean the Irish when I referred to the Romanov class of white males who controlled the country. I was talking about people who had cut their ties with whatever ethnic groups they had emerged from and were merely faceless, anonymous men for whom the corporation was the only nation they swore allegiance to; the corporation was their religion, their impersonal god.

Callahan said that blacks would probably do the same thing if they had power. At first I agreed, but upon further reflection it occurred to me that whites do a hell of a lot better under black rule than blacks do under white rule. I mean, you don't see whites sweeping the streets of Accra or Nairobi the way you see blacks doing the trash trades in Paris and New York.

I said that political systems really didn't mean that much because white men of the left and right behaved the same way when their interests and control were threatened. Herbert Hill, former labor secretary of the NAACP, said that he had more trouble dealing with labor over black jobs than with management.

Callahan said that a black Ph.D. was probably better off than he was. I answered that a dead black Ph.D. is just another dead nigger to the highway patrolman who shot him because he thought the Ph.D. was pulling a gun when he reached into the glove compartment for his registration. The victim's gun, of course, is never found.

The Haidas agreed with me.

This discussion took place a few weeks before the Oakland police, with guns drawn, burst into the office of the NAACP. Oakland has a black mayor, but he's like Bishop Abel Muzorewa; he can't do nothin' about it.

The argument continued over drinks, at times with raised voices. The Tlingits complained that the Haidas hadn't invested in the hotel as they promised, and the Haidas complained that the Tlingits had treated them as inferiors, and told Polish jokes about them.

The Haidas, according to the Sitka Tlingits, migrated to Alaska later and were given the permission to settle by the Tlingits. Finally, Callahan acquitted himself quite well. In fact, he got in the last word. "All nations are full of shit," he said. That was followed by a long silence. Callahan and the Haidas went off to the bar to continue the discussion. The next morning I had scheduled an interview with some of the Tlingit leaders to discuss the Sierra Club suit and their quest for land on Admiralty Island. I went to bed.

What am I doing writing about Native-Americans? Why ain't I in my place? Harper's wanted stories from me about education, race, crime. Why ain't I doing that? I could claim my Native American heritage. Native-Americans are always pointing this out. I was once in a motel room during a conference at Ellensburg, Washington, when a Euro-Iroquois writer and publisher tried on a headdress. Phil George, a poet, dancer, and descendant of Chief Joseph, put the headdress on me. "That's more like it," he said.

There is evidence of cooperation and cohabitation between Africans and Native-Americans in the Americas. One could even say that the first 300 years of Afro-European history in America were spent in bed. That's why it's about 300—some say 50,000 years—too late to talk about a pure race, the subject of quack discussions in newspapers and magazines these days. The Americas are creole from the Arctic ocean to the bottom of Argentina. President Andrew Johnson wrote of traveling through the postwar ghettoes of Tennessee and not being able to tell what was what, the black mothers had so many white-appearing children at their apron strings. In the Alabama Beacon, June 14, 1845, there appeared an ad asking for information on (the whereabouts of a runaway: "She is as white as most white women, with straight light hair, blue eyes, and can pass herself for a white woman."

There was an instance of the Seminole Chief fighting the American officials for the return of his captured black woman. Jim Beckworth, a black, fought on the side of the Crow Indians.

There have also been instances of friction and exploitation between blacks and the Native-Americans as well. The Cherokee owned black slaves. Buffalo soldiers, called that by Native-Americans because of their curly hair, did their patriotic bit in exterminating Native-Americans, but at the same time Native-Americans shot at anybody who came over the Rockies, black or white. Still, Native-Americans and blacks have more in common than both groups have with Euro-Americans. For example, they have the same national enemies. When American historians get nostalgic they think of Teddy Roosevelt. But Roosevelt aroused the enmity of blacks for his role in the Brownsville, Texas, riots which erupted when black troops became outraged at the treatment accorded them by their fellow soldiers and townspeople. Roosevelt gave the black soldiers dishonorable discharges. Roosevelt was also a well-known Indian hater. A relative, Franklin Roosevelt, wanted Japanese-American soldiers kept out of his sight—and guarded by shotgun—when he visited a World War II army camp. Black historians claim that the first Roosevelt didn't charge up San Juan Hill until black troops who captured it told him the coast was clear.

I always wondered why the Yorktown Bund exhibited huge posters of Jefferson and Washington at their Nazi rallies. I was a victim of that form of indoctrination we refer to as "the public school system," with its patriotic debriefing sessions during which we were told that George Washington, a slaver whose father's name in Sioux means "destroyer of Indian villages," never lied.

Native-American historians accuse Arthur Schlesinger, Jr., of omitting any reference to the Trail of Tears of the Cherokee Nation in his Pulitzer Prize-winning *The Age of Jackson*. Schlesinger, and others, prepare for leadership people like Reverend Billy Moyers, a former advisor to a President, who only recently found out that slavery wasn't merely the practice of some ignorant white trash overseers, but was endorsed by the judicial and legislative bodies of the time. His guest, A. Leon Higgenbottom, author of *In the Matter of Color*, was polite. He could have mentioned how American churches sold slaves to raise money to support their missionaries abroad, and how The American Government Sold Slaves to Raise Revenue!!

A few months earlier, Bill Moyers and a historian spoke in solemn tones as they strolled up and down Monticello, lauding the accomplishments of Thomas Jefferson, "an 18th-Century Man." Undoubtedly, Jefferson was a genius, in the same sense that Hitler, one of his disciples, was a genius, because Jefferson was the architect of Indian removal, which led to black removal, Jewish removal, Polish and Russian removal. Herd them into trains and get them out of our sight. Being a naturalist, and an environmentalist, perhaps Jefferson wanted an unobstructed view of the American landscape? Hitler, his misanthropic student, drew pictures of landscapes without people. Callahan mentioned the undertow of misanthropy in environmentalist writings, including those of Thoreau.

I had known about Jefferson's intimate relationship with a slave—the subject of the first novel written by an American black, William Wells Brown's *Clotel; or, the President's Daughter*—and now Indian removal. "Confine them to the narrower limits," for aren't ghettoes, reservations, and barrios the same,

the difference being that reservations contain enormous mineral wealth—
wealth encroached upon by white commercial interests, in collusion with the
government, so much so that "American Indian lands have been reduced, in
the past century, by over two-thirds, from over a hundred and fifty million to
fifty million acres" according to Roxanne Dunbar Ortiz.

The American solution to the Indian problem in the 19th century was
extermination. The Americans, with their war toys and true grit, were especially good at it. They had more than sixshooters. They had Gatling guns,
howitzers, cannons, rifles,muskets, and even with these armaments were
often defeated. The destruction of the Plains Indians was so vicious that the
"civilized world"—nations whose armies were exterminating people thousands of miles from their capitols—was appalled. John Toland argues that the
extermination of the American Indian provided the model for the mass murders which took place during Nazi Germany's rise and fall.

The "conquest" of California provided a new model for American aggression toward cultures which had inhabited the southwest and California for
thousands of years. The Californios fought the Americans to an honorable
peace at Guadalupe-Hidalgo. American squatters invaded the land promised
to the Californios and "American law" intervened on the side of the squatters.
By the time a settlement was made the squatters had squatted up the land.
Just as squatters and the "law" were used to win California, they are being
used to win Alaska. Squatters have been able to do what American might
wasn't able to do, squat up Alaska.

In New York people live in their heads. People call me up to tell me about
the latest cultural, intellectual controversies and trends. In the west it is physical: body building, the land. Private property. You can get arrested in Los
Angeles for walking down the street. Good people own cars. Good people
own condominiums. Why don't you buy a house? People ask.

In New York one rarely sees a bird. Nature is manmade, indoors. Art.
Conversation. Poetry about Nature. The west is laconic. In New Mexico,
New York poet Quincy Troupe wanted to see a mesa, and so a Native-American showed him one. No words were spoken. Out here the land talks, or
people talk for it.

The ancient white-Indian feud was expressed in an exchange between
poet Gary Snyder and Indian writers Geary Hobson, a Cherokee, and Leslie
Silko, a Chicana-Laguna. Silko is a Marman whose people arrived in New
Mexico in the 14th century. She is the author of *Ceremony*, a novel. The
younger generation of Native-Americans are asking for hegemony over their

culture and their land. In his "The Rise of the White Shaman as a New Version of Cultural Imperialism," Hobson traces the "white shaman" fad to Gary Snyder, author of "Shaman Songs." He doesn't blame Snyder, and even praises Snyder's poems, saying they contain "great vitality, and are, I believe, sincere efforts on Snyder's behalf to incorporate an essential part of American Indian philosophy in his work. Importantly, nowhere does Snyder refer to himself as a shaman." Hobson blames the Snyder imitators for the "white shaman" cult. Crossover poets.

In Ms. Silko's "An Old Time Indian Attack Conducted in Two Parts," she writes, "Although Snyder goes on at length about the land, the earth, and the Native-American's relationship to it, he does not deal with the facts surrounding his ownership or use" if you prefer, of the acreage in the Sierras. He clearly acknowledged that land he is occupying is

> the land that was deer and corn
> grounds of the Nisean
> branch of Maidu

Hobson's and Silko's criticisms were quite mild and the writers didn't neglect to praise Snyder's poetic accomplishments. Snyder's reply smacked of the scolding, missionary tone typical of so much environmentalist thought. After equivocating about Proposition 13, the Pacific White Republic's latest effort to drive poor people out of the state, close the schools, libraries, and other intellectual centers so despised by cowpokes and the agri-business, Snyder replied to Silko: "I'd have no difficulty smiling as the suggestion that all of North American occupancy is 'Illegal' and that the USA is founded on stolen land, went floating by. Does anyone expect these borrowed liberal ideas to change the facts of the world?"

The Indians accuse the whites of ruining their land, paving over the soil with cities. They criticize the hunting, mining, fishing, and herding techniques of the whites as cruel and wasteful. For example, the natives catch only as many salmon as they need, while the canneries strive to supply a market, and in the process deplete the fish resources. William Johnson, a Tlingit "Big Man" said of the canneries' techniques, "They frighten the fish! The fish pile high on the beach. They stink! They stink!" The differences don't end there. The Indians use every part of the animal not only to provide food but shelter, boats, clothing, and even musical instruments. The Kayak, an Eskimo invention, was made of sealskin. The whites, they claim, hunt for sport.

The conflict between the two world views was evident in Snyder's answer to Hobson. He defined the power of the Shaman as resulting from one stepping outside of the "social nexus" and making contact with "a totally non-human other." For Snyder, making contact with "the non-human other" means walking the deserts or mountains in solitude. The problem with this explanation is that the Indians do not view the mountains and the deserts as "the non-human other" but as human, as people. For the Indians the land and the animals are people. They speak of fish-people and bear-people. According to Tlingit history every human is descended from the Raven creator. Clan emblems are wolves, ravens, frogs, etc.

All but a small part of the mountain had been taken. The reservation boundary included only a canyon above Encinal and a few miles of timber on the plateau. The rest of the land was taken by the National Forest and by the state which later sold it to white ranchers who came from Texas in the early 1900s. In the '20s and '30s the loggers had come, and they stripped the canyons below the rim and cut great clearings on the plateau slopes. The logging companies hired full-time hunters who fed entire logging camps, taking ten or fifteen deer each week and fifty wild turkeys in one month. The loggers shot the bears and mountain lions for sport. And it was then the Laguna people understood that the land had been taken, because they couldn't stop these white people from coming to destroy the animals and the land. It was then too that the holy men at Laguna and Acoma warned the people that the balance of the world had been disturbed and the people could expect droughts and harder days to come. —Leslie Silko, *Ceremony*

The word "Alaska" is derived from the Aleut word "Alaxaxq," meaning "the object toward which the action of the sea is directed."

When the Russians first reached Alaska, bearing the eagles of the Romanovs, the Natives had already discovered it some thousand years before. Archaeological finds at Tangle Lakes, Anangula Island, Ground Hog Bay, provide evidence of cultures dating back 10,000 years. The Birnik finds uncovered hunting and fishing gear, utensils, musical instruments, and the remains of kayaks and sleds made 1,500 years ago.

It's been speculated that the Tlingits were members of a family of tribes of the Nadene or Athapasca language groups who crossed the Bering Straits. (Cultures 30,000 years old have been found in the southwest United States.) The Eskimos were the last to arrive, possibly 2,500 years ago.*

Oral histories begin as early as there is evidence of the existence of people in Alaska and the southwest. William Johnson, chief of the T'akdeintaan people, a Raven Clan, said that when archaeologists informed him of a "discovery" at Hoonah, he told them, "We knew that already." Johnson said that when the whites came to Alaska the land had already been marked, certain streams had been set aside for fishing for different Clans. Clans would never fish in a stream or river belonging to another Clan.

In June 1741, a two-ship expedition led by Vitus Bering, the Dane, of whom it was said he used "tobacco and brandy excessively," left the Siberian port of Petropavlovsk for the east. Sailing on a body of water which would later carry his name, Bering's ship, the St. Peter, lost contact with the St. Paul in the Aleutian Islands. On July 17, 1741, the St. Paul, commanded by Alexei Chrikof, reached an island characterized by "gloomy woods." One boat was sent ashore for the purpose of reconnaissance. After a few days, another boat was sent to rescue the first. It disappeared, too. Twenty-eight Russians had been led into ambush by a Tlingit disguised as a bear.

From that time the Tlingits' attitude toward the Russians alternated between tolerance and hostility. "The Russian American Empire" consisted of little more than a string of mom and pop trading posts. "There were never more than 823 Russians in the colony. Apart from Kodiak and Sitka, permanent settlements were very small, often including as few as a dozen Russians. Most locations were simply trading posts, often manned by one or two Russians."

In 1798, Alexander Baranof established, by trading some goods with the Natives in exchange for land, a trading settlement at Sitka. The trading post was separated from the Tlingit village by a fence.

Alexander Baranof, manager of the Russian American Company which had received its charter from the Emperor, was "a hard drinking" Russian whose treatment of the Natives was harsh. As for the character of Baranof, who appears in a painting bald and wearing an equilateral cross on his chest, a witness said of Baranof's behavior in church: "I could not help but marvel

---

* Inuit poet, Sister Goodwin, disagrees. She cites oral Inuit history which contends that the Inuits (the name "Eskimo" is considered derogatory; a word given the Inuits by the French, it means "eater of raw meat") were in Alaska before man got up from all fours.

at Alexander Baranof who stood and listened, crossed himself, and had a response at the proper time and joined in the singing with the same hoarse voice with which he was shouting the obscene songs the night before, when I saw him in the midst of a drunken carousal with a woman seated in his lap."

After a number of provocations, the Tlingits, who were known to retaliate, as the Russians, and the Americans later, would discover, were led into an attack on the Russian settlement by Katlian, Andy Hope's ancestor, wearing a Raven's head and swinging a blacksmith's hammer against some Russian skulls. This became known as the Sitka Massacre of 1802. Katlian was a member of the Kiksiad' warrior clan. According to oral history, he was shot in the back by one of Baranof's men.

The Russians were in Alaska with the Natives' permission. Alexander Baranof was no "Lord of Alaska," as he styled himself, because the Russians never controlled the region. Therefore, it came as a surprise to the Natives when they learned that the Russians had "sold" Alaska to the United States for $7,200,000. Not only had their land been seized but they didn't receive a dollar for the sale! It was after the Americans arrived in Sitka on March 30, 1867, that William S. Dodge, customs collector, described Sitka as "a grand house of ill-fame." Americans, whom the Tlingits referred to as "Boston men," previously came as whalers and fur hunters. John Jacob Astor had equipped an expedition.

Major General Jefferson C. Davis commanded an army of "desperate and immoral men" that maintained law in Alaska. It went on constant drunken rampages through the town, raping Native and Russian women. Cohabitation between the Russians and the Aleut women, the Portuguese sailors and Eskimo women had already given rise to a race of what the historian Bancroft refers to as "creoles." The Russians wanted furs and didn't interfere with the Natives' claims to Alaskan land, nor were the claims disputed during the ten years of army "rule" in Alaska. In 1877, Davis's army was withdrawn to fight Nez Perce "uprisings" and Sitka was left to "aboriginal" rule. "They had been accustomed to stern treatment under Russian rule, to brutal treatment under American rule, and now there was no rule. They found themselves living with Americans, Russians, creoles, Chinamen, Eskimos, men of all races, creeds, and colors, in a condition of primitive republican simplicity." The threatened massacre of whites for wrongs which occurred during the American rule never happened.

Then the Navy came. Davis's regime was marked by infamy and depravity. The Navy's occupation saw atrocious treatment of the Natives. Before the

Navy came, the only sign of the American presence was a custom's office. Over a misunderstanding, which happens so often in this country of uninterrupted white-male-settler government, the Angoon people were bombarded, an incident that the Tlingits speak of with bitterness even today. In another incident, neglected by American "historians," before this event, the Navy was defeated by the Klukwan Tlingit people who have, from that day in 1880s to the present, used as their emblem a Navy uniform.

The Americans, according to the Treaty of Cession, viewed the Natives as "uncivilized," which meant that they would be treated in the same way the Plains Indians were treated: exterminated, placed on reservations the government held in "trust" for them, or compensated. On the flight to Alaska, Jim Pepper had joked that as part of the U.S. settlement with his people he receives 50 cents every Christmas. Jim Welch, a Blackfeet, said that he receives $50 annually. The only difference between that policy and today's is that formerly the Indians were removed from their lands, today their lands are being removed from them in the same old scam—they are frozen, locked-up for the "national interest"; they become "parks" and "recreation" areas so that the American Romanovs can go up and cruise about in their float boats. The Sitkas joked about a Sierra Club lobbyist who, after riding about Admiralty Island in a kayak, an eskimo invention made of sealskin, announced that he "now had a special interest in that land." The Tlingits accused the Forest Service of looking out for the interests of big companies. William Johnson said that Fish and Wildlife and Business were like brother and sister.

If a people is uncivilized, you have to set up a mission to civilize them. This gave the Americans an opportunity to take 640 acres for "missions." The encroachment on Native lands accelerated until 1971 when the Natives, who had claims to all of Alaska, settled for one-ninth of the country. To some it was history's biggest swindle.

The further deterioration of Alaska as a "holistic ecosystem"—a deterioration which had begun with the arrival of the Russians-occurred in the 1880s and 90s: The Alaska Gold Rush. In 1880, armed prospectors forced their way through Tlingit country by threatening the Tlingits with a Gatling Gun. In their assault on "the non-human other," they were joined by an international army of vigilante squatters. Some settled in Juneau, Alaska. By 1904 the non-Native population outnumbered the Native population. By 1908, according to the Alaska Native Land Claims, published by the Alaska Native Foundation, $140 million in gold had been removed from Alaska. Although Kowee, an Aukwan Tlingit, and Tom Garrick, an Eskimo, located the first gold deposits, they didn't receive the benefits because they weren't "citizens," but members of "uncivilized tribes."

The invaders caused the supply of moose, sea otters, and whales to diminish. The invention of the debarring machine led to the demise of the seal herd so that by 1911 the fur seals had been reduced from a population of four million to 110,000. The cannery and mining techniques destroyed the salmon streams and threatened the survival of the salmon. In some instances the Natives cooperated in this destruction. The Russians had to get their furs from somewhere. The Aleuts hunted seals for the Russians, and the Eskimo were paid to kill whales. Even the ice was sold. A company in San Francisco bought Alaskan ice at $30 a ton, and sold 20,000 tons. It was the same San Francisco ice house that the Russian American Company originally offered to sell Alaska.

The Organic Act of 1884 made Alaska a U.S. District with an appointed governor. Although the act promised to protect land "used and occupied by Natives," it legitimatized the theft of land by miners during the previous 17 years. The Alaska Natives had learned as blacks, Chicanos, Puerto Ricans, and Natives of the lower 48 have learned—the white man's laws favor the white man. Murderers walk the streets of the south. The "alleged" assassin of Medgar Evers even ran for office. His slogan was: "You know where I stand." The government policy toward blacks was similar to that traditional policy toward Indians, that of "confining them to narrower limits." On the reservation question, Chief Ivan of Coskaket said, "I tell you that we are people on the go. People 'on the go' don't always understand the notion of 'private property.'" In the later Alaska government said that in their selection of land the Natives were not to claim "private property" for conveyance.

At the same meeting, where "Big Man" Ivan of Coskaket made his statement, held in July 1915 at the Thomas Memorial Library in Fairbanks, Chief Joe of Salchaket said: "We are suggesting to you just one thing, that we want to be left alone. God made Alaska for the Indian people, and all we hope is to be able to live here all the time."

Chief Alexander of Tolovana told the government not to "let the white people come near us. Let us live our own lives in the customs we know."

Wickersham, Alaska's delegate to Congress, told the chiefs that "as soon as they have established homes and live like white men, and assume the habits of civilization, they can have a vote."

For the purpose of "naturalizing" the Indians the Alaska Native Brotherhood was formed in 1912. It was open to all "English-speaking Natives." In order to become a member of the organization, which chose, as its colors, red for salmon and gold for gold, one had to have abandoned "aboriginal customs," which included the ceremonial Potlatch, a "feeding of the dead," characterized by extravagant gift-giving, a historical pageant of Tlingit history. The Christians viewed the dancing and singing as "pagan." (In 1982, the second year of the Reagan presidency, a "new right" Congressman said that rock and roll played backwards revealed Satanic codes.)

In the last major ceremonial feast of 1904, the Tlingit men posed in costumes bearing geometric representations of the animal crests which indicated Clan or subclan. They wore fabulous hats and held carved staffs. In the photo of the Alaska Brotherhood, members wear plain suits and sport European hairstyles. "Cutting his hair would humble the Indian and give him pain, for he took pride in his hair; and to the white man long hair was the symbol of Indian ways, so he wanted to blot out the symbol and then believe he had civilized the Indian," explained historian Clark Wissler of an Indian Affairs Department policy.

The mission-Native generation yielded its mind, customs, soul, dancing, and singing; it changed its style to win the approval of the whites, and as a way of gaining "citizenship." In the "lower 48," the black mission-Natives graduated from Morehouse and used the white men's religion as a tactic to embarrass him into acting right. A mission-Native generation of blacks, reds, and yellows went to war against the white man's enemies in order to prove their loyalty to the flag, even if it meant killing their distant relatives. In John Okada's Japanese-American classic *No-No Boy*, Ichiro, a C.O., is subjected to taunts and violence for his refusal to fight on the side of the United States. One attack on him is led by his brother.

In Leslie Silko's *Ceremony*, Rocky, an All-American Indian, hallucinates that the Japanese soldier he kills is an Indian. He has to undergo "aboriginal treatment"—treatment by a medicine man—in order to be cured of combat fatigue. The mission-Native generation was sometimes followed by a "neo-aboriginal" generation. In the 1960s, a black generation of neo-aboriginals abandoned the polite English-speaking "eloquence" of a generation of black mission-Native writers for "aboriginal" street talk, folklore, investigations of a past covered up by the mission-Natives and their missionary tutors.

What the neo-aboriginal generation succeeded in doing was to modernize the "aboriginal" ways. A modern hotel decorated with Tlingit art; new totem poles.

The Dawes Act held that any Native who "severed tribal relationships and adopted the habits of civilization" could become a citizen. Still the American government ignored the Natives' "aboriginal claims," and continued to use the "law" as a way of hustling more land. According to historians, the Americans who entered Alaska were "speculators, politicians, office-hunters, tradesmen, laborers, loafers, harlots, gamblers, bunko men, conmen, and sure-thing men." There were so many crooks in Skagway, a town run at one time by a gang of outlaws led by one Soapy Smith, that it was said a traveler would arrive in the evening with money and the next day wouldn't have enough to buy breakfast. There were constant shouts of "murder!" in the streets. Wyatt Earp was up there.

In 1935, Congress passed a law permitting the Natives to sue the United States for land taken. This led to the 1959 Tlingit-Haida decision which claimed that the Tlingit-Haida people had "Indian title" to most of the land in southeastern Alaska. But it was a hollow victory for it had been preceded by the Statehood Act of 1958, which set aside 104 million acres of land for the new state.

Shortly before 1 P.M. on December 22, 1971, a little more than 100 years after the Russian-American Company "sold" Alaska to the United States, Richard Nixon signed the Alaska Native Claims Settlement, awarding the Natives of Alaska 40 million acres of land, about half the size of California, and $962,500,000. The money would be distributed to shareholders through regional and village corporations. Regional corporations would control subsurface rights; village corporations would own surface rights.

After two years of enrollment operations supervised by John Hope, Andy Hope's father, the Shee Atika Corporation incorporated and made a land selection proposal to the Ford Administration. Following the guidelines of then Secretary of the Interior Rogers Morton, they chose land within a 50-mile radius of Sitka.

At 9 A.M. Tuesday, March 27, I ordered two pots of coffee and awaited my guests—Nelson Frank, Jack Barry, Andy, and his aunt, Ellen Hope Hays, Alaska Native liaison to the National Park Service, Nora Dauenhauer of the Cook Inlet Native Association, and Bob Callahan. I planned to proceed cautiously. Last visit, Bob and I were accused of being outside agitators. Up here, I was a liberal. An Eskimo artist accused me of attempting to "deAlaskanize him" because I asked him to submit some of his drawings to my magazine. In one series of his work, giant reptilian creatures reap revenge upon the earth as fossil fuel. There were unsolved Eskimo murders of whites along the route of the Alaska pipeline which cut through Eskimo country.

Mrs. Hope claimed that with the Alaska Native Claims Settlement, new forms of planning and organization were imposed upon the Natives which had nothing to do with "Indian culture." The Tlingits had governed themselves through Clans and associations before the missionaries arrived. She said that the Angoon people and the Sitka people are the same. "We are part of them, they are part of us." Now they were competitive corporations. The Hope ancestors were Angoon people. Andy said that the Angoons had sold their aboriginal rights twice over and were victims of bad investments through the machinations of their former executive director, who disrupted a compromise reached by the Sitka Tlingits and the Angoon Tlingits.

The Angoons, she said, had become welfare Indians, and had a welfare mentality, always counting on the whites to bail them out. The Sierra Club, Hope said, was providing them with assistance and so were the Friends of the Earth; the Angoons' lawyer, Steve Volker, was a Sierra Club member whom Nelson Frank had accused of misleading the Angoons about their prospects on Admiralty Island. He accused the lawyer of unethical conduct. The Sitka Tlingits said that the land dispute was turning Native against Native, an old colonial tactic. "The fact that these interior tribes are better morally than their brethren of the coast is so apparent that even the dullest observer must see the difference between the two, and wonder how it happens that these natives who have been brought into contact with our boasted civilization are more objectionable in their manners and less trustworthy than those who have not enjoyed these advantages" (J.C. Cantwell in *Cruise of the Revenue Steamer Corwin in the Arctic Ocean in the Year 1884,* by M.A. Healy. Washington, D.C.: Government Printing Office, 1889).

The Shee Atika Corporation of Sitka said they'd compromised too much and attributed Angoon's desire to keep them off Admiralty Island "altogether" to Shee Atika's willingness to compromise and negotiate. The lawsuit against the Sierra Club has been in court for five years and, as a result, the Sitkas are $500,000 in debt. When the Sitkas wrote a letter supporting a bill which guaranteed compensation for their court costs incurred during the land selection claims and land on Admiralty Island, their lawyer, Edward Weinberg, accused them of behaving like "petulant children."

When the vote affecting the Breaux-Dingell-Huckaby bill was defeated some blamed it on the "backlash" against the oil companies. How did Shee

Atika feel about being on the same side as Exxon and the multinational oil and timber companies? Hope said he didn't agree with the objectives of the multinationals; he saw the bill as a way of obtaining the land the Sitkas had been promised.

What about the arguments that the Alaska Native Claims Settlement, which the Alaska Federation of Natives, a statewide group, adopted by a vote of 511 to 56, was a swindle? Hope said that the settlement, which gave millions of acres of land and a billion dollars to 75,000 Natives, was fine as long as the land was going to be given to them.

Callahan felt that the Sierra Club environmentalist policy was "reactionary" and the most progressive environmentalists were supporting the concept of multiple land use, the approach taken by the Breaux-Dingell-Huckaby bill, which would have set aside land in Admiralty Island for subsistence, recreation, wilderness, as well as development. "The Europeans who came here had a one-use, one-plant, mentality and are often startled when they go to the Caribbean and see a variety of plants growing in a person's backyard." "The Sierra Club," Callahan charged, "were Teddy Roosevelt conservationists who viewed the wilderness as a place where the bosses could get away from the poor who worked in their sweatshops." Callahan said he thought it ironic that the environmentalists, who'd viewed the Indian as an ecology symbol for years—the TV image of the Indian tearfully watching the litterbugs—would now oppose an effort by Indians to show what they can do with multiple land use.

Nelson Frank said that the corporation had consulted experts about the land they chose. Their cultural Tradition Bearers judged the historical value of the land; their people in the forestry school and their scientists made tests for surface and subsurface values—the Sitkas had submitted the land in question to thorough scrutiny. For doing their homework, and being good bargainers—the early fur traders testified to that—the Sitka Tlingits are called capitalists, plunderers, and slavers. One of the best forestry people in Alaska, I was told, is on the Shee Atika staff. Andy Hope referred to the Tlingit scholar who'd written his dissertation on the cannery industry's wasteful and harmful fishing techniques. The land elsewhere in the 50-mile radius is "scruffy" in comparison to that on Admiralty Island, Nelson Frank said.

To add to their problems, President Carter, under a rarely used Antiquities Act, had set aside 50 million acres of Alaska land for the "national interest"; some of this land was located on Admiralty Island. The Sitka Tlingits' land selections on Admiralty Island would be surrounded by "national monuments."

The Carter Administration has been worse than the Administration on the land question, the Sitkas claimed: When the Tlingits went to Washington with their land proposals, each department they talked to had a different position. The administration told them it wouldn't "yield to their pressure." Nelson said the government "had the wrong maps," and didn't know the land "up here," and was besieged by environmentalists like Stuart Eisenstat, who, in a memo to President Carter, attempted to pass the blame for the present oil crunch to OPEC.

The Sierra Club expressed fears that the Sitkas planned to use the land for lumbering. Japanese interests are expanding in the Pacific Northwest. The hippest capitalist of them all, in 1978 the Japanese government had a surplus of over $100 billion. The Japanese had bought into the Alaska timber and fishery industry. "They will soon own the whole Pacific rim," Ellen Hope Hays said. The Tlingits spoke of Japanese who lived in the hills and kept to themselves. Other Asian immigrants didn't fare as well. All you see on the plane to Kodiak, Jack Barry said, "are Filipinos and Vietnamese." They're on the way to the canneries where they murder each other.

Congressman Morris Udall, in a white male settler's speech made in favor of the environmentalists' Udall-Anderson bill, which would bar development on Admiralty Island, argued that the Japanese would use timber from Admiralty Island to make television sets, which they would then sell to the United States.

Udall accused the supporters of the Breaux-Dingell-Huckaby bill of attempting to turn Admiralty Island into a pulp bank.

Andy Hope said that Udall was ignorant of the facts. The environmentalists claim Admiralty Island as a "virgin forest." Hope said that there've been 135 timber sales on the Island in the last 100 years.

He said that Congressman Udall erred when he said that offshore drilling causes less ecological damage than land drilling. Hope said that an Arctic slope borough had made a study which proved that off-shore drilling was more damaging ecologically.

Frank and Hope claimed that the Sierra Club desired to turn Admiralty Island into a rich man's weekend playground. A Romanovs' Winter Palace. William F. Buckley, Jr., wrote: "It is easy enough to get to Alaska, and to enjoy the peripheral feasts of the table, but to get into the sexy parts, you need such things as private airplanes, and guides, kayaks, bear-and-mosquito-killing equipment, and ideally radio communications with a convenient satellite." These and other pleasures are available to the Romanovs while their serfs line up around the block for gas in the Bronx and El Cerrito, half alseep and whipped at 6 A.M. Lawrence Rockefeller, member of a group called "Americans for Alaska," paid $25,000 for the Angoon Tlingits to travel to Washington where they presented President Carter with the Tlingit title of "Great Nation in Migration." That night, May 3, 1979 when the Kootznoowoo Corporation presented Carter with the Tlingit beaded vest, Andy Hope called me from Washington to accuse the Angoons of selling out the people of Southeast Alaska. The following Sunday morning, CBS reported that the way the polls looked, the Tlingits may be Carter's only constituency.

The discussion that morning went on for three hours. Toward the end, the gathering concluded that the administration and Congress viewed the Udall-Anderson bill as a cheap environmental vote. They could point to Alaska as a way of ignoring environmentalist reforms in their own districts. Udall called the land the nation's "Crown jewels." What about the "Crown jewels" in Udall's own state of Arizona, or the "Crown jewels" of Georgia. "There are only 400,000 people in Alaska," someone remarked. Not enough votes to be of significance.

The Sitka Tlingits feel they are being blamed for all the bad ecology that's taken place over the years. They are being blamed for New Jersey.

"Have you seen Coney Island recently?" asked Nelson Frank. "Looks like a ghost town." Frank couldn't believe that a deserted Coney Island was in proximity of a population of seven million. Finally, Callahan said that the Europeans had looked upon America as a frontier, as a way of making a fresh start. He said that there was never a frontier in Frederick Turner's sense, because when the whites came west, they met cultures which had been in existence for thousands of years. He said it was a case of people who had had their land taken away latching on to other peoples' land. He accused the English of "de-foresting" Ireland, and said that Ireland was "off-broadway" for colonial practices in "the new world." The Monarchies of Europe were disturbed by the thousands of beggars lining their highways and filling their cities. The solution? Remove them to the colonies.

Later I took in an art exhibit by Native artists Daisy Phillips, Mathilda Peck, Ida Kadasnan, Sam Fox, Joe Senungetuk, Tony Glazier, Martha Nelson, Kathleen Carlo. They used sealskin, horsehide hairs, wood, abalone shell, and fungi, to create representations of ravens, whales, and human faces. Senungetuk's work was entitled "The Shaman Beckons." Kathleen Carlo's black walnut mask in two faces won a prize. A group of us posed next to a huge, menacing-looking stuffed Grizzly. Then, travelling through Sitka, passing the remnants of old Russian "rule"—St. Michael's Church, a roundhouse, a hill upon which rested a few cannons—we headed for the Pioneer's bar. The walls were covered with photos of fishing boats. St. Michael's Church was the real landmark. Three years ago when I visited Sitka, I peeked in and saw some Russian Orthodox priests going through their maneuvers before a rococo altar.

That night, surrounded by large totems, Missoula, Montana's Jim Welch read from his works at the Sitka Visitor's Center. The Tradition Bearers listened respectfully as he read from his new book, *The Death of Jim Loney.* The 15-minute reading was from a scene in which a man kills another man while hunting, but isn't certain whether it was an accident or deliberate. Welch's book was published in October, 1979 by Harper and Row. In his first novel, Welch exhibited some satirical deftness in dealing with American land-management practices: "The white men from the fish department came in their green trucks and stocked the river with pike. They were enthusiastic and dumped thousands of pike of all sizes into the river. But the river ignored the fish and the fish ignored the river; they refused even to die there. They simply vanished. The white men made tests; they stuck electric rods into the water; they scraped muck from the bottom; they even collected bugs from the fields next to the river; they dumped other kinds of fish in the river. Nothing worked. The fish disappeared. Then the men from the fish department disappeared...."

On Thursday, May 4, Andy called from the Holiday Inn in Washington to tell me to turn on the television. Members of the Kootznoowoo Corporation were presenting Carter with the Tlingit beaded vest. The photo in the next day's *San Francisco Chronicle* reminded me of the mural in the Sitka airport. A primitive oil painting depicting the Alaska Day Pageant. A scene from Baranof Castle. Alexander Baranof, Prince Maksutoff, Princess Maksutoff, Walt Massey, imbibing vodka, while Charlie Olson of the Eagle clan presents them with a samovar.

The next morning, Andy attempted to get in touch with Congressman Ron Dellums and other members of the Congressional Black Caucus to do some last-minute lobbying. Dellums, he said, was key. I had received a pro-environmentalist letter from Dellums, and when the Udall-Anderson bill passed in the House on May 15, it was with the support of Dellums. Hope's calls weren't returned by Dellums. Andy also talked to the Seal Alaska Corporation, a regional corporation, to Chip Dennerling of the Alaska State Division of Lands (formerly rivals, the State and Shee Atika were working together for the Breaux bill), and to the Citizens for Management of Alaska Land, the main lobbying group for Alaska. Dennerling inspired Shee Atika to write the letter supporting the Breaux bill—the letter which aroused their attorney's ire. They also talked to some of the attorneys for the Native corporations. They were told that the corporations' attorneys were neutral. Shee Atika reminded them that some of the attorneys had written letters in favor of the Udall-Anderson bill. The Native corporations were threatened that if they didn't support the Udall-Anderson bill, they wouldn't get their Native amendments into the bill. Up until then, Hope said, the corporations were united. He said 95 percent of the people of Alaska supported the Breaux bill and that since there'd be reapportionment in 1981, there would be a backlash vote against the Natives. The Alaska Federation of Natives, he said, was "waffling" on the issue.

On the day of the vote I talked to Hope. He was discouraged, tense. Udall-Anderson had passed 268 to 157. Under the bill 67 million acres of land were designated wilderness; 10 million acres with oil potential were closed; 91 percent of the state would be open to sport hunting; U.S. Borax would have sufficient surface access to its molybdenum deposit in the southeast. The timber allowed to be cut annually was reduced to 345–350 million board feet. Two thousand jobs would be lost in southeastern Alaska, according to Bill Horne, minority consultant for the House Interior Committee. Hope said that this too would begin a backlash. The unemployed whites would expect the Shee Atika Corporation to hire them. "We'd have to hire Natives first," Hope said. The Forest Service didn't think that the reduction in timber board feet could support the existing mills. I asked Andy to stop by Berkeley on his way back to Sitka.

On the 17th of May we attended a benefit for *City Miner* magazine at San Francisco's Fort Mason. I picked up Hope at Berkeley's Durant Hotel, and we drove to San Francisco. He seemed listless, preoccupied. After a showing of Les Blank's documentary on Mance Lipscomb, I introduced Hope. "Yesterday," I said, "a Congress which can't get a decent health bill through, which has allowed the cities to go to rubble, which is responsible for widespread discontent and suffering in the United States, expressed its love for the Caribou." The youthful pro-environmentalist audience was polite, but didn't think the remarks funny. Andy made a short speech giving the background of the land dispute.

"Make it quick," Mike Helm, *City Miner's* editor, kept yelling from the sidelines. Andy told the audience that the land controversy was complicated and that they should listen with an open mind. He was given a well-mannered reception. He was followed by Wavy Gravy, an intelligent humorist dressed as a clown. I wondered how many of these people could afford float boats and guides.

On June 8, 1979, Andy called to say that he had been elected manager of the Sitka Community Association, an organization made possible by the Indian Reorganization Act of 1935, and open to the younger generation born after 1971, who, according to the Alaska Native Claims Settlement, weren't eligible to be stockholders in regional, village, or urban corporations, set-up by the Omnibus bill of 1976. Hope said that the structure of this organization would be similar to that of the old clans and associations. The Udall-Anderson bill would go to the Senate. With 34 millionaires sitting in that august democratic body, you can guess what its fate will be.

The Natives couldn't subsist the way they did successfully before the Russians came, and now, under the American system with its "territories," "commonwealths," "states," and other organizational ideas, masks for aggression, their cultures had been smashed. *(In Recife it was forbidden to "shout, scream or cry out in the streets," a measure aimed at the religious observances and festivals of the Africans.)* It was against the law for Aleut children to speak Aleut. We hear much about the early colonial persecution of the Quakers; in Alaska, the Quakers threatened parents who didn't send their Inuit children to Quaker schools with jail.

Andy Hope and his generation were going to bring it all back. They were going to recover their Black English. And so now they had a hotel, and when it looked as though their corporation would succeed, it might have to go into receivership because some missionaries thought they should seek land elsewhere. Andy Hope said that the Sitkas were interested in land of value, not cliffs and glaciers.

On June 25, I called the San Francisco Sierra Club. The previous Friday I'd called Paul Swater, who was referred to me as the Club's conservation man. He never returned my call. When I phoned again on the 25th and talked to the Alaska "person," Ms. Winky Miller, she repeated the Sierra Club's desire to preserve Admiralty Island as a wilderness area. She said that the Tlingits agreed with the Sierra Club's position and asked if I had seen them in the White House ceremonies with President Carter. I told her that the Sitkas didn't agree and had asked me to ask her what the Club expected them to do for economic subsistence. Ms. Miller said that the question was a "toughie" and she'd call me later.

Later that day, she called to say that the Sitkas had taken a hard line on the Admiralty Island question; the Angoons wanted it for subsistence but the Sitkas wanted to log it. Ms. Miller said the Sierra Club and Gold Belt had settled out of court, and that Gold Belt has chosen land elsewhere. Ms. Miller said she didn't have sufficient facts to answer my other questions; she suggested I call Ms. Lin Sonnenberg, the Sierra Club person who was Conservation Committee Chairperson for the State of Alaska.

On June 29, I called Lin Sonnenberg who told me that negotiations were still going on with the Sitkas. She termed "absurd" Shee Atika's claim that it would fold if it didn't receive its land on Admiralty. "Who would lend money to a corporation which didn't have clear title to the land?" she asked. She said the Sierra Club wanted Admiralty as a designated wilderness area because it possessed qualities none of the other islands had: The largest population of brown bears in North America, and the largest eagle population in the world. She said Admiralty was an "intact ecological unit" which was "virtually untouched."

What about the 135 timber sales Andy Hope mentioned. She denied the timber sales. "There were contracts but the contracts never came through." There was only one small logging spot in the 1800s, she said.

If the environmentalists saw the Indian as a symbol of good ecology, why not give the Sitkas a chance to show their stuff—teach us multiple land use, I asked.

"Multiple land use on a nonrenewable climax forest is not possible," she said. "A climax forest is nonrenewable habitat." She claimed that if you cut down trees in southeast Alaska, it would ruin the forest permanently. "The trees may grow back later, but you'll never have the forest again."

"Logging affects the fish population, affects the actual use of the area by deer and bear." She cited a study done by the Alaska Department of Fish and Game which concluded that through logging you lose 90 percent of the deer population in the logging areas, and then you lose bears, and so on.

I asked what she thought of the Natives' claim that if they didn't receive their Admiralty land selection the unemployment rate would climb to 50 percent in Sitka. "Absurd" and "Illogical," she said, Gold Belt made a selection elsewhere and didn't fold.

I repeated Shee Atika's claim that no land of equal value could be found within the 50-mile radius.

Ms. Sonnenberg said she wasn't acquainted with the 50-mile radius provision and suggested I talk to the local Angoon Sierra Club attorney, Steve Volker.

Reached at his Angoon office later that day, Volker said that negotiations were still going on with Shee Atika. He praised Gold Belt's decision to settle out of court. They'd received 23,000 acres at Port Houghton, Hobart, and Berner's Bay.

What about Shee Atika's concessions to the Sierra Club, I asked. First, Volker said, there'd been no concessions. I went over the history of concessions as told to me by the Shee Atika directors.

Volker said that he wasn't the lawyer at that time, and that the former Sierra Club lawyer, James Moorman, now worked for the Justice Department. He said that since the suit had begun there'd been no concessions. He repeated Ms. Miller's and Ms. Sonnenberg's suggestion that Shee Atika select land off Admiralty Island.

"There is land of comparable value off Admiralty," he said, and the Sierra Club had assisted the Forest Service in locating the land. Shee Atika, he claimed, had declined their proposals. When I asked about the Shee Atika's economic situation, Volker said he didn't know the facts of their situation.

Volker claimed that the Sitkas had no "ancestral ties" to Admiralty as the Angoons had. "It was their traditional land for fishing and hunting," he said. He said that the Tlingits inhabited all of southeast Alaska but were of different tribes.

I restated what the Shee Atika Corporation had said, that the Sitkas and the Angoons were the same people; that the division among them occurred when the Americans brought in their organizational ideas. The "corporation" structure, I said, had nothing to do with "Indian culture." Clans and associations are different from the cold-blooded corporation which was introduced as a type of modern business organization in the 1800s.

Volker suggested I talk to Sterling Bolima, land planner for the Kootznoowoo* Corporation of the Angoons. He would give me the Angoon position, Volker said.

What about the charge that only the rich could use Admiralty's "wilderness" and recreational lands. If this was so, how would making Admiralty Island into a "wilderness" or "national monument," as President Carter had done, be in the "national interest"? To the charge that only the rich could use the island, Volker said, "So what." He then amended his remark to say that

---

* Tlingit for "Bear Fortress." It is said that there are so many bears in Angoon that the people walk on one side of the street, the bears on the other.

people could take a ferry from Seattle to Admiralty for $90. (If you don't eat for three days and can sleep in a chair.)

On June 26, the *New York Times* ran an ad sponsored by the Jewish Press headlined: "An Angry Public Charges President Carter CAUSED THE GAS CRISIS." Among the ad's charges was that President Carter's land freeze had prevented developers from getting at over 10 million acres of oil-bearing land. According to the ad, the Jewish Press's interview with Senator Ted Stevens of Alaska revealed how "the environmentalists put us in the gas crisis mess." Stevens claimed that there was enough underground oil in Alaska to meet American oil needs for the next 30 years. Later, the State of Alaska took out a $15,480 ad in three New York papers, in which it claimed it could fuel the nation for 20 centuries but that federal control of much of its land prevents development of the State's resources. The State had received only 21 million acres of the 104 million acres it had been promised.

With the high cost of food, shelter, and clothing, and the threatened collapse of the western economic system, the long gas lines, the despair and uneasiness among the American people because of the oil crisis, I asked Volker if the Sierra Club was running the risk of being accused of caring more about bears and eagles than about people.

Volker said there was no oil in southeast Alaska, and that the Alaska oil reserves weren't affected by the Udall-Anderson legislation. He said the only question was the two million acres on the Northern Slope, and he said it was doubtful whether oil could be found there.

I reached Sterling Bolima in Seattle on June 2. He said that the Angoons and the Sitkas had been fighting for 10,000 years, and that half the Angoon "stories" were about warfare with the Sitkas, and Yakatats. The Goldschmidt Haas report of 1947 carried ancestral claims made by the different clans. Bolinas said nobody challenged the Angoons' claim to Admiralty Island as well as to some of Baranof and Chichagoff. To Hope's claim that the Angoons originally migrated from Sitka, Bolima said that Sitka was merely a stopover for the Angoons, who were returning to Admiralty after the Ice Age, 10,000 years ago.

The Sitkas' off-Admiralty Island selection was Chichagoff, but the Sierra Club challenged them. When they chose Chaik Bay, the Angoons and the Club rejected the selection because Chaik Bay was supposedly the most historical place for the Angoon people. Five Shee Atika shareholders grew up in Chaik Bay. According to Bolima, the Shee Atika corporation sued the Secretary of Interior because Mitchell Bay and Chaik Bay weren't included in the

Hood Bay withdrawal. A month later Angoon sued the Secretary of Interior to keep the Sitkas off Admiralty altogether. Bolima denied that the Sierra Club was picking up the tab for Kootznoowoo's court and lobbying costs. He said they were paying these expenses with money they'd received from 23,000 acres of land. As for unemployment among the natives in Sitka, Bolima said that when the Angoons and the Sitkas met, the Sitkas claimed they'd lose only 40 jobs if they didn't receive their land conveyance on Admiralty. He cited a Forest Service report which held that no jobs would be lost as a result of setting aside wilderness areas; in fact, more jobs would be created. In 1976, Bolima said, the state issued 1,675 unemployment checks totalling 1.2 million dollars to out-of-state workers, people who worked in Alaska seasonally or with the pipeline. As for the proposal to Shee Atika for off Admiralty land of equal value, Bolima said that the Final Environmental Statement carried a proposal which would give Shee Atika $10 million as well as higher acreage than that selected on Admiralty Island.

"If we thought that the Sitkas had a valid existing claim to Admiralty Island, we wouldn't be in court," Bolima said. Far from disrupting a compromise reached by Sitka and Angoon, Richard Powers, the forester Nelson and Hope referred to, had actually sought a political compromise with the Sitkas, and after six months was released as executive director of Kootznoowoo, the Angoon corporation, which felt that he was "too lax" with Shee Atika. "He studied political science in school and was always talking about compromise," Bolima said.

Bolima praised the Udall-Anderson bill. He said that it provided better subsistence rights for the Natives, a tax-free land bank, and provided for Visiting Centers to be set up next to the "National Monuments."

Sterling Bolima, land planner for the Kootznoowoo Corporation, is half-Filipino and half-Tlingit. Does that disqualify him as a spokesman for Kootznoowoo? He thought not. "My mother is Tlingit and Tlingit succession is matrilineal," he said. "I'm also a member of the Juneau Filipino community," he chuckled.

I called Andy Hope to get his responses to Miller, Sonnenberg, and Volker. To Miller's charge of the Sitka "hard line" on the land question, Hope said that the Sitkas had a valid existing claim to Admiralty, and if that constituted a hard line, then "so be it." He accused the Juneau Gold Belt Corporation of selling out by settling out of court with the Sierra Club. "Gold Belt wanted some cash and didn't want to stay in court forever," he said.

He termed Sonnenberg's and Volker's claims that negotiations between the Sierra Club and Shee Atika were still going on "a lie." "They say this so that Congress won't seek a legislative solution. If Senator Jackson thinks the issue is about to be resolved between the Sierra Club and Shee Atika, Jackson would be hesitant to push through legislation." By challenging Shee Atika's claim to Admiralty Island, Sonnenberg, Hope said, was in fact saying that the Alaska Native Claims Settlement, under which the Sitkas had received the land, "was a farce."

He also doubted Sonnenberg's claim that Admiralty Island has been "virtually untouched." He cited several timber sales which had been made in West Bay, Hood Bay, and Winning Cove, the last sale made as late as 1974. As for the bears, "The Angoon people lead white hunters to shoot those damned bears," Hope said. He said that most of the land they'd chosen didn't technically fit into the category of "a non-renewable climax forest," because there were Sitka spruce trees and hemlock on the land.

I told Hope that Volker had no knowledge of concessions made prior to the lawsuit, and that James Moorman was now assistant Attorney General in charge of national resources. He called it "a fucking joke" that this environmentalist was in charge of defending the government and the Sitkas against the Sierra Club suit. As for the charge that the Forest Service and the Sierra Club had made proposals to the Shee Atika for off-Admiralty land of equal value, Hope said that this was a lie. There was no proposal to resist since, in nine years, no proposal had been made. Andy Hope did not deny aboriginal claims to Admiralty made by the Angoons. He said, however, that these claims had been extinguished when the Angoons accepted the Tlingit-Haida decision and the Alaska Native Claims Settlement.

He disputed Volker's claim that the Angoons and the Sitkas were "different tribes." "We're the same tribe. We're different clans. There are Angoon clans in Sitka, and Sitka clans on Angoon," he said. Tlingit history is one of continuous migration. He also denied Volker's claim that it was doubtful that oil could be found on the Northern Slope, or what Hope referred to as "The Gates of the Arctic." President Carter, in a July 15 speech, urged development of the Northern Slope. "The resulting oil pollution would ruin the ocean forever because this kind of disruption is permanent due to the cold and the ice," Hope said. He said that the Arctic Slope Borough had made a study and found oil. There are also huge coal deposits and oil on Admiralty Island. George Davis, an 80-year-old Tradition Bearer, had discovered it but wasn't telling where it could be found.

Hope said that Bolima's notion of a 10,000-year Tlingit history in Alaska was largely conjecture. Evidence indicates that the Tlingits migrated to Alaska anywhere from 12,000 to 250 years ago. They are a racially-mixed people of Polynesian and Mongolian background. They also assimilated with the Athapascans, and intermarried with the Filipinos. He said that there was warfare between the clans 150 years ago, but it had been settled at a peace conference in 1904. The friction between Angoon, Kake, Hoonah, and Sitka had been settled in the ancient manner. Hope said that the Angoons were trying to have it both ways; first they give up their ancestral rights to the Island, required in the first paragraph of the Alaska Native Claims Settlement, then they attempt to hold on to them, only this time they were using "White Man's Law." To Bolima's denial that the Sierra Club was paying Kootz-noowoo's expenses, Hope recalled a letter Bolima showed him in which the Sierra Club said it would.

Hope said he was concerned about the out-of-state unemployment cases, too—people who got paid by Alaska and spent it in Seattle—but that this had nothing to do with Native unemployment in Sitka.

> Where we going to get our hunting?
> where we going to get our fish?
> where we going to pick our berries?
> where we going to dry our salmon?

Chief Johnson told me that before you cut down a tree you say to it in Tlingit, "Tree, I need you." And the tree would fall where you wanted it to fall and would replenish itself. "They are alive like you and me."

Chief Johnson is a Tradition Bearer. Andy Hope is the neo-aboriginal, armed with facts, a room of Sitkas answering those questions he didn't have information about. They relaxed by playing softball. At the Sitka Community Association, the phone is answered by women with soft voices. They are like eagles, nobody knows where they go, nobody knows where they come from. What brought them out of Asia? Repression. Were they refugees or explorers trying to find out where the moon lived? What very ancient political, social, or natural upheaval brought them across those straits or from the south.

Once, the Tlingits owned all of southeast Alaska. William Johnson said his ancestral home included Glacier Bay National Park. When he returned he was turned away by shotgun. His smokehouse was burned down. "They let the white people use it, but turned me away." On the bombing of Angoon, another Tradition Bearer, George Davis, told me that in 1880 an American ship tried out a cannon-like gun and hit a whale. The whale leaped out of the ocean and "screamed like a wolf," he said as he told me a story part fiction, part autobiographical, part nonfiction (the new fiction is at least 20,000 years old). The Medicine Man, Tlingit for "Dog Salmon," said this was a bad sign. The next cannon shot killed the Medicine Man. The Tlingits took two days off from building a dock to mourn their Medicine Man. The singing and dancing made the Navy so nervous that they went in and mowed down the village indiscriminately killing women and children. They warned the survivors that if they ever told the story they'd come back and get them, too.* You see, the Navy thought they were the Plains Indians performing the ghost dance. In the official report the Americans said they did it because they found a still. Somebody had broken the law. Alaska had been declared "Indian country," which meant you couldn't drink. Notice all the things you can't do when the colonialists march in and set up their trading posts. The colonialists had been replaced by the squatters. Now they were telling the Natives what they could and couldn't have.

Andy Hope said they'd turned down land near Deer Island, and it wasn't, as Volker had said, the Forest Service and the Sierra Club which proposed this land, just the Forest Service. This land, Hope said, was piecemeal. Scattered about, which meant expensive management. He said the trees were few, and there was lots of muskeg, or swamp. He said they'd been offered a million dollars in cash, not ten million as Bolima said, but even this amount was vetoed by the Office of Management and Budget. "We don't want a monetary settlement," Hope said. "If they bleed us to death in court then that's the way it has to be."

To the charge that Shee Atika never consulted the Kootznoowoo corporation before making a land selection, Hope said that they'd discussed land selection with Mathew Fred and Danny Johnson, members of Kootznoowoo board. Sitka and Angoon had originally selected lands contiguous to one another as a way of cutting down on administrative costs.

"Bolima is a stone-age mercenary. A warlike person. He should go to Vietnam if he wants war," Hope said.

Hope accused the Angoons of putting too much faith in the Carter Administration. The Carter Administration isn't going to be around much

---

* The bombardment and burning of Angoon by combined military forces of the United States government on Oct. 26, 1882 is remembered by the Kootznoowoo Heritage Foundation with much bitterness; the foundation is requesting that the United States government make restitution for the deed.

longer, Hope said, and when it falls, "Kootznoowoo is going to be up shit's creek." The Sierra Club would be opposed to Sitka even if Sitka and the Angoons were together, Hope said. "Our quarrel isn't with Angoon, it's with the Sierra Club." The Sierra Club doesn't give a damn about the Angoons. They want both Sitka and Angoon off the Island.

Hope based his ideas of conservation on Felix Cohen's *The Principle of Conservation*. The aim of conservation, Cohen said, was to look out for future generations. Chief William Johnson pleaded, "What the kids going to do?" Hope said that if Angoon wanted to protect future generations, it would try to create some jobs for the youth. He said he respected the Tradition Bearers on Angoon, but thought they were being misled. If Bolima wanted to be seen as a Tlingit that was fine, Hope said. "But he should have enrolled to Kootznoowoo and become a shareholder to show that he really meant it."

I asked Hope what Shee Atika was going to do next. He said they'd try to get a summary judgment against the Sierra Club.

"You can't appeal to the Sierra Club's sense of conscience," he said. "You must have leverage."

What was Udall to gain from all of this? "He wants to have his bust next to Teddy Roosevelt's in the Conservationist Hall of Fame," Hope replied. "He's one of these new missionaries." A new missionary. That brought up a joke. I think maybe I made it up. Why did the missionaries switch from human rights to animal rights? Because bears and seals can't challenge them for leadership of the movement.

September 1979

## THE TLINGIT MARKET

I'm from the Tlingit market
Did someone say the Aztecs came here by boat when
the ice melted?
Here so long
We got beaches
We got tides
We got rain
We got water

Here so long
We had gold, it slipped, someone shipped it away
Lost
We got tourists
We got hotels
We got recreation
Give me a tour
We got leisure
We got trees
We chop wood
We carve wood
We burn it
We got poles
We got clans
We got old living
Here so long
We got spirit
Look me in the eye when I talk and you'll remember what I say
— *Andrew Hope*

I WAS TEMPTED to title my remarks about George Orwell "White man's Utopia Is a Black Man's Dystopia," after Muslim Minister Louis Farrakhan's 1960s calypso hit, "The White Man's Heaven Is a Black Man's Hell," until it occurred to me that, although any journalist or critic can refer to me as black, my very use of the word "white" marks me as a racist. This points to a double standard regarding what ethnic and racial designations mean, and the personal motives of those who use them. In fact, one could argue that the very words "white" and "black"—terms created by ancient American slave masters in order to create a cheap labor supply—are polarizing, given the conflict between these concepts in English, a conflict that has been frequently documented.

A sign of how enormously the media influence political trends in American life can be found in Theodore Bernstein's account of how the newspapers chose the term "black" over "Afro-American," because the word "black" was easier to set in headlines. I have noticed over the years that critics have often referred to me as a "black" without revealing their own ethnic backgrounds. This matter has become one of the themes of a new novel entitled *Reckless Eyeballing,* which means that people can define me and even profit from interpreting what they call "the black experience" (think of all of the millions non-Afro-American producers, artists, and writers have made from interpreting "Afro-American culture" through novels, film, music, and television—so much so that it's debatable whether the culture is "ethnic").

Afro-American culture, it often seems, is every American-European's third heritage. Even my writing students who are not Afro-American do not hesitate to create Afro-American characters and to employ what they feel are Afro-American speech patterns and styles, yet when Samm-Art Williams, an Afro-American playwright, wrote about the Nazi holocaust from the point of view of its victims, or when novelist Willard Motley created characters with an Italian background, their attempts were viewed as out of line.

Richard Wright's *Savage Holiday*, a novel which includes major "white" characters, has been viewed as a curiosity. However, no one blinks an eye when Francis Ford Coppola produces a film based upon Afro-American culture, *The Cotton Club*, or when John Sayles produces a miserable racist film that he calls a "black" horror movie; indeed, critics often write about non-white cultures as though their only reason for existence is to influence American-European artists. Fifteen thousand years of Native American poetry is important because it inspired what the Native Americans call "white shamans," like Walt Whitman. Rock and roll is important because it inspired Mick Jagger. We are spear-carriers in this great epic entitled "Western civilization," or "Judeo-Christian" culture, a phrase which makes you wonder why the Christians have given the Jews such a hard time for hundreds of years. Our attempts to write about other major cultures are considered a case of "reckless eyeballing." What you lookin' at? This is none of your business.

Some may view my attempt to comment on George Orwell's *1984* as a case of reckless eyeballing. Looking at something that doesn't concern me.

After viewing the science fiction movie *2001*, many Afro-American patrons commented about the absence of Afro-Americans in Arthur C. Clarke's and Stanley Kubrick's future world. In Ernest Callenbach's novel *Ectopia*, about a future quiche-and-sushi California paradise, the Afro-Americans are shunted away into pogroms. It's not that there is no room for groups other than privileged European males in the future; the problem for talents like Clarke and Callenbach is that they are writing from a limited point of view. They live in a world blind to the existence of what they refer to as "minority men," and to women. It's their viewpoint that's ethnic, if the word "ethnic" has come to mean narrow-minded. They cannot face the facts of a world of diverse cultures and people. *1984* is the monocultural nightmare. Writing from a restricted point of view, Orwell failed to see that for millions of his contemporaries, 1984 had already arrived. In the United States, Afro-Americans have been witnessing 1984 for over three hundred years. One can conclude that it is better to suffer from Reckless Eyeballing than to suffer from the disease that afflicted Winston Smith and his group of elitist intellectuals who provide the Big Brothers of the world with their information and attitudes. The disease of cultural astigmatism.

George Orwell's vision of a grim totalitarian dictatorship that he predicted would be in place by the year 1984 has provided Communists and anti-Communists with an opportunity to indulge in their usual name-calling and finger-pointing. Anti-Communist ideologues claim that the party and political order of 1984 resembles the regime that controls the Soviet Union. Orwell's Eurasia could very well be the Soviet Union. People of the West refer to the Russians as "Mongolian hordes" when they get mad at them, as when the South Korean Flight 007 jet was shot down over Soviet territory, Ms. Jeane Kirkpatrick, in a private speech before the Heritage Foundation, attributed the existence of a "totalitarian" system to Russia's history of "Oriental despotism," indicating that the political feud between the Soviet Union and the United States might be more racial than ideological.

Further evidence that Orwell had the Soviet Union in mind might be garnered from the fact that 1984's secret doctrine was based upon a slogan used to popularize one of Stalin's five-year plans. Certainly Goldstein, the party's archenemy, bears a relationship to Stalin's archenemy, Trotsky, in physical description, and like Trotsky, Goldstein wrote a book about a revolution being betrayed. Yet the author points out in several passages during the course of the book that the techniques used by the Soviet Communist party and the German Nazi party are quite crude in comparison with those exercised by the party in 1984. "The German Nazis and the Russian Communists come very close to us in their methods but they never had the courage to recognize their own motives. They pretended, perhaps they even believed, that they had seized power unwillingly and for a limited time, and that just around the corner there lay a paradise where human beings would be free and equal. We are not like that," Winston's interrogator, O'Brien, says at one point. The fact that the Soviet Union has banned the book 1984 has been viewed as proof that their government sees the book as being critical of their system. For the Soviet Union, Orwell was a "Socialist renegade," and in December of 1984 a Latvian dissident was arrested by Soviet authorities and sentenced to seven years hard labor for having a copy of the book in his possession. On January 26, 1983, a Soviet publication called *The Literary Gazette* went so far as to charge that it was really the United States Orwell had in mind when he invented the totalitarian government of Oceania, and pointed to parallels between life in that made-up country and life in the United States, which like Oceania lies in the middle of two oceans. The article argued that Newspeak, doublethink, and the Thought Police can be found in American life. One might reply that a government that bases its principles upon the often wordy and obscure jargon of Karl Marx has a lot of nerve accusing a rival government of using Newspeak and doublethink. Both governments are guilty of that. One could even say that those neoconservative critics who use the book 1984 a way of condemning Soviet society are also guilty of Newspeak and doublethink. (I have a hard time deciding whether it's neoconservatism they're pushing, or whether they use the term as a cover for neo-Nazism.)

Speculation concerning the author's intentions and the accuracy of his prophecies has become a blue-chip industry. I'm amazed that the people who gave us Monopoly haven't invented a game called 1984. United Technologies placed an ad in *Harper's* magazine that claimed that Orwell's vision of a sinister technology used to keep its citizens in line was wrong. "Technology has not enslaved us, but freed us," the ad announced, which ought to reassure those who are worried about the military uses of space or chemical and nuclear technology. Even the contemporary manufacturers of telescreens speakwriters got into the act. Apple Computer Company portrayed Big Brother as the IBM Company, while Apple's MacIntosh computer presumably represents the proles who would one day overtake Big Brother and overthrow Big Brother and his party. (If Orwell had a chance to write 1984 from the vantage point of 1984 instead of 1948 perhaps he would have seen the class of hackers instead of the class of proles as a threat to Big Brother's rule.)

Whose side was Orwell on? He has been called a capitalist, but most of his comments about capitalism are ironic and descriptive and do not constitute an endorsement of the capitalist system over the socialist system. The description of capitalist attitudes toward the proles given by the old men Winston encounters in the pub during his search for clues about the past seem pretty accurate to me.

> "They owned everything that there was to own. They lived in great gorgeous houses with thirty servants, they rode about in motor cars and four-horse carriages, they drank champagne, they wore top hats.... they and a few lawyers and priests and so forth who lived on them—were the lords of the earth. Everything existed for their benefit. You—the ordinary people, the workers—were their slaves. They could do what they liked with you. They could ship you off to Canada like cattle."

And it does in no way serve as a vehicle for the author's praise of capital-ism. Orwell's cynicism, which comes through in his biting descriptions of characters, who are often mangled by the author, indicates a "plague on both your houses" attitude toward capitalism and communism as economic sys-tems. His misanthropic inclinations might be traced to the tuberculosis he suffered while writing the book and may also account for the book's apoca-lyptic vision.

Even though the author's praise for the proles—eighty-three percent of Oceania is prole, and they are permitted a freedom the Party members are denied and even sass the Thought Police—his description of the proles is reminiscent of those employed by American literature's archsnob Henry James in his story "Brooksmith." They don't speak English correctly. Their tastes are bad; their children are savages; they smell of "hideous . . . sour beer"; they're the only members of the population permitted to enjoy sex, for the Party believes that "only proles and animals are free." The Party doesn't even deem it necessary to install telescreens in their homes. (In fact, one could say that the proles in 1984 are better off than the contemporary proles. The 1984 proles are encouraged to reproduce while there is evidence that many of today's proletariat women—Native American, black, and poor —have been sterilized without their permission.) While Winston Smith shares the attitude of 1984's author George Orwell regarding the proles, that "If there was hope, it must lie in the proles, because only there, in those swarming disregarded masses . . . could the force to destroy the Party ever be generated," Smith's ambivalent view of the proletariat reminds one of the attraction-revulsion ideas concerning the working class held by a group of intellectuals, sanctioned by the American media as the United States' official intelligentsia, the New York intellectuals, or the Family. Those who aban-doned Marxism and leftwing politics for the religion of aesthetic traditional-ism, or neoconservatism, after being disillusioned by Joseph Stalin and hounded by Joe McCarthy.

Their attitudes are mercilessly satirized in Mary McCarthy's superb book The Oasis. Although they spend a lot of time denying their power, they set the trends of not only American literature but Afro-American literature as well, a literature they view as part of a separate tradition, treating it as such in their journals, in which all "black" writers are lumped together.

Many of these ex-socialists have made their career out of criticizing popu-lar culture, the Third World, the grass roots, populism, the underclass, and the rest of the labels they apply to the rest of us. Like them, Winston Smith, whose favorite word seems to be "rubbish," wanders about searching for a lost tradition and commenting on the decline of good tastes. The book includes endless dawdling about the lack of "good books," chocolate, cigarettes, wine, whiskey (Party intellectuals drink Victory gin; the masses, beer), and good English (though the author of 1984 constantly confuses "one another" with "each other"). Winston Smith longs for antiques: china, glass, brass candlesticks, all suggesting a nostalgia for what the Party condemns as ownlife, and what the Marxists referred to as bourgeois individualism. If the world of 1984 is one of dystopia, then utopia for Winston Smith would be a long dinner party on the Upper West Side of New York that would include much prattle concerning abstract things, or a gourmet tour of Berkeley.

As a novel, 1984 contains flaws that creative writing students are always warned to avoid. The author bullies both the readers and his characters with lengthy amateur psychoanalysis (another New York intellectual pastime) of their motives, which puts him in the position of a literary Big Brother submitting the characters in his fiction, for whom he has little regard, to thought control. His repetitious and often confusing and contradictory descriptions of the political system of his fictional world interrupt the story line, his narrative often deteriorates into cant and polemics, and his often meanspirited prejudices seem odd and puzzling. Some of his scenes are embarrassingly and unintentionally funny, as when he has the lovers Winston and Julia meet in a church that has been A-bombed thirty years before. His love scenes contain descriptions that one associates with pulp writing: "She twisted herself round and pressed her bosom against him. He could feel her breasts, ripe yet firm, through her overalls. Her body seemed to be pouring some of its youth and vigor into his." For a book touted for its glimpse into a future sinister technology, most of the technology—the telescreen and the speakwrite rockets—is based upon primitive prototypes that were available in Orwell's time.

However, at least Orwell had the daring to make a guess and take a chance in a form—the novel—whose practitioners often take the easy way out, writing books with conventional plots and predictable characterizations that indolent critics demand be "well-rounded"; books that lack the fresh imagery one expects of the poet. One can say that Orwell's is at least interesting and different. He deserves a high mark for imagination and it is a tribute to him that many of his predictions about the state of things in the year 1984 have come true. Two political cyclops that one might call Oceania and Eurasia are at loggerheads and a world, scared to death, looks on helplessly. Giant and mindless bureaucracies inspect the actions of citizens as though they were

Orwell's "beetles under a microscope." (It's not the crude torture devices or the horrors of Room 101 that ultimately get Winston Smith to confess, but the endless questioning by bureaucrats: "Their real weapon was the merciless questioning that went on and on hour after hour, tripping him up, laying traps for him at every step of lies and self-contradiction, until he began weeping as much from shame as from nervous fatigue." Anyone who's ever had a driver's test knows the feeling.)

How accurate was George Orwell's projection concerning the surveillance of contemporary citizens by a totalitarian government? A survey conducted on September 1, 1983, of 1256 people, paid for by the Southern New England Telephone Company, found that the percentage of Americans who are, "very concerned" about threats to personal privacy had increased from thirty-one percent in 1978 to forty-eight percent in 1983. Those who believed that their privacy was being invaded cited collection and sharing of data about them by the IRS, FBI, census bureau, phone companies, banks, loan companies, credit bureaus, and other agents of the private and government sectors as a cause for alarm. Modern citizens not only have to fear surveillance conducted by their government, but surveillance by enemies of the government as well.

According to *The Berkeley Review,* 2 February 1984, "competent technical sources" indicated that "the Soviet Consulate in San Francisco has the resources and capability of intercepting important microwave telephone transmissions in the area."

Microwave interception is just one of the toys used by governments and the private sector to keep tabs on citizens. Also available, according to *Security World,* the trade journal of the industrial security field, are "infra-ultrasonic detectors sensitive to noise or motion, electric eyes which activate cameras and silent alarms in stockrooms and other 'high security areas,' infrared detection systems, motion detectors, bugging devices, debugging devices, paper shredders, and virtually everything else the imagination can conceive."

Orwell was correct, and his prediction concerning the extent of surveillance to which contemporary citizens are subjected by government and the private sector falls on the conservative side.

Moreover, the physical torture inflicted upon dissenters and ownlifers continues. It sometimes seems that torturing other people still ranks as one of mankind's chief pleasures and pastimes. In April 1984, Amnesty International described the methods of torture that are used in at least one-third of the world's nations, including the Soviet Union and the United States. They include pain-inducing drugs given in "psychiatric clinics," "beatings, electrical and acid torture, the spraying of tear gas into the faces of prison inmates." In Iran's Evin prison, the report noted, "small children are forced to watch their mothers being tortured."

Some people didn't have to wait until 1984 for this kind of relentless torture and surveillance to happen to them. For Afro-Americans, it could be argued that every year they've spent in this country since they arrived in chains to perform forced labor has been 1984. For the first three hundred years, those who considered them to be property kept tabs on their every action, or relegated this task to a class of Overseers and Patrollers, Big Brother's human surveillance equipment of the time.

As Julia and Winston's love affair was broken up by the authorities, many slave men and women were forced to go their separate ways or betray each other for fear of torture and now, because of welfare eligibility requirements in some states, they must live apart or starve. The knock at the door at night has always meant for Afro-Americans the possibility that white men have arrived to take you somewhere to torture you or to lynch you: the Klan, the Nazi party, the FBI, the state, county, and local police, as well as any number of vigilante groups.

Behavior modification involving drugs and other technologies has been regularly practiced on Afro-American men and women, and quack scientists have been permitted to use them as guinea pigs in infamous and Nazi-styled experiments such as the Tuskegee syphilis experiments. When Nixon's adviser, Arnold Hutschnecker, proposed to test children for antisocial behavior, he had Afro-American children in mind.

There are other parallels between the terrors experienced by the Party members in 1984 and those Afro-Americans have experienced throughout their history in the United States.

In 1984, literacy is discouraged by the state. When Winston Smith is arrested, his diary is used as evidence against him. During the period of slavery, a slave who read or wrote could be maimed or killed, and even in modern times an AfroAmerican writer's words have been used against him, as both Langston Hughes and W. E. B. DuBois discovered when they testified before the contemporary version of the Thought Police, the House Un-American Activities Committee. Even though European-Americans were humiliated and psychologically tortured by the same forces, Afro-Americans always seem to get the worst of it. No white man has been spied upon the way Marcus Garvey, Malcolm X, or Martin Luther King, Jr., who was encouraged by the FBI to commit suicide, were spied upon.

But we found out about the hideous surveillance of those men through the Freedom of Information Act, and this is the reason why I feel that it is Winston Smith's class of elitist intellectuals and monoculturalists (called the "Town Set" by populists of the 1880s) who are more likely to bring about the kind of world that George Orwell envisioned than any American government, for no matter what totalitarian tendencies it might have, no matter how many Huston Plans a government might be tempted to try, sooner or later an administration, no matter how abhorrent its policies, will leave office, and there's always the possibility that whatever excesses it may have condoned will be exposed.

But there seems to be no way to remove the party intellectuals whose ideas control the media, and by media I mean any industry involved in communications: television, radio, newspapers, the universities, and culture; in fact, it has sometimes been the government that has made an effort to moderate the resistance of this class to multiculturalism in American society, and to the participation of women and minority men in the communications industry. It has been government reports that have exposed the domination of the media by men of the same class and interests. It is members of this class—sometimes referred to as "the brightest and the best"- – who counsel politicians, and they who train politicians how to think.

Winston Smith's attitudes toward women and minority men are typical of the attitudes held by this class. The women who appear in 1984 are either stupid or childlike. It is they who are the most susceptible to the teachings of Big Brother. They are zaftig slumgoddesses with mountainous, earth-mother bodies—the salt of the earth—or they are fallen women like Julia, who admits to having slept with a number of men, among them hypocritical Party members. That's all right, Winston Smith says. I don't like pure things anyway. In 1984, a Third World man has a walk-on. He is described as "the little yellow-faced servant . . . carrying a tray with a decanter and glasses." The other nonwhites are off somewhere in Asia or Africa, scene of Orwell's Armageddon.

For "the brightest and the best," the Party intellectuals, the cultures of women and minority men have been vaporized and flushed down the memory hole. Winston Smith's job is that of doctoring history, of vaporizing and distorting things. Winston Smith accuses his interrogators of embracing a primitive solipsistic philosophy, "the belief that nothing exists outside of your own mind," but cannot see his own solipsistic attitudes and those of his Brotherhood.

What went wrong in Lebanon? How did we lose Vietnam? Where are we? What's going on? the politicians ask as they lurch from disaster to disaster. For the Party intellectuals, nothing exists outside of their monocultural view of things. They don't explain to the Big Brothers they serve that with the shrinkage of the world that has occurred because of modern communications technology, lazy and inarticulate responses—brute force—no longer work.

The ambassador to the United Nations is the author of a number of crude remarks expressing a contempt for internationalism and what she and her staff refer to as the "Third World." She caught the eye of the administration after her articles appeared in *Commentary* magazine, a hangout for the right-wing branch of the New York intellectuals. These monoculturalists discourage any contact with other cultures abroad and at home. The Party discourages the learning of foreign languages, reminiscent of the contemporary antibilingual education campaign here at home (when the American hostages were seized, nobody in the American Embassy could speak to the Iranians in their language). They desire that everybody be ignorant like them, yet the mass media refer to them as intellectuals when one Paul Metcalf, or one Wendy Rose, or one Toni Cade Bambara is worth more than the whole crowd.

Instead of attempting to communicate with other cultures at home and abroad, members of the Family like Midge Decter and Nathan Glazer attempt to engage them in endless competition over who is going to be their most beloved "minority."

Nathan Glazer wants to know why Afro-Americans haven't made it while the Indians and the Hispanics have. Nathan Glazer wants to take a peek at our chromosomes to see if that's the reason why Afro-Americans haven't made it. The New York intellectual is bent upon "making it." To be in a position to influence public policy. To be invited to dinner by the White House and be told that the president liked your arguments opposing affirmative action. Making it.

Their counterparts in the television, movie, and newspaper industries are constantly subjecting women and minority men to "Hate Week," exciting the population with inflammatory disinformation smears against them, the way

the media in 1984 stir up hatred against the Eurasians and the East Asians.
We're criminals and brutes to them; they like us to be like Mr. T, a playful
though menacing brute who is in a constant state of belligerency. Savages.
They even hate mild-mannered people like Michael Jackson and Larry
Holmes and Mayor Bradley, excoriating them and their achievements in hate-
ful vitriolic column after column. It is this malice and cultural astigmatism
that will eventually lead to the downfall of the Party, Winston Smith's people.
They can't see us but we can see them. They don't know us but—as multicultural writers—we know them at their worst and at their best. To them, we
are ethnics; to them, we are the proles, a name I'm sure they would apply to
writers like Leslie Silko, Lorna Dee Cervantes, Andy Hope, Sister Goodwin,
Nash Candelaria, and Simon Ortiz, American aristocrats whose ancestors
were among the first families of North America.

Their almost-religious clinging to monocultural values and their insis-
tence upon intellectual obedience to what they and Winston Smith refer to as
"tradition" has contributed to the United States' warped perception of the
world and of cultures at home. They have given the American eye a bad dose
of cultural astigmatism. They are the true Thought Police, and what's the
difference between the current fundamentalists' drive for an Establishment
Church and their desire to impose their values upon the rest of us in what
was meant to be a pluralistic society?

Orwell's 1984 is rich in resonance and lends itself to many interpretations,
the essence of modern art. It is poetic, and packed with sharp and insightful
proverbs, but at the same time prolix and speckled with bad writing. But it is
still a great book and a great work of art in the same sense that *Uncle Tom's
Cabin* and *Native Son* are great works of art, because they inspired, and
because they sprang from, the soul, which is the source of all great art. Han-
del said that when he wrote the *Messiah* God had visited him, and with 1984
the spirit visited George Orwell, and the result is this handwriting on the
wall, this warning to future generations of what happens when truth and art
disappear from a society.

Will Orwell's idealistic hope ever come true? Will the proles overthrow
Big Brother and his intellectuals, the Party? That game is still being played,
but it's quite possible that this generation will witness the final outcome of
this old battle. As the middle class vanishes all over the world, this weary,
beat-upon class that has served as a buffer between the rich and the poor, the
world will be divided between Big Brother and the proles, and if the proles do
overthrow Big Brother and his overclass intellectuals, maybe they will have

the tolerance that was never shown toward their cultures, maybe they will have the good sense to spare the Party its greatest nightmare, that the cultural annihilation they practiced toward others will not be aimed at them, and that the abuse and the torture they meted out to others will not be meted out to them.

It is significant that George Orwell, who served British imperialism in Burma, casts Winston Smith's chief interrogator as the Irishman O'Brien.

## BIGGER AND O.J.

IN Richard Wright's *Native Son,* Bigger Thomas, a part-time hoodlum and welfare recipient, lives in the slums of Chicago with his dysfunctional family. He gets a job in the rich household of the Daltons, a wealthy white family, whose philanthropic patriarch is also a slumlord. His wife is blind, and his daughter flirts with radical politics and has a lover. After driving the drunken daughter Mary home one night, he tries to put her to bed, all done in innocence, but so as to avoid detection by her blind mother, who enters the room, he suffocates Mary. The narrator calls this an accident. The rest of the novel covers Bigger's flight from justice, capture, and imprisonment. Unlike today's middle-class writers who write about underclass characters, the Boyz in the Hood, Richard Wright knew what he was talking about. Not only had he been poor, but as a youth radical worker he got to know many Biggers and, on the basis of this experience, was able to draw a character so convincing that Bigger has become an archetype for the inner-cities' disaffiliated youth.

During the O.J. Simpson trial, Simpson was compared to Shakespeare's Othello, which seemed stretched, since it is apparent that while Othello was a naive patsy, O.J. Simpson's cunning and intellect contributed to his legal team's overwhelming one of the most formidable adversarial armadas ever assembled: forty prosecutors, an international police force, including Interpol, the FBI, and media investigation teams so biased as to appear as operatives for the prosecution. In addition, a hi-tech paradigm constructed by a Silicon Valley computer, which concluded that Simpson was the killer, was used by the prosecution. Moreover, Nicole Simpson was no Desdemona.

On other occasions, Simpson was compared to Bigger Thomas. On the surface, the two have little in common. Bigger Thomas was a poor, rootless slum-dweller whose opportunities were slight. O.J. Simpson, though of humble origin, graduated from college, became a football star with the Buffalo Bills, a celebrity salesperson for Hertz Rent A Car, and a movie actor. While Bigger Thomas was one who used violence to communicate with his associates, O.J. Simpson is highly articulate. I saw him deliver a stand-up monologue on *Saturday Night Live*. It was flawless.

O.J. was comfortable in a world of whites, while Bigger remained in a psychological and mental slum, even though the hand of white philanthropy reached out to him. What Bigger and O.J. Simpson do have in common is that both were arrested for the murder of blond white women, both were subjected to a mob-rule public opinion that convicted them before all of the evidence was examined, and both were tried in the media, which, instead of serving as an objective reporter of the facts, inflamed the situation and contributed to a racial divide. (A caller into NPR's "Talk of the Nation" on March 28, 1996, asked why the media never repeated its showing of a split screen that showed both an all-white bar in Buffalo, New York, and a gathering of blacks, cheering the announcement of the acquittal. Christopher Darden, the show's guest, agreed with the caller that the media contributed to a racial divide by depicting all whites in favor of a guilty verdict, and all blacks favoring an acquittal.) This wouldn't be the first time. A book titled *The Betrayal of the Negro* by Dr. Rayford W. Logan documents how, historically, the American media have contributed to racial discord and riots between whites and blacks. For example, the Carnival Riot that took place in New Orleans in 1900 was the result of a newspaper publisher's agitation, both public and editorial.

Richard Wright's book also indicates that the relationship between African Americans and the racist criminal justice system hasn't changed since Richard Wright wrote *Native Son*.

The views of the characters and the narrator about politics, class, gender, religion, economics, and the media also have a contemporary ring. Bigger's arrest, imprisonment, trial, and execution provide Wright with an opportunity to explore racism in the criminal justice systems, which is still an issue— especially when black youth are five to ten times more likely to be incarcerated than white youth for committing the same crime, and when blacks are receiving mandatory five-year sentences for possession of crack cocaine while white crack possessors are not, and when there exists a disproportionate number of black prisoners on death row. My examination of Uniform Crime

Reports (U.C.R.), a system that critics accuse of being flawed, leads me to conclude that blacks don't commit more crimes: they're arrested more.

The institutions that manipulate the crime figures are often institutions whose racist attitudes toward blacks have been documented. The police departments and the FBI have been investigating and often smearing black celebrities and political leaders at least since 1919. In the Simpson case, it was obvious that the police were willing to lie in order to convict a black defendant, and the FBI's role was also designed to benefit the prosecution. In fact, during the last phase of the trial, a witness was ready to testify about an FBI scientist's willingness to produce results favorable to the prosecution. The FBI agent in question agreed with the defense about some crucial sock testimony but, after being contacted by the prosecution, changed his testimony.

Bigger travels through the novel complaining about his lack of freedom in a white society that controls him and orders him around. After the Simpson verdict, Tammy Bruce, head of Los Angeles NOW, proposed that Simpson leave the country and be removed from the culture. Media commentators like Geraldo Rivera urged that he be ostracized. Both Rivera and Bruce were attempting to restrict Simpson's movements, to control him. Nothing could be more revealing of the attitudes of some whites toward African Americans than Jeffrey Toobin's remark that Simpson was now treated like a "pariah." Obviously, Simpson has been greeted very warmly by African American audiences. For Toobin, being a pariah means ostracism by the wealthy whites of Brentwood. Where do pariahs go? To the African American community, which, for Toobin, is occupied by intellectually inferior lepers. Professor Dennis Schatzman described the Toobin book as the second bell curve in which blacks are characterized as stupid and incapable of understanding hard evidence. Though he found no evidence to accuse Colonel North of drug dealing, Toobin is convinced of Simpson's guilt. It figures. Mr. Toobin's ideas about blacks are consistent with his employer's, the *New Yorker*, attitudes toward blacks. Its founding editor, Harold Ross, characterized "negroes" as "dangerous or funny." The soft treatment accorded Toobin by the media was typical of how pro-prosecution writers and pundits were coddled and nurtured. Former Los Angeles Police Chief Darryl Gates told the networks that he never used the "N" word. However, former Chief of Police of San Jose Joseph McNamara, now a fellow at the Hoover Institute, said that he had heard Gates use the word "nigger" frequently. When I called a local television station to ask McNamara, a guest on the show, to elaborate, the screener said that she didn't think the question important.

Bigger tells his lawyer, Max, "...a guy gets tired of being told what he can do and can't do. You get a little job here and a little job there. You shine shoes, sweep streets; anything..." Elsewhere he mentions the penal-like condition of African Americans. "Not only had he lived where they told him to live, not only had he done what they told him to do, not only had he done these things until he had killed to be quit of them; but even after obeying, after killing, they still ruled him. He was their property, heart and soul, body and blood." Like Bigger, Simpson became a commodity, making fortunes for television networks and publishers, rescuing careers, and even providing a man who hated him, Chris Darden, with an opportunity to make more money than he ever would have had he remained an obscure Los Angeles prosecutor; and his fellow prosecutor, Marcia Clark, received the third highest advance in history to write a nonfiction book about the case. Geraldo Rivera's show was about to be dropped, which would have jeopardized his $500,000 per year income, before he began to do hundreds of shows about Simpson. The ratings of CNN were described as "languishing" before the onset of the Simpson trial. Afterwards its ratings increased sevenfold and put Ted Turner in a position to bargain with CBS and Time–Warner. Though journalists and politicians complained about the $13 million that the Simpson case cost Los Angeles, they rarely mentioned the millions made by the city as the result of it being the site of the trial, including $400 million, in hotel taxes.

Moreover, an industry of mostly white pundits and commentators, some of whom didn't even follow the trial yet had opinions, was generated as a result of the trial. CNN's Greta Van Susteran and Roger Cossack and Entertainment TV's Kathleen Sullivan deserve congratulations for their fair and unbiased coverage of the trial. *Newsday's* Shirley Perleman also deserves kudos for her avoiding the lurid stampede toward the tabloid exhibited by many journalists covering the case, but in their general coverage, the media were on bended knees before the prosecution. Katie Couric, Geraldo Rivera, and Gloria Allred became little more than advocates for the Brown family, abandoning any pretense of objectivity.

Steve Brill's *Court TV*, which has been accused of commercializing and tabloidizing the criminal justice system, ran ads for the O.J. trial, and Brill was quoted by the *New York Observer* as saying that he was the happiest man on the planet when O.J. didn't commit suicide, a quote that Brill denied having made. At one point, the amount of money made by some businesses from the O.J. phenomenon totaled $300 million, more than the economy of Grenada; yet, when Simpson attempted to earn money by promoting a video that explained his side of the case, he was chastised by others who were making money from the case themselves, including Dominick Dunne, who expressed his disgust about Simpson marketing his video, even while writing his own book about the case. Mr. Dunne, one of a number of commentators who pronounced Simpson guilty before the defense began its case, wrote vicious, gossipy articles in *Vanity Fair* (published by a tabloid-happy import named Tina Brown). Dunne called the jury, which included nine African American women, stupid for acquitting Simpson; yet he was also used by NBC as an objective reporter about the trial.

Of Whites, Bigger says, "They choke you off the face of the earth...they don't even let you feel what you want to feel. They after you so hot and hard you can only feel what they doing to you. They kill you before you die."

In another section Bigger says, "We black and they white. They got things and we ain't. They do things and we can't. It's just like living in jail. Half the time I feel like I'm on the outside of the world peeping in through a knothole in the fence...."

This remark by Bigger expresses the feeling that many African Americans, Hispanics, Asian Americans, and Native Americans have when viewing a media that's fifty years behind the South in their efforts to diversify. Having their points-of-view excluded from a media discussion during which their enemies often discuss their lives and culture contemptuously and without risk of rebuttal is for African Americans and others like peeping into the world from a knothole in a fence. During the recent protests over Hollywood's lack of black Oscar nominees, it was revealed that the number of black writers who are members of the Screen Writers' Guild totals two and a half percent. Minority representation in newspapers and television is slightly higher, and so the dialogue regarding race in this country is monopolized by white males, who are ignorant of black history and culture, talking to each other, or to themselves. This characterized the media discussion in the Simpson case. The *New Yorker's* Jeffrey Toobin, who carried on like a prosecution plant, even went so far as to serve as a consultant to other white journalists about the mores in the African American community. Because he presumably was able to read the minds of the mostly black female jury, he predicted, the night before the acquittal, that they would convict Simpson. Shortly before the verdict another white male expert on black psychology predicted that the black women would vote for conviction because black women can tell when black men are lying.

The most conspicuous representative of white society for many blacks, and the only whites whom they may see on a day-to-day basis, are the police, who are often viewed as members of an invading force, which arrives in the community to impose brutality and engage in illicit activities. This image is reinforced by the large percentage of policemen who don't reside in the inner city. In Oakland, California, where I live, eighty percent of the police reside outside of the city, including one officer who commutes from Denver, Colorado. Every time the citizens of Oakland attempt to change this situation, they are opposed by the policeman's union.

As in the case of the 1992 Stuart case in Boston, in which a white man claimed that his pregnant wife was murdered by a black man, and the 1994 Susan Smith case, in which a white woman accused a fictitious black figure of murdering her children, the murder of a white person, especially a Nordic-appearing white woman, as in the Simpson case, puts the entire black male population under suspicion. Police suspend with the Bill of Rights and employ the kind of tactics that the United States says it despises in totalitarian regimes. In *Native Son,* the police and the vigilantes search every black home under a blanket warrant from the mayor. The police in the Simpson case were accused by the judge of a reckless disregard for the truth when they concocted a probable cause for entering Simpson property without a warrant.

After it is discovered that Bigger is responsible for Mary Dalton's death, thousands of police and vigilantes throw a cordon around the Black Belt. For whites, all blacks become culpable for the actions of one black and must be punished. Since the Simpson case, America's yellow journalists, who feed upon racial psychoses for profit, have been speculating about how whites are going to pay blacks for the verdict. Will affirmative-action programs be curtailed? Will welfare policies become more stringent? Some have suggested that this is how whites riot—economically—though whites still engage in physical riots as well. Thirteen percent of those arrested during the 1992 riots that took place after the Rodney King verdict were white (and probably from two-parent households), yet no black or Latino mob has given as good a riot as Irish Americans did in New York in the late 1800s. The *Wall Street Journal* and Los Angeles mayor Tom Bradley said that whites were responsible for burning down restaurants in Koreatown.

Since the typical recipient of both affirmative action and welfare is white, this retaliation will affect whites as well. Mob psychoses cause one to cut off one's nose to spite one's face. Self-maiming is the kind of action that results from a psychosis.

In Wright's time, the whites perpetrated physical assaults upon African Americans when a black man was accused of a heinous crime against a white. After Bigger has escaped, black men are beaten and the homes of black people are assaulted. One thousand homes are raided. The *New York Times* of October 25, 1995, reported that interviews conducted with students on American campuses revealed an anger among whites about the outcome of the Simpson trial. Oprah Winfrey reported that tips given black doormen declined after the Simpson verdict. (A week after Ms. Winfrey made this remark, the black doormen at New Orleans's Fairmont Hotel told me the same thing.) Economic reprisals were also visited upon blacks after Bigger Thomas's escape. Bigger reads a newspaper that reports "several hundred Negro employees throughout the city" had been dismissed from jobs. A well-known banker's wife phoned a newspaper that she dismissed her Negro cook "for fear that she might poison the children." Just as, in some instances, groups of Native Americans were slaughtered because of the actions of one or two, and the German Jews paid with Krisstalnacht after a Jew assassinated a high-ranking Nazi official, the fact that all blacks are still blamed for the actions of some blacks is an indication of how much racism in this country persists. In fact, freedom can be measured according to the degree of anonymity that the society offers to members of a particular group. Though Irish American Andy Rooney offered a reward for the capture of Ron Goldman and Nicole Simpson's killers, no one in the media blames Andy Rooney for the actions of Irish-American Timothy McVeigh, who is suspect in the bombing of the Oklahoma City federal building, nor were Irish-American leaders like Daniel Moynihan required to condemn Irish-American extremists like Pat Buchanan. (In fact *Newsweek*, which ran a scurrilous article about Simpson, presented what for some was a sympathetic portrait of Oklahoma bombing suspect McVeigh and *Time*, which issued a controversial cover portrait of Simpson, printed a benign one of McVeigh.)

As soon as Bigger encounters the police he is accosted with "N" words, "A" words, and "B" words. He's an animal, a black son of a bitch. The "array of faces, white and looming," threaten to kill him, to lynch him. After the Simpson verdict, a white woman called one of the talk shows and said that the people in her town were saying that the "nigger" ought to be lynched, that the "nigger" ought to be burned. For me, the low point of the ugly and racist journalism in the Simpson case occurred when A. J. Benza, a reporter for the *Daily News*, appearing on Entertainment Network's *The Gossip Show*, encouraged Fred Goldman to shoot Simpson.

In *Native Son*, Bigger is called a black ape. Black men are animals, and the inner cities are the jungles that we inhabit. Bigger is described as a "rapacious beast who is driven from his den into the open. He is a beast utterly untouched by the softening influence of modern civilization. He seems out of place in a white man's civilization, according to the *Tribune,* the rabble-rousing newspaper that carries the story of Bigger's flight, capture, imprisonment, and trial. Such descriptions of African Americans are not limited to contemporary ultra-right publications; but they are the kinds of things one might read in the *New Republic,* where *The Bell Curve* was favorably discussed, or *The End of Racism,* where an imported demagogue named Dinesh D'souza (who was once associated with the anti-black, anti-Semitic *Dartmouth Review,* and who is backed by powerful interests, including William Simon, a former cabinet member, the Olin Foundation, and the American Enterprise Institute) writes that blacks have a civilization gap. Mr. Dinesh D'souza suffers from the same historical amnesia as the Irish police captain who is quoted in the same *Tribune* article in Wright's novel describing Bigger as a beast, a man without civilization. A governor general of India said that Indians had the intelligence of a dog, and the British said that the Irish were the earlier missing link in the human species, which matches the description of Bigger in the novel. It has been noted that in the United States, the former victims of racial oppression practice racist oppression against blacks.

Animal imagery was also used to describe Simpson. A savage. A beast. The networks kept rubbing the 1993 tape recording in the public's face, without informing them that during the time period of this tape Simpson didn't strike Nicole Simpson. Photos of her bruised face were shown to worldwide audiences without the media stipulating that there was no proof that Simpson was responsible for inflicting these bruises. In one of a number of salacious *Vanity Fair* pieces about the case written by Dominick Dunne, Nicole Simpson's reference to Simpson as an animal was gleefully highlighted in bold type. In a phone call to the *Larry King Show,* Louis H. Brown, Nicole Simpson's father, a man who has benefited from Simpson's largesse, called Simpson an animal when it was suggested that the defense might call Sidney Simpson as a witness. Whether Brown expressed indignation at the actions of his daughter Dominique is not known; she sold pictures of a topless Nicole, and of the Simpson children, to tabloid publications for $100,000.

While Wright mocks the novel's journalists with scathing gusto, these early journalists behave like Freedom Forum Fellows in comparison to today's journalists, those who work for outfits whose ambition is not to create good journalism but to make money. So sleazy was the coverage of the Simpson case that when the editor of the *National Enquirer* appeared on ABC's *Nightline* to discuss the case in the company of some prominent mainstream journalists, he seemed right at home. In the Thomas case, as in the Simpson case, the media behaved as a sort of public relations department for the police and for the prosecution, inflaming the public with sensational copy unfavorable to the defendant. From the time of the Simpson arrest, the police and the media began a partnership—the media doing its part by leaking damaging information, much of which was false. Remember the ski mask and the scratches on O.J.'s body? Five days after Simpson's arrest, CBS ran a poll to which respondents were asked whether, if convicted, Simpson should receive life imprisonment or death. There was no question in CBS's mind about Simpson's guilt.

A gullible American public, which reveals its ignorance about the world in poll after poll, is an easy prey for manipulation by the media that keeps them confused and naive. A white public, large segments of which expresses shock frequently when some outrage upon the black community is exposed, is fair game. They're shocked that the CIA is cooperating with drug dealers who've been selling drugs in Oakland, San Francisco, and Los Angeles. They're shocked that Susan Smith lied about blacks kidnapping her children. They're shocked that the government permits plutonium injections upon unsuspecting blacks. They're shocked by the brutal beating of Rodney King. They're shocked by Mark Fuhrman's testimony about the kind of torture and cruelty practiced against blacks and Latinos in police stations throughout the country. Even the pundits and the commentators showed themselves to be as naive as the average white about the police's attitudes toward black Americans. Jack Ford, who was then a commentator for *Court TV* (before his looks got him a job on NBC), said that the idea of the police planting evidence was absurd. The white commentariat and segments of the white public also expressed a naivete about how the drug trade works in California. Willard Scott hinted on the *Today* show that cocaine is the drug of choice among media personnel, and so they must reside in a world where the drug dealers extend unlimited credit and make appointments before arriving to slay deadbeats. The white public dismissed the theory that drug kingpins murdered Nicole Simpson and Ron Goldman, yet Colombian nationals are regularly arrested for drug dealings in California. Many whites showed their naivete about how the criminal justice system affects blacks when they were seduced by Mark Fuhrman's testimony. Even the media lavished praise upon

Fuhrman. He became a hero to many whites and had the McKinny tapes, during which he revealed his hated of blacks and Mexicans, not come to light, it's quite possible that he could have become a powerful political figure, running on a fascist platform. Not only did Fuhrman express a bias toward Mexican Americans and African Americans, but he also displayed Nazi paraphenalia. In addition, two Jews told *Hard Copy* that Fuhrman beat them up.

This early trial by leak, and the subsequent siding with the police and prosecution by the media, its pundits, and pro-prosecution commentariat, did much to influence the polls that saw the majority of whites convinced of Simpson's guilt long before evidence had been introduced and the defense had begun its arguments. I followed the case on a daily basis and found the media coverage to be full of errors and a pro-prosecution bias. Those seven thousand daily callers, who followed the trial, instead of relying upon news reports, and who were polled daily by the Entertainment network, consistently favored the defense in their voting, and at the end of the case voted overwhelmingly for acquittal. Whites telling white pollsters that they believed in O.J.'s guilt may have been a result of their desiring to express solidarity with pollsters belonging to the same race. When they voted by phone and were able to be anonymous, those who followed the case on a daily basis voted for the defense. If the majority of whites do believe in Simpson's guilt, it could be the result of the media siding with the prosecution. In taped network news reports which were blatantly of such a nature, often the networks failed to even cover the defense's arguments. When Johnny Cochran attributes the animus toward Simpson to pontificating pundits and biased wrapups, he has a point. Alan M. Dershowitz pointed to one glaring example of media bias when he mentioned a report on the case by the *New York Times*, whose copy was consistently pro-prosecution and whose reporter, David Margolick, seemed to spend most of his time hanging out with Faye Resnick. After the glove demonstration, Margolick said that the gloves fit "snugly" even though he didn't witness the demonstration. During an exchange with a black lawyer, Margolick pompously ridiculed the legal profession. Pundits like Jeffrey Toobin also raised questions about the ethics of the legal profession. Toobin works for the *New Yorker* magazine, whose editorial policies are being influenced by Roseanne Barr, a Denise Brown confidante, leading to the resignations of some of its finest writers. Certainly the legal profession could use some reform, but so could the media. But we won't hear about it because the media resent criticism. They can dish it out but they can't take it.

Their attitude toward Simpson is typical of their attitude toward black people in general, which hasn't changed since the time of Wright's novel: Blacks are guilty until proven guilty. CNBC's Jay Monahan, expressing regret that the public will have to rely upon media reports of the civil trial instead of being able to watch it on television, said on October 3 that "the bad reporting and bad commentary which characterized the media's treatment of the first trial contributed to the polls which saw the majority of whites convinced of Simpson's guilt, while those who actually followed the trial came to the opposite conclusion." He also questioned the methodology of the polls.

Bigger's lawyer accuses the press of being part of a conspiracy to kill not only Bigger but the Communist party in the hearts of its readers. The press then, as now, reaps revenues by whipping up irrational fear on the part of the white population, and being used as a weapon against minorities and unpopular beliefs. And instead of engaging in serious debate with one's opponents, slogans are substituted for thought. Those who disagree with media pundits are politically incorrect or out of touch with reality. Bigger's lawyer says, during the trial, "The hunt for Bigger Thomas served as an excuse to terrorize the entire Negro population, to arrest hundreds of Communists, to raid labor union headquarters and worker's organizations, indeed the tone of the press, the silence of the church, the attitude of the prosecution and the simulated temper of the people are of such a nature as to indicate that more than revenge is being sought upon a man who has committed a crime." The media, in the Simpson case, was used as lynch-mob leader just as it was used against Mike Tyson and Clarence Thomas.

The behavior of some media feminists in the Simpson case confirms my suspicion that some elements in the white feminist movement, and their African American surrogates, pose the most serious threat to African American men since the Klan. Michelle Carouso, of the *Daily News*, said on *Larry King Live* that she was glad that there were eight women on the jury, implying that she was hoping for a conviction, and Leslie Abrahamson and Gloria Allred recommended the death penalty for Simpson—yet both were hired by ABC and CNN to be objective consultants on the case. Ms. Allred was even accused by one defense witness of phoning her and trying to badger her into revealing her testimony. The *Nation* printed an article about how the white women who ran for office as Anita Hill feminists abandoned women's issues and voted with their male colleagues. During the Simpson trial, Ms. Hill was used as a prosecution prop, putting her on the side of a team that gave Mark

Furhman a clean bill of health, possibly planted evidence, had the defense teams' experts followed and harassed, and withheld exculpatory evidence.

The Simpson case also provided some high-profile white male journalists and pundits who hypocritically posed as women's rights advocates with an opportunity to posture. They included Geraldo Rivera, who admitted in his autobiography that he abused his first wife, Edie Vonnegut, causing Kurt Vonnegut to refer to Rivera as the vilest human being he knows; a talk-show host who was accused of sexual harassment by a woman employee, and a former attorney general who functioned as a consultant on the Simpson case for different networks. This man's use of women to entrap a black mayor was termed pandering by a *New York Times* columnist, yet he wasn't subjected to the sort of feminist harassment to which black men have been subjected, portrayed as poster-boys for sexism by women who are silent about such practices that occur in their ethnic groups. The case also revealed a split between white feminists and black women. After the jury came back with the not-guilty verdict, a prominent feminist appeared on television to denounce the verdict. She said that this verdict arose from black women being accustomed to abuse by black men. Yet statistics show that the rate of black men murdering black women and black women murdering black men is about the same, due to the tendency of black women to retaliate.

Also never mentioned in places like the *New York Times*, the *Village Voice*, and NPR, where misogyny is viewed as an exclusively black male problem (but where we never learn how women, who share the ethnic backgrounds of the men who direct these media outfits, are treated), are statistics which show that the murder of black women by their husbands and boyfriends has declined by 40 percent since 1976. The split between white feminists and black women, exemplified by the racist comments of Tammy Bruce, the grand dragon of the feminist movement, continues. In a review of journalist Jeffrey Toobin's *The Run of His Life*, *Times* critic Wendy Kammer came to Marcia Clark's rescue by rebutting characterizations of Ms. Clark which Kammer considered sexist, but failed to defend her black sisters on the jury from Toobin's assault upon their integrity. Mr. Toobin said that these black women were swayed by the demonic Negro oratory of Johnnie Cochran to vote for Simpson's acquittal, but the jurors themselves said that they were more impressed with Barry Scheck's testimony than with Cochran. During his book tour none of his interviewers, including Bryant Gumbel, asked whether the two white and the one Hispanic juror were enchanted by Cochran's spellbinding Negro oratory. Just as Bigger Thomas was used by the establishment to smear all blacks, O.J. was used to signify on all black men, and the black women jurors were used to do the same for black women. Indeed, for some white men and white women in the media, Faye Resnick, whose wretched past has been exposed in Joe Bosco's new book, had more credibility than the black women jurors.

Though the criminal justice system and the media are treated in Wright's novel, the theme that gives umbrage over all others is the theme of miscegenation. (Though Johnnie Cochran and Robert Shapiro have both been accused of playing the race card, one could argue that Christopher Darden introduced the race card when he accused Simpson of having a fetish for blondes, an accusation he would never have used against a white man.) The high-priced model of international capitalism is the White woman, preferably Anglo-looking and preferably thin. Her face and body have launched millions of products. She is the, icon that adorns the motion-picture screens and the fashion magazines. Black fashion models complain that they can't find work and that there's racism on the runway. Though many claim that the enormous attention paid to the O.J. Simpson case was a result of Simpson being a celebrity and a presence for many years in every living room due to his role as an NBC sportscaster, the miscegenation angle is what excited many viewers, just as Nazi newspapers like *Der Stuermer* and magazines like *Jugend* fascinated their readership by printing sensational stories about relationships between Jewish men and Aryan women. But many wondered whether such attention would have been paid if the murdered woman in the case had been a black woman. In *Native Son* the murder of the white woman by a black man excites more interest than the murder of a black woman, Bessie, by Bigger. Moreover, when Richard Goldstein of the *Village Voice* sought to discover whether as much attention had been paid to black and Latino women who were murdered in Central Park as there was to the highly publicized crimes against white women, he complained that the New York authorities gave him the runaround. (Gerry Spence, who received an education about race during the trial, said that many whites believed that Simpson had taken something that belonged to them. Their property—our woman.) The commentary on *Native Son* and even the narrator says that Bigger's murder of Mary was an accident. But a closer examination of the text reveals that Bigger has a motive. He kills Mary because he doesn't want to be caught in the bedroom of a white woman. Black men have been lynched for less. Black men have been arrested for recklessly eyeballing a white woman. During the Simpson trial Kathleen Bell testified that Fuhrman told her that he'd arrest a black man driving in the company of a white woman. Deeply embedded in African American folklore is the notion that a black man shouldn't be caught dead coming into contact with a white woman. There are tall tales about black men walking up the side of buildings so as to avoid passing a white woman who was approaching them on the street from the opposite direction. But like many taboos the possibility of black men and white women sharing intimacy raises excitement, some of it sexual. When Bigger is captured by the police, they want him to simulate his raping of Mary. They desire to get their kicks by having this entrapped black man tell them how he did it to a white woman. How many commentators about the Simpson case revealed a similar voyeuristic attitude? A San Francisco attorney sought to answer those who believed that Mark Fuhrman planted the infamous bloody gloves by suggesting that Fuhrman could not possibly have done so because he didn't know whether Simpson had an alibi. He could have been in bed with Paula Barbieri, he explained on several occasions. Was this commentator thrilled by the prospect of Simpson being in bed with one of his bimbos? Would he have liked to have been in some creepy corner of the bedroom, in the dark, panting heavily and, perhaps, manipulating himself?

One of the most vicious attacks on Simpson, the prosecution, and the defense team has come from Mark Fuhrman defender Vincent Bugliosi, former Los Angeles district attorney. He told talk-show host Charles Grodin, whose flagging audience appeal was lifted by one-sided pro-prosecution commentary, and panels that were hostile to Simpson and the defense, that to believe police would plant evidence was "blasphemy." He is the author of *Outrage,* a book that the publisher, Norton, described as putting the "noose around Simpson's neck." Christopher Darden, who was criticized in the book, said on June 12 that Bugliosi hadn't even read the transcripts of the trial, or watched it on television. Moreover, he said that Bugliosi hadn't tried a case in thirty years, and was out to cash in on the case. The book's arguments were demolished by Alan Dershowitz, who debated Bugliosi on June 11, reducing him to a rubble of sputtering invective. Previously appearing on the Geraldo Rivera show, Bugliosi complained about Simpson's returning from Bermuda with "lipstick all over his face."

For her part, Ms. Barbieri told interviewer Diane Sawyer that her father warned her that if she were ever raped by a black man, she shouldn't come home, which is what an Anglo father may have said to an Anglo woman about associating with Italian-American men—about thirty years ago. In a review of Spike Lee's film *Jungle Fever,* Professor Lawrence Di Statsi said of this movie (about a relationship between an Italian-American woman and an African American male) that taking white women was the charge originally made against Italians. Other comentators said that if Simpson were let out of prison, he'd be at the Riviera Country Club with white women. Geraldo Rivera, who revealed his homoerotic yearnings for Mick Jagger and Rudolph Nureyev in his autobiography, *Exposing Myself* (yet referred to Simpson as a "punk"), seemed particularly aroused over the prospect of Simpson appearing on the beach in the company of white women. During the trial, the Entertainment network announced a poll that revealed most women would rather watch the O.J. Simpson trial than have sex.

Even the most progressive and intellectual people have bought into the myths surrounding black men and white women. Some highly educated African Americans, including those who can figure out what on earth Foucault and Derrida are driving at, sound like your typical backwoods peckerwoods when discussing miscegenation. Those who make a career out of scolding folks about their sexism, homophobia, and misogyny also get steamed up when the discussion of miscegenation is brought up. Today, as in Bigger's day, the eerie sexual fantasies that revolve around the black male presence in the United States present a danger to black men in everyday life.

Even feminists like Susan Estrich, who is beginning to sound more like the late Lee Atwater with each new column, have bought into myths about black men and white women, In a column, she warned white women about coming into contact with black men, and justifies this on the basis of crime statistics (even though interracial crime is rare). Young professional black men often complain that white women are scared to ride in the same elevator with black men. Well, if a woman is usually raped or killed by somebody she knows, then white women should be fearful of riding elevators with white men. If Jesse Jackson is fearful of walking down the street at night with a group of blacks following closely behind, then why, given the fact that 70 percent of the violent crimes committed against whites are committed by other whites, aren't whites afraid of walking down the street while being trailed by other whites? Though sexual contact may have been in Bigger's thoughts, there is no sexual contact between Bigger and Mary Dalton when he "accidentally" murders her. Yet from the very beginning of the case, the newspapers charged Bigger with rape. One headline reads, "Troops Guard Negro Killer's Trial, Protect Rapist from Mob Action"—this being the kind of singling out of blacks for crime, especially when the victim is a white, that we read in the newspaper daily. The narrator of the novel says, "To hint that he had committed a sex crime was to pronounce the death sentence; it meant a wiping out of his life even before he was captured; it meant a death before death came, for the white men who read those words would at once kill him in their hearts."

There's something crazy about thinking about race in this country, and Richard Wright was among the first to point out the ironies and paradoxes of the American racial situation. Maybe the question of race shouldn't be left to a crime system that buys into the logic of race, or a media devoted to zebra journalism that only exacerbates the problem by photographing only those whites who were disappointed about the Simpson verdict but providing no photos of those who cheered, and by photographing blacks who cheered but editing out pictures of blacks who were disappointed. Maybe the question of race shouldn't be left to academics in disciplines that require little empirical proof, the kind of field where demagogues with Ph.D.s are allowed to run wild, such as members of the African American literary tribal council who are attempting to disappear AfricanAmerican male writers, including Ralph Ellison and Richard Wright, with the charge of misogyny, which is like calling somebody a Communist in the 1950s. They object to Wright's treatment of Bigger's mother and his girlfriend but are silent about his treatment of the black males in the novel, Bigger's associates, and even Bigger himself.

Maybe it's time to bring the question of race into the clinic room or the emergency room and treat it for what it is: a public-health crisis. Miscegenation has made people hysterical. Joel Williamson reports in his powerful book *The Crucible of Race* (1984) that one of the causes of the Atlanta race riots was a rumor that black men were drinking from a bottle with pictures of white women on them, and a great black Cajun singer was murdered by white men because he used a handkerchief given him by a white woman to wipe the sweat from his face. Miscegenation is also an issue that hovered over the Simpson trial, yet Americans, black and white, though often feigning repugnance at the mixing of the races, are more familiar with this demon than anyone might admit. In fact, interracial sex may be the taboo that millions of Americans have enjoyed the most. There is a saying in the South that white men didn't know that white women could have sex until they got married. While visiting Memphis, I was told by Professor Brett Singer, the niece of the great Yiddish writer Issac Bashevis Singer, that she asked her classroom of whites how many had engaged in sex with a black person. Everybody raised their hand. (I also asked her why feminists belonging to her ethnic background ignore the copiously documented misogyny-spousal abuse that occurs in their community, while blaming all of the world's sexism on Simpson and black men. She said that she was taught by her father to keep the sins of her community a secret.)

The parallels between the racial climate of Wright's novel and that of the Simpson case are endless. Nineteen nineties California, where the criminal trial took place and the scene of the civil trial, very much resembles the Jim Crow Chicago of Wright's novel. Scene of a drive against affirmative action, financed by ultraright forces and led by a governor who ties his career to wedge issues, and a right-wing legislature, a number of what might be called Negro laws have been introduced, including the notorious Three Strikes Law, which affects black defendants disproportionately. These laws have been advocated by the same attorney general, Dan Lungren, who negotiated a plea bargaining deal that let Mark Fuhrman, a white policeman, off with a light $200 fine and three years probation, shocking even Melanie Lomax, the Simpson prosecution's best friend and the darling of the "lynch Simpson" media. Tough on crime for Lungren apparently means tough on the poor and the black. These racist laws follow the historical pattern in which, at one time, Chinese Americans and Japanese Americans were excluded from California. During one nineteenth-century legislative session, called "The Legislature of a Thousand Drinks" because most of its participants were drunk at the end of the session, blacks were nearly excluded. Proposition 187 indicates that such enmity toward nonwhite immigrants still exists since the over one hundred thousand illegal European immigrants residing in California are never mentioned in the debate. And so it's not surprising that the California legislature has intervened three times in the Simpson case, most recently in an effort to change the rules of evidence so that Nicole Simpson's diary could be admitted, a diary that would usually constitute hearsay. Previously, another get-a-Negro measure, a terms limit proposition, was passed as a way of ridding the assembly of Willie Brown, whom California racists considered too uppity. Given California's attitudes toward Asian Americans and the rising number of hate crime against Asian Americans, it's not surprising that two Japanese-American judges would side with the prosecution so as not to raise anxiety among some whites about Japanese Americans who were interned during World War II. Republican appointee Judge Lance Ito, in the minds of the media and many whites, failed to do the job, even though he did his damnedest to convict Simpson, consistently siding with the prosecution in his rulings. His failure has put pressure on the new Japanese-American judge, Hiroshi Fujisaki, who has to prove to the media and many whites that he can deliver a verdict holding Simpson liable for the wrongful deaths of Goldman and Nicole Simpson. Apparently he is doing a good job. The media are congratulating him as being no nonsense, and praising his toughness with Simpson's team in the civil case. As of this writing Judge Fujisaki has gutted the defense's arguments and has permitted the plaintiffs' attorneys to dismiss fifteen prospective black jurors who had doubts about Simpson's guilt, while keeping white jurors who expressed belief in his guilt. One observer, the law partner of the late William Kunstler, was right to term this civil trial "the revenge of the white establishment."

The media lynching of Simpson by prominent feminists, lawyers, intellectuals, and journalists, without exploring the evidence, has not only been disgraceful but should be alarming to black men. Not only was the defendant lynched but also his lawyer has been subjected to media inspired hatred. A *New York Times* feminist referred to Johnnie Cochran as "odious."

Bigger Thomas gets into trouble because this poor black stepped out of the box that society had created for him. While his friends are petty thieves, he gets a job working as a chauffeur, which, in view of what was expected of him, was a step up. He is surrounded by liberals who are interested in his welfare and who give him lectures about self-improvement. Stepping beyond his bounds was the kind of adventure that got his creator, Richard Wright, into trouble. When he left the themes that made him famous—the conflicts between white and black Americans—and abandoned the United States for Europe, Wright was written off by the critics and dismissed as a one-novel writer, that novel being *Native Son,* when *The Outsider,* written in exile, might have been his best novel.

Simpson's troubles may have also arisen from his transcending the fate that awaited him had he not been a talented athlete: imprisonment, death, or a slave to a low-paying service job. On a recent trip to Los Angeles, I passed by his Rockingham estate and found it to be the kind of residence that kings and presidents possess in many countries. He associated with the high and the mighty and dated women with international reputations for their beauty. This was too much for some whites–those who couldn't wait for him to fall, like the four policemen who told us that they all abandoned the crime scene just to inform Simpson of his wife's death, even though he wasn't the next of kin; those who told us that they were so worried about Mr. Simpson's health that they climbed over his wall without a search warrant. One detective, Philip Vannatter, in a remark that the white commentariat overlooked, said it all when asked about the activities of Simpson's maid on the night of June 13. Mr. Vannatter said wryly, I don't have a maid."

Both Wright and Simpson have been accused by those who still wish to play the racial extortion game of abandoning the "black community." But if all Wright had done was to write *Native Son,* he contributed to the African American community immensely by exposing the racist forces that are arrayed against black achievement, and he did it in a manner that was artful, profound, and with an acid sense of humor. Whatever dues Simpson owed to the community have been paid because never before has the deeply rooted hostility toward African Americans by the police, prosecutors, and other components of the criminal justice system been revealed to the whole world as they were in the Simpson case.

*Native Son* excels as a novel in my mind because, though published over fifty years ago, the issues that are addressed by the author still exist. A classic is a book that though written decades or even centuries before the present time could have been written today. Thus, *Native Son* is a classic novel, as true now as it was when it was published on March 1, 1940, and its truth was certified in 1995, the year of the trial of the century.

I DISTRUST the monoculturalist point of view so much that when they praise something I become suspicious, and when they condemn something, I feel that there must be something praiseworthy about it. This hunch is not always justified, since, from time to time, both they and I agree about the quality of a work, but in the case of Wole Soyinka's play, *Death and the King's Horseman*, I think that the establishment's critics lacked the understanding to appreciate one of the most powerful, and most memorable—possibly unique —experiences I've had in the theater. Their narrow-minded reviews, to put it politely, discouraged many theatergoers from sharing this experience, and for this reason they proved Soyinka's point about the monocultural view of the world and the lack of understanding that goes with it.

Acceptance of African and Afro-American artists depends upon the political fads of the time in this country. Soyinka said as much in the course of an interview with the *New York Times*. Currently, the American intelligentsia (the only difference between the Right and Left of which is the Left's more creative racism), embrace a smugly blind attitude toward "the other," the fashionable metaphor for the Third World. For them, the problems of the Third World are traceable to a lack of "the work ethic," as one columnist put it. According to the current political daydream, the invasion of Africa and its catastrophic consequences never happened, and slaves, who did "slipshod" work, continued to be imported to the Americas, presumably because the slave masters were lonely. The uplift of the Third World will only happen through the graces of "Western civilization," a term that gives some penurious minds an opportunity to hang out with Aristotle.

Therefore some of the publications that bashed Soyinka's play had sonic kind words to say about V. S. Naipaul's *The Enigma of Arrival*, a book whose racism was soundly rebuffed in a devastating review by Derek Walcott in the April 13, 1987, issue of the *New Republic*. The *Village Voice* critic, who came to the play with an obvious chip on her shoulder searching for evidence of patriarchal oppression (she works for a newspaper owned, directed, and published by men, as Olunde would point out), took Mr. Soyinka to task for his "tribalism," yet Mr. Naipaul's book was listed in the *Voice* as "our kind of bestseller." Mr. Naipaul told the newspaper *India West* (25 April 1980) that Negroes were "the most stupid, primitive, lazy, dishonest, and violently aggressive people in the world." As for the charge of "patriarchal" oppression in *Death and the King's Horseman*, Iyaloja, "Mother of the Market," is the strongest character in the play. She scolds the king's horseman, Elesin Oba, and defies Simon Pilkings's order prohibiting Iyaloja from stepping across a line during her stockade interview with Oba. In scene 3, schoolgirls ridicule and humiliate the Muslim patriarch, Sergeant Amusa.

Perhaps some of the critics were offended by the portrayal of Simon Pilkings, the district officer, and his wife Jane, because, according to the current political line that has trickled down from Washington and taints American cultural life, they were bringing the values of a superior culture to "savages." They accused Soyinka of "comic-strip" and "agitprop" creations with the Pilkingses, even though in scene 5 Pilkings gets in some good lines during an exchange with Elesin, whose death the Yoruba religion requires for the sake of cultural continuity. For her part, Jane, who offends the local religion by joining her husband in wearing a confiscated juju costume to a ball, shows sensitivity to other aspects of the culture, so much so that her husband chides her for being a "social anthropologist"; a comic-book character would be incapable of the kind of intelligent dialogue that she conducts with Olunde, Elesin's son, in scene 4.

It's a good guess that some critics and members of the audience, who identified with the Pilkingses, are descendants of people who suffered under colonialism as much as the play's Nigerians, but took the Pilkingses' side because, in the United States, the fastest route to "whiteness" is to identify with the "Upstairs" of "Upstairs, Downstairs" and other imports that American television borrows from the BBC. This is the reason that the British royal family receives more coverage per year than all of the black-ruled nations of Africa.

Moreover Americans, both black and white, have always had trouble understanding African religion. African religion, for example, has always been ridiculed, misunderstood, and suppressed in this hemisphere. The reviews of the play show that such attitudes are difficult to change. A religion that claims millions of followers (its key zones being New York and Miami) was referred to as a "cult" by one critic. The *Christian Science Monitor* dismissed Yoruba religion as being based upon "tribal superstition," Mary Baker Eddy's theories presumably being based upon fact.

Critics have difficulty dealing with a "pagan" religion of such potency that even Amusa, the play's Muslim, respects it and Olunde, the "been to," and "not quite," remains a follower. Responses to this religion by bigots have often produced disasterous results. During the famous Witchcraft Hysteria, when some of Salem, Massachusetts's young women were possessed by some of the same gods mentioned in Soyinka's play, many of the citizens were executed. Tituba, the slave who was held responsible for the young women's trance, was imported from Barbados, where a variation of African religion known as obeah is practiced. She was jailed.

Mr. Soyinka reports that some of the members of the Vivian Beaumont audience, as well as members of the cast, became "overwhelmed" during the performances of the play as the powerful *gbedu* drum did its work. As Pilkings observes in scene 2 of the play: "It's different, Jane. I don't think I've heard this particular sound before. Something unsettling about it." This is not your ordinary theater, and it's quite possible that the term "play" doesn't begin to encompass what Mr. Soyinka achieves in *Death and the King's Horseman*. His theater has more in common with the ancient religious possession dramas of the Greeks that included gods that were parallel to those of the African ones—human gods with human appetites, who, unlike Jehovah, could accept ridicule from mortals.

The Greek connection is appropriate since, rather than polarizing cultures, Mr. Soyinka gently draws parallels between them. While in some societies the king's horseman is required to accompany the king to the otherworld, it is the custom in others for captains to go down with their ships. Costuming and dancing are universal. Soyinka is not the first to explain European tribal wars and World Wars I and II as instances of mass suicide; Carl Jung and poet Wilfred Owen have said as much. So that empires don't tilt, some societies require that their royalty take risks, such as making dangerous trips to their far-flung outposts. Writer Robert Maynard has even suggested that President Kennedy's trip in a convertible through a hostile Dallas was an act of hubris.

Mr. Soyinka is a cultural relativist who uses different literary and dramatic traditions in order to create a theatrical synthesis. In the play both Yoruba and English are spoken by the actors, while the music of different cultures, including indigenous dances, the waltz and the tango—a dance of love and death that arose from the slums of Argentina—are performed.

Speaking to me in one of the Vivian Beaumont offices, shortly after the play's production on Sunday, April 22, Mr. Soyinka was quite upset, to put it mildly, about the critical reaction. He believes that the "Irrational" misunderstanding displayed in some of the reviews reflects a larger problem. A problem of perception that many of the nation's outsiders, including Ralph Ellison and Richard Wright, have reflected upon in their masterworks, *Invisible Man* and *Native Son*, a book in which blindness is a frequent image and metaphor. The sort of cognitive dysfunction, or plain arrogance, that would lead a president to send a Bible as a goodwill gesture to a people whose sacred book is the Koran.

After another discussion with Wole Soyinka of the critics' reactions to *Death and the King's Horseman*, the following Friday morning, by coincidence, I had an engagement at Bob Fox's class at the University of Suffolk on Beacon Hill in Boston. Professor Fox, a Polish American who grew up in Buffalo, New York, is one of a growing number of young Euro-American writers, scholars, and critics who don't treat African religion in the usual Tarzanized manner. One thinks of Robert Gover, author of *Voodoo Contra*, and Bob Thompson at Yale, whose work on African religion has led to his ostracism by some of his colleagues; the campus issue of *Newsweek* ridiculed one of his courses on the subject. *Newsweek* is the same magazine that sighed relief when Lisa Bonet, star of *Angel Heart*, the standard exercise in Hollywood "voodoo," promised that she wouldn't be doing any more voodoo dances. (The term "voodoo" has come to denote Americanized African religion; some speculate that it is based upon the word "vodu," used by the Fon people to refer to the orishas, loas, or "spirits" of their Yoruban neighbors.)

I asked Bob Fox, a friend of Soyinka's in Nigeria, for his reaction to some of the critics' comments about the religious aspects of *Death and the King's Horseman*. He said: "For anyone to term African traditional beliefs 'tribal superstition' demonstrates vividly that Eurocentric arrogance and ignorance are alive and still kicking. Whatever stands outside our monological enterprise troubles us, and if we can't control or influence it, we put a pejorative label on it. But this demeaning terminology can be turned back on us. After all, the linkage between apartheid and fundamentalist theology in South Africa reveals a racist system built on Afrikaner tribal superstition. And I think this is a clue to what lies behind some of these radically misinformed statements about Soyinka's work. My impression is that there are people who want to put him 'in his place' because instead of ingratiating himself with his 'masters,' he had the nerve to use the occasion of his Nobel Prize to attack Western hegemony in general and apartheid in particular. But then Soyinka has always refused to be 'Westoxicated,' and the richness of his Yoruba cultural heritage has enabled this resistance."

Before climbing Beacon Hill to Bob's office, I paused in front of the statue of Mary Dyer. A Quaker, she was hanged in the 1600s for her membership in an unconventional faith. As I examined her proud stone face, staring out at me from underneath a bonnet, I thought of Pilkings's line in *Death and the King's Horseman:* "You think you've stamped it all out but it's always lurking under the surface somewhere."

## WRITER

Though the young African American hip-hop intellectuals picture Malcolm X as an apostle of armed resistance—their favorite poster is that of a rifle-bearing Malcolm, peering out from behind curtains, preparing to do battle with his enemies—the revolutions that both Malcolm X and Martin Luther King, Jr., precipitated were textbook Sun Tzu. They produced change, King in the law, Malcolm in consciousness—without throwing a punch (at whites), or firing a shot. And though they are regarded as opposites, it was Malcolm's threats that were partially responsible for the establishment's agreeing to some of King's demands.

Malcolm made wolfing and jive into an art form, and though his battles were fought on television (Marshall McLuhan referred to him as "the electronic man") and his weapons were words, he was a symbol of black manhood; "our shining prince" was the way Ossie Davis put it, in a eulogy delivered at Malcolm's funeral. Black men were in need of such a prince, manhood being very much on the minds of black men during the sixties. Their frustration was heightened when some black children were blown to bits during church services in Birmingham, Alabama; King Jr.'s macho critics thought that he had "punked out" when he used children in one of his nonviolent demonstrations.

Black nationalist poet Askia Muhammed Toure wondered aloud, "But who will protect the women's quarters?" the desperate cry of men whose women were being poked with cattle prods and beaten to the ground by white thugs in uniform. I wrote a long noisy rambunctious poem entitled "Fanfare for an Avenging Angel," dedicated to Malcolm, and, after reading it, Malcolm told me, charitably, that it reminded him of works by "Virgil and Dante."

That's how we saw Malcolm X. He would make them pay. Pay for the humiliations we suffered in a racist country. Young black intellectuals were out for revenge. They were in a Kikukyu warrior mode. On the west coast, a young black prisoner was using the Spanish dungeon of the sort that used to hold slaves as his personal library. Eldridge Cleaver was also impressed with Malcolm X and took Malcolm X's position over that of Elijah Muhammad, whose generation called whites devils, because they had come out of the southern racist hell where the whites had shown themselves to be capable of the most fiendish acts.

As in the case of his hero, Malcolm X, Eldridge Cleaver went to school in jail, reading, writing, meditating, and practicing his intellectual style on mentors, who were obviously no match for his probing, hungry intellect. In his book *Soul on Ice*, he confessed to a former career as a rapist and admitted to relationships with white women (still the cardinal taboo in the eyes of white and black nationalists).

He assured his readers, especially the eastern Left, which had the power to make celebrities of those who supported its issues, that he was a recovering racist, a former black Muslim, who read and admired Norman Mailer's *The White Negro* (the usual bit of Noble Savage gibberish), but the recurrent theme in the book is that of an eternal struggle between the black supermasculine—a struggle that menial and the white omnipotent administrator continues in various forms, to this day. While white males were on the receiving end of criticism by black writers during the sixties and early seventies, some white male writers and media commentators have since gotten even by bonding with the black feminist movement and criticizing the treatment of black women by black men.

In this war, women are regarded as bargaining chips and loot for both sides, the black ones, Amazons, the white ones, gullible Barbie dolls. A white guard objected to Cleaver having pictures of a white woman on his cell wall. This guard, like many white men, regarded all white women as their property, while black men feel that black women belong to them. Both groups were upset when the women declared that they owned their own bodies, their souls, and their minds. In *Soul on Ice* the women are either Madonnas or whores. In some gushy, heart-wringing letters, Cleaver professed his love for his lawyer, Beverly Axelrod, and her responses, printed in the book, were equally cloying.

Cleaver was first pushed as a celebrity by the New York Old Left and its branches in Northern California and Los Angeles. They had given up on the worker (at the time depicted by Robert Crumb and other underground cartoonists as a bigoted, flagwaving, Budweiser-guzzling hard hat and incipient Reagan democrat) and in his place substituted the black prisoner as proxy in their fight against capitalism. In the *New York Times Magazine*, in an article that was preceded by a quote of mine that if Thomas Jefferson were around he'd be reading Eldridge Cleaver, Old Lefter Harvey Swados referred to Cleaver as the quintessential American. And he is, in the sense that Tom Sawyer, Huckleberry Finn, Ellison's Rinehart, Gerald Vizenor's Bearheart, and the creatures in those African-Native American animal tales who use guile, wit, and flattery to accomplish their ends are quintessential Americans. (In a classic tale a snake says to a benefactor, who expresses dismay after being bitten by the creature it has rescued, "You knew I was a snake.")

I was in Leonard Bernstein's apartment the week before he gave a party for the Black Panthers (a party made notorious by Thomas Wolfe, in whose latest book, *The Bonfire of the Vanities,* blacks are likened to rats) and Bernstein, pointing to Cleaver's book on the coffee table, asked me had I read him. I hadn't read him at the time, but figured that the New York Left was going to make use of Cleaver and the Panthers, for whom he became Minister of Information. I said so publicly. I was hip to the eastern intelligentsia which was dabbling in Marxism at the time and knew of the intelligentsia's "contradictions." Leonard Bernstein, who was sympathetic to the Panthers' cause, was having trouble with black musicians like Arthur Davis, who accused the conductor of discriminating against black musicians.

After the collapse of the Black Panther party, Cleaver, like Doug Street in Wendell Harris's extraordinary film *Chameleon Street*, went through different changes. In *Soul on Ice* he refers to himself as though he were different people: "I was very familiar with the Eldridge who came to prison, but that Eldridge no longer exists. And the one I am now is a stranger to me." He went into exile and lived in Cuba, Algeria, and France (where it was rumored that he shared a mistress with a prime minister), returned to become a fundamentalist minister, campaigned for the Republican senatorial nomination, designed clothes that highlighted the penis, and began a church devoted to the male reproductive organs and the preservation of sperm. Recently, he was criticized for poaching curbside recyclables, on behalf of his "Church of the Great Taker," that were intended for the nonprofit Berkeley Ecology Center. Once in a while he appears in the local newspapers, in trouble with the law over some petty charge, or for assisting an elderly white woman from being evicted from her house. Sometimes the local media uses him for comic relief.

He wrote a second book, *Soul on Fire*, which in many ways was as absorbing as *Soul on Ice*. But, like Till Eulenspiegel, he had worked his tricks too many times; the book was ignored and his description of his conversion to Christianity, mocked (he said that he joined the fundamentalists because they had brought him from exile, and if the Panthers had brought him home he would have sided with them).

Each group of Cleaver's supporters claimed that it had been taken by the head of the Church of the Great Taker, but it could be argued that they did quite a bit of betraying themselves. Besides, if they had read *Soul on Ice* instead of marveling at the fact that a black prisoner could hold such a gifted mind they would have learned that Cleaver's most persistent intellectual quality is doubt. And doubters aren't followers and are distrustful of structures, which is what perhaps inspired Amiri Baraka to describe Eldridge Cleaver as a "bohemian anarchist," a highfalutin name for the trickster.

His supporters used him, but he used them too. And who could blame a black man for using his wits to get out of one of these Nazi-like pits, often guarded by depraved sadists, where this society had cast him to rot and die at the age of twenty-two? Today, thousands of young black men like Cleaver languish in the country's prisons while the inside traders receive light sentences for nearly wrecking the economic system, while the Justice Department spends millions of dollars to trap a black mayor on a misdemeanor charge, while the BCCI money-laundering enterprise, perhaps the biggest drug scandal in history, is ignored, and in a society where most of the S&Lers won't even come to trial.

Had Cleaver remained in prison without the publicity that ultimately led to his release, he'd probably be dead.

By the end of the sixties the Left and the Right, like lovers, began to trot toward each other so that at the beginning of the eighties they were in bed together. Cleaver hurt James Baldwin (so did I) who was deemed politically incorrect by the young lions who were so paranoid about their manhood. Baldwin was also considered a sellout, and "radical chic" was the expression introduced by the late Seymour Krim to chastise Baldwin for permitting *The Fire Next Time* to be published in the *New Yorker*, the epitome of uptown pretensions and snobbery. Baldwin pretended that he didn't care. Baldwin used to tell me that he didn't mind my criticisms of him because, "Ishmael, you're a writer, but that Cleaver. . . ." Cleaver and Baldwin underestimated each other. Far from being a clown, Cleaver is a writer, too, and though Baldwin comes in for some vicious criticism from Cleaver, it is obvious that *Soul on Ice* is influenced by Baldwin's flamboyantly eloquent taxidermist's style, just as Baldwin's *If Beale Street Could Talk* reminds one of Eldridge Cleaver.

But Baldwin proved to be more reliable than Norman Mailer, who is championed in this book. Baldwin went to his grave protesting the injustices committed against the underdogs of the world by forces and institutions more powerful than they, while, by the end of the sixties, Norman Mailer was saying that he was "tired of Negroes and their rights," and there is only a thin intellectual partition between his recent comments blaming blacks for the drug trade and those of the new policy elite at the *New Republic* (whose neo-conservative about-face can be gauged by the fact that an endorsement from the pre-Right wing *New Republic* appears on the paperback edition of *Soul on Ice.* The publisher, Martin Peretz, who seems to spend all of his waking hours making up fibs about the "underclass," formerly had ties with SDS, wouldn't you know). Cleaver supporter, the *New York Review of Books,* which, during the sixties, carried instructions on how to make a Molotov cocktail, now prints long, unreadable pieces by Andrew Hacker denouncing affirmative action and seeking to divide Asian Americans from black Americans with ignorant comments about the model minority.

The New Left, which sought to use the Black Panthers to foment a violent revolution, by the late seventies had joined the Reagan consensus, or had begun to wallow in a selfish consumerism. Others became Second Thoughters, denouncing the Panthers before neoconservative banquets of the sort that get carried on C-Span. Sylvia Ann Hewlett describes the spirit of postrevolutionary America as that of "a therapeutic mentality . . . which focuses on the self rather than a set of external obligations."

Cleaver believed that the younger generation of whites would be wooed away from their omnipotent administrator fathers by African American dance and music. Whites began to dance better, but that didn't make them more humanistic. Rock and roll made billions for white artists and became the entertainment at white-power rallies and accompanied the black-hating lyrics of Axil Rose. Even the creator of the Willie Horton campaign, Lee Atwater, received a better review in the *New York Times* for his rock and roll music than Miles Davis. *Rolling Stone,* which was the voice of the counterculture during the sixties, went Republican and upscale, and Malcolm X, the symbol of black sixties manhood, has been "outed" in a new book by Bruce Perry.

The groups that are the subjects of so much abuse in *Soul on Ice,* women and gays (the Cleaver of *Soul on Ice* considers homosexuality to be a disease), have placed their oppression front and center and have even made villains of the former black male machos who fantasized a revolution (while borrowing their strategies). These groups could even be accused of trivializing the oppression of the white and black underclass because once you propose that all women, including Queen Elizabeth, or all gays, including Malcolm Forbes, are oppressed, then everybody is oppressed, even the omnipotent administrator—white males with Ph.D.s, the new oppressed, whom the media would have us believe are being set upon by a politically correct multiculturalism.

And now Hollywood, which poured money into Black Panther coffers, will get its money back with interest, with a slew of films now in the works about the Black Panthers demonstrating that Cleaver's scientific socialism was no match for the witchcraft of capitalism. (One of these films is being scripted by Anna Hamilton Phelan, the writer for *Gorillas in the Mist*, the favorite film of the gestapo wing of the LAPD.) Capitalism could even transform a group that once advocated its overthrow into boxoffice receipts and T-shirt revenue.

I always wondered what would have happened if Cleaver and Huey Newton and the Panthers hadn't been used as pawns in a struggle between the white Right, who destroyed them, and the white Left, who piled an agenda on them that went way beyond their original community concerns, and who viewed them as cannon fodder. (They wanted "a nigger to pull the trigger" as one Panther put it.) Thanks to the Panthers, the downtown Oakland political establishment is black but that doesn't seem to prohibit the police from continuing to beat the shit out of black people in Oakland (and as elsewhere in the case of these black ceremonial governments, the cash is controlled by whites). They also elected a Congressman.

Huey Newton was shot dead in the gutter and was bitterly denounced, before his body was even cold, by a post-New Left Berkeley "alternative" newspaper whose editorial line mirrors the confusion of the Left—one week printing a long piece sympathetic to still-imprisoned Panther Geronimo Pratt, another week printing an article favorable to University of California anthropologist Vincent Sarvich, a member of the new oppressed, who maintains that women and blacks are intellectually deficient because of their small brain size (the same argument that Hitler's "scientists" used to advance against the professor's ancestors).

In this political and cultural environment Cleaver seems a has-been and the villains in his book, Lyndon Johnson (promoter of the Great Society) and

Barry Goldwater (who challenged the CIA's mining of the Nicaraguan harbor)—in comparison to the sinister crowd in power now—seem like populists from the quaint old days of the American Weimar.

But I suspect that history is not finished with Eldridge Cleaver. If he never does another thing in his life, he wrote this book. It's not just a book about the sixties like those books and films written by his former white allies that prove that the authors were white nationalists all along because they omit, or give scant attention to, the role of, blacks, who created the political and cultural matrix for that decade. The conclusion of one recent film, Mark Kitchell's *Berkeley in the Sixties*, most of whose narrators are white women, seems to be that the significance of the political and cultural upheaval of the sixties was that it led to the formation of the middle class feminist movement.

The reissue of Eldridge Cleaver's *Soul on Ice* will challenge the current bleaching out of the black influence on the cultural and political climate of the sixties. This book is a classic because it is not merely a book about that decade, regarded as demonic by some and by others as the most thrilling and humanistic of this century. *Soul on Ice* is the sixties. The smell of protest, anger, tear gas, and the sound of skull-cracking billy clubs, helicopters, and revolution are present in its pages.

The old cover's image of the lilies juxtaposed with the young prisoner's rugged face and unkempt hair is apt.

Out of the manure that American society can often be for black men, the growth and beauty of their genius cannot be repressed. Cannot be denied.

## BOXER

IN THE films *Mandingo* and *Drum* former WBA Heavyweight Champion Ken Norton plays a slave boxer, moving through scenes, his flesh handled by people who have such intense feelings for him they wish to stab him or boil him in a pot. The women want to ball him, and the men want to do battle with him; some people want to do both.

The Heavyweight Champion of the World is, most of all, a grand hunk of flesh, capable of devastating physical destruction when instructed by a brain, or a group of brains. I'm not saying he's stupid. He may be brilliant, but even his brilliance is used to praise his flesh.

Edy Williams, 37–23–37, a "raven-haired" woman, jumped into the middle of the ring between rounds and took her clothes off, revealing flesh the color of the hotdogs they were serving in the press room, and a few shades lighter than the red ring ropes.

Describing herself as a "Naturalist from California," she said, "If Muhammad Ali can use his body to be a success in the ring, why can't I?" One newspaper described her show as "the most exciting event of the evening." Many were using their flesh for success outside the ring as well; it seemed that every whore and player from the Mississippi Valley and points beyond were there.

The Heavyweight Championship of the World is a sex show, a fashion show, scene of intrigue between different religions, politics, class war, a gathering of stars, ex-stars, their hangers-on, and hangers-on's assistants.

It's part Mardi Gras with New Orleans Jazz providing the background for the main events while the embattled Be-Boppers, led by former Sonny

Rollins and Ornette Coleman sideman Earl Turbington, held forth in one of the restaurants facing the Hilton's French Garden bar.

Driving into town on Route 61 past the authentic Cajun music and food joints, motels with imitation French-styled balconies, car lots heading on Canal Street towards Decatur, I heard Dick Gregory on the car radio. A saint of the prime flesh movement was naming "Carlos," a New Orleans man, as a conspirator in JFK's assassination. Gregory was one of Ali's advisors, though an insider told me that Ali didn't pay attention to Gregory's nutritions.

Hotel Bienville, named for the founder of New Orleans, Jean Baptiste Le Moyne Sieur de Bienville, was located in a red-light district of the French Quarter. Nearby, two Greek restaurants stood in the direction of Canal Street and some small time players' bars. I checked in, changed, and then followed the hugh Hilton H the way you'd follow a holy asteroid: the sign resembled a blue star on the New Orleans skyline. The Hilton is located on a 23.3 acre $250 million international river center. It has 1,200 rooms, five restaurants, three lounges, parking lots of 3,550 cars, tennis courts, and rises to 30 stories above the street. It was designed by Newhouse and Taylor Architects.

Entering the press's hospitality room I was greeted by Sybil Arum, a Japanese-Korean woman who got me a drink and introduced me to her husband, Bob Arum. They both were dressed casually; she was wearing proletariat pigtails and later someone said she was the best-looking woman in the hotel. Arum was seated next to Leslie Bonanno, a heavy, wavy-haired sheriff who is heavyweight Jerry Celestine's manager. Arum was confident that Spinks was going to win the fight. He had great admiration for Ali but it was his theory that "elements of deterioration" had set in during Ali's "exile" from 1967 to 1970. I was introduced to an ex-UPI reporter who followed Ali's career during those years, and we were about to head upstairs to the bar to discuss them when Mike Rossman's family arrived, wearing Mike Rossman T-shirts. They told me they were bringing in three planeloads to witness what turned out to be Rossman's victory over Victor Galindez for the WBA Light Heavyweight Championship of the World. After the fight, Rossman's dad said, "If he weighed fifteen more pounds, he could beat Ali."

The man from UPI talked like Jimmy Stewart and didn't want his named used. He had that glint in his eye—the glint I'd see in the eyes of the other Ali disciples, Norman Mailer, Budd Schulberg, and George Plimpton. The Ali glint belonging to the true believer.

He remembered an argument that broke out in the UPI press room when Ali fought Frazier for the Heavyweight Championship the first time. They didn't know what to call him. They decided, finally, to call him Ali if he won the fight, Clay if he lost.

A black promoter from Charleston offered Ali an exhibition fight which was to be held on a dirt track. The UPI man and a reporter from the *Detroit Free Press* were the only ones there to cover it. The city council voted against the exhibition bout, and it was cancelled. At three o'clock that day they came to Ali to tell him there'd be no fight. Ali took it philosophically, got into a car, and headed for the airport wearing the same suit he'd worn for two years.

The punishment and cruelty visited upon Ali during those three years for refusing to step forward at the induction center have become part of the Ali Legend. It seemed that the whole nation wanted to spit in his face, or skin The Grand Flesh. Not only, to them, was he a draft dodger but also a member of a misunderstood religion which the media had hyped into a monstrous black conspiracy. The Muslims were different from many of the other black organizations of the time. They had rhetoric but they also accomplished things. They built a multimillion dollar business from mom-and-pop stores and newspapers. They were the Bad Nigger, the Smart Nigger, the Hard Nigger, and the Uppity Nigger epitomized by one organization. Ali had to pay a heavy price for his religion and for his politics. My favorite story from that period occurred when an imprisoned Ali was ordered to serve breakfast to prisoners on Death Row. One prisoner looked up and said, "My God, I must be in heaven, the Heavyweight Champion of the World is serving me breakfast."

There was a flurry in the lobby. Some of Spinks's people began showing up. Tourists were standing on the second-floor balcony staring down at the scene. Shortly, Spinks came in. With that black crest he resembled a black-silk-shirt-wearing iguana. I approached the gathering with my brand new Realistic tape recorder I'd bought at Berkeley's Radio Shack. Spinks's bodyguards made a scene. They demanded that I turn the tape recorder off. Later I understood why. A *Playboy* writer using a tape recorder had betrayed Spinks's confidence by writing that Spinks smoked some grass. Because I was standing with Leroy Diggs, Spinks's sparring partner and bodyguard, a tourist came up and asked for my autograph. It was that way the entire week. People signing autographs for each other; photographers snapping pictures of other photographers.

The next afternoon, people from both camps began to show up in the French Garden bar, a stunning environment lighted by sun rays which poured through a skylight above. Ali's brother, Rachaman Ali, his freckled-faced mother whom Ali calls "Bird," and his father, wearing a checkered sports jacket and white hat. Bundini arrived and, judging from his ringside antics, I thought he'd have an expansive sense of humor. He didn't. He was wearing a white leisure suit. Bundini always wanted to be an actor, someone told me later.

In the evening, Mayor Ernest N. Morial, New Orleans's "Black" mayor, who'd be considered white in most parts of the world, gave a reception at the Fairmont Hotel honoring Muhammad Ali and Leon Spinks. I walked into the lobby toward a big room on the first floor. There was a commotion behind the door. The first man to exit was Ali. I was standing face to face with a $100 million industry which included everything from candy bars to a forthcoming automobile capable of travelling across the desert. He was huge and awesome looking, but not the "Abysmal Brute" Jack London had pined after. "Hi, Champ," I said. I shook hands with the black man they let beat up Superman.

He was followed by his wife, Veronica ("Veronica belongs to me," he said later). A procession followed the couple to the upstairs ballroom, the whole scene illuminated by photographers' flashbulbs. I fell in behind them. When Ali reached the top of the escalator I heard a loud exchange between Ali and a figure who was coming down. It was Joe Frazier. He would sing "The Star Spangled Banner" before the fight and perform at the Isaac Hayes victory show at the Hilton Friday night.

Slave power allowed southern women to spend hours at the mirror costuming, preening, and painting their faces. In the New Orleans French Quarter you can buy any kind of doll you want. Black. White. I bought a black doll which turned inside out and became a white doll (no jokes, please!).

There was that eerie ad for Georgia Life Insurance carried on a billboard. It was a picture of a child done in the kind of oils with which Rod Serling used to introduce "Night Gallery." She was dressed in a Victorian outfit, and was heavily made-up, under the caption, "What about Her?" The southern woman was supposed to be this life-sized doll who occasionally produced a fake aristocrat while the old man went about impregnating the countryside.

Some of my very talented female writer friends have jammed up the media with their woeful tales regarding the black male's proclivity toward the Macaroni style. It took me some serious reflection to reckon with the truth in this. But if black males were that—if Emmet Till was a rogue as a demagogic feminist, so hard up for a victim, has claimed—then they certainly had a great teacher.

The doll style of the women in this ballroom, in their synthetic fabrics, bloused and belted-in at the waist, showed that even though the institution was razed, certain habits of the old South have endured. The women were what we used to call "beautiful," and the men were youthful and virile look-ing. Attractive and adorned bodies gathered to witness the most wonderful body in the world. A flesh ball. The mayor was standing behind Ali's people, beaming. Don Hubbard told me that the fight would bring the city $20 mil-lion in revenue, bigger than the Mardi Gras.

Ali has so much control over his body he can turn the juice on and off. In contrast to the sombre and downcast-looking fighter I'd seen emerge from the downstairs room, with whom I was alone for about 15 seconds, the upstairs Ali began to shuffle up and down the stage, jabbing at invisible oppo-nents, dancing, all the while speaking rapidly. He doesn't have the brittle dry irony of Archie Moore or the eloquent Victorian style of the bookish Jack Johnson, but he is more effective because he speaks to Americans in Ameri-can images, images mostly derived from comic books, television, and folk-lore. To be a good black poet in the 60s meant capturing the rhythms of Ali and Malcolm X on the page. His opponents were "Mummies" and "Vam-pires"; he was "The Man from Shock." In his bitter press conference he dis-cussed "The Six Million Dollar Man." His prose is derived from the trickster world of Bugs Bunny and *Mad* comics. The world of Creature Features. Thus, after victory, he was able to get a whole room of grown and worldly men and women to chant with him; "Mannnnnnnn, Mannnnnnnn. That's gone be the new thing," he said, "Mannnnnnnn."

"I don't know what to say," he said. "Where's the champ? If he stays out of jail, I'll get his tail." Ali referred to Spinks as a "nigger," then caught himself to explain that "Niggers can say niggers, but white folks can't," which is as good an answer as any to the man running for office in Alabama who requested that he have the same right to say "nigger" as "the Jews" and "the niggers."

Ali's style was a far cry from the nearly catatonic humility of Joe Louis and Floyd Patterson, but then, these are different times. Can you imagine the uproar which would have happened if Louis came up with "No Nazi Ever Called Me Nigger"?

When the question-and-answer period came, I had my hand up and so he pointed to "the young man over there." I was on his side after that.

Mr. Ali, do you plan to run for Congress as the *Nation* magazine has sug-gested?"

"No, I plan to run for vice-president, that way the President won't get shot." He called himself the "Saviour of Boxing," and predicted that he'd punch Spinks out of the ring. "Spinks," he said, "will become the first spook satellite." He flirted with the ladies and praised his body.

Dick Gregory followed Ali with some familiar jokes about Spinks's arrest for driving without a license and possessing $1.98 worth of cocaine (St. Louis cocaine). Gregory strongly believes that the coke was planted on Spinks. "Why did they alert the press before he was brought into the station?"

I asked Gregory to repeat what he'd said on the radio, that the killers of JFK resided in New Orleans. I figured that since the mayor and the police were on the stage the conspirators would be arrested, immediately. The laughter vanished. The mayor and Ali stood silently. Dick Gregory refused to discuss it.

During the broadcast he urged black-Italian cooperation. "If the Mafia is so big," he said, "why won't Henry Ford invite it to his next garden party?"

After Ali left, Gregory came over to the bar where I was standing. The black waiters, dressed in black bowties and green satinish jackets, weren't serving beer or wine, so I asked for what Gregory was drinking. Vodka and orange juice. UMMMMMM.

A long table covered with white linen held hors d'oeuvres under silver tops which resembled Kaiser helmets. The South knows how to lay out the dog when it wants to. Chopin on the piano stand. Silver laid out in case somebody's coming for supper.

I got a plate, returned to my seat, and found myself being choked to death from behind. It was Hunter Thompson. Choking people, I learned later, was his way of showing affection. He was wearing dark glasses, and looked like he'd just stepped off a space ship. They're filming his life and the crew was coming to New Orleans with his two lawyers.

The DeJan's Olympia band began to second line about the floor playing some old music. They were led by this lithe flesh wearing top hat and tails, symbolizing what to some may be a spirit imported from Haiti. The carrying of the umbrella may be an African retention. I fell in behind the band and began doing the second line around the room with them. Few joined in. As we made it about the door, Spinks appeared. His eyes seemed to roll about his head. He was wearing a droll grin. He seemed very, very happy. He took the umbrella from the band's majordomo and second lined toward the stage. He stood and signed autographs for a while.

I went back to the press hospitality room and met some old timers, some trainers, and some boxing buffs.

Like there was Sam Taub. As Irving Rudd of Top Rank tells it, "Sam Taub was 92 on September 10. He was born on Mott Street on the Lower East Side and was working as an office boy when he got a job through the *New York*

*Times* with the *Morning Telegraph*, a magazine similar to the *Police Gazette*. He worked many years for Bat Masterson, a lawman who came west to be a fight official and sports writer. It was Sam who found Masterson dead at his desk of a heart attack. I was looking through the record books and I found out that Masterson was the time-keeper for the Sullivan-Corbett fight which was held in New Orleans, September 7, 1892.

"Sam did the first radio broadcast from Madison Square Garden, in the 1920s, and the first telecast of a bout from Madison Square Garden in 1939. For many years Sam broadcast for Adam's hats and Gem razor. He has a popular show on WHN called 'The Hour of Champions.' Never took a quarter from anybody. Never put the shake on anybody.

"During the last riot in the Garden he climbed to a chair to call the rioters 'hooligans,' and had to be carried away by the police, bodily." Sam Taub told me about the time Jack Johnson worked at the 42nd Street Library and was obsessed with these sandwiches which they were selling four or five in a bag. Taub went out and bought some for Johnson. "And when Sugar Ray appeared on 'The Hour of Champions' for the first time, I said, 'Now you watch this fellow; he's going to be the champ one day.'"

As I approached Taub to be introduced he was threatening a man who could have been 40 years younger than Taub with "Take a walk, buddy!" The man moved on.

Thursday, hundreds of people were pushing into the Grand Ballroom for the official weigh-in ceremonies. Bright, unnatural lights from the television cameras. Total confusion. People were standing on chairs, craning their necks to see celebrities. It was 10:55 when Angelo Dundee arrived. He looks like a mild-mannered math teacher at a boys' high school. Jimmy Ellis, who has a teenager's bright face, and Ali's brother, Rachaman—whom I mistakenly called Rudolph Valentino Clay – -following. He could have been Valentino standing against the pillar in the French Garden bar, dressed in a white suit.

The platform was so full of the press that it began to reel. Arum threatened to cancel the press conference. I see Don King.

He is followed by Ali, toothpick in mouth, and Veronica Ali. A man next to me says, "Ali is the best-known person in the world." Ali weighs in at 221 pounds, Spinks 201. I'm tempted to bid.

After the weigh-in I asked former Light Heavyweight Chainpion of the World Jose Torres to assess Ali's chances. Torres was pessimistic. He'd seen Ali work out and he didn't like his color. "Too grey." He thought Ali's eyes were "dead," and that he was bored. "Ali no longer enjoys fighting and despises training," Torres said. "I want Ali to win for nostalgic reasons." He liked Spinks. "The more criticism he gets the more I like him," Torres said. Leroy Diggs, Spinks's bodyguard and sparring partner, standing behind Torres, said that Spinks looked real good.

Up front, Emile Brumeau, a wizened wild turkey, the head of the Louisiana Boxing Commission, was holding a press conference. Somebody asked him if he voted to strip Ali of the crown in 1967 when he was sitting on the World Boxing Association. The Commissioner told the reporter to leave or go "to a cemetery."

Another person asked if there would be a dope test following the fight. It seemed that Ali's corner had complained about a mysterious bottle given to Spinks between the rounds of the last fight. Whatever was in it seemed to give Spinks extra vigor. He asked the Commissioner what kind of water would be allowed in the corners. He answered, "Aqua water."

I saw Don King's famous crown poking above the crowds in the aisle, moving and mashing their bodies against each other. He was blandly praising Ali but at the same time voiced hope that he would retire. He said that Ali was the most identifiable man in the world. "Strong on the inside as well as the outside." He praised Larry Holmes, "the other champion," in a short speech dotted with words like "cognizant." The most frequent adjective people use in talking about King is "flamboyant."

I went up to the second floor to inquire about my credentials. A white-haired Norman Mailer was standing in the middle of the room. I met him in 1962 at Stefan's and had gone to a couple of his parties. Gone were the pug breaks and the frantic fast-talking. He seemed at peace. We exchanged greetings.

Albert C. Barnes, writing in *The New Negro* in 1925, extolled Primitivism in Negro Art with his, "It is a sound art because it comes from a primitive nature upon which a white man's education has never been harnessed." He said it reflected "aspirations and joys during a long period of acute oppression and distress."

Man in distress was existential man. Mailer popularized this idea with his "White Negro." To be Negro was to be hip. Jack Kerouac studied Negro Art, and for his dedication Bird did a tune called "Kerouac." What Mailer and Kerouac failed to realize was that the average black would have thrown Bird out of his home, or giggled at his music, or charged him with not combing his hair. It was hard enough to be a Negro but to be that and Bird too was real hard. Joe Flaherty writes in *Managing Mailer* about the freeloader blacks Mailer surrounded himself with—hustlers who turned Mailer sour on blacks in general. Kerouac and Mailer tried. As they grew older their intellectual positions regarding blacks became more obtuse than right. As obtuse as their prose styles.

Reading *The Fight* again, on the way down, I realized that what I had mistaken for racism in Mailer's writing was actually frustration—frustration that he couldn't play the dozens with Bundini and them; frustration that he couldn't be black. Maybe one day the genetic engineers in their castles rocking from lightning will invent an identity delicatessen where one can obtain identity as easily as buying a new flavored yogurt.

It's kind of sad. The trench-coated verbal and physical scrapper I used to trade jokes with at Pana Grady's salons in the Dakota. His benign eyes indicated that he had realized he could never really become a "Wise Primitive," and this had brought tranquillity like the look that comes over the face of the werewolf who finally realizes his agony is over.

I asked Mailer who was going to win? He gave me one of those answers for which he has a patent. "Ali. He's worked the death out." So had Mailer.

The black entrepreneur is caught in a bizarre crossfire. On one hand, black intellectuals view him as a sellout to the system, even though many of them have bank accounts which help sustain the system.

The 1960s social and cultural programs brought prosperity to some, and with this prosperity came the guilt feelings experienced by other aspiring immigrants toward the "brothers left behind." He is expected to kick back his gains to them, "the sub-proletariat." In Oakland, the Black Panthers, joined by white children of the prosperous middle class, picketed black merchants. He also has to struggle against the banks and creditors who grudgingly lend him money, and against the myth of black ineptitude. He has to struggle against blacks who seem to try their damnedest to prove the myth.

He knows that if he gets too big, they'll axe him down to size.

Don Hubbard, the 38-year-old president of Louisiana Sports, sits on the arm of a couch in the second-floor lobby of the Hilton. He is confident, proud, cocky even. He blames Top Rank for the disorderly weigh-in ceremonies which had just taken place. "Only people with gold passes should have been admitted."

The Vegas fight between Spinks and Ali was the first fight he'd attended; the first time he'd heard the "moans and groans" of the sport.

Hubbard met Butch Lewis, Top Rank's former vice-president, at the fight and invited him down to New Orleans for the Superbowl. He proposed to Lewis that New Orleans would be a good scene for a rematch between Ali and Spinks. Lewis scoffed at the suggestion, reminding Hubbard that he'd never promoted a fight before and there was some strong competition, including Anheuser-Busch, groups from Las Vegas, Casino owners in South Africa, and a Miami group led by Chris Dundee, Angelo Dundee's brother.

"Spinks agreed to come to New Orleans for the YMCA and didn't show. The mayor's limousines, police escort, and everything were waiting for Leon Spinks. I looked at the five-o'clock news and Spinks was in Detroit. My wife had cooked dinner and was mad enough to jump on Spinks.

"Butch Lewis came down to save face, and raised the money for the YMCA. I started needling Butch because there was a rumor that the fight was going to South Africa. How the hell can Ali stage his last fight in South Africa? Top Rank got a whole barrage of protests from the Urban League and others, and I kept bugging Butch.

"Butch called one evening and said, 'Don, you're bugging the hell out of me. I'm coming to New Orleans at 11:30. From that time you have 48 hours to raise $3 million.'"

Hubbard said he met with the mayor to get his blessings on the international event, obtained a letter of credit for $350,000, and kept $2,650,000 in escrow. At the time I talked to Lewis, which was about 12 o'clock on the Thursday before the fight, the $3 million investment had been returned. Hubbard's partners were Sherman Copelin, a black, and two Italians, Jake DiMaggio and Phillip Ciaccio. Hubbard said he didn't know whether to call the Italians white because some Italians are white and some are Italian.

"The boxing crowd spends more money than the football crowd," he claimed; "When the Superbowl fans come it's with clubs on chartered buses, but the fight crowd arrives in Rolls Royces, Mercedeses, private planes."

Seventy thousand boxing fans spent $6 million to see the Ali-Spinks fight at the New Orleans Superdome. New Orleans chauvinists say that the Superdome is so big you can put the Astrodome inside and still have 60 feet around. A Muslim reporter wrote an article describing it as "a white elephant."

Back in the press room I ran into Harold Conrad, who'd promoted the Liston-Patterson fights and traveled to 22 states seeking a license for Ali to fight during his three-and-a-half-year exile. He said that if Ali won, the only fighter he'd get money for fighting would be Larry Holmes. I had just seen

Holmes encounter Angelo Dundee in the hall, when Dundee said to Holmes, "My kid thinks you're the ugliest and biggest man she's ever seen."

Conrad was completing a novel called *A Rare Bird Indeed,* which he says will be the story of a newspaperman of the 1930s and 1940s, the end of a great era when you could get a table at Lindy's and Reubens at 5:00 A.M. and everybody knew Winchell, and nightclub openings were as big as Broadway openings. Conrad, tanned and wearing a plaid sport jacket, slacks, and a thin mustache, could have been a Runyon character. He worked for Damon Runyon, a "strange man from Kansas City, who didn't have many friends and liked to be left alone." Humphrey Bogart played Conrad in *The Harder They Fall,* his last role.

My friend Sam Skinner, from San Francisco's Channel 44, and I posed for a gag picture with Larry Holmes, WBC Heavyweight Champion and one of the brightest students of the Ali style and a trickster like Ali. Holmes wanted to know where the women were. A young hostess told me that the demand for women was incessant from the Spinks people. They bragged about all the "ladies" they had coming down from St. Louis.

Skinner introduced me to a black-haired, short, and tough looking man, Richie Glachetti, Holmes's trainer. I asked him how Holmes had made Ken Norton look so bad.

"I studied the Norton film. He can't back up, he's vulnerable to uppercuts, straight right hands; when he throws a left hook he telegraphs it; his overhand right is only effective on the ropes; he can't throw it in the middle of the ring because he drags his foot.

"So the way you fight Norton is to stay in the middle of the ring and fight and jab—jabs nullify him better than anything else. You neutralize a slugger with jabs, you back him off, you fluster him."

How would Spinks fare against Ali? "Spinks is still an amateur. In football you go through high school to college and then to the pros. Spinks went through high school- – but he hasn't had enough fights to have gone through college.

"Spinks makes a lot of mistakes, but at the same time he's fighting an old fighter like when Marciano went up against Louis. Spinks would not get the recognition because he will have defeated an old man, a man who contributed so much to boxing; a living legend. Spinks has nothing to gain and everything to lose by defeating Ali."

How should Ali fight Spinks? "Go out and take the first rounds, don't give up anything, stay away from the ropes and fight in the middle of the ring; Spinks's best attack is a combo left hook followed by a right hand. Ali should sidestep him, throw short left jabs, counterpunch him, and there will be no contest.

"I'm for Ali. Got to go with Ali. But if it goes over ten rounds, Spinks will win the fight."

Spirit City had become keyed up for the fight. Boys and girls in red Stetsons and fringed jackets were bused to the Hilton to provide a marching band. The town was heavy into disco. Hilton employees, dressed in black skirts, pants, and white blouses, tossed black and white balloons in the alley next to the Hilton as they second lined to a Jazz band. There was a fireworks display overhead at this New Orleans sun temple. On the second floor, celebrities moved through the English bar, or sat on the sofas. Souvenirs of the fight were for sale all over the French Quarter. They ranged from cheap and expensive dolls to T-shirts to the $100 officia fight poster by LeRoy Neiman, on sale at the Bienville Exchange where the Louisiana equestrian crowd brunch on Saturdays. Even in the airport there were waitresses dressed in glossy boxing shorts, and wearing Ali and Spinks training jerseys. The fight coincided with the Hilton's first anniversary and so it got real goopy. Baron Hilton, the son of "the man who bought the Waldorf," was greeted with a kingly reception as he walked into the lobby with a woman who wore a fur coat, even though it was about 90 degrees outside. The humidity was making life miserable. There was a huge cake near the French bar about 15 feet high, blue and white in color. Two chefs were standing next to it. I asked how many pounds of flour went into the making of the cake. They said that the cake wasn't edible.

I had dinner Thursday night with Hughes Rudd, whose appearance in experimental anthologies alongside Barthelme and Barth is a well-kept secret. CBS's eye should be replaced with a peabrain for removing Rudd from the CBS morning news. It got us all up at 6:30 A.M. so that we wouldn't miss those long rambling anecdotes of his which were about as close to writing fiction as television will ever approach. We ate and went through a couple of bottles of Pouilly-Fuisse in Winston's Room, on the second floor of the Hilton. It was done up in the style of early Frank Lloyd Wright and included some teachers of chinoiserie which became popular in the 20s when the missionaries were looting China.

He talked about an incident during World War II when they sent him an airplane that was worth less than the crate it was shipped in. Rudd said some things about the "TV Industry" which led me to think that it ought to be sunk beneath the ocean in cans so that it won't disturb mankind for maybe 200 years.

On the day of the fight you couldn't touch anything without getting a shock, so high was the tension. The night before I made a bet with a Reuters reporter that Ali would K.O. Spinks in three rounds. I overheard Angelo Dundee telling someone, "The Champ's going to do a number on Spinks."

In the morning José Fuentes and Jane Senno took me up to Luis Sarria's room, to the man some people referred to as the "mysterious Cuban." He was eating breakfast alone, gazing from time to time at the barges and sightseeing boats on the brown Mississippi, or watching the cartoons on television. I'd met him Wednesday night, and watched him as he stood on the periphery of the crowd, hardly speaking, contemplative, studious. He was the calmest man in the whole place. I must have asked him a hundred times whether he thought Ali would win; José or Jane would translate to Spanish, and he'd usually nod his head. José showed me a photo he'd taken of Sarria, "laying hands" on Ali's face. Sarria's face was black and his features were ancient, like those of the people who came over on the first boats.

We went to Ali's private suite, room 1729, only to learn that Ali was living in a private home in West Lakeside. He was inaccessible to all but TV and media stars. Television put up $5 million for fight coverage. There were some men sitting about the suite, silent, not talking. I was reminded of the time I was snowed in one Seattle night with the Cecil Taylor group only to hear a tape of the three-hour concert I'd just left. Nobody said a word. Drew Bundini Brown filed in with Pat Paterson and some others only to file out again. It was like a religious cult. The night before, an insider had praised Ali as Christ, Abraham, Moses. What influence would he have on international politics in the future? The newspapers were beginning to say that he was naive about the Soviet Union. Others were saying, that his entourage was protecting him from the world and that he was "easily deceived."

We went to Pat Paterson's room; he was the permanent bodyguard whom Mayor Charles Daley of Chicago had assigned to Ali. My eyes were blinded by a crowd of blazing trophies laying on a dresser, glittering like idols to the sun. I had read that there's a crunch in the dressing room after the fight and asked Pat Paterson, who was wearing a green leisure suit, my chances of getting in. He said I'd have to take my chances like everybody else.

The packed press bus headed for the Superdome at four o'clock. I felt sorry for the working press. I thought about the newspapers they worked for.

The cities they had to return to. I was standing next to Ed Cannon, a Muslim reporter who was wearing a sweater which read "There Is No God Greater Than Allah." That night he was hassled on the floor by a "famous movie star." The Superdome resembled a giant concrete jaw jutting out at the end of the street. Soon we were inside the jaw. There were a lot of police. After one round a few rows of state troopers gave Ali a standing ovation. Spinks looked like the kind of guy who'd say "motherfucker, kiss my ass," as they put the handcuffs on him. The seats were of red and blue hues and extended to the roof of the building. Strobe lights blinked on and off. Processions of flag bearers headed up and down the aisle.

One blue flag carried the letters "Moron." Nobody would believe me. I asked Nick Browne of the *Soho News*, who was sitting next to me, to examine the flag through his binoculars and sure enough it said "Moron." After the chaotic weigh-in there had been a threat to call out the National Guard. Fistfights broke out on the floor during the bouts.

I decided to take my press pass and rove about the floor. Spinks's cars were on the main floor near the dressing room, all white. I went to Ali's dressing room and was stopped at the door by two whites. I moved through the crowds on the main floor who were gawking at the celebrities entering to take their seats at ringside. People were putting on a fashion show, and hardly paying attention to the bouts. Three black women dressed to the hilt in 1940s costumes walked up and down. One was wearing a gold-sequinned dress the color of her hair and skin. There was a group of men who made a ring about another man. Nobody was paying any attention to them. I walked up to see Chip Carter standing in the center of the ring.

"Who's going to win the fight?" I asked.

"Ali," he said.

"What about Spinks?"

"He's good too."

"You're really a politician."

"I hope so."

I made my way down the aisle toward ringside, past the guards who were sending people back. Up close I could see an ugly dark red wound about the eye of Victor Golindez, who was defeated by Mike Rossman for the WBA Light Heavyweight Championship.

This was real blood, and some of it had sprayed on the referee's shirt. Somebody in the front row yelled "get out of the way," and I spun around and flashed on the people at ringside. It resembled one of Dadaist Lil Picard's

Beauty Shop satires she used to do in the East 60s art galleries. I saw no eyes, noses, nor mouths but what appeared to be blank faces smeared with pancake make-up which seemed unnaturally dry under the lights. My mind flashed back to the Norton films, the eager and richly fed faces, despising his body but at the same time lusting after it.

I headed back toward the press box which was way up in the balcony, nearly touching the ceiling. The fighters in the ring looked like dolls from where I was seated. So I watched some of the fight on one of four giant TV screens suspended from the ceiling. As I moved toward the elevator, Veronica Ali was entering the Superdome, protected by bodyguards.

All during the fights, even the championship fights, people were entering and exiting. "They don't care about this crowd," somebody said, "what they care about is television." Over 200 million people watched the fight.

Nick Browne's remarks were more interesting than the preliminary bouts. It was the kind of grim, deadpan, jaded humor you hear traded across the bar at the Club 55. When Featherweight Champion of the World Danny (Little Red) Lopez knocked out Juan Malvarez, Browne said, "I can understand ethnicity in boxing but a guy who's part Irish, part Amerindian, and part Chicano is taking it too far."

When Rossman came on to the strains of "Hava Nagila," he quipped: 4,000 years of history and only one song.

As the main event approached fistfights began to really break out, "over bets" I was told. About six rows of state troopers spilled over one another just to stop two guys. It was like a rowdy 1890s audience which used to hurl liquor bottles at the actors, or mercilessly heckle politicians on the stump.

Sylvester Stallone, Joe Frazier, and Larry Holmes had entered the ring, Holmes receiving a few boos, but much less than the Governor of Louisiana received when he was introduced. Isaac Hayes did a disco version of "America the Beautiful," and Joe Frazier sang "The Star Spangled Banner," grimacing as if in pain. Somebody seated beneath me said, "I ain't gonna stand."

When Ali entered he was mobbed. He was alternately lifted and buried by the crowd. His party seemed to sway from side to side and as they moved him down the aisle the crowds pressed in for a souvenir of The Greatest's flesh.

"My thing was to dance, come right out and start moving, win the first, win the second, win the third, get away from the ropes, dance, do everything I know how to do. Get my body in shape so that it could do what my brains tell me. The fight's almost over, if you lose eight rounds, you lose the whole fight – -so after I won about ten rounds, naturally, the opponent gets frustrated. He

can't win unless he knocks me out, and I get more confident," was the way
Ali described his victorious strategy at a later press conference. He fought the
way the pros said he had to fight in order to win. "He cut out that rope-a-
dope bullshit," as one old timer said to me.

His left jabs worried Spinks silly, and Spinks looked like a brawler,
engaged in a St. Louis street fight, the most vicious east of the Mississippi.
His trainer, George Benton, left his corner during the fight, in frustration at
the amateurs Spinks; had at ringside yelled to him "wiggle, Leon, wiggle."
Arguments broke out among them over who should give Spinks advice.
Spinks; was 25, lacked craftsmanship, was a sensational head-hunter. I
remember a trainer at an exhibition fight pleading with Spinks to go for the
opponent's body. Ali had followed the advice Archie Moore had given to an
Old Man in the Ring. "You hone whatever skills you have left."

A reporter from the *Washington Evening Star* told me that it was Ali's most
serious fight in three years. At the end of the 15th round there was no doubt
in my mind that Ali had won, and so I headed for the dressing room without
hearing the decision. Veronica Ali, Jayne Kennedy, members of the family,
boxing people, and show business personalities were watching a small TV set
as the decision was being announced. Stallone entered, and John Travolta
was standing off to the side chatting with some people. I asked Liza Minnelli,
who was standing in front of me, wearing a red dress, what she thought of
the fight. She thought it was "sensational."

As soon as Ali left the ring, the crowd began swaying and moving like a
papier-mâché dragon, moving through the interview room to the dressing
room. When Ali finally entered it was impossible to gain entrance unless you
were a celebrity or an important member of the Champ's entourage. "Make
way for Wyatt Earp," they said when Hugh O'Brien walked by. I spotted
some of the old timers I'd met on Wednesday evening. I wanted to hear what
the craftsmen had to say. James Dudley is black, greyhaired, and looks like a
classical American trainer, old style. Suspenders and glasses, starchy white
shirt, and a smile that makes his eyes shine.

James Dudley managed Gene Smith and Holly Mimms. When I
approached him he was being congratulated. His new fighter, Welterweight
Johnny Gant, had won a shot at the title.

"Ali made him miss a lot. Spinks tried to weave and bob, and weave and
bob, but wasn't able to do anything. Any time Ali's left hand is working he's
unbeatable, and his left hand was jabbing and hooking. Ali hit him with anything he wanted to hit him with.

"Spinks comes straight to you and any man who'll come straight to you—you hit him. You move from side to side and hit him with a right hand, hit him with hooks, hit him with anything you want to hit him with." I asked Dudley when he thought Ali had the fight won.

"In the tenth round, because I'd given Spinks only three."

"What was Spinks's biggest mistake?"

"Taking the fight," he chuckled. "Ali," he continued, "lost the last fight because he stayed on the ropes and gave away six rounds."

"How would Ali do against Larry Holmes?"

"I think he's serious about retiring. He's done everything you can do in the fight business. There ain't nothin'else you can do."

"How would Ali rate against Joe Louis?"

"Ali has the style that always gave Louis trouble. Any boxer who could move gave Louis trouble and Ali is the fastest heavyweight of all time."

Louis, I thought, might have had a harder punch. Judging from his films, his K.O. victims take a longer time to rise than Ali's.

Congratulations were going all around as well-wishers entered the dressing-room area. Ali's brother was standing in the middle of the room chanting Muslim phrases. In English he kept repeating, "He said he's from the world of shock." Ali had told the inner circle that he would surprise everybody and he was from the world of shock. I decided that the silence among his aides that afternoon was not due to sullenness but to gloom. Ali had to cheer them up.

I caught up with Dick Gregory. Gregory said he was surprised that the fight went as long as it did. "It was a lesson for the world, a health and body lesson. If you take the physical body God has given you and purify it, there's nothing that the body won't do for you. Anything made by the universal force won't get old. That's what it was, with the right mineral balance and combination of nutrients you can make it." I overheard one of the trainers remark, "He did 6,000 calisthenics. Six thousand. No athlete has ever done that."

New studies had come out which indicated that we know less about aging than we thought. Senility was being seen as a social, not physical,* phenomenon. The idea of waning intellectual powers among the elderly was under challenge. George Balanchine, the dancer, had a body which put many a teenager's to shame. I remembered a story from an old boxing magazine, about someone running into the retired Jack Johnson. He was eager

---

* A new theory, announced in 1982, says that senility is physical in origin and can be cured.

to fight Louis, and bothered Louis so he was banned from the Brown Bomber's training camp. The story revealed that Johnson knew of Louis's weakness—dropping his left after a lead—before Schmeling spotted it on film. How would a retired Johnson have made out against Joe Louis?

But then there was something unique about Ali. Bob Arum had put his finger on it. He argued that "elements of deterioration" had set in during Ali's layoff, just as they had to Louis during his army stint, and Jack Johnson after his exile abroad. But then he spoke of Ali's regenerative capacities. He said he'd seen three Ali's—The Supreme Court victory, the victory over Frazier, the defeat of George Foreman—and that Ali might win if he had a fourth Ali in him. That night in the Superdome we'd seen a fourth Ali.

He had his skills, he had his personality, and he had the will; what else did he have at ringside? Spinks's manager, George Benton, mentioned a "mystical force guiding Ali's life. . . ." After the Zaire fight, George Foreman's corner complained that Foreman didn't fight the fight that was planned. That he seemed distracted. After Spinks lost he said that his "mind wasn't on the fight." Was an incredible amount of "other" energy in Ali's corner? His devotion to Allah is well known.

Bob Arum said that Dick Gregory warned him to call home because his son had an accident. Arum called and it was true. Was Dick Gregory laying more than physical protection on the Champion? Did Dick Gregory have "second sight"?

A Miami customs official said that with the immigration laws as they are now, half of South America will be here in the next few years. On my last trip to New York I noticed storefronts to the Goddess of the Sea, Yemanya, were springing up around the West 90s. Among the people who came were the Cubans who hold Santaria ceremonies in their Miami apartments. The Cubans brought their cults. This Cuban, Luis Serra, was protected by Chango, the perfect loa of boxing, the warrior god of fire, thunder, and lightning.

It was a "mystical" night. The Superdome audience had watched a man turn the clock back, a rare event. I noticed pigeons inside, circling the Superdome, flying above the heads of the crowd.

Spinks's six-door white Lincoln Continental was brought up by a bald man, wearing dark glasses and an earring, named Mr. T. He was surrounded by a few people including his brother Michael. Spinks waved at some people who stood on a balcony. Nobody waved back. Somebody announced that Ali was holding a press conference upstairs. He was seated, flanked by Veronica

Ali and Jayne Kennedy, the actress, who resembled each other so they could be sisters.

"Immona hold it six months. I'm going to go all over the world. Do you know what I did? I was great in defeat, can you imagine how great I am now? How many endorsements, how many movies, how many commercials I will get? I was great when I lost fights. I got eight months I can hold my title . . . mannnnnn.

"See how big I am? Can you imagine what will happen if I walk down the street in any city?

"Do you know I danced 15 rounds with a 25-year-old boy? I'm 36 years old. Man, do you realize how great I am now? The doctor checked my temperature and my blood, and took it to the hospital, and told Dick Gregory what I needed. Do you know how my stamina was up? Do you know what he told me to do?

"Take honey and ice cream 30 minutes before the fight. Half a pint of ice cream and five or six spoonfuls of real honey. My doctor told me to eat ice cream and honey. He gave me a big hunk of honey and melted ice cream. I didn't get tired. Did you see me explode all during the fight? I said, go!

"Spinks is a gentleman; he held my hand up. Spinks will beat Larry Holmes. Spinks will be champion again. He's going to be the second man to regain it twice. He'll have to do a lot to do it three times. But Spinks will be champion again. He's young, he's in good shape, he's going to fight Larry Holmes and be the champ.

"I'm the three-time champion. I'm the only man to win it three times. The greatest champion of all time. [Audience: "Of all time."] Of all time. Was I pretty? [Man in audience: "You was pretty."] Was I moving? Was I fighting? Was I sticking? Was I a Master?

"In eight months I'll let you know, I'll either retire or fight. Hold it eight months. Why give it back as hard as I worked? I'm getting old. Somebody is going to get me. I'm lucky I came back. See, I had you thinking I was washed up. You thought I was washed up. You really didn't know how great I was. You didn't know I just didn't train for the first fight. You thought I had trained and that was my best. Wasn't I much better this time than the first time? I'm older. I'm seven months older. Wasn't it a total difference?

"Mannnnn.Mannnnnnn.Mannnnnnnnn.Mannnnnnnnnnn. I was the best in this fight, let me tell you. I was training six months. My legs were running, I was chopping trees, running hills, watching my food. I said I cannot go out a loser; Jack Johnson went out a loser. Sugar Ray went out a loser. Joe Louis went out a loser. Of all the great fighters only Marciano and Tunney—two white ones—went out winners and everybody's talking about how great Marciano was, and how great Tunney was.

"I said, some black man has got to be smart enough to get by all these people. I got to be that black man who gets out on top. I went training early. I put all my tools together. I tricked you. I was separated from my wife, all my friends. Mannnnnn. Mannnnnnnn. [Audience, including urbane, sophisticated sports writers: "Mannnnnnnn."] Man, I got ready a book coming out for all school children. I hang up my robes, hang up my crown, and my trunks. A Champion Forever. A champion forever. A champion forever. Mannnnnnnn."

A reporter asked Ali did he think we'd hear from George Foreman again.

"You'll hear of George Foreman no more. I don't think he'll ever come back. Spinks will win the title. Spinks is not finished. He just couldn't beat me. He'll beat Larry Holmes [takes a swig of Welch's grape juice].

"I have an announcement. Kris Kristofferson and Marlon Brando have just signed to make my movie, 'Freedom Road.' We have a $6 million budget. Couple of more questions then I gotta celebrate. Mannnnnn, you come over to the Hilton and we gonna ball. Mannnnnn. My victory party. All y'all playboys come on over. "

Trainer James Dudley said Ali won because "Class will tell." Ali's camp did everything according to script down to even the right kind of music. In the first fight with Spinks he was introduced with a movement from a Brahms symphony. In the second fight, "The Saints Come Marchin' In." Spinks's entrance was accompanied by the macho "Marine Hymn" which boasts of an illegal invasion of Mexico. So the people were joking about Spinks's style. A friend of mine predicted that Spinks would win the fight if he weren't arrested between leaving his dressing room and entering the ring. Ali made a joke at the mayor's reception about Spinks still owing a thousand dollars on his $500 suit. Not only did Spinks lose the fight but they had trouble backing his huge white car out of the Superdome.

The political, cultural, and entertainment establishments were rooting for Ali. His victory would be seen as another sign of sixtomania now sweeping the country because, even though some of his most heroic fights occurred in the 70s, he would still remind us of the turbulent decade, of Muslims, Malcolm X, Rap Brown, The Great Society, LBJ, Vietnam, General Hershey, dashikis, afros, Black Power, MLK, RFK. He represented the New Black of the 1960s, who was the successor to the New Negro of the 1920s, glamorous, sophisticated, intelligent, international, and militant.

The stars were for Ali, but the busboys were for Spinks. They said he lost because he was "too wild." His critics claimed that he drank in "New Orleans dives," where the stateside Palestinians hang out—the people the establishment has told to get lost. The people who've been shunted off to the cities' ruins where they live next to abandoned buildings.

They could identify with Spinks. If they put handcuffs on him for a traffic offense, then they do the same thing to them. If he was tricked into signing for a longer period in the armed forces than he thought, the same thing happens to them. For seven months, he was "The People's Champ."

Ali and his party left the stadium, with people lined up on each side to say farewell to the champion. The night before, the streets were empty, but now they were crowded, reminding one of the excitement among the night crowds in American cities during the 1930s and 1940s, or when the expositions were held in St. Louis and Washington. The black players' bars were filling up. The traffic was bumper to bumper. Hundreds were standing outside the Hilton, or standing body to body inside of the hotel. In the French Quarter, many more moved down Bourbon Street as the sounds of B. B. King and Louis Armstrong came from the restaurants and bars. Every 36 year old had a smile on his face.

After returning home I learned that Butch Lewis had been fired from the Top Rank Corporation for, according to Arum, taking a $200,000 scam. Don Hubbard told me that the press conference had been called by Ali, who had remained an extra day to blast two officers of Louisiana Sports, Jake DiMaggio and Phillip Ciaccio, for filing suit against the black partners, Don Hubbard and Sherman Copelin. Ali was joined by Joe Frazier and Michael and Leon Spinks. They wanted to show support for Butch Lewis. Ali said that those who control boxing believed that "the black man's role in the sport should be limited to boxing and carrying the bucket while the white men count the money."

He said that if he heard any more about a suit against Copelin and Hubbard, he'd go see President Carter about the matter, or bring it up during his world tour. "I don't know all the details of this suit," he said, "but I know this is a racist suit."

I called Top Rank's Bob Arum. He said that Ali had apologized to him for the press conference. He'd talked to Ali the night before and accused Copelin, Hubbard, and Lewis of "steaming Ali up" so bad that Ali "got intemperate."

"Ali is contrite," Arum said. "Jesus, when they steam him up they almost make him drunk on rhetoric. Everybody in Chicago is concerned. Herbert Muhammed leapt to my defense. Hubbard, Copelin, and Lewis concocted the press conference to attack me, but Ali thought they were attacking the other guys [DiMaggio and Ciaccio]. Ali was ill-used and is going to say so today. I talked to Muhammed last night."

"Why did Spinks lose?"

"I thought Spinks was going to win based on his having George Benton as trainer," Arum said. "He lost because he received no guidance from his corner. None." I asked him about the quote attributed to him by *Newsweek* that Spinks was "drunk every night." *Sports Illustrated* repeated the claim.

"I didn't see him every night, but every time I saw him he was drunk. A young fighter can drink and abuse himself and not affect his conditioning, but it has a mental effect. Spinks has great raw talent. His wife, Nova, reputedly has joined the Muslims. If he joins the Muslims they will straighten him out. If he goes on like he is now, forget about him ever fighting again. His life will end up being a personal disaster."

Arum said he'd fired Butch Lewis because "I found out he was working a scam on me amounting to $200,000." It had been reported that Lewis received the amount as kickback from the fight in the form of letters of credit. I thought it incredible that Ali didn't know the contractual details of the "Battle of New Orleans" and asked Arurn why he thought this was the case.

"He's easily deceived," Arum said. Would Arum promote another Ali fight? He said that he'd do nothing to encourage Ali to fight again. There was a rumor making the rounds, the source of which he said was Dr. Ferdie Pacheco, Ali's former doctor, whose book *Fight Doctor* annoyed Ali. The rumor was repeated in *Newsweek* and *New York Magazine*, whispering that Ali is showing the symptoms of brain damage. I taped a press conference that Ali gave after a grueling 15 rounds in the ring with a 25 year old man and detected not one bit of slurring or any lapses in his usual comical brilliance. In fact, he could have been a Bible-toting Kentucky evangelist on the stump; the audience in the room belonged to him. They were spellbound by his oratory. Had he commanded, they would have permitted him to walk out of the room on their backs.

DiMaggio and Claccio sued Hubbard and Copelin, but later withdrew the suit saying it was the result of a misunderstanding.

The "internal problems," Hubbard said, "had been resolved." "We don't want to spread our dirty linen all over the nation." But according to a report from KDIA Oakland Thursday night, September 28, the linen would be spread and the scavengers would dine. A grand jury was going to look into the promotion of the second Spinks-Ali fight.

Ali apologized just as Arum said he would. He termed his press conference "unfortunate."

"Certain people whom I regarded as my friends gave me a distorted version of events, which so enraged me that I made unthinkable, angry remarks. I never met Mr. Ciaccio or Mr. DiMaggio and hold no personal animosity. Even if they are wrong I should not have called them a name, particularly a name which offends a whole nation of people."

DiMaggio had threatened Ali with a $10 million suit unless he returned to New Orleans to "apologize" for the remarks Ali made against him.

In defending Arum, Herbert Muhammed said, "He came to me with a contract to guarantee Ali $3 million, $250,000 for training expenses, and $250,000 for any other sources of expenses, and Butch Lewis came to me working for Top Rank, and Arum's a white man. And Lewis is a white man. And Top Rank is a white organization, so I think Ali was not that informed."

Toward the end of his extraordinary Monday press conference, Ali indicated that "Blue-eyed Jesuses" and "Tarzan, King of the jungle" were on his mind, which reminds us of Tarzan's Anglo origin and that, in many black churches, Jesus resembles Basil Rathbone. This brings us to Ali's last challenge: The Anglo-Saxon Curse on black Heavyweight Champions.

"The white hope" legend was born in the mythic Pacific White Republic of California—Atlantis—with its Anglo-Saxon ruling capital, the city by the golden gate. Early California poetry boasts of how the Anglo-Saxons were destined to conquer and rule California and become its supreme race. Jack London was the lingering myth's chief philosopher and fantasist and, for London and others, when Jack Johnson defeated Jim Jefferies, the claim of Anglo-Saxon superiority received a severe setback, and they went scrambling about to find someone to break Jack Johnson. Finally, as a historian observed, the white hope appeared in the form of legislation: the Mann Act.

The pride blacks felt in Johnson's victory led them to celebrate.

They were lynched for "boasting." Other victims were accused of "strutting about." "Frenzied Negroes Exasperate the Whites," screamed headlines in the *London Daily Express,* July 6, 1910.

A curse seemed to be laid that, thereafter, black champions would retire in defeat, "the good ones," like Joe Louis and Ezzard Charles, suffering as much as the "bad guys," Sonny Liston, possibly killed. If he's a historian as I believe he is, Ali will retire, undefeated. If he's a "businessman" as he said at his press conference, he'll fight Larry Holmes for "the other" championship, and Miss Velvet Green, the phantom woman who attends his fights, her chauffeur-driven car outside the stadium, will be there at ringside, awaiting Ali's destruction. She won't be the only one.

PURISTS refer to it as Vodou or Vodoun, a word with Dahomean, and Togo, origins meaning "the unknown." In the Americas, it has come to mean the fusion of dance, drums, embroidery, herbal medicine, and cuisine of many African nations whose people were brought to Haiti during the slave trade. It is an element in many of the syncretistic religions of South America (Pocomania, Umabanda, Santeria), which, combined, claim more followers than Christianity. There has been a religious war in Brazil for years with the Vodoun cults now gaining the upper hand. Vodoun has always had a remarkable ability to blend with other religions, even those considered its rivals. Edmund Wilson writes: "I was once in Haiti near Christmas and found that the Christmas cards, along with 'Joyeux Noel,' were sometimes decorated with a snake." (The snake represented St. Patrick and was based upon the symbol for Damballah, the oldest loa of the cults, said to be a white python which appears every thousand years.) Haitian Vodoun is said to be more "African" than the "African" religions who've been influenced by the colonialists. The Haitians always kicked the rascals out, a feat which struck dread in the hearts of southern slaveholders, who felt that the spirit to revolt (Ogun, loa of iron, and war) might be catching. Adalbert Volck, that genius of Confederate cartoonists, the American Bosch, depicted Lincoln as a satanic figure, signing the Emancipation Proclamation, with grinning demons next to the ink bottle and peering through the room's windows. Above Lincoln's head, in a painting entitled "Santa Domingo, and Haiti," Negroes are seen putting the machete to the struggling whites. The Southerners felt that what happened to the colonial French would happen to them.

In the United States, Vodoun became "HooDoo," a word which appeared in about the 1890s, when Marie Laveau, the First, a HooDoo Queen, held power in New Orleans. Dimmed were the Haitian practices, which one scholar has described as "Baroque." The ceremonies were no longer secret and whites were invited, by Marie Laveau, the First, an extraordinary show woman, to attend the rites. HooDoo might be called Vodoun, streamlined. In New Orleans it's all over town, invisible to all but the trained eye. Faced with curious and sometimes comical suppression by the police, it never went underground; it merely put on a mask.

In New Orleans, one of the forms it took was what we call "Jazz," a music possibly performed in whorehouses whose madames were "HooDoo Queens" like Marie Laveau, and Mammy Pleasant of San Francisco, who catered to the local captains of industry and finance including officers of the Bank of California. A fearless abolitionist, she was active in the Underground Railroad, and was constantly pursued by the authorities until smuggled out of New Orleans by Marie Laveau.

Vodoun is based upon the belief that the African "gods," or loas, are present in the Americas and often use men and women as their mediums. Men and women of all races, and classes. Fifty per cent of the followers of American HooDoo have been white, including the masters and mistresses of some southern plantations where the "conjure man" or "HooDoo man" was the most powerful figure. Whites who operate temples in some parts of South America, are possessed by African loas, and are, in some cases, loas themselves, for example Mademoiselle Charlotte, a French loa who possesses illiterate peasants to speak impeccable French. Augusta, a "tall, blond" woman was Marie Laveau's assistant and was reported to have been quite good at orgies. The African loas, like the Greek, and Norse gods are very human in their behavior. They love, hate, get jealous, mess around, drink rum, and cause mischief, injury, and even death, on the other hand they are healers, doctors, scientists, intellectuals, artists, warriors, and counselors, and they are great dancers; they crawl up and down the side of trees dancing, as certain women do when possessed by Damballah.

They are also tough and persistent. In *All Men Are Mad,* by Philippe Thoby-Marcelin and Pierre Marcelin, a zealous young priest, unaware of the tacit agreement of tolerance between Catholicism and Vodoun attempts to uproot the local Vodoun shrines. The peasants become possessed by Baron

Samedi, the aristocrat of a family of loas known as guedes, and associated with the cemetery. Baron Samedi addresses the young priest through a host the loa has borrowed: "It's me, Baron Samedi, talking to you. What do you think you're doing, knocking down my cross? It's made of wood. You can burn it. But I, who am a loa from Guinea, you won't burn me. You won't chase me away from this country either."

Mardi Gras is also of ancient origins, when it was a celebration involving fornication, self-castration, human sacrifice, and flagellation with goatskin whips. Therefore, it's appropriate that it takes place in the South, where, in a former time, whipping was the chief entertainment. Mardi Gras is polytheistic, just as Vodoun is; it involves drumming and dancing as in Vodoun; both "religions" include ritual masking and costuming. Heathen and Christian rites blend. Mardi Gras is French for "Fat Tuesday," the Tuesday preceding Ash Wednesday. In Mardi Gras, there is a captain who stage-manages the ceremonies for each "krewe," or organization, or cult. In Haiti this role is taken by the Houngan (loosely translated "Priest," a word of Fon origin) or Mambo (priestess). One of the big song hits of this Mardi Gras season was "Mardi Gras Mambo," by the Hawkettes.

Both Mardi Gras and Vodoun include secret societies equipped with flags, songs, and other rites unique to each.

On March 3, 1699, a few Frenchmen, with bread and fish, celebrated Mardi Gras at a place called "Pointe du Mardi Gras," or "Bayou du Mardi Gras." Over a century and a half later, in 1857, six young men, from Mobile, Alabama (the only other American town where Mardi Gras is observed), of the Cowbellion de Rakin Society, organized the Mystick Krewe of Comus, which presented, on February 24, 1857, a New Orleans street parade. Its theme was "The Demon Actors in Milton's Paradise Lost," a Vodoun pageant if there ever was one, since Milton consigns African gods to hell.

Later came Rex, the carnival's elite krewe, which was hurriedly put together for the occasion of the visit to New Orleans of his Imperial Highness Alexis Romanoff Alexandrovitch, heir apparent to the Russian throne. A militant womanizer, the Prince, who had just hunted bison with Buffalo Bill, apparently followed an actress, Miss Lydia Thompson, to New Orleans. She was the star of the musical comedy called *Bluebeard*, according to contemporary accounts the Prince was a little too formal, and "stiff" in the land of hospitality and the Colgate smile. He is remembered as being rude to his hosts and refusing to shake people's hands. The Rex song that year, dedicated to his Royalvitch, contained the lines: "If ever I cease to love, If ever I cease to love,

May the Grand Duke ride a buffalo/in a Texas rodeo." Some historians claim that this song contributed to the Prince's irritable mood. The song, however, has endured.

Since those days, in the middle 1850s, many other krewes have been added, some formal and some outlaw, as this year's Krewe of Constipation, whose maskers dressed in boxes of Ex-Lax.

The history is interesting, but all but ignored by many of the Mardi Gras revelers. Vodoun interpretations vary from town to town, from family to family, and from individual to individual. Although the forms are similar, no two humfos (temples?) are alike.

"You get together with your friends to eat and drink," is the way San Francisco novelist Ernest Gaines defines Mardi Gras. The college girl, sitting in the aisle seat, on the Delta plane said: "It's like Halloween, I think."

I didn't know that if you planned to travel to New Orleans during the Mardi Gras season you had to book at least six months ahead of time. The motels are full within an eighty-five mile radius of New Orleans. I wound up in the Tamanaca Hotel on Tulane Avenue. It was like Alcatraz if Alcatraz were a ticky tack. I was down for a double but one of the beds had been removed to accommodate other Mardi Gras visitors. It was also a headquarters for some of the students who were attending Mardi Gras. Students are all over town; the place looks like Fort Lauderdale, or some other nesting place for students during the intercollegiate mating season. During the night they spent a lot of time knocking on each other's doors, asking for ice. "Got any ice?" "Hey, where's the ice?" I was feeling cranky. In my day we got our own ice.

Before the young girl and the businessman, who looked like a congressman, got on at Dallas, my companions were a middleaged couple, which, though nice people, middle-aged is all I could remember about them. They looked like the handsome couple on the Geritol commercials tainted with forties sepia. They were discussing the Patty Hearst case. The front page of the San Francisco *Chronicle* said something about Patty Hearst being dehumanized. A modern word for "sacrificed." Months before I had written a piece, "An American Romance," about how the defense would concoct a story in which Cinque would be the sex-crazed Beast who shambled off with the society girl and traced 'the plot to Richard Wright's *Native Son,* and Tarzan, *The Ape Man,* both produced during the thirties. The *Los Angeles Times* couldn't handle it; the *Washington Post* said it was too short; the *New York Times,* too long.

I was reading this big book Steve Cannon lent to me, and the nice Geritol lady with the tinted-blue silver hair said, "Is that a heavy book?" I didn't know how to take the remark. The last time I went to New Orleans to visit the principal HooDoo shrine, Marie Laveau's tomb, two white men, who were deplaning at Dallas, noticed the book I was reading and said: "Niggers reading books. Educated niggers."

Besides, I was a little miffed because there was a fly in my coffee. Being a Negro in this society means reading motives in a complicated way. We write good detective novels. Was the stewardess deliberately putting insects into the coffee cups of Negroes? Was this an accident? It was an accident. The stewardess went to fetch me a hot cup of coffee. The lady sitting next to me wasn't the Texan in Dallas. She was genuinely interested in the book. It was a book with exciting and informative illustrations. I told her that I was going to New Orleans and was reading about Mardi Gras. The couple became so interested in Mardi Gras they decided to change their plans and go from Dallas to Mardi Gras.

Everybody ended up laughing like integrated ads on television where black football players dash through airports on behalf of Hertz car rentals.

An Older Man and a Flower Child got on the plane in Dallas.

He is going to meet his family in New Orleans; she, her boyfriend. This is her first Mardi Gras. He is a Mardi Gras pro.

The plane is full of Mardi Gras visitors. There's a gay contingent. Mardi Gras is gay. Female impersonators. "Baby Dolls," as they are called, are everywhere in drag. These gays are dressed as cowboys. They wear turquoise and other jewelry in their belt buckles. They make ambiguous cracks to the male passengers and titillate the women. They pass out champagne and candy to the passengers. New Englanders considered the old Mardi Gras to be wicked. It does have a kind of Louis XIV light-opera decadence. "We bought twenty-two bottles of champagne and have drank twenty-three." In case anybody doesn't get it the man squeals it again.

"The men dress up like women, and do you know, some of them look better." The pro tells her. She's a freshman, eighteen, majoring in political science at the University of Arizona. I would hear this statement a few more times in the coming days. He was discussing Endymion, one of the krewes I'll catch later in the evening. The Older Man tells the Flower Child, "Mardi Gras is a big show, a freak show, which doesn't cost anything." He gave her something before they got off the plane. She clasped it in her hand and said, "I'll never forget you." I'm touched.

I headed from the Tamanaca to Canal Street, where the carnival suddenly came in upon me. One could see people, sitting on the curbs, watching the marchers and floats, all the way up to the Marriott Inn at Canal and Chartres streets. I caught images of corn hot dog vendors with Confederate flags waving from their carts, fried chicken, cotton candy, decorated lampposts, and electricity. The streets were lit up. People were sitting on deck chairs, or on the street curbs, watching. They were drinking beer, wine, and whiskey from thermos bottles.

It was the old populist crowd. Rednecks, country-western types in vans bearing spray-painted illustrations you could bar-b-cue from. Blacks. Not the urbane *New York Magazine* glossy "Superfly" or Negro Gatsby types but people who put on overalls and walk down the street holding their children's hands. This is the "field" division of Negro society. They're a taciturn hardworking bunch. "Their deepest dissent is silence," a slave master once said. They drink corn whiskey and dance at clubs with names like The Honey Hush and do their wash in the Splish Splash Washateria. Sometimes, they stand on the side of roads next to the old Buicks selling crayfish. Mardi Gras' past is not only scandalous and violent, but racist. The Irish of the 1860s used Mardi Gras as "Get Nigger Day," and amused themselves by invading Negro neighborhoods to murder and shoot up people. In the same decade, maskers dressed as apes delighted the crowds by chasing Negroes. Baron de Rothschild, a Jew, was denied entrance to Comus, and Proteus (elite balls formed in 1882). Even today, the floats carry caricatures of Indians with the kinds of faces on the old Cleveland Indians emblems.

For one day the establishment permits the old gods to parade up and down; gods it crushed, often mercilessly. The old gods of the Confederacy are people like Stonewall Jackson, Jefferson Davis, and Robert E. Lee, the last of whom generations of children have been taught was a kind of tragic Prince Valiant who led a noble but lost cause. The Confederate gods are those who tried to restore an imitation Middle Ages, a land of serfs, of Fair Ladies, and cruelty. During Mardi Gras, the old Romance is stirred, and floats bearing "colonels" and soldiers in those dreaded gray uniforms; I even caught a photo of a young man in full Confederate regalia, stranded in a Fiat, as yelping, hooting, "Black Indians" blocked traffic. He was wearing the Confederate battle flag as a head-rag.

The Stars and Bars, America's swastika, waved from everywhere. From balconies, from rooftops, from windows, from corndog carts of peddlers, right alongside the cotton candy. Designed by P. G. T. Beauregard, this symbol of that gothic anachronism, the old South, flies all over America these days. Waving on the lawn where President Ford greeted President Giscard, right alongside the Stars and Stripes; there it was, the morning after Jimmy Carter's Ohio win, on the left side of the future President. Is this harmless, or an omen? I'm thinking, like many other Negroes think when they see this hated flag. A reminder that when the North withdrew its troops, the old Confederate officers, through murder and terror continued slavery as usual, leading Henry Adams, a Louisiana freedman, to say, in 1877, "We lost all hopes. The whole South—every estate in the South—had got into the hands of the very men that held us slaves." Jefferson Davis died with a smile on his face, and down here they celebrate his birthday, and name freeways after him. A man who referred to Africans as a "weak" race, which shows how stoical, and coolheaded Negroes are in the face of so much hurt. "Grudgeful hearted," as 133-year-old Charlie Smith would say. Grudgeful hearted politics. Busing! Busing! Busing! "The bus is us," as Jesse Jackson put it. Grudgeful hearted art. People can't even have fun without hurting or bullying somebody. What kind of fun is that?

The Mardi Gras loves Kings and Queens. Another ambition of the old Confederacy. A southern monarchy. Maybe that's why Huey Long tried to eliminate Mardi Gras, he must have seen through this attempt to revive the Confederate dream, old populist that the Kingfish was. The southern aristocrats paid Kingfish back by having their maskers satirize the Kingfish with a procession of marchers in robes and crowns who ridiculed his famous election promise. In the 1976 parade there was a Boat honoring Huey Long with "Every Man a King" spelled out in flowers.

I am standing in this crowd, catching the tail end of Endymion Parade, Saturday night. The American Endymion is not only in a coma but dreams bellicose floats in his coma dreams. The theme of the parade is "Hail to the Chief." There was a "giant" of JFK and his PT boat. Other floats rolled by with giants of other Presidents; Truman, MacArthur in dark glasses with corncob pipe, Eisenhower, "who supported the anti-communists in Guatemala," and others are remembered for being tough, standing up to the Russians, refusing to bug out. Guns, and missiles roll by. In contrast, Alice Cooper, the rock person, is the grand marshall of this parade and somebody named Irving Wallace, the King. The black Southern University Bands march by doing K.C. and the Sunshine Band's "'Get Down Tonight," and it goes on, Endymion, with a Nixon float even, with what appears to be a picture of John Ehrlichman on the side. After it was over I followed the Negroes who were

heading towards Shakespeare Park because I figured they knew where something else was going on. There were hundreds of us moving uptown, walking
towards the Promised Land for all I knew. It must have been this way when
Negroes found out that "slavery," at least on paper, had ended and dropped
what they were doing and started walking through the gates of the plantation. Hundreds of them. Walking. To Ohio, for all they knew. As if moving to
freedom. From slavery to vagrancy. They got thrown in jail and were forced
to work on plantations as punishment. Some of their descendants are in this
bunch. Nobody writes about them as well as Ernest Gaines. "I spend time in
the country and then, on Mardi Gras day I come into New Orleans," he said.
The destination turned out to be the Greyhound bus station. I went into the
bar and ordered a Budweiser, lest someone thought I was loitering about
Greyhound bus stations these days in my leather jacket, and jeans. Barry
Manilow was on the jukebox singing, "I write the songs . . ." The Negroes
were boarding their buses, leaving this white Mardi Gras, or "Caucasian"
Mardi Gras, as my acquaintance Rudy Lombard, an architect, sneered.

Nobody in an ape's costume chased them this night. Mardi Gras had
become civilized, far removed from its sordid past, when the New Orleans
newspapers dismissed it as a gathering of rowdies. In fact, the next night, a
leading Pan-Africanist intellectual, an independent man who publishes his
own poetry, made a speech that could have been delivered by a Kiwanis.
About how in a place like Russia he couldn't write his poems for fear of being
censored. How America had made progress. This man was a dedicated and
serious militant and he said, "Why, ten years ago, I wouldn't have been able to
even stand here to watch Mardi Gras." I didn't know whether to faint or to
salute. I did neither. There had been a lot of jargon, and political abstruseness
about the political movement in the 1960s. I became cynical very early when
I saw some of the militants picking up the habits of the oppressors. Like people who'd participated in Freedom Rides criticized our magazine, *Yardbird,*
for printing an interview with George Schuyler, a brilliant political satirist
and thinker from the Harlem Renaissance, a high point in American creativ-
ity. They wanted to suppress his free speech. They wanted to do to him what
they accused white people of doing to them. The revolution had moved to
the suburbs. The revolution had a carport.

When I got back to the Tamanaca from the bus station I went to my cave
and watched some television. Yul Brynner, playing a Hollywood robot, was
chasing some guy through sets from different periods of time. Finally Yul

Brynner's cowboy face melted. I went to sleep and dreamed that a Mardi Gras of melting masks was chasing me.

The next morning I headed towards the French Quarter, where the HooDoo shrines are located, the principal one being Marie Laveau's tomb at St. Louis #1, though the name on the stone reads, "Glapion, the Widow Paris." The "VooDoo" museum is located at 1139 Rue Bourbon in New Orleans. It's dives like this that give HooDoo a bad name, associating it with "Black Magic" and "Devil Worship," when the Houngan (from the Fon) is known for his curing abilities, not hexes, and the "devil" does not exist in the Vodoun pantheon, this creation having to do with a Western quarrel—the conflict between the Christians and the old Pan cults, the cults of the "Golden Calf," and other homed gods. Inside was the cliche tourist display of dolls, and "hex" powders. No wonder HooDoo has received such an abominable reputation. Mr. Charles Gandolfo, the curator, unloading boxes. Though there was a "closed" sign on the door Mr. Gandolfo opened the door for me. "I don't usually do this," he said. He was unpacking a box shipped from Samuel Weiser's famous "occult" bookstore in New York City. A box of Tarot cards, a watered-down deck at that, with Camelot figures on it—a bogus deck since the Tarot originates in Africa. As phony as the old South. A black man entered the shop. It was the famous Prince Kyama, or "Chicken Man" as he is known, internationally. America's HooDoo Prince and, according to the Prince, the incarnation of Marie Laveau. "They coming next month to make a film on me," the Prince said. Tourists travel from Canada, and from all over the United States to see the Prince; they live in campers outside of town and send in emissaries to make contact with him.

"How about a photo for the folks in Detroit, Prince," said some collegiate-looking Negro kids as we walked down Bourbon Street. He makes a living "geeking," lying in caskets, handling rattlesnakes, and putting on shows for tourists who happen into the "VooDoo" museum. Some innocent-looking college girls entered the shop. He invited them to come on his "VooDoo Underground" tour. When they declined, he invited them to attend a concert, happening that night, in which he would perform with Doctor John. "He isn't the original Doctor John," I said. Prince Kyama was unacquainted with the original Doctor John. This should have deterred me from taking the "Underground" tour, but I decided that this was a case of consumer fraud which might be interesting. I had, a week before, paid fifty dollars to a plumber for sticking a pole down a stuffed toilet. A few weeks before I paid for the same automobile repair job twice and when I told the chief mechanic that I thought his operation was slippery he looked at me as though I was crazy.

The Prince was wearing beads made of turquoise and silver, fringed jacket, a bamboo hat shaped like a Stetson, a red and yellow checked jacket, and Bruce Lee T-shirt with Bruce Lee painted on it posing before a Dragon all done in snazzy graphics. He said that Bruce Lee was his student. The Prince had a lot of stories. He was bom in Haiti, and had come to New Orleans only a few years before and now he had the whole scene. Oh, the police had busted him a few times for the chicken act, but outside of that he was well known and would star in a film. He told one fellow he owned 1,000 acres of land in Texas. For ten dollars he showed me Marie Laveau's tomb, a cottage reputed to have been invaded by the HooDoo Queen, on St. Anne's Street, an intersection where the first black was said to have been hanged. I already knew about the tomb and the house.

Reluctantly, and impatiently the Prince pointed out a beauty salon, on the reported location of one owned by Marie Laveau. It's very hard to separate the Laveau legend from fact. Were there two Marie Laveaus, or even three? Was it a title given HooDoo Queens after the death of the original Marie Laveau? There is evidence that there existed a Marie Laveau, born possibly in 1794 and died in 1881. Another "Marie Laveau" lived until the 1920s. So confusing are the accounts of the deeds of both that it's possible to speak of them as one person. For example, although thousands of pilgrims visit the St. Louis cemetery to pay homage to Marie Laveau, there is evidence that the daughter, not the mother, is buried there. The original Laveau is said to have disappeared from the earth without a trace. I shall speak of them as "Marie Laveau." There are accounts of the activities of a Marie Laveau in the nineteenth-century New Orleans *Picayune* newspaper. She was said to have conducted "ceremonies," which sound like orgies, attended by people of both races not excluding prominent men and women of New Orleans society. She has also been accused of murdering and driving her rivals out of town or even driving them mad. On the other hand, just as there are many aspects to the Haitian Venus-loa Erzulie, she has also been praised for her good deeds. The tomb of "Marie Glapion" (a lover's name) or "the Widow Paris" (a first husband) reads in French: "She was a good mother." Erzulie of the Dahomean rites is often a virgin and child figure. Marie was a kind of patron saint of prostitution and was supposed to have performed a miracle which postponed the hanging of a prisoner. She operated a house of prostitution called The Maison Blanche, where "Negro Balls" took place, an astonishing name since no black males were admitted.

It was in these plush and opulent interiors that white men would rendezvous with Negro women called "quadroons," racially mixed women on whose beauty an Englishman commented: "[They resemble] the high-class Hindus; lovely countenances, full, dark, liquid eyes, lips of coral, teeth of pearl, sylphlike figures; their beautifully rounded limbs, exquisite gait, and ease of manner might furnish models for a Venus or Hebe."

"Marie's" chief rival in those days of "The Business" was Doctor John. Jean Montanet, Jean La Ficelle, or Jean Latanie, or Jean Racine, or Jean Grisgris, or Jean Macaque, or Jean Bayou, or VooDoo John, he went by many names but has come down to us as "Doctor John," reputed to have been a Bambara, from Senegal. Lafcadio Hearn, New Orleans writer known for his "jewel-like" words, and reputed to be one of Marie's lovers, described Doctor John as "a man of middle height, very strongly built, with broad shoulders, well-developed muscles, an inky black skin, retreating forehead, small bright eyes, a very flat nose, and a woolly beard. . . ." Hearn also says, "He had a resonant voice and a very authoritative manner." Doctor John was a wealthy man of expensive tastes and often received scorn from sections of New Orleans because of his adherence to the polygamistic ways of his Bambara tribe. He is said to have had an international harem of fifteen wives, in a Christian country, where only white men are allowed that many. He had knowledge of Obeah, the West Indian Vodoun, sometimes referred to as Pocomania. He knew botany, the knowledge belonging to only the high priests of Vodoun, the Houngans.

Marie's background, on the other hand, wasn't all that great. Daughter of a slave owner, and the slave woman he "raped," at least modern feminists would claim, she constantly vacillated between Catholicism and HooDoo and is said to have denounced HooDoo on her deathbed in favor of Catholicism. One can imagine the conflict between the two: Doctor John perhaps dismissing Marie's HooDoo as humbug. He was "inky black," she was a quadroon. He knew the real thing, or at least the original thing. The HooDoo of the North Americans seems to be more muted, and faster; the phenomenon of Be-Bop can be interpreted as a HooDoo loa.

There was also an altruistic side to Doctor John. He was supposed to have distributed "gombo," and "jimbalaya" to the poor. His career was brought to an end when somebody cut his throat. Marie Laveau went to jail for the crime until it was discovered that some female members of his cult did it.

The conflict between Marie and John had been exacerbated over an incident concerning a slave girl named Pauline. It seems that a white man so fell in love with Pauline that he moved her in with his family. When he left town on a trip Pauline enslaved the family. When the authorities broke into the house they found his wife and children in a state of malnutrition. Doctor John was supposed to have provided Pauline with a charm to prevent her hanging. She was hanged anyway and so Doctor John was accused of bad gris-gris. A strange coincidence occurs when we find that the family's name was Rabbeneck, and Doctor John "The Nighttripper" spells his last name "Rabennack." Max Rabennack!

Like most of the tourists to New Orleans that week I had been "jacked up." It ain't all that free. They were even selling a Viva Mardi Gras lipstick on the radio. Now, if I were conducting a "VooDoo" tour I wouldn't have left out the church at 1229 Saint Philip Street. A most unusual church. I wouldn't have left out Congo Square, where African slaves fathered and performed ceremonies a few irrational observers have characterized as "stupid fetishism," I wouldn't have neglected the other shrines where slaves gathered and created such foment that the Spanish colonial Governor issued an edict against the importation of slaves from Santo Domingo and Haiti. "They are too much given to Voodooism and make the lives of the citizens unsafe," said the Guv. I couldn't understand why the Prince didn't point out the Pharmacy Museum at 514 Chartres Street, where HooDoo botany can be found. He left out the Quadroon Ballroom, located inside the Ramada Inn at 717 Orleans Street, where Marie set up quadroon "dates" for their fans who visited from all over the world for their favors. Royalty was into HooDoo! Queen Victoria was supposed to have consulted Marie Laveau.

I was getting hungry and the Prince recommended a place called the Vaucresson Cafe Creole, which was located at 624 Bourbon Street. Well, we went in and laid out five dollars for a scoop of something that looked like rice with some kind of red dye on it. The waiter, who looked "Latin," referred to the thing as jambalaya. He had on red jacket and black pants and came over to the table and made some motions about a bottle of wine. And so I said, "In Berkeley I buy this stuff around the corner at the Chinese-American Mom and Pop store at Cedar and California." There were these Belles at the next table with those white floppy Belle hats. They were wearing white gloves. They broke up. The other man, a manager, gave me an angry look. He looked Creole. Creole originally was a derisive term created by the Spanish as a put-down of the French who seemed to enjoy fucking everything. The cockhounds of the colonialists. Maybe that's why the intellectual black cock-hound's headquarters is Paris. Even some of those pushing "buy Black."

Nowadays, a Creole is someone who is of mixed white and black blood. It's kind of become confused with mulatto. There's a joke about New Orleans Creoles. Seems that during the freedom marches in New Orleans, an irate white person left her children with a Creole woman, saying: "Hold these children, we got to go down and do something with these niggers."

Well, after we'd eaten whatever it was, and drank a glass of wine and the Prince seemed as though he was real comfortable, I told him that I was writ-ing about his "VOODOO" tour for a magazine. He just about fell out of the chair. He asked me did I want to meet Doctor John "The Nighttripper." Would I like to go rattlesnake hunting with him? Did I want to see him lie in a casket in broad daylight. All I wanted was a receipt. With trembling fingers he signed his name under "VOODOO tour." I smiled and shook his hand. I headed up Bourbon towards Canal Street. Gerald Jackson, Bob Thompson, Jack Levine, or Ensor could paint this scene. The grotesque circus faces. Wine selling on the streets. More T-shirts than I'd ever seen. I felt like starting up a metaphysical bunko squad. America needs one. The hustling Charmers who give all the others a bad name. They say that most of the Vodoun ceremonies have been secret. Nobody hassling you at the airport with Swami books or knocking on your door all times of the day or telling you that you hate black people when you don't buy their paper. Senator Henry Jackson said: "Reli-gion is private and personal." Scoop's finest moment!

The next night was spirit night. I attended Bacchus with two poets, Tom Dent, Kalamu Ya Salaam, and their wives. Each Boat was dedicated to a spirit. The "Spirit of Exploration," "The Spirit of '76," etc. Perry Como was Bac-chus VIII, "the only Outside King," a citizen who knows his Mardi Gras sneered. He seemed to be resting his feet on the shoulders of some old smil-ing "Uncle" dressed in a red suit. In one of the segments some Negro grooms led horses ridden by white Knights. There was the "giant Bacchus, with the same blank, droll grin, clutching a goblet. The "Spirit of Courage" was a "giant" coonskin cap-wearing Daniel Boone clutching a revolver; it had the same sinister stare. The crowd cheered. Flashbulbs were going on and off like at a Muhammad Ali fight. Something cold hit the back of my neck and slid down under my sweater collar. It was a doubloon, Bacchus' doubloons were medallions with pictures of Bacchus on them. Somebody on one of the floats had thrown a doubloon and it landed in my collar? I was thinking of the odds for that. Others were hitting the deck for theirs. "Hitting the deck" is taken seriously at Mardi Gras; my friend dived for one only to have it trapped by some southern woman's foot. "Take a picture of this, Ishmael." I took a picture of it, but she wouldn't budge. She was staring straight ahead, determined to keep her foot on the doubloon. If looks could kill. I remembered this nice southern panel, at this nice university, in Winston-Salem. These southern ladies were saying that their plight was similar to that of the blacks and I asked did they know of a case where a man sent a bloodhound after a woman after she'd left him. "Race Issue Disrupts Panel." The Winston-Salem Journal said. A "giant" black raven is before me. "The Spirit of Literature," and there were the names of Twain and Poe. On the side of the tableau was the typewriter next to which a Confederate soldier held forth a bayonet. Now, this float was trying to tell me something.

After the parade we went to Lu and Charlie's for pitchers of beer and hamburgers. On the walls were jackets of Tom Dent's *Magnolia Street*. Performing was the New Orleans French Market Band, a white Dixieland band. The leader, Barbara told me, was the city coroner. Anyway, they were keeping the old New Orleans spirits in shape.

I spent dead Monday, the day before Fat Tuesday, or Shrove Tuesday, with writers Toni Morrison (*Sula*, *The Bluest Eye*), Toni Cade (*Gorilla, My Love*), and Gloria Smart. At one point they asked me why I referred to them as the Seven Sisters. The Seven Sisters was a single conjure woman from Georgia. At least one of the Seven Sisters is a working Mambo. Root woman. Wrote dialect right up front in the *New York Times*, and who don't like it? I think I'd get along with them even if there were no feminist movement. I'd said some harsh things in the past about women intellectuals, now I only teased them. Maybe man should give up every "piggy" habit except the right to tease. Women, the right to blush. They can have everything else. They can have the millions of female maniacs who have custody of your children and all you get back is an endorsed check and the courts and the law go right along with the arrangement. They can have dying younger. They can have all the wrestling the dragons, walking the moon, entering, unharmed, the caves where rattlesnakes hibernate, and all the other things men do for, or over, or to impress, a woman. Like clawing and knifing each other to death. Have any of you brothers out there ever found yourself in some woman's bed, and her man is ringing the buzzer and she gets up and rings it for him to come up, and you only got sixty seconds to get your clothes on, and she's enjoying your anxiety? We do need a metaphysical bunko squad to explain that. I saw the face once of a woman over whom a man had been murdered. It was one of the most peaceful faces I've ever seen. Like a saint's face.

Was there ever a "Hal of Troy?" What man has ever had people go to war over him just because he was pretty? Men sweat, yearn, and risk great reputations to lie in the arms of a woman. The congressman took sleeping pills but the woman got $200,000 and a spread in the big magazines. Is it fair?

I think that's it. Chester Himes said it. He tried to be "'fair." Like I've been clipping reviews by white male critics of novels, plays, and films by black women and you'd be astonished at the results of my research. People making love right in the paper!! They especially like this woman novelist who writes colored Norman Rockwell type stories about how Jesus was walking down the road with this old colored lady, and all about how Jesus had these "blue eyes," and "auburn hair"; the greatest American Romance has yet to be written. They hated the film *Mandingo* because *Mandingo* was accurate. Well, that day, we got along well. It was more than militant intellectual women and male chauvinist man but writer to writer. And when writers get together they talk about books. Their books, the competition's books.

We had lunch at a place called the Provencial. When I tasted the jambalaya I then could tell why it had achieved the status, through lore, of a holy food. It is better than Boston clams, Nathan's hot dogs, dinner at Wo Ping restaurant, Inc., on Pell Street, Prawns at Berkeley's Spenger's, Texas red at Schultzs in Austin, and Albuquerque's blue tacos. HooDoo food. Syncretic: Spanish, African, Native American, French-adaptable to all cultures. There was warm fellowship in this restaurant. The waiters and waitresses talked in a slow hum of good will. Not a drawl, but a hum. A hum that could put you to sleep. This was the sweet South of ambrosia, where people say yes mah'm and no mah'm, where there's always the best silver laid out, and places set in case somebody stops by hungry. Where the man sits at the head of the table and carves.

A land where the male leads are plaid by Clark Gable and Don Ameche, tipping their top hats, and escorting ladies to the ice cream parlor. And New Orleans is the thick cream of that sweet South. The South's vanilla. The city of po boy sandwiches, Frankie and Johnny, Louis Armstrong, the great Zulu, where the mayor's first name is Moon and every day a Frank Yerby novel. If you're a tourist they'll show you where Tennessee Williams lives and gossip about Clay Shaw. (Had whips in his closet!)

New Orleans like HooDoo is all over place and time. We walked from the

French Quarter of the nineteenth century to the Spanish Cabildo of the Middle Ages. There were even jugglers performing in the courtyard. It's so nice. Almost makes you forget that other South which lies buried in the New South's soul to surface once a year as this pageant. The day when portraits of Robert E. Lee are dusted off and placed alongside the Audubon bird displays (Audubon was an Afro-American) in the windows of antique bookshops. The South where the Klan and the White League used to terrorize Negroes for having saved enough money to buy a house, or for raising uppity crops. For wanting to go to "Quality" schools. The same things they "lynch" Negroes for today. That's why I'm always a little uneasy in the South. I never know which one I'm going to run into. The elegance of Chapel Hill and Lexington, Virginia, or North Carolina's chicken coop: Winston-Salem. The difference between Jimmy Carter, smiling on his face's right side, the Stars and Stripes behind him, and Jimmy Carter, frowning on his face's left side, the Stars and Bars beside him. They thought they'd buried the old South before, only to have it rise, like Frankenstein, to pillage, terrorize, and plunder in the hooded robes of organizations whose charters refer to fraternity in the feminine gender. Perhaps the most important question the United States faces in the next ten years is: has the South finally got rid of its monster?

When we arrived at St. Louis # 1, the cemetery, the gates were locked. When I visited, the day before, in the company of Chicken Man, the tourists were white too. They were making wishes before Marie's tomb. People from all over the South—HooDoos—still come here. There are fresh flowers at her grave, and visitors are invited to make an X for good luck, on her tomb. The surface of the tomb is crowded with X's.

Toni Morrison mentioned a place called The Cabaret. Once there I was able to snap a photo to add to my HooDoo altar, which consists of "evidence" and gifts from all over the world, including a Yemanja mask from some Argentineans. You see, above the bar, resting on a shelf, was a skull to each side of which were "bowling trophies" to the casual observer, but loas to the trained eye. Atop the skull's head lay a necklace beaded with snake vertebrae. It is what the Haitian Houngans call an Annet. There was a big butt woman standing at the bar. She had "kiss me" written all over her rump. Erzulie, no doubt.

Tom Dent and I are friends who spend a lot of time feuding with each other. Maybe it's "cultural differences." Like, Tom Dent eats lobster; I eat Kentucky Fried Chicken. He's a bourbon "black" as he once said to me, and his father runs a university. He's very "fair" looking, as they say. I'm brownish red. I left Toni Morrison, Toni Cade, and Gloria Smart at Tom's house because I didn't like the way Tom was "relating" to me, as they say. Plus he had this guest who was real boring. Real hung up on ideology. We couldn't even enjoy the Bacchus parade, he was spouting all of this uninteresting jargon I've heard, maybe a hundred thousand times. I made a joke. Something about tape recording everything he was saying from my Living History tape recorder bag where I had stuffed notebooks, evidence (menus, street maps, matchboxes, hundred-year-old postcards, doubloons, Kodak bulbs, Mardi Gras memorabilia), and other "junk" to go into the psychic vacuum cleaner. When I made the joke the dude took off like a hotblooded rocket. WHOOOOOSSSSSHHHH. Berated me on the street. Called me names. He was louder than the drums of the marching bands. Raised a Methodist, I didn't like to get loud talked in public. Why do all of you talk so loud? a Third World person asked me once. We are an exuberant people, I explained. But there's a difference between being exuberant and a political basket case, like all of the shell-shocked who can't believe the revolution didn't come when even a glimpse of American history would have proven that Apocalypse is usually a false arrival. Anyway, Tom had joined us at the Gov. Nichols apartment, where the women were staying, and we all headed out to his house after about three hours of Tom pacing up and down the floor, cussing me out, signifying, attitudinizing. He wouldn't help me find the car. We had been out all day walking around New Orleans. It was night, and the streets had French names, and so I couldn't remember which French street I left it on. "If you parked it illegally I'll have to come down to the police station to help you look for it," he said. You can think any number of pleasant nostalgic thoughts about the South until somebody mentions The Police Station, a land where many Negroes have disappeared. I'm thinking of the movies of big-bellied Dixie police shooting into nigger cells for target practice and feeding them cockroach meat for breakfast. I didn't want to go into a southern police station for anything. I remembered the Auschwitz type diggings that had taken place in Arkansas a few years ago, where the bones of "lost" prisoners, killed by guards, were dug up. I was relieved when I found the car, and drove to Dent's house, triumphantly, stormed in, ate Barbara Dent's gumbo, and then told the women, "Let's go, I'll drive you home."

"Suppose we don't want to go," Toni Morrison said. I didn't want it to sound so crass, but then went on to make another M.C. remark. There was no way for me to win that night and so I huffed out, got into my car, and drove off: fast; loud; so everyone would know I was annoyed. So when I met everybody the next day for the trip to see "Black Indians," things were a bit tense.

The important parades on Fat Tuesday were Comus, Rex, and Zulu. This year's Rex is Frank Garden Strachan, a businessman. He looks like the couple on the Delta, a shipper who looks as though he probably has no problems with regularity. His consort is Miss Alma Marie Atkinson. Mr. Strachan wore royal golden robes. His sacrificial maiden is surrounded by maids, and jonquils, ribbons of purple, gold, and green. Mardi Gras ladies wear laurel crowns. She wore a candy wool crepe suit. There's a "giant" ox. The Boeuf Gras, surrounded by huge berries and cocks. In the old days the oxen would have been slaughtered, a rite known as "burying the carnival." Interesting, when you realize carnival, loosely translated, means "farewell to meat." Other things, right out of the pages of the Golden Bough: wild men are all over town, carrying clubs, acting savage, black and white. I took a photo of one in a leopard skin outfit and club.

Mr. Strachan's favorite lines in the Rex poem, written by Ashton Phelps, were, "He dresses with care, never tatterdemalion/As becomes every proper Episcopalian." Anglicism, the church of the Confederacy. The theme was "Jazz-New Orleans' Heritage." The HooDoo shrines and the Jazz shrines are in the same neighborhood, suggesting a possible connection. The "HooDoo" guide book says that "jazz" is based upon VooDoo ritual music. I'm thinking of all of the musicians called "Papa." It was the one ritual in which the "Papa" or the "King" told people when to stop playing. There are Ragtime floats and Muskrat Ramble floats and an "Oriental" "Chinatown My Chinatown" float. The bakery equivalent of this aesthetic is blueberry cheesecake. But if you think that's rich, in 1838 the Mardi Gras procession contained "... several carriages superbly ornamented-bands of music, horses richly caparisoned-personations of Knights, cavaliers, horses, demigods, chanticleers, punchinellos, &c, all mounted. Many of them were dressed in female attire, and acted the lady with no small degree of grace." They knew how to put on the dog in those days. There seemed to have been more work put into the masks. Contemporary photos show the women of 1880, dressed in hoops, putting the masks together by hand.

Now, old-timers say that the Zulu Parade began as a response to Rex. Whereas Rex was white, mythical aristocratic, a Confederate pageant which once honored the daughter of Robert E. Lee, who was "took out" by Comus at the ball that 1870s night, the Zulu Parade involves an ancient Afro-American survival form. Adopting the oppressor's parody of themselves and evolving, from this, an art form with its own laws. I call this process loa-making.

If the whites had their King, Rex; we have our King, Zulu, a savage from the jungle like you say he is. While you're laughing at us we're laughing with you but the joke's on you. In the first Zulu Parade there was a jubilee quartet at each end of the parade. It was a proletariat parade of porters and laborers, who were put down by the Afro-American middle class, the colored six companies. What you put down you often join, someone once said, and so this year's Zulu King was Reverend Lawler P. Daniels of the great southern Negro industry: death—preachers, insurance men, and undertakers, the millionaires of the race. His court included Big Shot Soulful Warrior, and Witchdoctor. The social mobility of the Zulu Parade can be measured by comparing the style of this parade to that of earlier Zulu parades. King Peter Williams, the first Zulu King, wore a starched white suit, and for a scepter he carried a loaf of Italian bread. By 1914 the King could afford a buggy, and by 1922, the Zulus owned a yacht. This year's King wore turquoise vestments, and a jeweled crown. He waved a feathered spear. His wife wore a trailing turquoise gown. The reminders of former times were those wearing animal skins, grass skirts, and Afro wigs. Coconuts are Zulu's doubloons.

Rudy Lombard is a handsome bearded architect who was dressed in SNNC denims! Chic. I told him that Lombard was the name of a family which appears in Dante's *Inferno*. I'm always saying dumb shit like that. So when he said, "Yeah, I met him," after Toni Morrison introduced us, in that tone which sounded like a dismissal, I could understand where he was coming from. Well, he kind of made out that the Black Indians were a hermetic krewe, so secret that those who revealed them were not looked upon favorably. Jules Cahn, a film maker, has done a film on the Mardi Gras Indians, which was being shown at the Historic New Orleans Collection. Unkind remarks were made about his activities as we saw him walking down the street, during the Black Indian ceremonies. People have made so many billions of dollars from "The Black Experience," it ain't funny. And some wish to protect the last remaining secrets. I don't think the Black Indians are going to be so secret for long, if they ever were. I've seen them cited in a number of books concerning New Orleans and the carnival. Even Dick Cavett cited one book entitled *Gumbo-Ya-Ya* on nationwide television while touring the city in the company of Tennessee Williams.

I was told that they never cross Canal Street—"white zones"—but I followed them to Canal Street and beyond. But nobody had to tell me what to mention and what not to mention. In fact, some of the middle-class blacks with whom I visited somehow feel that New Orleans belongs to them and anyone interested in the city is an interloper into the New Orleans Nation. In her remarkable book *Black Dance,* Lynne Fauley Emery claims that none of the original HooDoo ceremonies has ever been witnessed. But the Black Indian ceremony was quite visible to blacks and whites.

The first thing I noticed at the black intersection, one of the stops for the Black Indians, was an old beat-up jalopy full of guedes. Guedes are states-men, clowns, artists, known to "show each man his devil." In *Canape-Vert, by* the Marcelin brothers, they are depicted as "Gay, rowdy, and a scandalous jester[s]." They are often proletariat gods who satirize government officials on their behalf, and are not afraid to mock the Houngan. Here they are on this New Orleans street, pouring beer Into the water tank of the car. Six hours later, I saw them in the same car, making that car run on beer. There's a whole ritual of greeting, mock competition, Chief-saluting, and unintelligible, for me, lingo the Black Indians go through. There was a little boy named Flyboy who was into some heavy discourse with Wildman, crowned with a bull's horn.

The most extraordinary feature was the costumes, richly decorated, and fantastic. People work on them throughout the year. They carried on with this procession, wending their way through the neighborhoods, then heading uptown on St. Claiborne Street. This krewe had no police escorts and traffic; at some points, became jammed. Some of the inconvenienced were good natured, like the fellow in Confederate battle dress with the Stars and Bars wrapped around his head. Others menaced the blacks with their auto bumpers and the blacks yelping and whooping menaced back, waving their flowered axes about their heads. It was a "mock" race war. I was trying to identify the costumes. Though whites consider the Black Indians to be odd some claim that cohabitation between Blacks and Indians has produced a new race in America. One theory has it that the geometric designs (*vé-vés*) made by cornmeal, on the ground, used by houngans to order "down" loas were a technique Haitians learned from the indigenous Indians of Haiti. They made the African gods meaner, they hated the Spanish so. Now, Bob Callahan, President of the Turtle Island Foundation, publisher of *Apalache* by Paul Metcalf, Melville's great-grandson, has a keen eye. We were sitting at the Golden Gate racetrack and from his seat he identified the golden grass—the original Spanish grass, behind the University of Califomia's football stadium. I showed him the photos I made of the Black Indians, and he said the costumes were Caribbean. I left the Indians, they were invading "white" territory like some kind of prophecy was taking place before my eyes.

Since the major American holidays seem to induce anxiety and depression Mardi Gras is a bright moment on the American Death calendar. During Christmas, for example, everybody goes about with those airplane stewardess smiles in the winter when it's cold. The plot of Christmas was deliberately scripted to cause guilt, and the only Mardi Gras figure is Santa Claus, who is for kids. Mardi Gras is one of the few art forms in which the whole community can become immersed, just as in HooDoo, which not only Negroes but the Irish practiced in New Orleans.

It's a day of joy when people can act the fool and wild instead of acting that way for the whole year around. They ought to have a Mardi Gras in South Boston. There could be San Francisco, Chicago, Detroit, and New York Mardi Gras as well as Mardi Gras in Atlanta, Denver, and Philadelphia. Cults all over the community could organize their floats and participate in parades. This could become a land of a million krewes. A non-political holiday could continue through July, where the only thing we have is the Fourth, a day set aside to commemorate feudal slave owners whom tennis court historians would have us believe spent most of their time talking like Alistair Cooke and sitting, hands clasped, in a winged Chippendale, saying profound things. How many people do you know who live in places like Monticello and Mount Vernon? I'd like to see each town work together to put its local histories, legends, and gossip on wheel and foot. Why not a sexy day during the month when the whole earth is doing sexy things, getting swollen to stand erect like the Legba symbol you find both here and in Africa? Legba is a loa who would appreciate Mardi Gras.

Mardi Gras is the one American art I have witnessed in which the audience doesn't sit intimidated or wait for the critics to tell them what to see. The Mardi Gras audience talks back to the performers instead of sitting there like dummies, and can even participate in the action. Oscar Wilde said, "Why shouldn't the Fourth of July pageant in Atlanta be as fine as the Mardi Gras carnival in New Orleans? Indeed, the pageant is the most perfect school of art for the people." Wilde, an admirer of the Confederacy, said he "engaged in voodoo rites with Negroes."

Just think of what artists could do with Mardi Gras. There could be Romare Bearden floats, and Marisol floats, and Ruth Asawa could do a float for the San Francisco Mardi Gras. I'd like to see a Mardi Gras band performing Donald Byrd's music. Amiri Baraka could design a whole parade.

I'd also like to see Karin Bacon, who staged those multi-media spectaculars during the last golden days of New York, co-ordinate a coast-to-coast Mardi Gras by video hookup.

I for one had been over-floated with this Mardi Gras. I headed away from the Black Indians and took one last photo of an interracial motorcycle gang all leathered up and giving the carnival some existentialist stares. I saw the last Black Indian chief, who was wearing those robes I imagined Quetzalcoatl of African and South American lore would be dressed in.

Sitting next to me on the plane was a brother man, dressed in an outfit and with the features of what could only be described as Barry White Cavalier. He stirred when the stewardess shook him.

"Did you go to Mardi Gras?" I asked.

"Yeah," he said.

"What did you think of it? An obscene Confederate pageant?"

"I don't know nothin about that," he said. "Mardi Gras, to me, is gettin together with your friends and eatin and drinkin."

He dozed off leaving me to watch the Mardi Gras southwest sky, and sipping a burgundy. Robert Tallant wrote in his book *Mardi Gras,* "Mardi Gras is a spirit." HooDoo, too. Watch out Christmas!

# POEMS

## The Feral Pioneers
### FOR DANCER

I rise at 2 A.M. these mornings, to
polish my horns; to see if the killing
has stopped. It is still snowing outside;
it comes down in screaming white
clots.

We sleep on the floor. I popped over
the dog last night & we ate it with
roots & berries.

The night before, lights of a
wounded coyote I found in
the pass.
(The horse froze weeks ago)

Our covered wagons be trapped
in strange caverns of the world.
Our journey, an entry in the thirty-
year old Missourian's 49 Diary.
'All along the desert road from the
very start, even the wayside was strewed
with dead bodies of oxen, mules & horses
& the strench was horrible.'
America, the mirage of a
naked prospector, with sand
in the throat, crawls thru
the stink.
Will never reach the Seven Cities.
Will lie in ruins of
once great steer.

I return to the cabin's
warmest room; Pope Joan is
still asleep. I lie down, my hands
supporting my head.

In the window, an apparition,
Charles Ives:
tears have pressed white hair
to face.

## There's a Whale in My Thigh

There's a whale in my thigh. at
nite he swims the 7 seas. on
cold days i can feel him sleeping.
i went to the dr to see abt myself.
'do you feel this?' the dr asked,
a harpoon in my flesh. i nodded
yes in a clinic room of frozen
poetry.
'then there's no whale in yr thigh.'

there's a whale in my mind. i
feed him arrogant prophets.

## The Wardrobe Master of Paradise

He pins the hems of Angels and
He dresses them to kill
He has no time for fashion

No money's in His till
You wont see Him in Paris
or in a New York store
*He's the wardrobe master*
*of Paradise; He keeps right*
*on His toes*

He works from ancient patterns
He doesn't mind they bore
His models have no measurements
His buyers never roar
He never cares to gossip
He works right on the floor
*He's the wardrobe master*
*of Paradise; He keeps right*
*on His toes*

The evil cities burn to
a crisp, from where His
clients go; their eyes
are blood red carnage, their
purpose never fluffed,
His customers total seven
they have no time to pose

*He's the wardrobe master*
*of Paradise; He keeps right*
*on His toes*

He does not sweat the phony
trends, or fashions dumb
decree; His style is always
chic and in, He never takes
a fee
In Vogue or Glamour or Harper's
Bazaar; He's never written up
*He's the wardrobe master*
*of Paradise; He keeps right*
*on His toes*

The ups and downs of Commerce
His shop will not effect:
the whims of a fickle market
the trifles of jet-sets
The society editor
would rather die than ask Him
for a tip; He sews uninterrupted
He isn't one for quips
His light burns in the pit-black night
I've never seen Him doze
*He's the wardrobe master*
*of Paradise; He keeps right*
*on His toes*

## My Thing Abt Cats

In berkeley whenever
black cats saw dancer &
me they crossed over to
the other side. alan &
carol's cat jumped over
my feet. someone else's
cat pressed its paw against
my leg, in seattle it's
green eyes all the way.
"they cry all the time when
ever you go out, but when
you return they stop," dancer
said of the 3 cats in the back
yard on st mark's place, there
is a woman downstairs who makes
their sounds when she feeds them.
we don't get along.

## Man or Butterfly

it is like lao tse's dream, my
strange affair with cities.
sometimes i can't tell whether
i am a writer writing abt cities
or a city with cities writing
abt me.
a city in peril. everything that
makes me tick is on the bum. all
of my goods and services are wearing
down. nothing resides in me anymore.
i am becoming a ghost town with not
even an occasional riot to perk me
up.

> *they are setting up a*
> *commission to find out what*
> *is wrong with me. i*
> *am the lead off witness*

## *Dualism*

IN RALPH ELLISON'S "INVISIBLE MAN"

I am outside of
history. i wish
i had some peanuts, it
looks hungry there in
its cage

i am inside of
history. its
hungrier than i
thot

## Report of the Reed Commission

I conclude that for
the first time in
history the practical
man is the loon and the
loon the practical man
a man on the radio just
said that air pollution
is caused by jelly fish.

## *This Poetry Anthology I'm Reading*

this poetry anthology
i'm reading reminds me
of washington d.c.
every page some marbled
trash. old adjectives stand
next to flagcovered coffins.
murderers mumbling in
their sleep.

in the rose garden the
madman strolls alone. the
grin on his face just
won't quit

## From the Files of Agent 22

a black banana
can make you high
bad apples can get
you wasted
the wrong kind of
grapes tore up
for days
and a rancid orange
plastered

know your spirits
before entering
strange orchards

## Railroad Bill, A Conjure Man
### A HOODOO SUITE

Railroad Bill, a conjure man
Could change hisself to a tree
He could change hisself to a
Lake, a ram, he could be
What he wanted to be

When a man-hunt came he became
An old slave shouting boss
He went thataway. A toothless
Old slave standing next to a
Hog that laughed as they
Galloped away.
Would laugh as they galloped
Away

Railroad Bill was a conjure man
He could change hisself to a bird
He could change hisself to a brook
A hill he could be what he wanted
To be

One time old Bill changed hisself
To a dog and led a pack on his
Trail. He led the hounds around
And around. And laughed a-wagging
His tail. And laughed
A-wagging his tail

Morris Slater was from Escambia
County, he went to town a-toting
A rifle. When he left that
Day he was bounty.
Morris Slater was Railroad Bill
Morris Slater was Railroad Bill

Railroad Bill was an electrical
Man he could change hisself into
Watts. He could up his voltage
Whenever he pleased
He could, you bet he could
He could, you bet he could

Now look here boy hand over that
Gun, hand over it now not later
I needs my gun said Morn's Slater
The man who was Railroad Bill
I'll shoot you dead you SOB
Let me be whatever I please

The policeman persisted he just
Wouldn't listen and was buried the
Following eve. Was buried the
Following eve. Many dignitaries
Lots of speech-making.

Railroad Bill was a hunting man
Never had no trouble fetching game
He hid in the forest for those
Few years and lived like a natural
King. Whenever old Bill would
Need a new coat he'd sound out his
Friend the Panther. When Bill got
Tired of living off plants the

Farmers would give him some hens.
In swine-killing time the leavings of
Slaughter. They'd give Bill the
Leavings of slaughter. When he
Needed love their fine Corinas
They'd lend old Bill their daughters

Railroad Bill was a conjure man he
Could change hisself to a song. He
Could change hisself to some blues
Some reds he could be what he wanted
To be

E. S. McMillan said he'd get old
Bill or turn in his silver star
Bill told the Sheriff you best
Leave me be said the outlaw from
Tombigbee. Leave me be warned
Bill in 1893

Down in Yellowhammer land
By the humming Chattahoochee
Where the cajun banjo pickers
Strum. In Keego, Volina, and
Astoreth they sing the song of
How come

Bill killed McMillan but wasn't
Willin rather reason than shoot
A villain. Rather reason than
Shoot McMillan

*"Railroad Bill was the worst old coon*
*Killed McMillan by the light of the*
*Moon*
*Was lookinfor Railroad Bill*
*Was lookin for Railroad Bill"*

Railroad Bill was a gris-gris man
He could change hisself to a mask
A Ziba, a Zulu
A Zambia mask. A Zaramo
Doll as well
One with a necklace on it
A Zaramo doll made of wood

I'm bad, I'm bad said Leonard
McGowin. He'll be in hell and dead he
Said in 1896
Shot old Bill at Tidmore's store
This was near Atmore that Bill was
Killed in 1896.
He was buying candy for some children
Procuring sweets for the farmers' kids

Leonard McGowin and R. C. John as
Cowardly as they come. Sneaked up
On Bill while he wasn't lookin.
Ambushed old Railroad Bill
Ambushed the conjure man. Shot him
In the back. Blew his head off.

Well, lawmen came from miles around
All smiles the lawmen came.
They'd finally got rid of
Railroad Bill who could be what
He wanted to be

Wasn't so the old folks claimed
From their shacks in the Wawbeek
Wood. That aint our Bill in that
Old coffin, that aint our man
You killed. Our Bill is in the
Dogwood flower and in the grain
We eat

See that livestock grazing there
That Bull is Railroad Bill
The mean one over there near the
Fence, that one is Railroad Bill

Now Hollywood they's doing old
Bill they hired a teacher from
Yale. To treat and script and
Strip old Bill, this classics
Professor from Yale.
He'll take old Bill the conjure
Man and give him a-na-ly-sis. He'll
Put old Bill on a leather couch
And find out why he did it.
Why he stole the caboose and
Avoided nooses why Bill raised so
Much sand.

He'll say Bill had a complex
He'll say it was all due to Bill's
Mother. He'll be playing the
Dozens on Bill, this
Professor from Yale

They'll make old Bill a neurotic
Case these tycoons of the silver
Screen. They'll take their cue
From the teacher from Yale they
Gave the pile of green
A bicycle-riding dude from Yale
Who set Bill for the screen
Who set Bill for the screen

They'll shoot Bill zoom Bill and
Pan old Bill until he looks plain
Sick. Just like they did old Nat
The fox and tried to do Malik

Just like they did Jack Johnson
Just like they did Jack Johnson

But it wont work what these hacks
Will do, these manicured hacks from
Malibu cause the people will see
That aint our Bill but a haint of
The silver screen. A disembodied
Wish of a Yalie's dream

Our Bill is where the camellia
Grows and by the waterfalls. He's
Sleeping in a hundred trees and in
A hundred skies. That cumulus
That just went by that's Bill's
Old smiling face. He's having a joke
On Hollywood
He's on the varmint's case.

Railroad Bill was a wizard. And
His final trick was tame. Wasn't
Nothing to become some celluloid
And do in all the frames.
And how did he manage technology
And how did Bill get so modern?
He changed hisself to a production
Assistant and went to work with
The scissors.
While nobody looked he scissored
Old Bill he used the scissors.

Railroad Bill was a conjure man
He could change hisself to the end.
He could outwit the chase and throw
Off the scent he didn't care what
They sent. He didn't give a damn what
They sent.

Railroad Bill was a conjure man
Railroad Bill was a star he could change
Hisself to the sun, the moon
Railroad Bill was free
Railroad Bill was free

## The Kardek Method

No son, I dont wanta draw
I hung up my *Petro* in the Spring
    of '68. Had got done with pick
    ing notches; and what with the wing
    ing and all, I ask you, was it
    worth it?
    So uncock your rod friend. Have
a sitdown.
    While I stand back about 15 feet
    think about some positive things. The
    gals at the Road to Ruin Cabaret at the
    end of the trail. The ranch in
    Arizona you have your heart set
on.
    Dont fret the blue rays emanating from
    my fingers. They aint gonna cut you.
    A-ha. just as I thought. Your outside
    aura looks a little grey. Your particles
    cry the dull murmur of dying. I detect
    a little green and red inside your
    protecting sheet. You are here but
    your ghost running cross a desert in a
    greyhound. It bought a ticket to
    No Place In Particular.
    Swoooooooooooooooooooosh!!
Yonder went the Combined Hand Pass
    Feel Better?

## Skirt Dance

i am to my honey what marijuana is
to tijuana. the acapulco gold of her
secret harvest. up her lush coasts i
glide at midnite bringing a full boat.
(that's all the spanish i know.)

## Poison Light
### FOR J. OVERSTREET

Last night
I played Kirk Douglas to
Your Burt Lancaster. Reflecting
20 years of tough guys I
Saw at the Plaza Theatre in
Buffalo, New York. I can
Roll an L like Bogart
You swagger like Wayne

Ours was a bad performance
The audience, our friends
Panned it. The box office
Hocked the producers

We must stop behaving like
The poison light we grew on

Ancient loas are stranded
They want artfare home
Our friends watch us. They
Want to hear what we say

Let's face it
My eye has come a long way
So has your tongue
They belong on a pyramid wall
Not in a slum
("Dead End"; 1937)

## The Katskills Kiss Romance Goodbye

### 1

After twenty years of nods
He enters the new regime
The machine guns have been
Removed from the block
The women don't wear anything
You can see everything

### 2

Hendrick Hudson's Tavern
Has slipped beneath the
Freeway where holiday drivers
Rush as if they've seen the
Hessian Trooper seeking his
Head

### 3

They get their goosebumps at
The drive-in nowadays, where
The Lady in White at Raven
Rock is Bette Davis and
Burton apes Major André
Hanging before the Haunted
Bridge

### 4

A New England historian has
Proof that King George wasn't
So bad.
Gave in to every demand
Donated tea to the American needy
Yankees are just naturally jumpy

### 5

Where once stood madmen
Buttonholing you
Gentlemen think of Martinis
On the train to Mount Vernon

### 6

R.I.P. old Rip
Cuddle up in your Romance
Your dog Wolf is dead
Your crazy galligaskins out
Of style
Your cabbages have been canned
Your firelock isn't registered
Your nagging wife became a
Scientist, you were keeping
Her down

### 7

Go back to the Boarded Up
Alley and catch some more winks
Dreaming is still on the house

## Mystery 1st Lady

franklin pierce's wife never
came downstairs. she never
came upstairs either.

## My Brothers

They come up here
Shit on my floor
Spill my liquor
Talk loud
Giggle about my books
Remove things from their
Natural places

They come up here
And crackle the snot-
Nosed sniggle about
My walk my ways my words
Signify about what is
Dear to me

My brothers
They come up here and
Hint at underhanded things
Look at me as if to
Invite me outside

My brothers
They come up here
And put me on the hot
Seat so I feel I am
Walking the last mile

My wrong, sorry, no
Manners brothers

I will invite them again
I must like it?

You tell me

Contest ends at midnight

## Al Capone in Alaska

or
hoodoo, ecology vs the judeo-
christian tendency to *let em*
have it!

The Eskimo hunts
the whale & each year
the whale flowers for the
Eskimo.
*This must be love baby!*
One receiving with respect
from a Giver who has
plenty.
There is no hatred here.
There is One Big Happy
Family here.

American & Canadian Christians
submachine gun the whales.
They gallantly sail out &
shoot them as if the Pacific
were a Chicago garage on
St. Valentine's day

## Loup Garou Means Change Into

If Loup Garou means change into
When will I banish mine?
I say, if Loup Garou means change
Into when will I shed mine?
This eager Beast inside of me
Seems never satisfied

I was driving on the Nimitz wasn't
Paying it no mind
I was driving on the Nimitz wasn't
Paying it no mind "Mr. 5 by 5"
Before you could say
I was doin 99

my Cherokee is crazy
Can't drink no more than 4
My Cherokee is crazy
Can't stand no more than 4
By the time I had my 15th one
I was whooping across the floor
I was talking whiskey talking
I was whooping across the floor

Well, I whistled at a Gypsy who was reading at my cards
She was looking at my glad hand when something came
Across the yard started wafting across the kitchen
Started drifting in the room, the black went out her
Eyeballs a cat sprung cross her tomb
I couldn't know what happened till I looked behind the door

Where I saw her cold pale husband
WHO's BEEN DEAD SINCE 44

They say if you get your 30
You can get your 35
Folks say if you get to 30
You can make it to 35
The only stipulation is you
Leave your Beast outside

Loup Garou the violent one
When will you lay off me
Loup Garou the Evil one
Release my heart my seed
Your storm has come too many times
And yanked me to your sea

I said please Mr. Loup Garou
When will you drop my goat
I said mercy Mr. Loup Garou
Please give me victory
I put out the beans that evening
Next morning I was free

*.05*

If i had a nickel
For all the women who've
Rejected me in my life
I would be the head of the
World Bank with a flunkie
To hold my derby as i
Prepared to fly chartered
Jet to sign a check
Giving India a new lease
On life

If i had a nickel for
All the women who've loved
Me in my life i would be
The World Bank's assistant
Janitor and wouldn't need
To wear a derby
All i'd think about would
Be going home

# The Author Reflects on His 35th Birthday

35? I have been looking forward
To you for many years now
So much so that
I feel you and I are old
Friends and so on this day, 35
I propose a toast to
Me and You
35? From this day on
I swear before the bountiful
Osiris that
If I ever
If I EVER
Try to bring out the
Best in folks again I
Want somebody to take me
Outside and kick me up and
Down the sidewalk or
Sit me in a corner with a
Funnel on my head

Make me as hard as a rock
35, like the fellow in
The story about the
Big one that got away
Let me laugh my head off
With Moby Dick as we reminisce
About them suckers who went
Down with the *Pequod*

35? I ain't been mean enough
Make me real real mean
Mean as old Marie rolling her eyes
Mean as the town Bessie sings about
"Where all the birds sing bass"

35? Make me Tennessee mean
Cobra mean
Cuckoo mean
Injun mean
Dracula mean
Beethovenian-brows mean

Miles Davis mean
Don't-offer-assistance-when
Quicksand-is-tugging-some-poor
Dope-under-mean
Pawnbroker mean
Pharaoh mean
That's it, 35
Make me Pharaoh mean
Mean as can be
Mean as the dickens
Meaner than mean

When I walk down the street
I want them to whisper
There goes Mr. Mean
"He's double mean
He even turned the skeletons
In his closet out into
The cold"

And 35?
Don't let me trust anybody
Over Reed but
Just in case
Put a tail on that
Negro too
*February 22, 1973*

## *Jacket Notes*

Being a colored poet
Is like going over
Niagara Falls in a
Barrel

An 8 year old can do what
You do unaided

The barrel maker doesn't
Think you can cut it

The gawkers on the bridge
Hope you fall on your
Face

The tourist bus full of
Paying customers broke-down
Just out of Buffalo

Some would rather dig
The postcards than
Catch your act

A mile from the brink
It begins to storm

But what really hurts is
You're bigger than the
Barrel

## Sather Tower Mystery

Seems there was this Professor
a member of what should be called
The Good German Department

Must have signed his name to
5,000 petitions in front of
the Co-Op on Cedar
and bought two tons of benefit
cookies
Blames Texas for the sorry
state of the oceans
Rode a Greyhound bus "Civil
Rights," Alabama, 1960
Found the long yellow war
"deplorable"
Believes John "Duke" Wayne's
values to be inferior to his

He said, "Ishmael, I'd
love to do the right thing
for as you know I'm all for
the right thing and against
the wrong thing, but
these plaster of paris busts
of deceased Europeans
Our secret ways
Our sacred fears

"These books, leather-bound
'copyright 1789'

All of these things, precious
to me, gleaming like the
stainless steel coffee urn in
the faculty club, an original
Maybeck, 1902

"I'd stand up for Camelot
by golly, even if it meant
shooting all the infidels in
the world," he said
reaching into his desk drawer

"Why, I might even have to
shoot you, Ishmael"

Staring down the cold
tunnel of a hard .38
I thought

*Most people are to the right*
*when it comes to where they must*
*eat and lay their heads!*

## Foolology

Shaken by his bad press, the wolf
presses north, leaving caribou to
the fox,
Raven, the snow player gets his
before buzzards with bright red
collars move in to dine near the
bottom of a long scavenger line

This poem is about a skunk, no
rather about a man, who though
not of the skunk family uses
his round-eye the way skunks do

After he eats, his friends eat
He is a fool and his friends are
fools but sometimes it's hard to
tell who is the biggest fool this
fool or his fool friends

By the time they catch us
we're not there
We crows
Nobody's ever seen a dead crow
on the highway

First moral: Don't do business
with people for whom April first
is an important date
they will use your bank balance to

buy eight thousand pies, tunics,
ballet slippers with bells and
a mail order lake in the middle of
a desert for splash parties

Second moral: Before you can spot the
fools in others you must rid yourself
of the fool in you
You can tell a fool by his big mouth

## *Sputin*

Like Venus
My spin is retrograde
A rebel in more ways than one

I click my heels
In seedy taverns
& pinch the barmaids
On the cheeks

Madeira drips from
My devilish beard
My eyes sparkle dart
Flicker & sear
Man, do I love to dance

Something tells me the
Tzar will summon me to
Save his imperial hide

I peeped his messenger
Speeding through the gates of
The Winter Palace

He's heading this way

Soon, my fellow peasants will
See me in the Gazette
Taking tea with the royal family

They'll say
That crazy bum?

## Sky Diving

"It's a good way to live and
A good way to die"
From a Frankenheimer video about
Sky diving
The hero telling why he liked to

    The following noon he leaped
    But his parachute wasn't with him
    He spread out on the field like
    Scrambled eggs

Life is not always
Hi-lifing inside
Archibald Motley's
"Chicken Shack"
You in your derby
Your honey in her beret
Styling before a small vintage
Car

Like too many of us
I am a man who never had much
Use for a real father
And so when I'm heading
For a crash
No one will catch me but
Me

The year is only five days old
Already a comet has glittered out
Its glow sandbagged by

The jealous sun
Happens to the best of us
Our brilliance falling off
Like hair from Berkeley's roving
Dogs

Even on Rose Bowl day
An otherwise joyous occasion
A float veered into the crowd
Somebody got bruised over the incident
Like a love affair on second ave.

It's a good lesson to us all
In these downhill days of a
Hard-hearted decade
Jetting through the world
Our tails on fire

You can't always count
On things opening up for you
Know when to let go
Learn how to fall

## Sixth Street Corporate War

Not all rats live in sewers
Some of them dwell in 100,000 dollar
rat's nests on the Alameda
and drive to work in a Mercedes
laboratory rat white
You wouldn't even know they were
rats
on the mailbox it says Mr. Rodent

As big as a coffee table book
(The only book in the house)
he spends his time nibbling ratboy
in a rathouse with its
cheesy rat kitchen or scampering
on a rat sofa or in a bed of
rats

Or you might find him at the Ratskeller
wetting his rat whiskers on
rat soup
"my favorite drink" said
This shareholder rat there he
go old bureaucratic rat investor
in rattraps where people live
like rats
As years went by he gained more
status until he became the esteemed
Doctor Rattus
Crashed a tomcat convention and

demanded to be put on the
banquet
This even woke up Scrounger
or Mr. All Claws,
the toastmaster tomcat
catnapping on the dais
after a night of pre-
convention howling
"whaddya say, boys"
said the thrice decorated
rat scrapper
"rat cocktail
rat of the day
rat a la carte
or rat mousse?"

The other cats being
democrats cast their
votes by secret ballot
gulp!

## The Reactionary Poet

If you are a revolutionary
Then I must be a reactionary
For if you stand for the future
I have no choice but to
Be with the past

Bring back suspenders!
Bring back Mom!
Homemade ice cream
Picnics in the park
Flagpole sitting
Straw hats
Rent parties
Corn liquor
The banjo
Georgia quilts
Krazy Kat
Restock

The syncopation of
Fletcher Henderson
The Kiplingesque lines
of James Weldon Johnson
Black Eagle
Mickey Mouse
The Bach Family
Sunday School
Even Mayor La Guardia
Who read the comics

Is more appealing than
Your version of
What Lies Ahead

In your world of
Tomorrow Humor
Will be locked up and
The key thrown away
The public address system
Will pound out headaches
All day
Everybody will wear the same
Funny caps
And the same funny jackets
Enchantment will be found
Expendable, charm, a
Luxury
Love and kisses
A crime against the state
Duke Ellington will be
Ordered to write more marches
"For the people," naturally

If you are what's coming
I must be what's going

Make it by steamboat
I likes to take it real slow

## Rough Trade Slumlord Totem

Here's how you put your enemy
atop a totem where the scavengers
get at him

This is for you, dummy
who hoarded our writings
in your basement, four solid months
like your brother landlord of
Sitka, Alaska, who chopped-up
the Tlingit totems for bar-b-cue chairs

The Raven will get you sucker
The Raven will hunt you down
Gaaaaaa! Gaaaaaaa! sucker

The thunder will empty its
bladder on your face you
seal-cow man who wobbles on
his belly with common
law fish in his mouth
May seagulls litter your
Punch-and-Judy corked eyes

May the eagle mistake your snout
for a mouse and sink
its claws into it
May the paint used on your
head be slum lord paint bound
to peel in a short time
And when you crash I hope

your landing place be
a maggot's hunting party

And while the rest of the
totem journey's into mother
soil
your segment remains
your sideshow providing
Laughing Forest
with a belly full

## Earthquake Blues

Well the cat started actin funny
and the dog howled all night long
I say the cat started actin very frightful
and the birds chirped all night long
The ground began to rumble
As the panic hit the town.

Mr. Earthquake Mr. Earthquake
you don't know good from bad
Mr. Earthquake Mr. Earthquake
you don't know good from bad
You kill the little child in its nursery
You burn up the widow's pad

The buildings started swaying
like a drunk man walking home
The buildings started swaying
like a drunk man walking home
The people they were running
and the hurt folks began to moan

Mr. Earthquake Mr. Earthquake
you don't know good from bad
Mr. Earthquake Mr. Earthquake
you don't know good from bad
You kill the little child in its nursery
You burn up the widow's pad

I got underneath my table
Had my head between my knees
I got underneath the table
Had my head between my knees
The dishes they were rattlin
and the house was rockin me

Mr. Earthquake Mr. Earthquake
you don't know good from bad
Mr. Earthquake Mr. Earthquake
you don't know good from bad
You kill the little child in its nursery
You burn up the widow's pad

I was worried about my baby
Was she safe or was she dead
I was worried about my baby
Was she safe or was she dead
When she phoned and said I'm
ok, Daddy. Then I went on back
to bed.

Mr. Earthquake Mr. Earthquake
you don't know good from bad
Mr. Earthquake Mr. Earthquake
you don't know good from bad
You kill the little child in its nursery
You burn up the widow's pad

## Points of View

### I

The pioneer stands in front of the
Old pioneer's home with his back-pack
walking stick and rifle
Wasn't me that Kisadi Frog-Klan
Indian was talking about when he
mentioned the horrors of Alaska
What horrors of Alaska?
Why Baranof was a swell fellow
Generous to the Indians, he was
known as far south as California
for his good deeds
Before we came the Indians were
making love to their children and
sacrificing their slaves, because
the Raven told them so, according
to them
"They couldn't even speak good
English and called the streams and
the mountains funny names
They were giving each other refrigerators
the potlatches had become so bad

We made them stop
They'd build a canoe abandon
it, then build another
We made them stop that, too
Now they have lawyers

They can have anything they want
If they want to go whaling

when we know they don't need to
go whaling
The lawyers see to it that they
go whaling
They're just like us
They buy frozen snow peas
just like we do
They're crazy about motorcycles
just like we are

We brought them civilization
We brought them penicillin
We brought them Johnny Carson
Softball we brought them trailer camps
They'd get married at fourteen
and die at 24
We brought them longevity

II

They brought us carbon dioxide
They brought us contractors
We told them not to dig there
They were clawed by two eagles
While uncovering the graves
of two medicine men

The white man has the mind of a
walrus's malignant left ball
We don't think the way they do
They arrive at the rate of one
thousand per month in cars
whose license plates read
texas oklahoma and mississippi
They built the Sheffield Hotel on
a herring bed
Everywhere are their dogs
Everywhere are their guns
Everywhere are their salmon-faced

women who get knocked up a lot
and sometimes enter the Chanel
restaurant wearing mysterious black
eyes, socked into their Viking-eyes
by men whose hair is plastered with
seal dung
It all began when
Chief Kowee of the Raven Klan showed
Joe Juneau the location of the gold
Now Mount Juneau is as empty as
a box of popcorn on the floor of
a picture show
When our people saw the first
Russian ship, we thought it was
the White Raven's return
Instead it was the Czarina's pirate
Dressed in Russian merchant's clothes
and a peacock's hat.
He shot Katlian in the back

## The Ballad of Charlie James

### I

Hunter's Point: Night
Papa Charlie James awakes
to see the 'Frisco police
at the foot of his bed
"Bring them hands from
underneath them sheets so's
we can see them. Let us see
what you got beneath those
sheets," they said, shooting
seventeen rounds of ammunition
into Charlie's bed

### II

He survived the crazy rhythms
in his chest
his lungs whistling like
ghost winds, but he couldn't
survive the police
Hazardous to your health
if you are poor, Indian, or
Chicano, or if you're a sixty
year old black man asleep in
bed "Bring them hands from
underneath those sheets so's we can
see them, let us see what you got
beneath those sheets"

Like in Count Albuquerque's
town, where underneath the freeway
a lone woman wears "I Want Your Body"

on her t-shirt, a black man can get
shot for just horsing around
They use the redman for target
practice, they hang the Mexican
in jail.
O ain't it a shame what they did
to poor Charlie James. Have mercy
and ain't it a shame
"He just played dominoes
drank soda water, and looked
out the window" his neighbors said
Thinking of his poor wife in a
Georgia loony bin
she saw her children die
one by one
Thinking of his mother out
there in the backwater cemetery
her shroud faded
her eye sockets, windows for
spiders, "Bring them hands
from underneath those sheets so's
we can see them. Let us see what you
have beneath those sheets"
The sign on Charlie's door
"Making Love Is Good For You"
shot full of bulletholes

His brains liver and kidneys
gone up in smoke
"Making Love Is Good For You"
His stomach will hold no more
beans
no more bad coffee
his lips have seen their last
cigarette
O ain't it a shame what they did
To Charlie James. Have mercy ain't
it a shame.

They said his homicide was justified
the parrot D.A. "concurred"
The police were just doing their
duty, they said, and the
parrot D.A." concurred, concurred"
O the parrot D.A." concurred"
O ain't it a shame what they did
to poor Charlie James
"Making Love Is Good For You"
"Bring them hands from underneath
those sheets so's we can see them.
Let's see what you have beneath those
sheets."

## Points of View

The pioneers and the indians
disagree about a lot of things
for example, the pioneer says that
when you meet a bear in the woods
you should yell at him and if that
doesn't work, you should fell him
The indians say that you should
whisper to him softly and call him by
loving nicknames
No one's bothered to ask the bear
what he thinks

## Datsun's Death

"Down in Puerto Rico, when
we didn't have no kerosene
we used the stuff to read by"
the stuff
he took his first drink
at twenty, and by the age of
40 had sauced up enough to fill
all the billboard bottles from
Lafitte's Galveston to Houston's
Texas
There's enough light in his belly
to fire all the gas lamps in
Cincinnati
He remembers getting burned in Cincinnati
his radiator was hot
his temperature was rising
like the white 68 Dodge grumbling
up Moeser Lane, as ferocious as a
pit-bull
The accident cop would later
say
It must have been built like a
tank
rammed into my piece of tail
a hit and run, you've been there
haven't you partner
haven't you?

It was A.T. and T. which reminded us
that the heaviest traffic occurs at
4:30 A.M.

All the phone circuits are busy
*I loves you baby*
*You know i loves you baby!*
Do you loves me baby?
I don't care what you women
say
Prometheus was a man
the X rays just came back
his liver looks terrible

For the ground crew
at the Kirksville
airport a sweetheart
is the otter jetstream
of Illinois Airlines
while the two-toned
Monte Carlo parked next
to the Robin breasted
cornfield is baby

For me heaven was
tooling around in the
driver's seat of my
280ZX
my honey of the midnight blue
my import car of the year
mutilated by the brazen chrome
of a snorting bull-car
hot and swerving under
the El Cerrito moon

Plymouth, Cadillac, Mercury
Montego, the automobile gods
rattled in their Richmond junkyards
Chrysler and Ford sales went down
30% the next day

And the shining new sacrifices on display
at banner-waving San Bruno
parking lots,
Wept from their windshields
Some used-up like my Datsun
Head mashed against the rhododendrons

## On the Fourth of July in Sitka, 1982

On the fourth of July in Sitka
Filipinos sold shish-ka-bob from their
booths in the park
On the fourth of July in Sitka, the children
dressed in deerskin jackets
and coonskin caps
On the fourth of July in Sitka, you
could buy fishpie in the basement of St. Michael's
Church, where the vodka-drunken Russians used to
pray
But the red white and blue cake was not for sale

On the fourth of July in Sitka the people
kicked off shoes and ran through the
streets, pushing beds
On the fourth of July in Sitka, tour buses
with yellow snouts and square heads
delivered tourists to the Shee Atika lodge
where they stared at floats designed by
Sheldon Jackson College and
the Alaska Women in Timber
On the fourth of July in Sitka the
Gajaa Heen dancers performed, wearing their
Klan emblems of Beaver Wolf Killer Whale
Porpoise, and Dog Salmon

On the fourth of July in Sitka the Libertarian
Party announced the winners of its five dollar raffle
1st Prize, a Winchester .300 Magnum
2nd Prize, an Ithaca 12 gauge shotgun
3rd Prize, a Sportsman III knife

On the fourth of July in Sitka the
softball teams were honored at the American
Legion Club and the players drank champagne till dawn
On the fourth of July in Sitka, the night was
speckled with Japanese fireworks
sponsored by Alaska Lumber and Pulp

On the fifth of July in Sitka
a Canadian destroyer brought to Sitka
for the fourth of July in Sitka sailed
through Sitka Sound and out into the
Northern Pacific
All of the men on board stood at
attention, saluting their audience
three bald eagles, two ravens, and me
watching the whole show from Davidoff Hill
the fifth of July in Sitka

## Petite Kid Everett

The bantamweight King of
Newark
He couldn't box
He couldn't dance
He just kept coming at
you, glass chin first
Taking five punches for
every one he connected with
you

Petite Kid Everett
He missed a lot
Slipped a lot and
By mid-life he'd
developed one heck
of a sorehead
Took to fighting in
the alley
Gave up wearing a mouthpiece
Beat up his trainers
Beat up the referee
Beat up his fans
Beat up everybody who was
in his corner
Even jumped on Houston Jr.
the lame pail boy
Who didn't have good sense

Petite Kid Everett
There's talk of a comeback

He's got new backers
He stands on one of the four
corners, near the Prudential Life
Building
Trading blows with ghosts
Don't it make you wanna cry?

## Turning Pro

There are just so many years
you can play amateur baseball
without turning pro
All of a sudden you realize
you're ten years older than
everybody in the dugout
and that the shortstop could
be your son

The front office complains
about your slowness in making
the line-up
They send down memos about
your faulty bunts and point out
how the runners are always faking
you out
"His ability to steal bases
has faded" they say
They say they can't convince
the accountant that there's such
a thing as "Old Time's Sake"
But just as the scribes were
beginning to write you
off
as a has-been on his last leg
You pulled out that fateful
shut-out
and the whistles went off

and the fireworks scorched a
747
And your name lit up the scoreboard
and the fans carried you on their
shoulders right out of the stadium
and into the majors

## Epistolary Monologue

My favorite lady-in-waiting is so loyal. She certainly can keep a secret. Every day at teatime she sneaks me three bottles of Beefeater. She knows that I can't stand tea. Today she brought me your note. This morning, she had to bring me two tablets of Myaatal. I still haven't recovered from my trip to America. Must have been the tacos and beans we ate at the Reagan's Ranch. That woman is so rude. You remember how she tried to upstage me during her trip to London? wailing about town with her motorcycle escorts. Got up in that tacky red dress and those wide-brimmed hats that make her resemble a witch. I was speaking to her husband, and the poor man fell asleep. Still telling the same jokes.

But back to your note, my sweet. Michael, I was so touched, but how would it look if another scandal happened to the Windsors? They still haven't gotten over Uncle Edward. If I ran away with you, the public would take away our allowances and evict us from Buckingham Palace. How would we survive? On hotdogs and beans. Our only experience is shaking hands and smiling. And there doesn't seem to be an awful demand for people who know how to walk in processions.

Somebody has to keep a level head. Andrew carrying on with that tart. Diana locked up in her room starving herself, all because she found out Charles's secret. The secret we've kept from the public all these years. Her look-alike is threatening to reveal the whole sordid business if she doesn't receive more money. And Princess Anne. Granted that she is my daughter, but sometimes I think that she's so ugly she should be arrested for public ugliness. The poor young man she's living with is always talking about leaving her. He says that he has to put a bag over her head in order to get a good night's sleep. So please understand, my darling. I do love you. Queens have feelings too, but if I married you, a poor laborer, who would feed my horses and my dogs?

Well, it's 2:00 a.m. here in the Palace. As the Americans say, "I'm in my gin." I just turned off all of the lights. Everyone here is so wasteful. Philip and my bodyguards are in the next room watching videocassettes of "Dynasty." O, I wish I could be like that Krystle. Always taking chances, going where her heart leads. But I've grown accustomed to my duty, my position, and the grand tradition of which I am a symbol.

And so, don't be cross with me when my lady-in-waiting delivers this note to you. Goodbye, my darling. And please forgive me for having you arrested. But when we were lying in bed that morning, and you complained about what you would and wouldn't do, I had to put you in your place. Though we were lovers, I was still your sovereign, which meant that my wish was your command.

Love,
Lilibet

## The Pope Replies to the Ayatollah Khomeini

My Dear Khomeini:

I read your fourteen thousand dollar
ad asking me why the Vatican waited
all of these years to send an envoy
to complain about conditions in Iran
You're right, we should have sent one
when the Shah was in power, look,
I'm in total agreement with you
Khomeini, that Christ, had he lived in
Iran under the Shah, would have led the
biggest damned revolt you ever saw

Believe me, Khomeini, I knew about
the Shah's decadence, his extravagance
his misdeeds, and how he lolled about
in luxury with Iran's loot
I knew about the trail of jewels which
led to his Dad's capture
but a fella has to eat and so when
David Rockefeller asked me to do something
how could I refuse?

You can afford to be holier than thou
What is it, 30 dollars per barrel these days?
You must be bathing in oil
While each day I suffer a new indignity

You know that rock record they made me
do? It's 300 on the Charts which is about
as low as you can get.

And I guess you read where I
had to call in all those Cardinals and
for the first time reveal the Vatican
budget?
I had to just about get down on my hands
and knees to get them to co-sign for a
loan
The Vatican jet has a mechanical problem
and the Rolls-Royce needs a new engine
The staff hasn't been paid in months
and the power company is threatening to
turn off the candles
To add to that, the building inspector
has listed us as having 30,000 code
violations
I'm telling you, Khomeini, that
so many people are leaving the church
I have this nightmare where I
wake up one day in Los Angeles and
I'm the only one left

Pretty soon we'll be one of those
cults you read about in the *San
Francisco Chronicle*
And so, Khomeini, I promise
you that when we pay off the
deficit, I won't send an envoy
I'll come visit you myself

I'd like to discuss this plan
that Patriarch Dimitrios, of
the Greek Orthodox Church, and I
just came up with

You know, we haven't spoken to
those fellows in 900 years but
when you are 20 million dollars
in the red
You'll talk to anybody

## Grizzly

He always prided himself on
never being caught with his paws down
The flying grizzly left his bear
tracks at fifty thousand feet
his life, a daily peach blossom
He always managed to find some
hot honey to dip into
He was smiling all the time
Licking his lips, till Mrs.
Grizzly discovered him in the
bush with some outside trim of
a wonderful red cabbage and Mrs.
Grizzly grounded her
Teddy Bear
the rough rider under her fur coat
she was not taken in by his sweet
word-bees
Last trip back to the cave
he felt like he'd entered customs
after a return from an enemy city
What are these claw marks doing on your back?
Are those huckleberry stains on the front
of your pants?
Why do you have that fishy smell?
The divorce left him belly-up
He's somewhere right now
dressed in white and black
checkered pants
being led at the neck by a rope

While he bangs on a dirty
bass drum
a little monkey toots a whistle
and little dogs taunt him
and little children tug at
his ears

## Judas

Funny about best friends
huh, Lord
Always up in your face
laughing and talking
leading the praise after
your miracles
That Judas, you had great
hopes for him
Good background
Good-looking, even in a
corduroy suit, made in
Poland, and thirty dollar
shoes
It was his quiet appeal that
kept the group in wine money

As soon as you turned your
back, he took your business
to the Goyim
Told them you going around
telling everybody you the
son-of-god
See how careful you have to
be about whom you go bar-
hopping with, Jesus
Now you're drowsy, Jesus

They've pricked you full of
Thorazine
They've given you electro-
convulsive therapy

You don't know where you
are
You have sores where the
straight-jacket doesn't fit
You're wringing wet from
where you've been sweatin
all night
You squirm on filthy straw

But stick it out, Jesus
where you're going
the drums don't stop
They serve Napa Valley
champagne at every meal
Everybody smokes big cigars
Sweet Angel hair be tingling
your back while you invent
proverbs in a hot tub

Where Judas is going
the people don't know how
to fix ribs
the biscuits taste like
baking soda
The wine is sweet and sticky
Flowers can't grow on this
landscape of jinxed hearts
the Field of Blood
to this day it's called
the Field of Blood

## Dialog Outside the Lakeside Grocery

The grocery had provided him with
boxes of rotten lettuce
He was loading them onto a
yellow pick-up truck
He was a frail white man and
wore a plaid woolen shirt and
frayed dungarees
I was sitting in a gray chevrolet
rent-a-dent
"I have eight adult geese and
twenty-six ducks," he said
and i said
"I'll bet you have a big management
problem," and he said
"They're no trouble at all. My
wife raised two of them in the house.
When she goes near their pen
the geese waddle towards her
and nibble the lettuce out of her
hand"
"I'd never think of killing them"
he said
"They keep me out of the bars"

## *Poem for Two Daughters*

Everybody wants to know
Where's your oldest daughter
Her first sentence was
phenomenon
Sixteen years later she
stands before you, drawing
on a cigarette
She says she's found you
out
She has exactly eighty dollars
to her name
she thinks she grown
She says she wants her emancipation
You tell her to spell it
She calls you a nerd, a dork
and other words you hear on the
3:15 Arlington #7 Bus
The Yo-Yo special

We used to chide the sightseeing
middle aged in those days when
we stood on our heads outside the Dom
Now, we are the ones sitting on the
greyline
We cannot figure out what it is
we are staring at

Our stomachs hurt
We gaze from houses with unobstructed views of the Bay

thirty years ago we couldn't come
up here
Nowadays the neighbors bring pies
Our daughters are either standing up
for the first time or flying

The youngest one puts everything
into her mouth, pencils, your hair
graham crackers, the cat, the car keys
even the Sesame Street book covered
with blue-fuzzed creatures with
purple noses and egg-shaped eyes
She trounces the trampoline in
the kindergym but's too plump for
the Olympics
Her first sentence was: "I see"

The oldest one, as fast as
Clifford Brown on Cherokee
Of another system, impatient
with your inability to cope with
the basic concepts of her world
grinds you up with her mind
Intellectually shoves you about
like you the
wildest Turkey in the state of
Georgia, guiding the hunters to
your roost
You have to fall back on
"It's so because I say it's so"

The differences between the three
would be revealed if someone were to
ask each what they would do if
the world was offered to them on
a silver platter

The youngest one would say
I'd eat it
or at least jump up and down
on it a few times
The oldest one would strut up and down
in front of the world, scolding the world
about its ancient corruption
She'd fast
By the time the question reached
you
the world would have run out of
bones

## The Middle Class Blues

MONOLOGUE

*I can't believe it's 1994. Back in 84 it meant something, but nowadays being middle class and a nickel won't buy you a cup of coffee. During the rest of the 80s the frig was still full and you could always mambo in Guadalajara during the discount off seasons. But by the beginning of the 90s, the only difference between us and the poor was that everything they owned was on their backs while everything we owned was being lent to us by the banks. The banks were on our backs. I was over my head in billy dues. Me and the Mrs. argued so about money that one day she just upped and left. And these were supposed to be our golden years. Some golden years. I can't seem to save over a couple of hundred dollars and I'm spending a third more than I'm making. It's only a matter of time before I have to visit one of those bankruptcy consultants. Talking about the new poor. Never thought it would happen to me. What happened to the old poor? I dunno. They were kicked out of the bus stations, the parks and the welfare hotels a long time ago. Some say they went South. Others say that the society people had them shipped to Central America because down there they know how to handle the poor. Wherever they are, they must have been desperate. They left behind their blues. I'm lucky I guess. I can still afford a martini.*

I

I got the middle class blues
I play by middle class rules
O, this middle class life
Is a life full of strife
The bourgeois state can be
A sweet and sour pill
When the first rolls around
You gotta deal with the bills

So hey, Mr. Bartender,
Bring me a dry vermouth and gin
Fix me a black olive and a big martini
Before I hit the wind

II

I constantly get headaches
And my back is often sore
Being the first one on the freeway
Is becoming such a chore
At work they got a robot
That soon will have my job
I'm too old to start all over
Too old to learn to rob

So hey, Mr. Bartender
Bring me a dry vermouth and gin
Fix me a black olive and a big martini
Before I hit the wind

III

The roof is always leaking
The plumbing needs some screws
Everybody on the block, it seems
Knows how to bar-b-cue
My next door neighbors are ticked at me
My lawn is turning brown
There's always something that must be fixed
Everytime you turn around

Hey, hey, Mr. Bartender
Bring me a dry vermouth and gin
Fix me a black olive and a big martini
Before I hit the wind

IV

My son is getting married
To a woman older than me

He just turned twenty the other
week
She's going on sixty-three
My daughter's on narcotics
Her eyes are always red
The car wouldn't start this morning
And I toss and turn in bed

So hey, Mr. Bartender
Bring me a dry vermouth and gin
Fix me a black olive and a big martini
Before I hit the wind

V

The communists say I'm an ingrate
The capitalists took my house
The old people say I neglect them
The young call me a louse
The tax man sent me a letter
He's coming here tonight
Sometimes it gets so heavy
At home, I'm never right

So hey, Mr. Bartender
Bring me a dry vermouth and gin
Fix me a black olive and a big martini
Before I hit the wind

VI

The Doctor says it's no good
To have this stress and mess
The ulcers that will get you
A classy middle class nest
A cat that won't eat store food
Must have its abalone
And don't forget the deadline
To pay the alimony

So hey, Mr. Bartender
Bring me a dry vermouth and gin
Fix me a black olive and a big martini
Before I hit the wind

### VII

Well, I'm tired of paying the dentist
And going under the knife
And doing all the things you do
To stay the bourgeois life
The rich they live in heaven
The poor they live in hell
And I live somewhere in between
A sign outside says for sale

So hey, Mr. Bartender
Bring me a dry vermouth and gin
Fix me a black olive and a big martini
Let me go on get this wind

## St. Louis Woman

He loves to see that orbed heat collapse behind the white Jefferson arc
as the downtown St. Louis sun temples burst

Orange as the inside of a Balaban's lobster they cater in the room
of Renoirish Third Reich Speer-room nude portraits where Wash. U.
grad student waiters resemble the t.v. crew filming a restaurant scene
in "As the World Turns." On a stool outside a black man in little boy's
cap and white butcher's coat attracts customers with the gleaming
stars of his gold teeth. For four days a storebought apricotheaded St.
Louis woman in poor white powder and tobacco-road mascaraed eye-
lashes told the other waitresses in the Forest Park Hotel to quit
putting cream and sugar in his coffee because "He looks spoiled. Big
and spoiled."

Daughters of Davy Crockett and Dan Boone with high-Cherokee
cheekbones, St. Louis women call closeted plantations with
monopoly-board street names, "home" behind fake second empire
gates which are locked at night to keep out the townies, Riding bicycles, their eyes buried in the streets, the only blacks wear supermarket
names on their t-shirts

They stand on the street's dividing line selling rush hour copies of
the St. Louis Post Dispatch like the apple-capped Irish lads in a book
about the life and times of Jacob Reiss

They are the last people in the nation who take out their billfolds
to show you their relatives and their girlfriends' and boyfriends' relatives and that time they went to Atlantic City

St. Louis is surrounded by ninety municipalities. Only a Filipino
with a Harvard M.A. in business can untangle the town, Emile said.
Emile said that St. Louis women are dumb blondes who stand you up.
Equal rights to them means the right to tantalize but not to put out,
Emile said.

"Are you Bruce Lee?" they asked Emile when he landed in Harlem.

Feeling tomorrow and twenty-two, a St. Louis woman told him she could run a whole radio station. She knew where you could fetch a Gucci raincoat for one hundred dollars. In her poetry she is "a black rose." He told her that if her skin really needed a flower why not an African violet to go with her yellow eyes. He told her that her eyes were all the evidence we needed to prove that ancient Asiatics reached Madagascar. He told her that a black rose was common and that she was anything but common and that she was as rare as a white tiger rarely seen in the jungles of India or rare as the image of a white owl carrying off a white ermine in the Bird Book we saw in the museum off Big Bend where we learned that the first words said on the telephone constituted a cry for help.

In the Steinberg auditorium he asked the Dalai Lama's stand in why there were black gods with nigger minstrel white lips and great Nigerian mound noses in Nepalese paintings dated 3,000 B.C.

Before rushing to the next question he said they represented Time. He told the "black rose" that she was as rare as Time hung on a monastery wall, while outside buddhists blow conch horns and chant like a chorus of frogs.

St. Louis women are rabbit-furred hookers who hustle to star wars in the steeple chase room of the chase park hotel where Gorgeous George dressed in sequined Evel Knievel jumpsuit discos to Elvis Presley and the hogged-necked bouncers in blazers threaten to break your arm. There are portraits in that room of horses, skins shining like chestnuts, life-sized statues of jockeys in polka-dotted blouses. The lamps are shaped like racing horns.

St. Louis women write body poetry, play the harp for the symphony and take up archery.

St. Louis women wash cook and clean for St. Louis women who write body poetry, play the harp for the symphony, and take up archery.

A St. Louis woman is the automatic writing hand for a spirit named Ida Mae of the red dress cult who rises from the Mississippi each night to check out the saloons before last call.

She rises from the big river G. Redmond calls Black River, Mike Castro's River Styx, and every body knows about Muddy Waters; St. Louis women are daughters of Episcopalian ministers who couldn't sit still for Grant Wood

Sternly scarfed they stare straight ahead inside Doberman
Pinscher station wagons. Their husbands work for McDonnell
Douglas, Ralston-Purina, and Anheuser-Busch.

(They still talk about how old man Busch was so rich that when
his son killed a man it was the trial judge who served time)

The great grandfather of a St. Louis woman appears in the 100
years of lynching horror book because he owned 300 acres and white
men wanted those acres

The grandmother of a St. Louis woman told her that no man can
say "I Love You" like a black man. "Velvet be dripping from his lips," a
unique experience like the one recounted by a man in the bar of the
St. Louis airport about the time when Nanette Fabray came into the
audience and sat on his lap, New Year's Eve, The Mark Hopkins
Hotel, San Francisco

On Sunday he stuffed the frig with dungeness crabs

You can find the quilts of St. Louis women patched with real chip-
munks and birds in the Jefferson museum next to the Lindbergh collection "Nothing like flying across the Atlantic in a one-seater" he
said, "When she rocks, you rock, when you thrust so does she, and
when she dives it's as if your soul bought the circus and you owned
all the ferris wheels, *The Spirit of St. Louis!*"

A black man wrote a song about a St. Louis woman that go Hello
Central, give me five o'nine, hello central give me five o' nine, the St.
Louis woman said she liked my line about a man entering a woman's
love pond, she thought i said love mine.

Like a Mississippi school boy loves his mint and rye i love to see
that evening sun go down when the St. Louis women come calling
around

Many St. Louis women are from Kansas City.

> The year was 1914
> W. C. Handy wrote a ragtime march with a blues
> tango introduction (The Tango, derived from
> the African Tangenda, was once banned all the
> way down to the Argentinian South Pole)
> but there was something missing.
> "What this music needs is a Vamp," the trombonist
> said, and that's how "St. Louis Woman" came into
> being

The big publishers wouldn't chance her.
They were only interested in Whiteman's blues
and so, at the age of 40, W. C. Handy went to
bat for his Vamp, publishing 10,000
copies of "St. Louis Blues" at his own expense
Handy flew up the Fatty Grimes diamond
from Memphis and presented it to her
(Hippolite's "Mystical Marriage")
He chauffeured her across the nation in
a whale-length white cadillac like the
one i once saw Bob Hope get out of
He introduced her to a Carnegie Hall
sell-out audience which she delighted
with her shanty-town ways
Sometimes she was as icy as the Portage glacier
in Portage, Alaska,
at other times she was tropical as the
Miami airport at 5:30 when the Santeria
jets sweep in

Resting under that mellow creole
river in a silver satin slip
the color of an enshrined coronet
mooning on the silky meat of a giant
clam
guarded by chocolate dandies
Irises on their creamy waistcoats
and a Tennessee billygoat covered with
cowrie shells
St. Louis Woman

## Bitter Chocolate

### I

Only the red-skins know what
I know, and they ain't talkin
So I keep good friends with
turkey whiskey
Or try to do some walkin
Don't want no lovin
Ain't anxious to play
And you want to know how
I got that way
Bitter Chocolate
Bitter Chocolate
Blood like ice water
Kisses taste like snuff
Why are all of my women
so jive and full of stuff

They call me a runaway father
But they won't give me no job
They say I'm a thief
when I'm the one gettin
robbed
Most of me was missing when
They brought me back from
Nam
My mama and my sister
cried for me
But my government didn't give
a damn

Bitter Chocolate
Bitter Chocolate
Sullied and sullen black
man

## II
When they come to lynch somebody
Always breaking down my door
When they lay somebody off
I'm the first one off the floor
Bitter Chocolate
Bitter Chocolate
Veins full of brine
Skin sweatin turpentine
Cold and unfriendly
Got ways like a lizard

## III
Well, it's winter in Chicago on
a February day
O'Hare airport is empty and
I call you on the line
It's 9:00 a.m. where you are
and the phone rings seven times
Hello, who is this? you say
in a sleeping heaving sigh
Your woman in the background yells
Who in the hell is that guy
Bitter Chocolate
Bitter Chocolate
I'm standing in the rain
All my love is all squeezed
out
All that I can give is pain
All that I can give is pain

## But Nobody Was There

I heard a crying child in the other room
I entered the room, but nobody was there
I heard a spider crawl across the silverware
I opened the drawer, but nobody was there
I heard your steps creeping up the stairs
I opened the door, but nobody was there
But nobody was there, but nobody, but nobody
But nobody was there

I saw your spirit sitting in a chair
I turned my head, but nobody was there
I heard a knock and the doorknob turned
I answered the door, but nobody was there
I saw my love in her funeral bier
I turned on the lights, but nobody was there
But nobody was there, but nobody, but nobody
But nobody was there

I heard your laughter on the summer's air
I called your name, but nobody was there
I saw you bare, riding your favorite black mare
I ran to the woods, but nobody was there
I saw you by the moon, you were combing your hair,
I rushed outside, but nobody was there
But nobody was there, but nobody, but nobody
But nobody was there

## Slaveship, German Model

### I

A pout is a thing with scales
Even when gliding across a marble
floor and tailored by Adolfo
I am in a room of pouts
the clothes they wear would set me
back three months rent
    Off camera, he displays a mink ring
    On camera, he talks about his
    "disenfranchisement
    his oppression"; a word that once
had its hand out has gone and gotten
a manicurist

### II

He said that he bought a Mercedes
because the holes on the side
reminded him of a slaveship

At the entrance to J. F. K.
there should be a sign:
"Welcome to New York
a rhetoric delicatessen"

## Lake Bud

Lake Merritt is Bud Powell's piano
The sun tingles its waters
Snuff-jawed pelicans descend
tumbling over each other like
Bud's hands playing Tea For Two
or Two For Tea
Big Mac Containers, tortilla chip, Baby Ruth
wrappers, bloated dead cats, milkshake
cups, and automobile tires
float on its surface
Seeing Lake Merritt this way is
like being unable to hear
Bud Powell at Birdland
Because people are talking
Clinking glasses of whiskey and
shouting
"Hey, waiter"

## I'm Running For The Office Of Love

I'm running for the office of love
My heart is in the ring
I'm bad at making speeches
So I guess I'll have to sing
A tune of moons and flowers
And things that go with Spring
And things that go with Spring

Love is so political
I don't remember it this way
They'll curse you if you play it straight
And kill you if you're gay
They say that love is dangerous
That it's best to do without
So somebody has to speak for love
That's why I'm singing out

I'm running for the office of love
My heart is in the ring
I'm bad at making speeches
So I guess I'll have to sing
A tune of moons and flowers
And things that go with Spring
And things that go with Spring

Love is like a loaded gun
A fool stands in its way
There was one man who was on the run
He was trying to get away
But love took careful aim at him
She brought him in her sights
He bought her wine and perfume

And all her favorite delights
He hadn't been paying attention
And given love her due
She took away his peace of mind
And plagued him with the blues

I'm running for the office of love
My heart is in the ring
I'm bad at making speeches
So I guess I'll have to sing
A tune of moons and flowers
And things that go with Spring
And things that go with Spring

They say that love is dangerous
It's on the radio
That holding hands is fatal
A kiss can bring you low
The papers they keep shouting
That "LOVE MEANS DOOM AND GLOOM"
So love is lying low for awhile
Until her next big bloom
Until her next big bloom

I'm running for the office of love
My heart is in the ring
I'm bad at making speeches
So I guess I'll have to sing
A tune of moons and flowers
And things that go with Spring
And things that go with Spring

## Life Is A Screwball Comedy

Life is a screwball comedy
life is a screwball comedy
it's Cary Grant leaning too
far back in a chair
It's Bill Cosby with a
nose full of hair
it's Richard Pryor
with his heart on fire
Life is a screwball comedy
life is a screwball comedy
it's Moms Mabley leaving her
dentures home
it's the adventures of Hope and Bing
it's Bert Williams doin' a buck and wing
It's Stepin Fechit sauntering before
a mule

It's matches in your shoes
It's April Fool
Life is a screwball comedy
Life is a screwball comedy
it's Scatman Crothers with his
sexy grin
It's W. C. Fields with a bottle
of gin
It's Maggie gettin' in her digs
at Jiggs
It's Desi and Lucy having a doozy
of a fight
It's Pigmeat Markham and Slappy White

Life is a Screwball Comedy
Life is a Screwball Comedy
it's Will Rogers twirling a rope

It's Buster Keaton wearing his
famous mope
It's Fatty Arbuckle in a leaking
boat
it's a scared rabbit
And a tricky Coyote
Life is a screwball comedy
Life is a screwball comedy
It's Eddie Murphy's howl
It's Whoopie Goldberg's stroll

It's Fred Allen's jowls
It's Pee-Wee Herman's clothes
It's Hardy giving Laurel a hard time
It's Chaplin up on his toes
Life is a screwball comedy
life is a screwball comedy
life is a screwball comedy
And the joke's on us

# PLAYS

ACT I: SCENE I

Oakland, California. About Fall, 1989

(*Home of the Warhaus's, a black couple living in the North Oakland section of Oakland, California. On the wall are pictures of a black Jesus Christ, Martin Luther King, Jr., JFK and a younger* SAM WARHAUS *in cowboy clothes. Also a young black man in Air Force outfit, goggles etc.* SAM WARHAUS *is sitting in a wheelchair with a blanket over his knees. Coughs a lot. He is listening to the baseball game. Enter* MILDRED WARHAUS, MABEL *and* JAKE NELSON. *They're wearing yellow jumpsuits, and caps and carrying flashlights. They wear badges that read "Crime Watch." All of the characters are in their middle sixties.* SAM WARHAUS *is clearly annoyed by this interruption.*)

MILDRED: (*Wearily*) Am I tired. Some of the people in the Crime Watch are in their seventies. I don't know how they do it. Walking up and down these streets. Looking out for suspicious behavior.

JAKE: (*Sits down, removes his shoes and begins to massage his feet*) My feet hurt so bad that when I go home, I'm going to soak them in a pan of hot water.

MABEL: Do you think that "take back our streets program" is really worth it?

MILDRED: I don't know. We go to these Crime Watch meetings and hear the people from downtown and nothing changes.

MABEL: Soon as the hoodlums move out of one neighborhood, they show up in another.

JAKE NELSON: It's all coming from that apartment building on Forty-fifth and Market Street. That's the headquarters of Crackpot. You see those runners out there all day with their bicycles. They use that bus bench, pretending to be waitin' for the bus so's the police won't notice them.

MILDRED: I knew that his lawyers would get Crackpot out. He was suppose to do ten years for running down Mr. Johnson, our block captain.

JAKE NELSON: He only did two.

MILDRED: You want some tea or coffee?

JAKE: Coffee.

MABEL: Not me. My doctor told me to cut back on caffeine. It's making me a nervous wreck. And with these gunshots going off half the night. I'm sorry I left Texas. (*She disappears into the kitchen.* MABEL *and* JAKE *glare at* SAM)

JAKE: It's all over woman. You know what your sister said in her letter from Houston. It's down there too. (*Turns to* SAM) Sam, we could use your help at the Crime Watch meetings.

SAM: I'm trying to listen to the ball game.

MABEL: If this drug war don't stop, you won't have a ball game. We'll all be dead.

JAKE: Crackpot and his gang are shooting up the neighborhoods and all you want to do is listen to the durn ball game.

SAM: That's my right, ain't it? Since when has it become against the law to listen to the ball game?

(*Announcer says "Home Run!"* SAM *leaves the conversation and returns to his radio. Enter* MILDRED *with two coffees and one tea.*)

MILDRED: You can forget about him. He ain't no help. (MILDRED *and* SAM *frown at each other.* SAM *waves her away contemptuously*)

MABEL: A lot of people are scared to come to the meetings, since Ms. Brown's house was burned down by them crack addicts. And that man down on Fortieth Street. They slashed his tires and killed his dog. They using these little boys to peddle their dope because they won't be prosecuted like the older boys.

MILDRED: Well, maybe the people are right not coming to the meetings. The police come out to talk to us. The district attorney comes and says that he's doing the best he can. But it don't change nothin'.

MABEL: Did you hear what that old crazy white woman said?

MILDRED: Which one?

MABEL: The one who tries to run the meetings every month and gets mad when she can't get her way. She said that we should go down to the council meetings and complain.

JAKE: The council meetings are televised. Every gang member in Oakland would know our faces. She must have been a fool to suggest such a thing.

MILDRED: White people live in a different world from us. They're free. They don't have to worry about these crack dealers. Yet they always complaining. Angry about the government. Angry about taxes. Angry about black people. Angry about who knows what else.

MABEL: I'll say, and that other white woman who represents us. The one who s'pose to be our councilwoman. We only get to see her once a year. She has a black man come in her place.

MILDRED: He's her liaison.

MABEL: Is that what he is? I was wondering what he was.

JAKE: Then what is she spending all of her time doing?

MILDRED: She's up at Rockridge where all of those young white professionals live. They worried about the ice-cream factory expanding.

(*They all laugh, except* SAM *who tries to silence them so that he might concentrate on the game.*)

MABEL: The ice-cream factory. We down here about to be driven out of Oakland by these thugs and she worried about ice cream. We have to drive ten miles to get ice cream. There ain't no stores or nothin'. We can't buy fresh vegetables.

JAKE: We have to go to the Arab stores.

MILDRED: You can go. I can't; Mabel can't. There are always these young people hanging out in front of those stores. Drinking whiskey.

JAKE: I thought that Arabs didn't drink liquor.

MABEL: They sellin' it all to us

MILDRED: Next time Jesse Jackson goes to the Middle East and be hugging and kissing—what's the name of that man who be wearing that old nasty headrag and look like he ain't shaved or took a bath in thirty years?

JAKE: Arafat. Yassir Arafat.

MILDRED: Well maybe he ought to ask that Arafat to close down some of these Arab liquor stores. (*Pause*) We got more liquor stores in Oakland than churches and that's the problem. (*Pause*)

JAKE: Sam sure has changed since Port Arthur. Remember?

MABEL: Everybody respected him....

JAKE: Because they know they'd get a mouthful of bullets, that's why....

MILDRED: Texas white folks used to push black people off the sidewalk....

MABEL: But not Sam.

JAKE: Even the white folks respected Sam. (*Chuckling*) I remember when we were kids. The depression. Times was hard and Sam's family got back on their rent. His mother used to take in the wash of these rich folks, but some of them was broke too. Well, the landlord came to collect the rent and when Sam's mother said she didn't have it, the landlord slapped her. Then he started calling her all out of her name. Sam took a brick and hit the landlord on the head with it. Nobody did nothin' because everybody thought Sam was crazy.

MABEL: What happened to him?

MILDRED: He hasn't been acting right since his retirement. He says he's sick, but the doctor can't find anything.

(*Shots are heard. Everybody scrambles for the floor except* SAM. *Spotlight on* SAM *who's still listening to the ball game. After the shots stop they slowly rise to their feet.*)

JAKE: This is gettin' bad on my high blood pressure.

MABEL: A whole lot of our friends are moving out of North Oakland.

JAKE: Or turning their homes over to their kids. Some of their kids are setting up crack houses. We can put some pressure on some of the landlords, but what do we do when they the landlords?

MILDRED: It's gettin' bad. But I'm not going to move. Nothin' will make me move. We been living in this house for almost thirty years. My child grew up in this house until he went to war. We plan to stay here.

MABEL: Yes, but sometimes I get discouraged.

JAKE: So do I.

MILDRED: I know that it gets bleak sometimes. Looks like we have been abandoned. Looks like nobody cares anything about whether we live or die. But you know what Martin King said.

JAKE: What's that Mildred?

MILDRED: He said: "Walk together children, don't cha get weary." Whenever I get discouraged, I think of Martin. (*She glances up at his picture*)

MABEL: (*Spontaneously, begins to sing*) "We shall not, we shall not be moved." (JAKE *and* MILDRED *join in.* SAM *becomes really annoyed*) "We shall not, we shall not be moved. Just like a tree standing by the water, we shall not be moved. We shall not, we shall not be moved...."

SAM: (*They sing over his lines*) Will you shut up and let me listen to my game?

## ACT I: SCENE 2

The Warhaus Home

(MILDRED *and a* POLICEMAN *are arguing.*)

COP: What do you want me to do about it, lady? I'm telling you that the department is undermanned. Go to the city council and ask them for some more money. We've tried our best to drive these bastards from the streets and into rock houses.

MILDRED: You ain't trying hard enough. We go to these meetings every month and you hand out the same jive. About how you don't have no money and you're working double shifts, yet that situation on Market Street has been going on for years and now with Crackpot out of jail it's getting worse. And tell me this. Another thing I want to know is why do the police seem so cozy with these thugs? Carrying on conversations and acting all chummy.

COP:(*Nervously*) You people don't understand how the system works Ma'am. It's not a matter of arresting these people. We have to have evidence—we have to be mindful of the law. The Constitution.

MILDRED: (*Angry*) You mean to tell me that the Constitution was some kind of suicide pact? That the men who wrote it went out and drank poisoned Kool-Aid afterwards. Crackpot sends these young people into our neighborhoods from that apartment building over on Forty-fifth Street. They talk nasty and look mean. They make filthy remarks to the women who walk by. They rob us. They mug us and break into our homes. The lady around the corner was raped and murdered and you talking about some durn system. Are you out of your mind?

SAM: (*Meekly*) No need to raise your voice at the man, dear. He's just doing his job.

MILDRED: (*To* SAM) You keep out of it. All you do is sit around, listening to the ball game all day. (To COP) If they spent the fifteen million dollars on this drug mess instead of puttin' all the money on that football team, there would be more money for the police.

SAM: Woman, what you got against the Oakland Raiders?

MILDRED: You shush. If you and the other men on the block would get together, you could get rid of these hooligans. Every time we have a Crime Watch meeting, a few more show up but it's mostly women and children show up. I wish that Mr. Johnson was still alive. He would do something. He would have chased these hooligans out of the neighborhood. They respected him. If James hadn't been shot down in Vietnam, he would have done something. He would have been right here with me. Standing up to these bums. Our son wasn't afraid of anything. Not like his father who is just a shell of his former self. You won't even get up from that chair so's we could take a trip to Washington to see the child's name on the Vietnam Veteran's Wall.

SAM: Aw Mildred, leave me alone. You know that I'm an invalid.

MILDRED: (*Ignores* SAM, *to* COP) It's been three months since I called you. You told me to organize a Crime Watch. So I went around and knocked on people's doors and got them to put those signs in the window saying that they would report any suspicious activities to the police. Next, we got everybody to make a phone tree. We call the police and call the police. We call that special number you gave us and a voice came on saying that the phone had been disconnected. We call all day and all night and they don't come. Sometimes we get a recorded voice and sometimes we don't even get that. It rings and rings. What will it take? One of us getting shot dead? Hell, I thought things would change after we formed our Crime Watch, but now that these boys see they can do anything and the police won't show up, they've gotten bolder. It's even worse now than it was before we organized.

COP: It takes time, lady.

MILDRED: Time? Time my foot. It's been a year. What are you going to do about Crackpot?

COP: (*Clearly uncomfortable with this question*) We haven't completed our investigation. Now if you'll just continue to write down license plate numbers and get the neighbors to call the police, it will be a big help and (*exasperated, looks at watch*), I gotta go. (*Heads toward the door*) You have my card. If there's anymore trouble, let me know ... (*She looks at him with disgust. He exits*)

SAM: You sure were hard on him. He's a nice young man. And I told you, you'd better leave those young people alone. You hear those automatic weapons going off half the night? They'll shoot you.

MILDRED: I wasn't raised to be no slave, and I didn't work thirty years of my life to spend my retirement in prison. (*Pause, then tenderly*) Why don't we get away for a while? You know they called up here last week and said I'd won that trip for two to Las Vegas.

SAM: But you know that I can't travel, the doctor said....

MILDRED: The doctor didn't say nothin'. You've been sent to twenty doctors and they can't find nothin' wrong with you, man.

SAM: It still hurts when I stand up.

(*Shots are heard outside.* SAM *cowers.* MILDRED *falls to the floor. Gets up slowly.*)

MILDRED: That does it. (*She reaches for an overcoat and picks up a purse*)

SAM: Mildred. Where are you going? You have to fix me my lunch.

MILDRED: The lunch can wait. (*Puts on coat*) I'm going downtown to *see* the council lady who represents our district.

SAM: For what?

MILDRED: This neighborhood, that's for what. These people come into this neighborhood every first and fifteenth of the month to buy drugs. Soon as they get their checks from the county ... everybody on the block knows about it, but nobody wants to do anything.

SAM: That's dangerous. Those young people don't respect nothin'. Why, one of these crack girls got into a fight with her own mother. You remember reading that? The child was selling drugs, and her mother wanted credit and she told her mother that she, her own mother, was just another customer.

MILDRED: We have to find some way to close down that apartment building. Get it condemned. The landlord don't care. He don't have to live around here. Probably live up there in the Oakland hills.

SAM: You just asking for trouble. You always was like that. Why can't you leave well enough alone? These are our retirement years.

MILDRED: And you want to spend it in that chair, listening to the baseball games, while I bring you lunch, dinner, and breakfast and rub your back. Wash your clothes. Everything for you, you. You and nothing for me. This is a time that we should be enjoying ourselves.

SAM: (*Puts hand on back as though he experienced a sharp pain*) Ohhhhhhh.

MILDRED: (*Concerned*) What's the matter?

SAM: My back. Please, Mildred. Rub it for me.

MILDRED: I can't right now. I have to catch the bus.

(*She exits. He returns to the baseball game.*)

## ACT I: SCENE 3

Interior of the private club The Vassals of the Celestial Ocean
(*Three club chairs, two facing the audience. A table with a pot of flowers on top. A framed portrait of Theodore Roosevelt in a safari outfit with bag, animal if possible.* KRUD *is a realtor who owns properties in Oakland, including the apartment building used by* CRACKPOT. *He's in his late sixties. Dressed in an expensive suit, shirt, cuff links, has blow-dried white hair.*)

KRUD: (*To audience*) Sure am glad to be somewhere I don't have to run into a lot of blacks. My club, The Vassal of the Celestial Ocean, allows me to be around my own kind. Men who think the way I do.

(KRUD *tinkles a little bell. Black waiter appears, in white jacket, black bow tie, black trousers and shoes. Gray sideburns, mustache. He wears a black patch over one eye. Very dignified. About sixty-six. He carries glasses on tray.*)

MARTIN: Yessir, Mr. Krud.

KRUD: Fix me a manhattan, Martin.

MARTIN: Yessir. (KRUD *hands him five dollars.* MARTIN *looks at the five dollars disdain-fully. Smiles. Puts it in his pocket*) Why thank you, Mr. Krud.

KRUD: Don't mention it, Martin. Sure wish we had more black people like you. They're down there in the inner city ruining the good name of the United States. Screwing like rabbits, and spending all of their welfare checks on crack and wine. You know, you can't blame the system or whitey anymore, Martin. You can't blame slavery or history either. Why, the Japanese are over here and you don't see them asking for any handouts. I'm trying to get Congressman Rapp to introduce a bill that would declare them honorary whites.

MARTIN: I lost an eye fighting the Japanese at Okinawa, Mr. Krud. We engaged the enemy in hand-to-hand combat.

KRUD: See? There you go. A prisoner of history. You and the other blacks ought to try to come into the twentieth century.

MARTIN: Yessir, Mr. Krud. (*With quiet anger. Looks contemptuously upon him when he's out of his view*)

(*Banker* KROCK *enters. Walks over to* KRUD *and gives him the secret handshake. Sits down in his chair, and begins to read* Baron's.)

KRUD: What's the latest?

KROCK: I feel great today. Deposits are up in the last two months, thanks to these black kids and their crack money. For a while there I thought we were going to have to get the Feds to rescue the company. I okayed so many bad loans to the club members and their friends. The Feds were about to audit our books.

KRUD: Those kids are getting all of us rich. I've rented out houses that I thought I'd never rent out. But I'm glad that we don't have to socialize with them as we do with the rest of our prime customers. It's a good thing that we have this club where we can get away from black people and our wives.

KROCK: You said it. I could make a helluva lot more money if I didn't have women in the way. A wife and mistress to support in that condo over near the lake. Only my daughter is making money.

KRUD: How is your daughter?

KROCK: Went to a stag the other night and they showed a dirty film. Guess who was the star?

KRUD: Who?

KROCK: (*Proud*) My twenty-year-old.

KRUD: What are you going to do?

KROCK: Buy half interest in the movie company. They've already drawn up the papers. You want in?

KRUD: No wonder you were able to build that chateau in the wine country. All of your investments. Your bank is holding the mortgage on half the property downstairs.

KROCK: These young ghetto kids are putting hundreds of thousands in the bank. Kid came in the other day and deposited ten thousand bucks in cash. The next day he deposited thirty thousand. They're making all of us rich. If anything happened to this cocaine traffic, the bottom of the economy would fall out. It's bigger than nuclear power and superconductivity. And the bio-tech industry—everybody thought this would be big in the late eighties? This crack stuff is bigger than that. And Jack Marsh, the gun dealer says he's making so much money he's talking about early retirement. Says these kids have bought so many weapons from him that they could supply three armies.

KRUD: We're getting ours, too. Crackpot, remember him?

KROCK: Do I remember him? He's one of the bank's best customers.

KRUD: He's renting that apartment building of mine over on Market and

Forty-fifth Street. Now he wants me to buy him a home in the country. Those bastards down there can all die if it were up to me. This crack stuff is merely hastening the day, but while the cash is coming in I'm going to get all that I can lay my hands on. (KROCK *looks at watch*)

KROCK: I'll be right back, I have to call the bank. (*Exits*)

KRUD: (*Rings the bell*) Where's that Martin?

(MILDRED *enters in her Crime Watch jumpsuit.* MARTIN *walks sheepishly behind her. Sets down* KRUD's *drink.*)

KRUD: What do you . . . .

MARTIN: We tried to stop her Mr. Krud. (*Out of* KRUD's *view, he grins*)

MILDRED: You the man who owns that apartment building on Forty-fifth Street? (*She hands him the address*) That's what they told me at the City Assessor's office.

KRUD: What's it to you?

MILDRED: You ought to be ashamed of yourself. We poor colored people work all of our lives to live in a quiet neighborhood and you come in with this apartment building. They got a rock operation going on. Some of our neighbors haven't had sleep in eight months. They leave these little packages all over the street (*flings a cellophane package at him; he recoils*), and that ain't the worst.

KRUD: (*Rises from his chair. She begins to back him up*) So what do you want me to do about it?

MILDRED: I want you to evict them.

KRUD: Evict them? Look, I have to rent to whomever can come up with first and last month's security. Hell, you people have been fighting for fair housing all of these years and you're asking me to evict some coloreds. (*Laughs*)

MILDRED: You can evict them if you wanted to. You know you can. Besides, I'll bet you wouldn't tolerate any rock houses in your neighborhood. Where do you live?

KRUD: (*Weakly*) Hillsborough.

MILDRED: That's where Bing Crosby used to live, ain't it? If some of these kids come to your neighborhood selling rock, they'd call in the army.

KRUD: I'm sorry lady. My hands are tied. Why don't you go see the council person. Don't bother me with your problems.

MILDRED: I called the police, and the police don't answer. They asked me to start a Crime Watch program and they still don't answer. I go to the councilperson and her assistant tells me to go to the vice mayor, and then I go to the vice mayor and he tells me to go to the mayor. The mayor is never in town. So I decided that since you own that place, I should come and see you about it. I don't blame some of these people saying that they want to take the law into their own hands.

KRUD: I'm sorry I can't help you. I know that you'd like to blame it all on the landlord, blame it on the system, blame it on anything but where the blame belongs. Your own self-destructive behavior. These are the nineties. We don't cater to special interest anymore.

MILDRED: Some landlord. That building is the worst one in the neighborhood. It should be condemned. You could at least cut the lawn from time to time. They use our sidewalks for a bathroom

KRUD: Look. Here's my card. If you can think of something that I can do legally, within the law, I'll do what I can. You people ought to band together like the Asians. You don't see them whining and complaining all of the time. You don't see them asking for affirmative action and welfare, or begging to be compensated for past acts of discrimination.

*(Glares at him while approaching him. Puts her finger on his chest. He recoils)*

MILDRED: Now you look here. I never asked for no welfare or anything else from you. Me and my husband worked all of our lives. I worked ten years on the night shift at Highland Hospital. Working with sick people. Praying with them, emptying their bedpans and changing their sheets. Bathing them and entertaining them. I was the one who cleaned them when they were dead and got them ready for the morgue.

KRUD: Now don't get violent.

MILDRED: My husband worked in the aluminum plant ever since we came up from Texas in 1943. We pay our taxes, and our only son was killed in Vietnam. So don't you ever accuse us of taking things from this country. We're the ones who are being bled. We do all of your dirty work and get treated like dogs. (MARTIN *comes in and takes her elbow. She yanks it from his grip and gives him a contemptuous look*) And all we're asking is that we have a little peace and quiet in our last years. Well, you're not going to help us, but I tell you one thing. That rock house will be closed if it's the last thing I do on earth, and as far as I'm concerned you're worse than those damned kids. You got them packed in schools like sardines and they don't learn nothin', you cut the money you was giving them for college, and you call them all kinds of dirty names, the TV, the politicians, and the newspapers, so what do you expect?

*(She exits. His son,* BOBBIE KRUD, *enters. He is dressed casually. He is accompanied by* JAKE HANDSOME, *and a man with an aviator's cap, knickers, boots, white scarf, dark glasses, and black gloves.)*

KRUD: Bobbie, my boy.

BOBBIE: What was that all about, Dad?

KRUD: One of these black malcontents. Blaming everything on the white male power structure. Demanding things. Some kids I rented an apartment to are operating a rock house. She wants me to evict them. (BOBBIE *looks to his companion,* JOE HANDSOME, *with anxiety)* Anyway, what brings you boys to the club?

BOBBIE: Thought I'd come over and take a swim. Meet my guest, Joe Handsome. (KRUD *shakes his hand)*

HANDSOME: Ciao.

BOBBIE: Joe's a pilot.

KRUD: Pilot? How exciting. You know, I always wanted to fly. Took a few lessons even.

HANDSOME: It's an exhilarating experience. I'd rather fly than eat, or be with a woman. Being up there with all of that mystery. What Swinburne calls "The Flowerless fields of heaven." A man is really alone with his thoughts. Sometimes when I'm flying late at night I turn on my tape deck and play Richard Strauss's "Also Sprach Zarathustra." *(Music comes up in the background.* KRUD *looks to his son quizzically. His son shrugs his shoulders)* And contemplate the moon. I think of the new man. The new god. I think of how we can transcend this puny shell in which we find our souls, or sometimes I put the ship on automatic pilot and read poetry. "When the bounds of spring are on winter' s traces / The mother of months in meadow or plain / Fills the shadows and windy places. With lisp of leaves and ripple of rain."

(KRUD *gives* BOBBIE *a puzzled look.)*

BOBBIE: *(Nervous. Trying to change the subject)* Joe's just made a trip up from Mexico. He's staying with me for a couple of days.

KRUD: That's nice. You must be really tired, Mr. Handsome. How do you like Oakland Airport?

HANDSOME: I didn't land at the airport, I ... (BOBBIE *takes his arm, eager to get him out of the room)*

BOBBIE: Dad, Joe and I should take our swim now.

KRUD: You boys come over for dinner tomorrow night. We'll barbeque in the back-yard and have a round of Old Fashioneds. (*They exit, and the banker* KROCK *enters*)

KROCK: Remember Richard Cummings, used to play golf up here with the boys?

KRUD: Yeah, what about him?

KROCK: Just called to ask for another loan. He's defaulted on three and he's two years behind in his mortgage payments.

KRUD: So what are you going to do?

KROCK: What the hell, I decided to go him another million. Anything to help a brother of the Vassals of the Celestial Ocean. Besides, at the peak of the Vietnam War he got my kid a cushy job in the National Guard. Cummings was a commander. He had influence.

KRUD: Can't let a lodge brother down. Say, you just missed my son. He's here to do the pool with a friend of his, a pilot.

KROCK: That son of yours is a comer. He's going to carry on the tradition. I wish . . . .

KRUD: Look, Krock. It wasn't your fault. Your oldest was just depressed. A lot of people suffer from depression.

KROCK: But when he jumped out of that window he took a part of me with him. I was such a hero to him, but when the Grand Jury indicted me for embezzlement, he took it real hard. Good thing the DA was a brother. He got the whole thing squashed, and fired the young zealot in his office who brought me up on charges. I don't know what I'd do if I didn't have the club, and my friends. Oh, did you hear? They're lettin' in a minority.

KRUD: They what? (*Shaken*)

KROCK: Aw you know the NAACP was raising such a fuss about our being on city land and being an all-white club. The board of directors decided to let one in.

KRUD: Are they out of their minds? Besides, it costs twelve thousand dollars per year to belong to this club. What minority can afford that? They must be crazy.

KROCK: That's what I thought, but they said that if we didn't do it, the city might scrutinize the operation and we don't want to have them up here. Suppose they find out that we're using up all the water keeping the golf club lawns green, while the people in the flats have to go without because of the drought, or that we're bringing prostitutes to our parties. The board decided that if we let one in, they'd call off the dogs.

KRUD: I don't like it at all. Have you met him?

KROCK: No, but I hear that he's an auto dealer.

(ROBERT HAMAMOTO *enters, snappily dressed, well-groomed*)

HAMAMOTO: (*Bows*) Gentlemen. My name is Robert Hamamoto of Hamamoto Motors. I'm the new club member.

(KRUD'*s jaw drops.* KROCK *rises and gives him the secret handshake. They both look at* KRUD. KRUD *glares at both of them. Angrily, returns to his newspaper rattling it in anger.*)

## ACT 2: SCENE I

The Warhaus's Home

(SAM *is sitting in the wheelchair. He's frightened. Cowering. Gunshots are heard offstage.* MILDRED *is on the telephone.*)

MILDRED: You can't send nobody right now? But they're out there shooting up the neighborhood.... What do you mean maybe an officer will be available in an hour? Somebody might be dead in an hour .... some neighborhoods are worse? (*To* SAM) It sounds like Vietnam outside and she talking about some neighborhoods are worse. (MILDRED *slams down the phone. She starts out of the door*)

SAM: Dear, where are you going?

(*She doesn't answer, but exits. Momentarily, the gunfire stops. She comes back in. She throws the Uzi to the floor.*)

SAM: (*Petrified*) Where did you get that thing?

MILDRED: I took it from one of those snotty-nosed punks. The rest of them ran away. He gave me some lip, but I aimed this thing right at his privates. He ran too.

SAM: Are you out of your mind? You took that gun out of that boy's hand? You could have been shot.

MILDRED: The way we livin', we better off dead.

SAM: But ... but they might come back. I'm scared. You know that I'm disabled. They might blame me for snitching on them or something.

MILDRED: Don't worry. I'll save you (*sarcastically*).

SAM: Mildred. You done gone too far with this. You becoming one of those vigilantes. Take the law into your own hands. Why, it's unchristian.

MILDRED: I'm like Charles Bronson in *Death Wish*.

SAM: Like what?

MILDRED: Charles Bronson. You know that movie we saw on TV last week where the man's wife and daughter are killed and he goes out and shoots him up a bunch of punks?

SAM: This ain't no movie. This is life. These punks will come back and blow us away.

MILDRED: We have to take a stand. I organized the Crime Watch in our neighborhood as they told us and that didn't work. I called 911 and nobody showed up. I went to the councilwoman's office and she made me wait. I think that she must have sneaked out the back after she heard the fuss I made in the reception area. I went to the vice mayor's office and they said he was in Chicago. It was impossible to reach the mayor. I went to the landlord and he laughed at me. What are we supposed to do? Nobody will help us. We have to do it ourselves. (*Knock on the door*)

SAM: (*Frightened, hiding under a blanket*) There they are now! (MILDRED *goes to the door. A black middle-class woman, well-groomed,* MARTHA WINGATE, *and a cameraman*)

WINGATE: Mildred Warhaus?

MILDRED: Yes.

WINGATE: We were in a neighborhood a few blocks from here, filming a crack bust when the call came on the radio about the shoot-out over here and when we arrived the people in the crowd told us that you'd disarmed one of the lookouts and chased him and his gang out of the neighborhood. The phones all over the city are ringing. We'd love to interview you for a few minutes. May we come in?

MILDRED: Word travels fast. Come on in. (*They set up for the interview.* MILDRED *sits next to* MARTHA WINGATE *on the couch. Smooths her dress, touches her hair*) Won't you give me a chance to change into some decent clothes?

WINGATE: You look fine. Don't worry.

CAMERAMAN: (CAMERAMAN *counts*) 10, 9, 8, 7, 6, 5, 4, 3, 2, 1 (*Points to* WINGATE)

WINGATE: This is Martha Wingate, Channel 8 News, in the home of Mildred Warhaus. Ms. Warhaus has become a celebrity within a half hour, and crowds are gathered in front of her house. This woman dared to disarm one of the members of the notorious Runners, an Oakland gang that's said to be responsible for the high homicide rate that has made Oakland the Miami of California. Many have begun calling it "Hubba City," Hubba being a nickname for crack. Ms. Warhaus, why would you risk your life by taking a gun from a dangerous drug runner?

MILDRED: It's about time somebody did something about these kids. This used to be a good neighborhood, but since Crackpot took over that apartment building on Forty-fifth and Market, life in our district has become a living hell. We have these hoodlums milling about on the street, and the children are scared to go out to play. Our elders are trapped in their homes. I just had enough of it. Just like that lady down in Montgomery who's feet was tired and she didn't give her seat to the white man because she had enough....

WINGATE: Rosa Parks.

MILDRED: Yes. I believe that's the lady's name. Just like Jesus when he chased the money changers out of the temple. He too had had enough.

WINGATE: Why didn't you call the police?

MILDRED: We been callin' and callin' the police. They told us to organize a Crime Watch. We did that. I called the city councilwoman. I went to the vice mayor. I tried to reach the mayor, the city manager. I even went to the landlord. He laughed at me. We patrolled the streets. We had a block party. Nothin' worked.

WINGATE: You certainly are a brave woman. (*Turning to* SAM WARHAUS) Mr. Warhaus, you must be proud of your wife?

SAM: (*Throws a blanket over his head*) Get those cameras away from me. Get them away. Those hoodlums might see me. Might blame me. You see what they do to snitches. You saw them burn up that woman's house. Besides, what she did was unchristian. You're supposed to forgive. There's no sin that can't be forgiven. It's in the Bible.

MILDRED: The Bible also says: "Wherefore lookest Thou upon them that deal treacherously, and holdest thy tongue when the wicked devoureth the man that is more righteous than he?" Habakkuk, first chapter, verse thirteen.

SAM: (*Waves her off*) Aw woman. Nobody can win an argument with you.

WINGATE: This is terrific footage. You getting it all?

CAMERAMAN: Got it.

WINGATE: Thank you very much, Ms. Warhaus.

MILDRED: Thank you. (*They exit.* JAKE *and* MABEL *enter*)

MABEL: Mildred. We just heard the news. You took that boy's weapon?

JAKE: Weren't you scared?

MILDRED: Something just came over me.

SAM: She puttin' all of our lives in danger.

JAKE: (*Ignores him*) It's all over town. People are calling up asking about Crime Watch. They asking Mabel and me where to sign up.

MABEL: All because of you, Mildred. (*They embrace*)

SAM: I don't like it. Strange people comin' in my house all day. The TV people will be parked out in the street all day. People will be calling up here. That ain't right. I can't concentrate on my baseball and, and ... Mildred this rock house mess is coming between us. I'll bet you going to be going out on these speaking engagements. Talking to club women. Doing interviews.

JAKE: Sam, she's done in an hour what the police and City Hall haven't been able to accomplish in years. Put heat on Crackpot.

MABEL: Seem to me you would be proud, Sam. What's come over you? You used to break all of the horses and kiss all of the women when we were young.

JAKE: You could zydeco better than anyone.

MILDRED: Remember his barbecue ribs? His standing up for people who couldn't take care of themselves? Back in Texas you wouldn't let nobody step on you. That, was the man that I loved, and that was the man that I married. Then when we moved here we had our child and you had a good job, working at the aluminum plant. Got your head busted when you led that strike back in fifty-three and then they gave you that foreman's job.

SAM: I was the first black foreman.

MILDRED: It all began to change, you got quiet.

SAM: It was different from the inside. You can't go through your life yelling and screaming.

MILDRED: Then they brought you down to the front office.

SAM: I earned it.

MILDRED: And as soon as you retired you got sick. I think that you're okay. You just sat at that desk for so many years you can't get up. They used you to keep out the other blacks, anyway.

SAM: I was qualified.

MILDRED: There were plenty others who were qualified. Every time they asked for a promotion the front office said they had you.

SAM: (*Sadly*) Why do you stay with me? A poor broken-down patient.

MILDRED: I stay with you because I love you and because one day you will stand up. One day you will be the man I married again.

MABEL: Come on Mildred, we have to go on patrol.

JAKE: It used to only be a few people walking out on crime patrol. But now, thanks to Mildred, we will have to turn people away. (*They exit.* SAM *returns to the baseball game*)

ACT 2: SCENE 2

(CRACKPOT's *apartment is filthy. Littered with empty fast-food boxes, empty bottles of Hi Life beer. Pairs of running shoes and clothes strewn around the room. Big sound system.* CRACKPOT, *about thirty years old, wears jeans and sweater, gold chains, sneakers, do rag on his head. Lying on a dirty mattress on the floor.* VEILED LADY IN THE RED DRESS *does her tape dance to the song, "Lady in Red."* CRACKPOT *is asleep on the sofa with a smile on his face. Toward the conclusion of the dance she kneels down and begins to take* CRACKPOT's *measurements with the tape.* SAM WARHAUS *comes on. He is smoking a cigar. He is dressed in white shirt, pants, and shoes. He glares at her. She sees him and recoils from* CRACKPOT. *She is frightened. She flees.* CRACKPOT *frowns and begins to toss and turn in his sleep.*)

SAM: Whatever you're doing son, you'd better quit. She's a bad one and she's got her eye on you. She wants to add you to her harem of lovers. The only catch is that you have to die to get the honor. She was taking your measurements for your coffin is what she was doing. (CRACKPOT *begins to thrash around and moan*) You'd better straighten up and get yourself together or you're going to find yourself somewhere where you don't want to be.

(CRACKPOT *wakes up screaming. Sits up. Two figures vanish. His bodyguard,* BUMP, *rushes in.*)

BUMP: Crackpot, what's the matter?
CRACKPOT: That dream. I had that dream again. This woman. There was this beautiful woman dressed all in red. And she was doing this dance. And when she finished she started to take my measurements. Then, a man dressed in white came on. He warned me that this woman wanted to take me as a lover, but I would have to die to get the honor. It was horrible. Must have been the Mama Rosa's pizza I ate last night. I ate two large sizes. Everything on them. (*Clutches his stomach*)
BUMP: Damn, Crackpot, I'm sorry.

(MOTHER *enters. She has a frantic look. She's ragged. Her hair is uncombed. She's a mess. No shoes. Hasn't had any sleep for days.* BUMP *and* CRACKPOT *are startled at first.*)

BUMP: Ms. Jenkins. (*Shocked*)
CRACKPOT: (*Contemptuously*) What do you want?

MOTHER: (*Drowsily, weakly*) Crackpot, I haven't had any sleep in five days, please Crackpot. (*She moves toward him*)

CRACKPOT: I told you to stay away from here. Besides, I'm busy.

(*She approaches him with arms outstretched*)

MOTHER: Just a bag, Crackpot. I'll pay you back. Honest I will. I won't bother you no more.

CRACKPOT: Yeah, that's what you said the last time.

BUMP: Crackpot. (*in sympathy with* MOTHER)

CRACKPOT: (*Shouts*) You keep out of this. (*To* MOTHER, *who is now trembling*) You owe me already. You'd better be glad that we have a special relationship. If you were anybody else, you'd be dead.

MOTHER: (*Drops to her knees. Clasps her hands. Begs.* BUMP *turns his head, arrogantly folds his arms*) I need just a little bit to get me through to the first. My check....

CRACKPOT: Your check. That's what you said the last time. And the time before that. Bump. Get her out of here.

(BUMP *moves to where* MOTHER *is kneeling. He takes her arm gently and she rises.* CRACKPOT *turns his back on them and folds his arms. She continues weeping. When they reach the exit,* BUMP *gives her a bag. She looks at* BUMP, *with gratitude, and begins to thank him but he moves her off the stage.*)

BUMP: Damn, Crackpot. Your own mother!

CRACKPOT: (*Calmly*) She got to pay like everybody else. Ain't no exceptions. Once you start extending credit, people start taking you as a chump. You get a reputation for being easy. I can't afford to give her any more credit. I'd be out of business if word got around that I was easy.

BUMP: But Crackpot, you're supposed to love your mother.

CRACKPOT: Love. Don't be givin' me that love shit. I'll tell you what I think about love. I agree with O. O. Gabugah.

BUMP: O. O. Ga-what?

CRACKPOT: O. O. Gabugah. He's this militant poet we used to read in that community college I went to for a semester. He said that: "Love is a white man's snot rag." That's the way I feel. Love is whitey's trick to keep the blacks soft so that he can mold them, and mess over them. The only one that I love is myself. There's no room in my heart for anyone but me. (*Pause*) Look, did they find that kid? The one who let the old biddy take his gun from him?

BUMP: Yeah. He was hiding at his mother's house, We had to waste his mother. While we were doing that he jumped out of the window. We had two of the runners outside waiting for him. They left his intestines in the middle of the street. It was a mess. Damn, Crackpot. The kid was only twelve. Couldn't you have given him a break? When that old woman took the gun from him he lost his cool.

CRACKPOT: We have to make an example. These kids don't know nothin' about discipline. Now we got people all over the city messing with our people. All because some punk let an old woman take his gun. They having neighborhood rallies and who knows what else. Block parties. This Mildred Warhaus is on TV all day. She's messin' with our credibility. All we have is fear. We keep those people afraid of us, but now that they've lost their fear, we've lost our greatest weapon. Now get back to guarding the front door.

(BUMP *exits. During the following monologue,* CRACKPOT *paces up and down the stage, haranguing the audience, smoking a cigarette.*)

CRACKPOT: I have to do all of the thinkin' for this group. That Bump is gettin' soft.

We have to enforce our way or people don't have respect. I don't care if the bitch is my own mother. If I find her snitching she would have to go, too. As far as the kid being twelve, you got to go sometime. We all got to go. You might be walking across the street and get hit by a car. I'm ready. I know that if I'm in the wrong neighborhood, somebody from another gang might get to me. But while I'm here I'm going to have all of the money, cars, and clothes I can buy. Homes, too. Never had no home. Lived with my mother in these shelters. In the street. Living room was a shopping cart and sometimes I was so hungry I cried myself to sleep. Now I got plenty of food and money. Boss hootchies. Respect. Ain't nothin' wrong with me gettin' mine. The way I see it, I'm supplying a need. A dirty need, but what I've found in my business is that in America, few people are clean. You either pimpin' or you ho'in. (*Beeper. Dials the telephone number*) Yeah. I told you that I can't give you no credit so don't be callin' up here. There's nothin' you have that I want. (*Hangs up*) You know who that was? Bitch's picture be on the society page every week. Always at some charity ball. She was down here yesterday crawling on that floor right there (*points*) naked, begging me for credit. Asking me whether I wanted her to do nasty things to me. She scared her husband will find out. Dude is a big stockbroker. She don't know that he's a customer, too. She don't want him to know, he don't want her to know. Meantime, I have all their money and their jewelry. She spends her whole day chasing the bag, and trying to get credit. You know these people you see who supposed to be so high and mighty? Be talking about family values and running down welfare mothers on TV? I know a lot of them. Lawyers, priests, accountants. You know that congressman that always be saying: "Just Say No." My best customer. Sucker be tweaked out all the time. Police, too. So the way I look at it, everybody in America is high on something. I'm performing a service. Some people are high on crack, some people are high on smack, and other people are high on things that you don't put in your mouth or up your nose or in your arm. They high on religion, or love. Or some other spacey thing. All these politicians who be passing these get-tough-on-drug laws? They drunk all the time. They just arrested the head of the vice squad last week for driving under the influence. Besides, what about all of the hubba they pushing? So why is everybody coming down on me? I read where one of these men who was running for President, Du Pont I think the fellow's name, ran a company that's responsible for the warming of the earth. Some chemical that you get out of an aerosol spray can and when it get into the space it makes a huge hole in the sky so that in five hundred years mankind will be dead. At least I ain't responsible for something like that—yet the people are mad at *me*. But this man who could be responsible for the oceans rising and skin cancer is allowed to run for President? And what about the government? They peddling dope, too. They sell cocaine and heroin in order to buy arms for the people down in South America who are killing babies and burning down people's houses, yet they talkin about the penalty for drug kingpins. So I don't see any difference between what I'm doing and what everybody else is doing. The way I look at it, the White House is the biggest crack house there is. (*Pause*) I don't be planning to be on the street all that long. I'm working with this partner of mine to go wholesale, so that all of these chumps will have to buy from me. I'll be one of the first brothers to be in on this. I can do what the whiteys do. Operate my business from home, with a fax, two computers and a Xerox machine. Get off the streets. You don't see whitey in the streets. He be operatin' from legitimate business fronts. You never see his name in the paper. (*Muses*) You never see him being dragged away in handcuffs, placed in leg chains, and strip-searched. That's only for the brothers.

When they put me out of school for stabbing the teacher, they said that my ass was going to end up dead. Now I'm making more money than all of the teachers in school put together. I'm making more money than the President. I'm a new breed. And one day—l may not do it myself—but somebody is going to take over this whole operation for the brothers who spend all of their money buying the very products that they're selling and getting us strung out as their customers. We'll put it in stocks and bonds and real estate. We'll start businesses in the community and hire people like Al Capone, Legs Diamond, Dutch Shultz, and Arnold Rothstein used to do. That time ain't here yet. But it's comin'.

(BUMP *enters with* MR. KRUD.)

KRUD: Crackpot, my boy. I have good news. Good news.

CRACKPOT: Yeah? What's the good news?

KRUD: That house you wanted to buy near Mount Diablo? It's all yours.

CRACKPOT: How much is it?

KRUD: Three hundred thousand dollars. I'll have to draw up the papers. There's usually a ten percent down payment, but I can get you in for five.

CRACKPOT: That won't be necessary. Bump, go over and get that bag.

(BUMP *goes over and fetches a bulky mailbag that rests in a corner of the room.* CRACKPOT *reaches in and removes some cash. He pays* MR. KRUD. KRUD *is shocked and his facial expression shows it.*)

CRACKPOT: Anything wrong, Mr. Krud?

KRUD: No, I just—do you mind if one of the boys help me carry it to the bank? I just don't want to walk around the streets with this kind of money.

CRACKPOT: Sure. Bump, get one of the fellas to take the money back with Mr. Krud.

KRUD: Nice doing business with you Crackpot.

CRACKPOT: Sure. And get the place ready. I want to drive up with my girls this weekend.

KRUD: I'll send the keys and the directions back with the boy.

(*They exit.* CRACKPOT *puts on a hip-hop cap, backwards.*)

BUMP: Where you going, Crackpot?

CRACKPOT: (*He picks up a pistol and puts it into his waist pocket*) Get the car. We're going to make a visit on this Mildred Warhaus. We have to teach these people to respect us. (*They put on ski masks*)

BUMP: But .... but, Crackpot. She's a sixty-eight-year-old woman. She ....

CRACKPOT: Did you hear what I said? (BUMP *looks at him for a moment. His fear is obvious*)

BUMP: But she was on television. She's all in the news. Aren't you taking a chance?

CRACKPOT: I know what I'm doing. One thing I learned in prison. You let one person walk over you, soon your body will be a highway. Bump, you actin' like a regular little ho these days. (*Mocks him in an effeminate manner*) "She's all in the news. Aren't you taking a chance?" Bump, I chose you to be second in command. Now if you becomin' some kind of pussy then maybe I should get somebody else. That means we'll have to burn yo black ass. You know too much.

BUMP: (*Trembling, excitedly*) No Crackpot. I'm ... I'm the same Bump. I just don't think we should be takin' chances. I'm lookin' out for you, Crackpot. (BUMP *glares at him with hostility for a moment*)

CRACKPOT: Okay. Let's go. (*They exit*)


ACT 2: SCENE 3


The Warhaus Home

SAM: (*Whining*) You hardly spend any time with me anymore. I have to go to the bathroom by myself. I have to shave myself. You always at meetin's or answering mail. Now you talkin' about running for city council.

MILDRED: I haven't made up my mind.

SAM: The phone rings all day. I can't hardly concentrate on the ball game. And now you want to travel to Washington to make a speech. Who is going to take care of me? Wash my clothes? Turn on the TV?

MILDRED: I'm taking you with me. With the contributions people have sent me, we'll be able to hire an assistant for you. While we're down there we can see our son's name on the Vietnam Veteran's wall.

SAM: I don't know about flying. Them planes ain't safe.

MILDRED: Sam, I'm worried about you. You haven't been out of the house in two years now. I'm thinking about getting a head doctor to come and look at you. You haven't been acting right ever since you retired.

(*Doorbell. She goes off to answer offstage.* SAM *hears* CRACKPOT *ask: "Are you Mrs. Warhaus? Mrs. Mildred Warhaus?" Shots are fired. Sam is shocked. Wearing an expression of great agony,* MILDRED *staggers onto the stage, holding her chest. Her blouse is bloody as she collapses.*)

SAM: (*Screaming*) Mildred!!!! Mildred!!! (*He slowly rises from the chair. With much effort he walks over to where she lies. He lifts her head.* SAM *looks at his legs. Goes to phone.*) Hello. 911. My wife has been shot. Please send an ambulance.... A half hour? What do you mean a half hour? I ... (*He goes to* MILDRED. *Struggling, picks her up and carries her offstage. Dark*)

(*Spotlight on* MARTHA WINGATE, *reporter.*)

WINGATE: Hundreds of people have gathered outside of Highland Hospital waiting for news about the condition of Mildred Warhaus who was shot earlier today by unknown assassins at her residence in North Oakland. Ms. Warhaus received national attention when she disarmed a crack dealer, one of many who had been terrorizing her neighborhood for over a year. For her heroism she has been called the Rosa Parks of the anti-drug movement. Ms. Warhaus has been in surgery for five hours, and according to attending physicians, the prognosis is not good. The police have no suspects in the shooting, but word has it that the shooting may have been a reprisal by the notorious Runners led by Crackpot Jenkins, a notorious drug kingpin who served two years as part of a plea bargaining deal struck with the District Attorney. The gang leader was charged with the murder of Ezekiel Johnson, a leader in the North Oakland community.

(*Spotlight out. Lights on Warhaus home.* JAKE *and* MABEL *are sitting at a table having coffee. They are glum.* SAM's *wheelchair is empty. The phone rings.*)

SAM: (*From offstage*) Will you get that?
MABEL: (*On phone, excitedly*) Hello.... She's out of surgery?... She's going to have full recovery? Well, thank the Lord for that. (*She puts down the phone*)
JAKE: That woman is made of lead. I knew that she would recover.

(SAM *enters. He is dressed in cowboy clothes. Campy, like in the movies. With sequins and other glitter.*)

MABEL: Sam, Mildred's going to be okay—what ... (*The sight of him shocks her*)
JAKE: Sam, what's the matter with you?
SAM: I'm going to take care of that punk who shot my wife.
MABEL: You don't have to be no hero, Sam. (JAKE *tries to block his way*)
SAM: Get out of my way, Jake.
JAKE: The police will take care of Crackpot. (SAM *laughs.* JAKE *realizing what he*

*said, backs away dejectedly. To* MABEL) You try to talk some sense into him, Mabel.

MABEL: Sam, what's the use of Mildred coming home to a dead husband? You don't have a chance against those boys. They'll kill you as soon as smash a bug. You know they don't care about life.

SAM: I have to do what I have to do.

JAKE: Sam, you ain't in Texas no more.

SAM: The hell I ain't. Texas is anywhere hell is. Now move out of the way and let me do my business.

(*Lights.*)

## ACT 2: SCENE 4

Crackpot's Apartment

(MARTHA WINGATE *is on TV . Picture of* MILDRED *flashes on. Then picture of* CRACK-POT.)

BUMP: Damn, Crackpot. They trying to trace it to you.

CRACKPOT: Change the channel.

(BUMP *changes the channel to a cowboy movie. They watch it for a few minutes.*)

WINGATE: Crackpot, you don't seem worried? The public wants to ice you for what you did to Mildred.

CRACKPOT: Don't worry about it. Just like the other times, they'll pick me up, and my lawyers will have me out the next day.

(*Same* COP *whom we've seen in the scene with* MILDRED WARHAUS *enters.* CRACK-POT *nods his head to* BUMP *and* BUMP *goes to the bag and takes out some bills and hands them to the* COP.)

COP: No, I didn't come for that this time, Crackpot.

CRACKPOT: What are you talking about? You know the arrangement.

COP: (*Nervously*) That Warhaus woman, Crackpot. There's a lot of pressure downtown to take you out, Crackpot. Why the hell did you have to go ahead and do it?

CRACKPOT: How am I going to maintain authority if I let a sixty-eight-year-old woman call my bluff? Everybody will be on my case. I won't be able to go nowhere without risking a drive-by by these people who think I'm weak.

COP: It was a big mistake.

CRACKPOT: What the fuck do you know about it? You livin' out there in the suburbs with your family. I clothed your wife and I sent your children to college. Every additional room you built on your house, I paid for. When your mother was sick, I paid for her bills. And now, with the first sign of trouble, you cut and run—why, you little cunt?! (*Grabs him by the collar*)

COP: I'm sorry, Crackpot. I won't be coming around anymore.

CRACKPOT: (*Shouting*) Well, run then, and I tell you what. If I go down, a whole lot of these high and mighty people downtown will go down with me. All of these people who drive in here in their Mercedes and BMWs will go down. I will name names and tell everybody where the dogs are buried. (*To* COP) Do you hear me?

(*Enter* HAMAMOTO, *the auto dealer*)

CRACKPOT: Hey! You get that order?

HAMAMOTO: Came in three days ago. It's in your garage next to the Mercedes and the Porsche. You have quite a collection.

CRACKPOT: Yeah. Well I don't like to drive the same car every day.

HAMAMOTO: I need eighty thousand dollars. (CRACKPOT *goes over to the bag and shoves some money into a bag*)

HAMAMOTO: Nice doing business with you.

CRACKPOT: Hey, didn't I see you in the paper last week?

HAMAMOTO: Yeah. Everybody in town must have seen it.

CRACKPOT: You got into some club?

HAMAMOTO: Yeah. They made me a Vassal. The club's name is the Vassals of the Celestial Ocean. I'm getting a lot of orders up there. Some of the big shots in Oakland belong to the club. We Vassals look out for each other and are always passing each other tips on the stock market and helping some of the brothers who suffer setbacks. We play tennis, golf, get massages, and have Christmas dinner together. It's a real fraternity. There are great opportunities for networking.

CRACKPOT: Maybe you can get me in. I have a lot of money. I have cars and houses.

HAMAMOTO: Takes more than that, Crackpot.

CRACKPOT: What do you mean it takes more?

HAMAMOTO: Look at it this way. You're black. They know that the kind of wealth you have is transitory. Guys like you are a dime a dozen. As soon as somebody takes you off the scene, somebody else will take your place. Mr. Krud will sell him houses. I'll sell him these Suzuki Samurai Hubba jeeps. And the Banker Krock will keep his money under lock and key. Every time they look at you they see a loser. Every time they look at me they see Japanese power, because even though my family has lived here for a few generations, I'm still an alien to them. But the biggest banks in the world are in Tokyo. That backs me up. You don't have any insurance. Suppose they legalize the stuff or somebody concocts a synthetic version and corners the market? You'd be back in some corner lot playing basketball.

(*He starts to exit, laughing.* BUMP *comes in the room with* BOBBIE KRUD *and* JOE HANDSOME. KRUD *and* HANDSOME *see* HAMAMOTO. BOBBIE *and* HAMAMOTO *exchange handshakes.*)

CRACKPOT: What was that all about, Bobbie?

BOBBIE: Oh, that was one of the brothers from the lodge. Every time we see each other we exchange the secret handshake. Look, I got some news.

CRACKPOT: What news?

BOBBIE: The guys in Colombia have come up with a new hit. Smokeable heroin. It should be on the market in the fall. And get this. It'll be five k's per kilo.

CRACKPOT: Man, can you imagine the profits? Joe, they're going to have you flying in day and night. Think you can handle it?

HANDSOME: Can I handle it? As long as they pay me the money I can handle it.

BOBBIE: All of mine goes to the stocks and bonds. When you come back from Rio next year, the operation will be in full swing.

CRACKPOT: (*Pause. Studies* BOBBIE KRUD) Rio. What are you talking about?

BOBBIE: We've decided that it might be a good idea for you to disappear for a while until the heat's off.

CRACKPOT: I don't understand?

BOBBIE: That woman. Look, I understand that you might have been under a little stress. I mean, hypertension is hereditary among black people, but you went too far when you shot that Mildred Warhaus. It's all in the papers and on television. I've decided that Bump should take over for a while. (CRACKPOT *looks shocked at* BUMP. BUMP *lowers his head. Shrugs his shoulders*) You're excitable. You need to rest your nerves on the beach for a while. If that woman dies, it'll be Murder One.

CRACKPOT: I'll be out on the street in an hour. You get that lawyer who's always defending me.

BOBBIE: He says you're at the end of your rope. He got you a light sentence for running down that old man, but now they have to give you some hard time. The cops say that they can't cover for you anymore.

CRACKPOT: They're gettin their cut. Anyway, Bump does what I say. Right, Bump? Bump, home? (BUMP *looks at his shoes*) Hey, wait a minute, man. Bump. What's going on man? Don't let this white boy come between me and you just because of some bread. Man, you and me, all the ass we used to chase, the way we used to get high together, remember when we took the principal and had him hanging out of a window, man? Remember when we stabbed that teacher? (BOBBIE *goes for his gun*)

CRACKPOT: Hey, Bobbie, what are you doing?

BOBBIE: Look, Crackpot, nothing personal, but the Cartel has decided that you're just too flighty to be of any use to us any longer. The days of wild men are over. We need a clean, efficient operation. We want this thing to be operated like IBM.

CRACKPOT: (*To* BUMP) Bump, help me, Bump. I'll give you all of my cars. My women, you can have them. Look, Bump there's all the money in the sack, you can have ... (BUMP *draws a gun. But before he can fire,* HANDSOME *shoots him*)

BOBBIE: (*Shocked*) Joe, what—what's going on?

HANDSOME: Drop it, Bobbie.

BOBBIE: Joe, I don't understand. (*Drops his gun and raises his hands*)

HANDSOME: I've decided to make it a two-man operation. Crackpot and me. (CRACKPOT *is relieved*)

BOBBIE: You, you siding with this ... this spade against me? Why, we were roommates together at Harvard and pledged for the same fraternities, double-dated at Yale Winterfest; I was the one who recommended you for the Elite club. We had that apartment in Greenwich Village.

HANDSOME: We've decided that we don't need you anymore. Cut out the middle man and I can deal directly with Crackpot. (CRACKPOT *laughs*)

BOBBIE: But, but ... (JOE *shoots him. He falls and begins to squirm in agony until he is dead*)

HANDSOME: Two less to share with. From now on when I fly in you meet me and I'll deliver the goods to you directly. Deal?

CRACKPOT: Look. You drop it, I'll distribute it. That Bobbie was slick but he wasn't as slick as you and me, huh, Joe? And Bump. How could he have ever thought that Bump could replace me?

HANDSOME: This is a big operation, Crackpot. Bigger than you ever thought. My orders come directly from the White House basement.

CRACKPOT: The White House basement? It must be big then.

HANDSOME: (*With a glazed look, begins to paint his vision with gestures. First few strains of Zarathustra music again*) I'll explain, Crackpot. You see, billions of dollars are going back and forth across the border. Some of it is making a lot of people rich. But some of it is making our country stronger, Crackpot. We're helping freedom fighters all over the world, Crackpot. From the jungles of Angola to the mountains in Afghanistan. Crackpot, you and I are patriots. Do you follow me, Crackpot?

CRACKPOT: (*Bewildered*) I guess so.

HANDSOME: Crackpot, there are people, bad people all over the world who are aligned with the traitors in this country to undermine our traditional values. Some of the profits from this operation are going to men and women who are keeping our liberties alive. Bobbie didn't understand that, Crackpot. He always felt that these sentiments were corny, Crackpot. He used to mock the small band of patriots who were outcasts at Harvard, Crackpot. There's plenty of red in that *Harvard Crimson*, Crackpot. He always had the fast cars and the women, Crackpot. He didn't understand what was at stake, and so when we got into this business after graduation, all he saw was an opportunity to make quick money. I saw it as a way to achieve a higher and nobler purpose. And I found plenty of brave and selfless men in the government who agreed with me, Crackpot. Crackpot, with the profits we're making from crack, we're stockpiling weapons in three western states and as soon as we get the signal that Armageddon is on—the final battle between the forces of good and evil—our patriots will heed Gabriel's call.

CRACKPOT: What call?

HANDSOME: For the day when we take back our government and restore justice to the American people. (SAM WARHAUS *has entered. He's dressed up like Gene Autry. Has two guns drawn. He looks comical. Both men laugh*)

SAM: I got your justice. Stick 'em up. (*His hand trembles as he holds the guns. They continue to laugh. They're in stitches.* SAM *tries to whirl the gun around his thumb, like in the movies. The gun falls to the floor. They really laugh then*)

HANDSOME: (*Laughing*) Who's this clown?

CRACKPOT: (*Laughing*) He's the husband of that woman we hit. Think we don't know that he's carrying a toy gun.

(*As* SAM *picks up the gun,* the gun goes off accidentally. This startles SAM, even. CRACKPOT and JOE are shaken up. SAM holds the gun again.)

HANDSOME: (*Panicky*) Look pal, I didn't have anything to do with it. It was this lunatic, Crackpot. He shot your wife. We can do without him. You and me. That's it. We can split the cash. Cut him out. I'll deliver directly to you.

(SAM *waves* JOE *away gesturing with the gun toward the exit.* JOE *flees.* CRACKPOT *gets on his hands and knees.*)

CRACKPOT: (*Sobbing*) Hey man. Let's talk this over. It was Bump's idea. I didn't want anything to do with it.

SAM: Bump. Who is Bump?

CRACKPOT: My partner. It was his idea to hit Mrs. Warhaus. He ordered me to run down that Mr. Johnson, too. He drove the car.

SAM: I don't believe a word you say. Now get ready to meet Satan. I'm going to give you the same chance you gave my wife.

CRACKPOT: Man you don't have to do it. Please (*sobbing*) don't kill me. Look, I got some cash. There's over a hundred thousand dollars in that bag over there. You can have it.

(SAM *walks over to the bag, and removes some cash. Examines it. While he is doing that,* CRACKPOT *reaches for a small pistol that he has in his shoe. He shoots* SAM *in the arm.* SAM *grabs his arm. He prepares to shoot again. Shots are fired from offstage, mortally wounding* CRACKPOT. SAM *turns to the entrance. This dramatic pause should be milked. Momentarily* JAKE *enters. He is dressed in corny cowboy clothes.*)

SAM: Thanks, partner. (*They embrace.* SAM *then goes over and picks up the bag*)

JAKE: (*Gazing upon* CRACKPOT's *corpse*) What a waste. Bright kid like that. No telling what he could have done with his life if somebody had given him a break. What's that? (SAM *removes some stacks of bills from the bag. Shows it to* JAKE. SAM *has a broad grin*) What are you going to do? Turn that over to the police?

SAM: That's not exactly what I had in mind, Jake. Seems to me that if we don't take it, these police will take it and spend it in the suburbs. If we take it, it goes back into the community.

JAKE: Put it back.

SAM: Are you crazy?

JAKE: I said put it back, Sam. (*Insistent. Growing angry. As* SAM *returns the bag,* JAKE *turns his back to* SAM *and faces audience. He folds his arms in a manner of moral superiority. He doesn't see* SAM *take a few stacks of bills and put this in his pocket, but the audience sees*) We have to be better than these people. We're Christian people. The Bible says: "Woe to him that increaseth that which is not his."

SAM: Yeah. Uh, thanks Jake. Thanks for reminding me.

(*They exit. Dark. Then, spotlight on* MARTHA WINGATE.)

WINGATE: We interrupt this program to bring you further news on the bizarre murders that were discovered this morning in an apartment building located in North Oakland. The bodies of three men, Crackpot Jenkins, Bump Disney his sidekick, and Bobbie Krud, son of the well-known realtor and community leader, Jack Krud. Neighbors said that they heard a number of shots and called the police. When the police arrived an hour later, they were too late to catch the assassin or assassins who escaped without being noticed by the drug kingpin's neighbors. The police had no explanation for how the three came to be found in the apartment together, but surmised that Bobbie Krud had been kidnapped by Crackpot and members of his notorious gang, the Runners, in an attempt to collect ransom from Mr. Krud's father. The young Mr. Krud's red Porsche was found parked outside the building, a clear indication, the police say, that he was a victim of a carjacking. Jack Krud, the civic leader and philanthropist, was in tears after identifying his son at the morgue. He said that the young man was doing well in his investment firm and was presently expanding his business to foreign markets. Mr. Krud offered a fifty thousand dollar reward for anyone who has information leading to the perpetrator or perpetrators of his son's killer or killers.

## ACT 2: SCENE 5

(SAM *enters carrying some luggage. He is dressed in a suit and wears a Stetson hat. He's smoking a cigar.* JAKE *and* MABEL *enter. They are also dressed well.* MABEL *wears a corsage.*)

JAKE: The car is ready. Where is Mildred?

SAM: Oh, you know that woman. Take her hours to get ready.

JAKE: (*Looks at watch*) Well, we'd better get going. The plane leaves in an hour.

SAM: What's the weather in Washington?

MABEL: Say it's going to be seventy.

(MILDRED *enters. Looks great. Hair done. Corsage. Mink. Walks with a cane.* SAM's *eyes widen.*)

MABEL: Mildred. Now don't you look nice.

JAKE: Like a million dollars.

SAM: She do now don't she? I knew what I was doing when I married the most pretty girl in Port Arthur.

MILDRED: (*Flattered*) Sam, you still know how to talk that trash, and it was awfully nice of you to arrange for all of us to fly to Washington. Then to New York. Puttin' us up in the Mayflower Hotel in Washington and this fancy New York hotel called the Plaza. Hiring that limousine driver ... we can see our son's name on the Veteran's Wall of Respect before we die. Thank the Lord.

MABEL: How are you able to afford all of this, Sam?

SAM: Oh, been saving a little on the side for all these years. (JAKE *and* SAM *have eye contact.* JAKE *frowns*)

MABEL: Well, I appreciate it, Sam. Jake and I never go nowhere.

JAKE: That ain't true, woman. I took you to Reno on that gamblin' special bus once.

MILDRED: When we go up to New York, I want to see Radio City Music Hall. The Statue of Liberty. The Empire State Building.

SAM: Maybe me and Jake can check out one of those fights at Madison Square Garden. Or even go to one of them OTB establishments.

JAKE: Harlem. I want to see Harlem.

MILDRED: And Abyssinian Baptist Church where Adam Clayton Powell used to preach. That man was a fighter. He took on the whole Congress and beat them. He's the kind of fighter that I want to be when I run for city council.

SAM: Now Mildred, you get that foolishness right out of your mind. (*All three of them glare at him. He backs down, sheepishly*) But on the other hand, I think that you will make a fine council person.

(*They exit, carrying bags. Turning down the lights.*)

The End

### PROLOGUE

RAPPER:
*Ladies and Gentlemen, we're turning down the lights*
*to show you a rap about a cultural fight —*
*about Three Strikes, a rapper, and Jack Legge*
*a preacher*
*I'll give you some background till I hear*
*from my beeper*
*The country's turned right and the*
*politicians have found*
*that the sure way to election*
*is by dissing black sound*
*the preachers and the journalists*
*are not far behind*
*Using columns and pulpits to*
*hasten rap's decline.*

CHORUS:
*The preacher and the rapper*
*One's dreadlocked, and one's dapper*
*A man of the cloth*
*and a man of the streets*
*The issues are old*
*and the passions run deep*
*and try as they might*
*will their minds ever meet?*

They're blaming hip-hoppers
for all that's gone wrong
that the source of all misery
can be found in its songs
that the children tune in
and get carried away
and pick up an Uzi
the very same day
that the women are bitched
and the women are ho'ed
and the mind of a rapper
is the mind of a toad

CHORUS:
The preacher and the rapper
One's dreadlocked, and one's dapper
A man of the cloth
and a man of the streets
They're on opposite sides
will their minds ever meet?
Now Congress is preparing
to put Rap on trial
claiming words on
these records
are nasty and foul
and the volume they're played at
is enormously loud
and that nudity and profanity
should be banished from sight
as a surefire way to end
this terrible blight.

CHORUS:
The preacher and the rapper
One's dreadlocked, and one's dapper
A man of the cloth
and a man of the streets
A man with a beat and a

> *sailor in God's fleet*
> *They're on opposite sides*
> *will their minds ever meet?*
> *(Beeper sounds. He exits.)*

## ACT I: SCENE I

*(St. John's Church.* REV. JACK LEGGE *is about fifty-five years old, prosperously robust with gold teeth. He wears an expensive black clergyman's outfit. Kunte cloth draped over his shoulder. His black shoes are fastidiously shined and he wears rings on three of his fingers.*

REV. JACK LEGGE *is praying. He has one follower. Sitting in a chair her back to the audience, she is dressed in Olosun cult clothes. White gown, turban, etc. On the wall is a poster of Charlton Heston dressed as Moses in the* Ten Commandments. *The* REV. *is on his knees, praying.)*

REV. JACK LEGGE: ....and Lord, we pray to you to end this drought. Replenish our congregation so that we may fight the evil of this time, Heavenly Father. Save St. John's Baptist Church. Fertilize our garden. Make us a well-spring of Christian hope. We call upon you, Heavenly Father.

You know our situation. You know that your membership has dwindled. That your children are being persecuted like never before. That thine enemies now rule this country. That our great and beloved United States of America has been taken over by worshipers of alien gods. Of strange and exotic idols. Serpent cults. Bizarre chants are being uttered in the streets of our capital and we are like Paul, a stranger in a strange land when he tried to spread the Gospel but finding opposition at every turn. They have driven your children into the corners of America. They have reduced our once powerful Church to a congregation trembling with fear as our rights are trampled by worshipers of the Mother Goddess. You must help up, O God! Restore us to the pinnacle as you did for Daniel, and Joseph, preparest a table for us in the presence of our enemies and have our cup runneth over. I implore you,O Lord! *(Rises from his knees. He begins to sing and clap his hands)* This little light of mine, I'm gonna let it shine. This little light of mine, I'm gonna let it shine. This little light of mine, I'm gonna let it shine. Let it shine, let it ... sister? Why ain't you singing along?

SISTER: I didn't come here to worship this morning, Rev. I came to say good-bye.

REV. JACK LEGGE: Good-bye. Good-bye. But you, the last faithful follower? At one time, St. John's Church had ten thousand members. Look at us now (*frowns*). People have abandoned Jesus for sin and fornication, and are living loose in a variety of new familial relationships. Sister, you give me strength. Because I know that if I just have one faithful follower, I can rebuild. Slowly build up a congregation so that we will be ten thousand strong as we were in the beginning. With far-flung missionary posts, Bible sales, and our television ministry theme parks, and the Rev. Jack Legge Bible College. Why, we built a replica of the Wall of Jericho, which is still the major tourist attraction for the state of South Carolina until this woman Barbara Sung and the Wicca Party began running things.

SISTER: I'm sorry. I've made up my mind.

*(Places his arm around her shoulder. She removes it.)*

REV. JACK LEGGE: What's the matter?

SISTER: I've joined the Yemaja Temple.

REV. JACK LEGGE: The Yemaja what?

SISTER: O da bo, Rev.

REV. JACK LEGGE: Ya-what? A-what? But, but you have been a member for twenty years. You're going to give up the Lord, just like that? You mean you're not going to worship in your home church no more? Sister, what's come over you?

SISTER: I'm sorry Rev. Legge, but according to our teachings, Christianity and Islam are invader religions. They are not indigenous to West Africa, the ancestral home of most African-American people.

REV. JACK LEGGE: Sister, who be putting these wicked ideas in your head? You know, you'd better be careful. God don't like one to put no strange idols before him. Jesus said: "He who is not with me is against me." You'd better not mess with the Lord!

SISTER: I'm sorry Rev., but we've been taught that Jesus is not our problem. (REV. *expresses shock*) Africans didn't kill Jesus, the Romans did. So why could we share the guilt for an offense that we had nothing to do with? Good luck, Rev. And may Olodumare be with you. (*Exits*)

REV. JACK LEGGE: (*Sits down, wipes his face with a handkerchief*) Another one gone over to the forces of Satan. What am I going to do? I'm six months behind in my Cadillac notes. Lost that TV hour, got evicted from my fifteen-room rectory. (*Pause*) That sexual harassment suit caused me a lot of damage. A lot of damage. But I weathered that storm. I had to pay one third of the Church's coffers to settle out of court. That greedy Jezebel. It was worth it, though. She had a butt that you could grow tomatoes on and a pussy as tight as a bulldog's grip. Still, things have changed since the 1990s. Boy, I was steppin' high then. The delectable juices of filet mignon dripping from my lips, banquets honoring me. Plenty of parish sisters in case I need to relieve the tension—that's an occupational hazard for a public man like me. The finest Scotch from Ireland and three kinds of wine. Hanging out with high-class folks. Statesmen, clergymen, and the most powerful business leaders in America. Invited to do op-eds in the *Wall Street Journal* in which I traced the problems of the black community to their forgetting to honor Jeeeeesssusss. I called for the politics of conversion. Congressional committees calling upon me to testify about the moral evil that was vanquishing America.

(*Stage goes dark.*)

## ACT I: SCENE 2

(*Lights up on a table topped with microphones with the call letters of different stations on them. A TV cameraman is photographing the scene. A black congressperson,* MABEL JOHNSON *with wide hat, fur collar, gaudy tasteless dress, wearing high heels and a blonde wig, is chairing a committee.* THREE STRIKES, *a rap star, is seated next to* REV. JACK LEGGE. *He wears dark glasses. Baseball cap and other hip-hop attire.*)

CHAIRPERSON: And Rev. Legge, tell the committee the threat that these nasty rap records are to the minds of the youth of today.

REV. JACK LEGGE: What effect do they have? They do have plenty of effect, sister. Plenty of effect. They have made them into licentious slaves to the passions of the flesh. They have turned them into violent predators. Why, when I look over my shoulder on a dark street and see that it's a white person walking behind me and not a black, I am relieved. They put evil thoughts in the mind of the young men. Get them to disrespecting they women. Using filthy words to express theyselves. Cussing out and issuing threats against our fine gentlemen in blue who provide a thin line between the jungle and we law-abiding citizens. I have a lyric right here that illustrates the viciousness of this nasty music. It's called: "Put It In the Butt," by Luther Campbell.

THREE STRIKES: That's not the title. It's "Put It In The Buck."

CHAIRPERSON: (*To* THREE STRIKES) Shut up, you!

THREE STRIKES: I've been sitting here for an hour listening to this ignorant rant.

CHAIRPERSON: (*Banging the gavel*) Three Strikes, if you don't shut your mouth, I'm going to have the Sergeant at Arms! . . . .

THREE STRIKES: This insane ignorant attack on rap by this—

REV. JACK LEGGE: Watch what you say, sonny. I'm a man of the Lord!

THREE STRIKES: Charlatan!

REV. JACK LEGGE: Charlatan? (*Rising in a threatening manner*) You call me, a man who walked with Martin Luther King, Jr., who was with the leader in Selma, Montgomery, and Birmingham—(*preaches*) whose clothes were soiled with the blood of the prophet as his life ebbed away on the balcony of the Lorraine Motel—you call me, a charlatan. Young man, you owe me an apology. (*catches the eye of* CHAIRPERSON *who nods in agreement*)

CHAIRPERSON: I'm going to hold you in contempt of Congress, Three Strikes, if you don't let the Rev. continue. You young people have no breeding. Your parents don't care anything about you. No wonder you're producing this pornographic smut.

REV. JACK LEGGE: As I was saying, Madame Chairperson, I think that it is time for the Congress to step in and stamp out this as though it were the evil serpent underneath one's foot. These vile records ain't doin' nothin' but putting people up to violence and misogyny. (*Applause*) They are causing the country to be threatened with a tidal wave of carnality. (*Applause*)

CHAIRPERSON: Now do you have something to say, Three Strikes? Make it brief. The committee has to take a lunch break. By the way, where did you get such a ridiculous name as Three Strikes?

THREE STRIKES: The way I look at it, Madame Chairperson and Rev. Legge, the black man has three strikes against him. He is born black, a man, and poor.

REV. JACK LEGGE: (*Laughing*) Ain't he crazy?

CHAIRPERSON: I sure do get tired of you young punks wallowing in your misery. You ought to go out and get a real job instead of disrespecting our women with these seedy songs of yours. Now proceed.

THREE STRIKES: Madame Chairperson, Rev. Legge, both of you are wrong about rap. What we do is merely reflect the attitudes of the community.

We didn't invent the social conditions that led to the breakdown of social values. We're merely the messengers.

REV. JACK LEGGE: That ain't no excuse.

THREE STRIKES: You can slay the messenger, but you can't slay the message. Besides, if you black leaders were more accessible to the needs of young ghetto people, maybe we wouldn't have a generation that's gone buck wild. It seems that you're using rap as a scapegoat for your inability to reach young people. Every time I see you in the papers, Madame Chairperson (*sarcastically*) you're playing golf or at some posh resort or on a vacation in Bermuda paid for by your big business sponsors who are doing more to pollute the country than all of the music ever written.

CHAIRPERSON: You're out of order, sonny boy.

THREE STRIKES: And you, Rev. Legge, the only reason that you're in on this is because of your insatiable need for publicity. Why, with all of the money that you raked in from your TV ministry, why haven't you built a recreation center for the youth? Or a senior citizen's home?

CHAIRPERSON: How dare you insult Rev. Legge. He is the kind of role model that our community needs instead of you rappers with your half-dressed nasty girls, your swimming pools full of Budweisers, and your gold teeth and chains. Look at some of these awful lyrics. (*Puts on glasses and reads from paper*) S my D, from New 2 Live Crew: "And won't you lick my clit, bitch." Such foul words, I have to gargle with mouthwash after uttering them (*pulls out a bottle of mouthwash, gargles, spits in a cup*). I've never had an occasion to use such words as shit, bitch, fuck, and dick (*said lustfully*) until I began this investigation. It makes me feel .... dirty all over. Needless to say, the experience has been trying.

THREE STRIKES: You artless tasteless boogee negroes. You tried to stop ragtime and you failed, you tried to stop the blues, you failed. You tried to stop gospel and you failed, you tried to stop rhythm and blues and rock and roll and you failed, you tried to stop the rhumba, the samba, and the salsa and you failed.

CHAIRPERSON: (*Banging gavel, furiously*) Mr. Sergeant at Arms!

THREE STRIKES: You tried to stop Be-Bop and Charlie Parker—

CHAIRPERSON: Mr. Sergeant at Arms!

THREE STRIKES: ...lives! (SERGEANT AT ARMS *grabs* THREE STRIKES *and begins to escort him from the hearing room*) When you stop rap here where do you go next? There's Hawaiian Rap, Japanese Rap, Togoland Rap, Italian Rap—

REV. JACK LEGGE: The boy don't respect nobody.

THREE STRIKES: People are rapping in Russia, Afghanistan, Madagascar. They're rapping in Beijing and Paris, Amsterdam and Hamburg, Singapore, Lagos and Tokyo, Kinshasa, you'll never stop it. Never, never. Viva le Rap! Rap libre! (*Exit with* SERGEANT AT ARMS.)

CHAIRPERSON: Rev. Jack Legge, I'm sorry for his outbursts. We have the votes. The votes that will outlaw this filthy music once and for all. Let me read the newest song by Three Strikes: (*Passionately*)

> *Ream my dick, my buttercup*
> *Lick it till it shrivels*
> *up*
> *Make me come all*
> *in your mouth*
> *Suck me, love me .*
> *Sex me, south*
>
> *Let me tickle*
> *your warm wet cunt*
> *stroke your bush*
> *with my hard thick runt*
> *you give me a pull*
> *and I'll give you a push*
> *and then I'll play with*
> *your cute little tush*

(*She stops, gazes into the distance, longingly.*)

REV. JACK LEGGE: You needn't read further, Madame Chairperson. (*She recovers*) Having to listen to these filthy CDs and watching these old MTV videos must have been trying for you. These wicked videos show half-clothed women, gyrating like savages in the darkest Africa. A ... er ... so I've heard. Every Christian in the country is grateful to you, Madame Chairperson, for coming down hard on this generation of youth who are a shiftless evil bunch. And I pledge my support and all of the resources at my disposal to fight to the end. We can win. With the help of the virtuous and moral individuals of this great nation, we will defeat rap. This ugly monster, this fiend from the bottomless pit who has put our Christian values at risk.

(*Dark. Lights go up. Spotlight on* NEWSPERSON.)

NEWSPERSON: Ladies and gentlemen, here is a late-breaking story. The Senate has followed an earlier House vote in banning Rap music from the airwaves. The President says that he will sign the bill that will make it a federal crime to record, disseminate, purchase or even hum a Rap tune, or even to imagine the lyrics of a Rap tune. Those convicted of breaking this law can be subject to a mandatory sentence of life imprisonment. So jubilant was a public weary of this filthy uncivilized music invading the sanctity of our alabaster land—America—that Monday has been declared a national holiday. Church bells will ring. The horns of ships will blast. Rev. Jack Legge, the sensible black leader who led the drive to ban Rap music, will receive the Medal of Freedom during ceremonies that will be held in the White House next week.

(*Stage goes dark. Then lights.*)

## ACT I: SCENE 3

(*St. John's Church.*)

REV. JACK LEGGE: Boy, those were the days. *Meet the Press. Face the Nation. People Magazine. The Times. Newsweek. Time.* My face was everywhere. (*Reveals empty pockets*) Now my bank account is about the size of a mosquito's peter. All these people are into this old Africa mess. Little do they know that lions and tigers are still walking through towns over there. Santeria. Yoruba, and this strange heathen belief that the chinaman's smuggled into the country. Goes by the name of Buddhism. What nonsense. God must be mad. A woman sitting in the White House. A follower of Sophia. S'pozed to be some kind of woman Earth Goddess. Saint John said that at the end of time women would be going with women and men would be lying with men. People don't seem to have the time for Jesus no more. They better get right or something terrible is going to happen to this nation. If the people and their leaders don't shape up, praying to false idols and ... and ... and worshiping a woman. Speaking of women (*pulls out small black book*), this stress is getting too much for me. I need a date (*soldiers arrive*).

IST SOLDIER: Rev. Jack Legge?

REV. JACK LEGGE: That's me.

2ND SOLDIER: You're under arrest.

REV. JACK LEGGE: For what? (*They carry him off kicking and protesting*) I know my rights. What is the meaning of this? Why, I marched with Martin Luther King, Jr. He wouldn't make a speech without having me okay it. I kept the shirt that bears the prophet's blood. Hey, not so rough. I'm a man who demands respect. You better not mess with a servant of the Lord. Hey, hold it, stop. Stop it.

ACT I: SCENE 4

(*The Oval Office.* THE PRESIDENT OF THE UNITED STATES, *an Asian-American woman. She is seated on the floor in a lotus position. Her eyes are closed. New Age music in the background. Incense floating up.* THREE STRIKES *enters now, older, grayer. He is the Attorney General. He is dressed in white, traditional sokoto and a fila.*)

ATTORNEY GENERAL: (*To audience*). She's in the Oval Office all day. Into her meditations she says. Not a single piece of legislation has been passed. The government is at a standstill. Mail hasn't been delivered in months. All of the postal employees are meditating. The Wicca members of Congress haven't returned from their retreat in Arizona. They're attending some spiritual edification conference. Our people can't do business for lack of a quorum. I don't know how long the Santeria party will be able to maintain an alliance with these people. Before the Chinese entered Tibet, a sizeable part of the adult male population was freeloading off of the working people. They justified this on the grounds that they were receiving wisdom and that this was work. With the Wicca people in power, this religion, a mishmash of Orientalism, self-improvement philosophy, California mysticism, and purist ecology, a similar kind of parasitism is happening here.

(PRESIDENT *blinks her eyes until these are fully open. She sees the* ATTORNEY GENERAL *and smiles. He smiles back.*)

PRESIDENT: (*To audience*) Him again. I made him Attorney General as a conciliatory gesture to the Santeria after the last election. I wonder, do they really sacrifice people? That's the rumor. All of the animals they sacrifice to spirits. And then that drumming. There are drums all over. The whole city sounds like Prospect Park. They're such a noisy people. When they call their members for a vote in the House of Representatives, they insist upon using a conch horn instead of the electronic system. I hope that they won't gain more seats in the House. It's a good thing that we Wicca people run the Senate. They talk a good game about their devotion to women's rights, but women priests or what they call "Babalawo" are very rare. Also, how can they revere such demanding egotistical and authoritarian gods? Gods who drink rum. Eat meat. And have sex with people.

ATTORNEY GENERAL: Ms. President, I consulted with members of the department. We've decided to arrest the Christian leaders and reprocess them. Close down the remaining churches. Of course, there will be those who will complain about the infringement upon First Amendment rights, but it'll blow over. The public has lost its patience with these Christians. The violence. The misogyny.

PRESIDENT: I think this is the best course of action.

ATTORNEY GENERAL: Outside of the mayhem and the grisly murders still taking place in the Christian sections, the country is at peace. The temples are filled with people. Crimes of violence are way down. People are not shouting at each other anymore more. Everybody goes around talking like Avery Brooks in *Star Trek: Deep Space Nine*. But in the Christian corridors, crime, violence, child and spousal abuse are still taking place. People in these areas lose their tempers with the slightest provocation. Everybody is armed.

PRESIDENT: They're nothing but trouble. They have these shoot-outs in their places of worship. On the day they celebrate their so-called savior, even. Some of the bloodiest battles occur on Christmas and Easter. Crazed disciples enter temples, mosques, and synagogues and engage in shoot-outs. Seems that religions that originated in the Middle East are hotheads. Nothing but Jihads, Crusades. Witch hunts. Maybe it has something to do with their all worshiping a volcano god.

ATTORNEY GENERAL: The public is through with the behavior of these Christians. Nothing but homicide and genocide wherever they go.

PRESIDENT: What do you propose, Mr. Attorney General?

ATTORNEY GENERAL: We're going to ban the Bible, the Koran, and the Torah. These books, as you know, Ms. President, are full of sexist comments and instructions. Hostility toward women is the hallmark of these religions.

PRESIDENT: Do you suppose their unruliness had something to do with their diet? Their breathing methods? Maybe a crackdown is in order. (*To audience*) This is an election year, right? If I can get rid of these people I will win reelection with no problem. The Wicca Party will come in with another landslide.

ATTORNEY GENERAL: (*To audience*) Fat chance. I sense a growing disillusionment with this regime. Everything is so cool and calm. People miss the excitement of former times. The Wiccas have declared a curfew all over the country—from ten P.M. to eight A.M. is the national quiet hour. There's no fun in Wicca, unless you're on the inside. People want to party. To let the good times roll again. Carnivals. Mardi Gras. We'll go through the motions of cracking down on these Christians. Get rid of their leaders. Then their followers will be up for grabs. They will have no choice but to side with us. With their support we will have a new religious majority in the country. After all, we use Christian saints as ways. Ways to get to our loas. The Christians have nowhere to go. They will have to join us. They hate the Wiccas. Christians used to burn people like her at the stake.

PRESIDENT: (*Starry-eyed*) Just think. Twenty years ago I was a minor poet and then I won a fellowship from the Only Oil Foundation to spend three weeks in residence at a country estate.

ATTORNEY GENERAL: That was the beginning of a notable career. (To *the audience*) She tells this goofy story at every occasion.

PRESIDENT: And one day while strolling through the meadow, a beautiful white horse galloped up from nowhere and spoke to me. Told me that destiny had great plans for me. That I would bring peace to a country nearly destroyed by random mayhem and violence. It was then that I swore off porterhouse steaks forever. Much later Sophia came to me in a dream and revealed to me that yes, indeed, she was that horse. The rest, as they say, is history. I defeated an obese freak who was addicted to country hams. So grossed out on hydrogenated oils he was until he couldn't go two minutes without fatigue. This glutton was a symbol of the Age of Greed. For breakfast he ate steak and eggs. Those awful calorie-laden western omelets. After I was elected, meditation centers were established in every neighborhood. Compulsory low-fat diets were forced upon the public. Fruit, natural grains, cereals, beans. A big market emerged for Psyllium Hydrophilic Mucillod.

ATTORNEY GENERAL: (*To audience*) There have been riots all over the country protesting this bland diet. We'll promise to restore Barbeque. French fries. Hi-fat ice cream. Steak. There are so many sacred cows wandering around that traffic is tied up from Pittsburgh to Riverside, California. The black market in steaks is making millions in profit. The compulsory diet issue alone should gain us seven states.

PRESIDENT: The first thing I did after the election was to declare war on meat eaters. I banned the marketing of steaks. But now some person is involved in a hot black market in steaks. Oh, I wish that I could get my hands on that person. I'll put him under the jail. Why haven't you caught him?

ATTORNEY GENERAL: We're doing all that we can. (*Hands her a document*)

PRESIDENT: What's this?

ATTORNEY GENERAL: It's the executive order that will allow our soldiers to raid the mosques, churches, and synagogues. Drastic steps must be taken to end the Judeo-Christian threat to civilization once and for all.

PRESIDENT: You have my unequivocal support. And once again we show the country that the Santeria and the Wicca, regardless of their differences, are capable of working in harmony for the common good. (*They eye each other suspiciously for a moment*)

ATTORNEY GENERAL: Thank you, Ms. President. (*He exits*)

PRESIDENT: One thing about them. They certainly wear beautiful clothes. I wonder who his designer is? (*Female* AIDE *enters*)

AIDE: Your Excellency, we have the final draft of the official prayer in school that all school children will be required to recite before the beginning of classes.

PRESIDENT: Read it to me.

AIDE: "Our maker Sophia. We are women in your image. With the old blood of our wombs we give form to new life. With nectar between our thighs we invite a lover. We birth a child. With our warm body fluids we remind the world of its pleasures and sensations."

PRESIDENT: Wonderful. Simply marvelous.

AIDE: I have a question, though.

PRESIDENT: What?

AIDE: Won't the boys be upset having to recite this prayer?

PRESIDENT: Women have had to recite creeds for thousands of years that addressed a god of the male gender. It's time for payback. (*Snaps fingers, vogue-like gesture made popular in the film* Paris Is Burning)

AIDE: And the Santerias?

PRESIDENT: Don't worry about them. They're very adaptable. You see how quickly they incorporated Sophia and Gaia into their pantheon? They're just two more spirits to them. I think they feed Sophia macrobiotic food. Those people have so many spirits to obey that they spend all of their time in ritual. No wonder they were the runners-up in the last election. They didn't have enough time to campaign. And listen, I'll tell you something. If we win the House in the next election, we may have to crack down on the Santeria. I don't trust them. We can run ads accusing them of Satanism and cannibalism. They're meat eaters like the rest. Only they have an exemption from the Supreme Court. They say it's part of their religion. After the next election, we'll see about that.

### ACT 2: SCENE I

RAPPER:
*What you visit upon others*
*can happen to you*
*Now Jack Legge the preacher*
*is in a hell of a stew.*

*In the 1990s*
*He was riding a wave*
*Now it's twenty years later*
*and he's considered a knave*
*A different regime*
*Is running things now*
*And they and the Christians*
*don't see eye to eye.*

*The prisoners in jail*
*include eaters of steak*
*And that's not all strange*
*in this off-the-wall state.*

*So sit back and chill out*
*and hear this weird tale*
*about Three Strikes and Jack Legge*
*and a Pope making bail.*

CHORUS:
*The preacher and the rapper*
*One's dreadlocked, and one's dapper*
*A man of the cloth*

*and a man of the streets*
*The issues are old*
*and the passions run deep*
*and try as they might*
*will their minds ever meet?*

(*Jail cell.* POPE *is being interviewed by the* NEWSCASTER. *He's playing solitaire and isn't looking at her.*)

NEWSCASTER: The world press is focused upon this federal prison today. Inside this jail cell is a man who used to be one of the world's most powerful men. But now, as a sign of the declining power of the Christian church, the Pope has been thrown in jail after being seized on the eve of his American tour. Your Holiness, how are you holding up?

POPE: I've had better days.

NEWSCASTER: The Sung government has said that because of your stand on abortion and women priests they couldn't guarantee your safety. That they have placed you in protective custody. But insiders say it's because of a complaint made by a young boy.

POPE: A baseless lie. I am not guilty.

NEWSCASTER: It's going to be hard to prove it, Holy Father. After the scandal of the last three decades and the cash the Church has paid out to quash suits made in connection with these complaints, people are wondering whether the charges are true?

POPE: Let them believe what they want to believe.

NEWSCASTER: How do you feel when you see your photo on the cover of all the magazines? The lurid copy. The press being almost obsessed with every development, every detail about your private life on display in supermarkets?

POPE: I don't feel a thing to tell you the truth. I just want to get the whole thing over. Clear my name.

NEWSCASTER: Thank you for giving us this exclusive interview, your Excellency.

POPE: My pleasure.

NEWSCASTER: This has been an exclusive interview with the Pope, who had been held in an American prison for six months. The government says it's because there have been threats against his life as a result of the Church's stand on abortion and women priests. But few believe the official story.

(*She writes a check and hands it to him.*)

POPE: Thank you.

NEWSCASTER: Don't you think it's degrading for a man of your stature to benefit from checkbook journalism?

POPE: Hey, I'm just trying to make bail.

NEWSCASTER: Thanks for the interview, anyway. (*She exits*)

POPE: A thousand bucks more and I'll have my bail money. (*Goes over to his tape recorder and puts in a tape. Some music by Giovanni Gabrielli. Begins to do push-ups. Momentarily* REV. JACK LEGGE *is roughly shoved into the cell that holds the Pope. Brushes off his clothes.*)

REV. JACK LEGGE: (*To guards who are leaving*) You'll pay for this! You'll pay. Why, I marched with Martin Luther King, Jr. It was I whom he asked for advice when he was composing his famous "March on Washington" speech. I was with him in the Birmingham jail. I wear his blood on my clothes. I have proof. (*Turns around and notices the other jail occupant. To himself*) Well, at least they put me in a cell with a white man. I'm afraid of these young brothers. When I walk down the street and someone is following me, I'm relieved when I discover that it is a white person behind me.

Aren't you—why yes, your Excellency (*kneels and kisses his ring*). It's an honor. I'm sharing my cell with you ... I read about your ... er ... troubles —they're persecuting us Christians all over the globe, it seems. Look at me. Why, I was one of the top strategists for the Southern Christian Leadership Conference—thrown in jail like a common tramp.

POPE: Take it as a learning experience. I've learned a lot in these past six months of incarceration. I've read much of the opposition's work. Marx. The Protestants. Buddhism. Santeria. I've even delved into this Sophia business that's been sweeping the West, posing the greatest threat to the Christian Church since the cult of Isis.

REV. JACK LEGGE: A woman god, ha! That'll be the day.

POPE: I wouldn't be so sure. As I said, I've had a lot of time to think. This isn't the same as viewing the world from my Vatican apartment of plush red carpets and pre-Raphaelite paintings. This is real. This is, what my fellow inmates would call, the nitty-gritty. You know what I'm saying? What are you in for?

REV. JACK LEGGE: They won't say. Came to my church. Hauled me away.

VOICE: Help me! Please, somebody help me!

REV. JACK LEGGE: What's that?

POPE: It's a young *Village Voice* reporter. He was always praising prisoners as the true voice of the disenfranchised masses. Said that they are the vanguard of the revolution. Said he read it in a book. He got himself arrested so that he could write a book from the inside. Poor fellow. The Ass Bandits got hold of him. They're passing him around and trading him for cigarettes and candy.

REV. JACK LEGGE: That's not going to happen to me. I'll be out of here as soon as my lawyer hears about this.

*(Television comes on. New Age spacey music.)*

NEWSCASTER: This is Violet Ray with the main points of the news. Thousands of people from all over America converged upon Florida today for the annual Odun rites. Master priest drummer Babatu Olatunji, his dancers and chorus excited Miami's largest stadium, which was filled to capacity. Many African deities came down and joined in the celebration. Shango, Oshun, Oya, Orungan, Dada, Babalu, Ifa and many others. Unlike the old Christian days, not a single episode of violence was reported. President Barbara Sung congratulated the worshipers for being so well-behaved. Though she disapproves of animal sacrifice and meat eating, she said that she would continue to observe the religious freedom of the Santeria, guaranteed by the Supreme Court. In other news, President Barbara Sung has declared the January Holiday of Martin Luther King, Jr., the prophet of nonviolence, to be a day of national celebration. If the celebration is not observed in New Hampshire, President Sung has promised to send in troops. As you know, the observances for George Washington, Abraham Lincoln, and Columbus have been eliminated from the calendar due to President Sung's having declared it inappropriate to celebrate the births of men associated with violence. And finally a repeat of the lead story. Troops are beginning to withdraw from occupying the Christian zones where they were sent after the Christmas riots. Each year during Christmas the Christians get drunk and begin to engage in a rampage of violence. The 9–1–1 calls increase beyond the capacity of our law enforcement agencies to handle them. On Easter, as you know, many of the more fanatical devotees of the Christian cult drive nails through their hands in imitation of their Lord about whom the preposterous claim was made that he rose from the dead. Experts say that one of the reasons that followers of desert religions are so violent is that their core belief is based upon mutilation and blood sacrifice.

*(Newscaster shivers with disgust.)*

Ms. Sung has decided to take stern measures against the Christians who are still engaged in misogyny and are promoting violence and racism, all of which are against the law. Millions of Bibles have been confiscated and burned. As part of the new crackdown, several prominent ministers have been arrested and will be reprocessed (REV. JACK LEGGE *is stunned*) as a way of cleansing society of Christianity and its cousin religions, which have led to the deaths of millions over the centuries. The charlatan and imposter Reverend Jack Legge has been seized and now shares a cell with the criminal Roman Pope who was arrested on the eve of the Pope's tour of America after a youngster came forth and identified the Pope as the man who molested him in a fantasy.

REV. JACK LEGGE: Re-processed. What is that? I ain't done nothing wrong. Why, that's crazy! (*Goes to bars*) Guard. Guard. There has been a mistake. I was with Martin Luther King, Jr., from his early days. Why, I used to write his term papers in college. It was me who researched his Ph.D. dissertation.

*(ATTORNEY GENERAL approaches the cell.)*

REV. JACK LEGGE: Who are you?

ATTORNEY GENERAL: I'm the Attorney General.

REV. JACK LEGGE: Well, that's more like it. The government has realized its mistake and sent you to apologize, right?

ATTORNEY GENERAL: (*Ignores* REVEREND) Pope, you're free to go. The child has changed his testimony. He says that it wasn't you who seduced him in his fantasy, it was Elvis. There's an all-states bulletin out on the King of Rock and Roll and he's been sited in a number of places. We believe an arrest is imminent.

POPE: (*Rising, exiting from the cell, shaking his head*) You Americans are crazier than anybody would have ever believed. You arrest me as soon as I land in New York on the first leg of my American tour. You throw me in jail and won't allow me to consult a lawyer. All because of some kid's fantasy.

ATTORNEY GENERAL: A fantasy, huh? What would you call the notion of virgin birth, or the Ascension?

REV. JACK LEGGE: Look, you. Me and the Holy Father ain't going to stand for none of your blasphemy. (POPE *and* ATTORNEY GENERAL *ignore him*)

POPE: Young man, you have a lot to learn. (REVEREND *nods in agreement*) And even you would admit that those truths that were revealed by faith are much stronger than some emotionally disturbed youngster, bringing charges of such a bizarre nature against me.

REV. JACK LEGGE: You tell him, Pope.

ATTORNEY GENERAL: Half the graves in Europe are filled with heretics whom your church put to death for denying those revealed truths as you call them. Fantasies as I call them.

POPE: How did a fantasy become the same thing as reality in American law?

REV. JACK LEGGE: Good question, Pope. Answer the man. How did it?

(*Challenging, gets into the* ATTORNEY GENERAL's *face.*)

ATTORNEY GENERAL: (*Ignores him*) *You* know as well as I, Pope, that in the West it begins with Plato's cave allegory and continues through Immanuel Kant's *Critique of Pure Reason*. Both argue that objective reality can never be known, right?

POPE: God knows objective reality. Besides, Plato was a pagan and Kant couldn't make up his mind about whether to be a pagan or a Christian.

REV. JACK LEGGE: You're right, Pope. God knows everything. (*To* ATTORNEY GENERAL) I guess he told you, chump!

ATTORNEY GENERAL: You don't know whether God knows objective reality because you cannot know God.

POPE: His being is manifest.

REV. JACK LEGGE: I know Him in my heart.

ATTORNEY GENERAL: Max Weber's comment that the objective interpretation of human meaning necessarily involved the subjective viewpoint of the observer is echoed in Heisenberg's principle of indeterminacy. The Japanese have a concept known as Shin-nyo, which closely means "suchness," the true nature of things that eludes all description for which the word "fu-ka-shi-gi" is used.

REV. JACK LEGGE: What's the Japs got to do with it? Stick to the subject. You're changing the subject because the Pope is beating your argument.

ATTORNEY GENERAL: (*Ignores* REVEREND) Of course, the Yoruba were into indeterminacy thousands of years before Plato. They even have a god Eshu, who is a god of indeterminacy, of chance and uncertainty, just as the Haitians reaffirm Plato's theory of knowledge, with their belief that the real world is alive beneath the sea, and that the world perceived through the senses is a pale reflection of this world. For the Akan people of Ghana, dream life is just as true as real life.

REV. JACK LEGGE: There you go with that old heathen Africa mess again.

You embarrassing me. You make the Pope think that we still savages. In the jungle. There ain't nothin' in Africa but reptiles and drums.

POPE: He's a real *fregniacciaro*.

ATTORNEY GENERAL: *Fregniacciaro*. That's bullshitter, right? (POPE *nods*) We're just amateur bullshitters next to you fellows. You invented the cosmological and teleological and ontological proofs for the existence of God. This real con-job in which the proof for the existence of God was rigged in the premise. Something like God exists because God exists.

POPE: Those proofs lasted for seven hundred years. You should be so lucky. (*Pause*) Besides, what about your god, Olodumare?

REV. JACK LEGGE: He got you now, infidel.

ATTORNEY GENERAL: Olodumare is rarely mentioned in Santeria. We respect his intermediaries who provide us with services. Unlike your God who allegedly interferes in the affairs of men, Olodumare is sort of like a C.E.O. who presides over a large staff of messengers. Also, unlike your God who has sent armies into the field for centuries, sometimes backing both sides, there is seldom an army that can claim its mandate from Olodumare. Olodumare never punished children who mocked a prophet. Olodumare never turned cities to sand simply because the inhabitants within engaged in unorthodox sexual practices. We even have a hermaphrodite god-Olokan. She/he lives on the ocean floor. Other Santeria gods are also gender neutral. Christianity condemns gays and lesbians to death. Leviticus says: "They shall surely be put to death." 20:13.

POPE: (*Pause*) You have a strange country here. You can be sure that when my lawyers sue you for false imprisonment, that it won't be a fantasy. It will be real. Am I free to go? (ATTORNEY GENERAL *nods*. POPE *gathers the Bible and rosary, puts on his skullcap. Begins to lift suitcase*)

REV. JACK LEGGE: Can I give you a hand, Pope? (*Reaches for suitcase*)

POPE: No, that won't be necessary.

REV. JACK LEGGE: I insist. (*They begin to struggle with the suitcase*)

POPE: (*Annoyed*) I said I'd handle it.

REV. JACK LEGGE: I know that we have had fallings out, your Excellency, but maybe now that the Church is under attack, we Protestants and Catholics ought to make up. Bury the hatchet.

POPE: Maybe so. (POPE *begins to exit*)

REV. JACK LEGGE: As for you (*to* ATTORNEY GENERAL) you should be ashamed of yourself, humiliating the Pope. Putting a Pope in jail for the first time in history.

POPE: Not true.

REV. JACK LEGGE: What?

POPE: Pius VII was detained by Napoleon. The Church survived Napoleon. In the 1840s, Pius IX was imprisoned by a revolutionary Committee of Public Safety. The Church survived that challenge, too. (POPE *and* ATTORNEY GENERAL *are studying each other as he delivers these lines*) We'll survive you, too.

ATTORNEY GENERAL: Pope?

POPE: Yes?

ATTORNEY GENERAL: Didn't you wonder why there was no outcry against your arrest?

POPE: That didn't bother me. How do you explain it?

ATTORNEY GENERAL: The Church is dead in this country. The Mother Goddess, which your early Church supplanted, has made a strong comeback. Maybe back there in the nineties when you had a chance, you should have ordained women priests.

REV. JACK LEGGE: Ha! Ha! That's crazy. Don't listen to him, Pope.

POPE: He has a point.

ATTORNEY GENERAL: And your stubbornness at the Cairo conference, refusing to make even the slightest concession to the Pro-Choice movement didn't help.

POPE: You're right, we didn't budge. Maybe we'll change. This time in jail has given me time to think. When do you have time to think? To sort of kick back and mull things over?

ATTORNEY GENERAL: I don't follow.

POPE: You and the New Agers are in charge now, but the same crowds who are applauding you today may be shouting for your crucifixion tomorrow. History always seems to be eager to get on to the next act. Good day, Attorney General. And Rev. Legge, keep carrying the cross. The forces of the Lord are down but not out. Maybe all of what is happening is merely a wake-up call. (*He exits*)

REV. JACK LEGGE: Good-bye, Pope. Have a good trip back to Italy and I'm sure that the rest of America's dwindling Christian band apologize for the awful treatment you've suffered at the hands of these heathens and idol worshipers. A wake-up call from the Lord. Yes indeed. (*To* ATTORNEY GENERAL) You are on top now, but we are united. Catholics and Protestants. Why, even though we may have disagreements, me and the Pope believe in the same thing.

ATTORNEY GENERAL: How about celibacy?

REV. JACK LEGGE: (*Pause*) Well ... I ... a (*removes a handkerchief and begins to wipe his brow*).

ATTORNEY GENERAL: Do you recognize me?

REV. JACK LEGGE: (*Stares for a moment*) Can't say that I do.

ATTORNEY GENERAL: You don't remember the Congressional hearings in the 1990s. The hearings that led to the criminalization of Rap music?

REV. JACK LEGGE: Oh yes! Mabel Johnson and I were successful in our attempt to get rid of that nasty music. Made it a federal crime to create, manufacture, disseminate, and listen to Rap music. That hothead Three Strikes desisted, though. Made a bootleg version of the music, was arrested, and got a long ... (*recognizes the* ATTORNEY GENERAL *as* THREE STRIKES) ... sentence—hey! It's you. Three Strikes!

ATTORNEY GENERAL: That was my name before my transformation. My new name is Ogun Jagun Jagun. (REVEREND *bursts out laughing.* ATTORNEY GENERAL *ignores it*) That long prison sentence gave me a chance to think. I decided that you were right, Reverend. That violence and sexist attitudes toward women should be curbed. The way they're smacked around, humiliated, bruised, beaten, raped, murdered. I read a lot of books in prison and decided that of all of the books that I read, the most influential was the Bible.

REV. JACK LEGGE: I'm glad to hear that, son. Glad you see it my way.

ATTORNEY GENERAL: Not exactly. The Bible, as you know, is the paradigm, the frame of reference of the Judeo-Christian religion and it was after a close line-by-line reading of the scriptures that I decided that it was the Bible that created the basis of our culture's attitudes toward women and violence. From the beginning of the Bible, the book of Genesis, when women are made from the rib of a man and one woman is blamed for the introduction of sin into the world to the end when women are called whores. The Bible is a manual for women haters. Not only that, but there are constant instructions to commit violence against women—"thou shalt not suffer a witch to live" Exodus 22:17—which led to the extermination of women during the Middle Ages or women's holocaust, to the reference to Babylon the great, the Mother of harlots and abominations of the earth in Revelations 17:5. There are constant admonitions in this Bible of yours to fight against the enemies of this psychotic god that your people worship. A god who receives fiendish pleasure from the sufferings of his followers and even his own son. A god who unlike our Orishas can't eat and can't dance, won't make love to a woman—a brooding, dangerous and melancholy god who dwells alone. The greatest taboo in Yoruba is to dwell alone. I regret the songs that I recorded back there in the nineties which disrespected women and were filled with scatology.

I joined the Santeria temple and became a follower of the Orishas. I dedicated my life to eliminating violence and misogyny from American life. And Reverend, you gave me the idea by leading the fight to banish Rap from the airwaves. You struck a blow for women's rights. I am to blame for making those underground recordings that got me arrested. But it was during that time in jail that I learned the truth. (*Slowly, deliberately*) That if criminalizing Rap was a good way of ridding the world of the misogynist culture, then criminalizing Christianity and its associate religions—Islam and Judaism—would help to end misogyny and violence once and for all.

REV. JACK LEGGE: Look here, buddy. You'd better not fool around with God —God don't like ugly.

ATTORNEY GENERAL: Your God is a racist, sexist, homophobic, and a misogynist. Throughout your Bible there are demands that women be subservient to men. "Wives submit yourselves unto your own husband, as unto the Lord," says Ephesians 5:22. "The husband is the head of the wife," again, Ephesians 5:23. "...the head of the woman is the man," says Corinthians 11:3. Your God doesn't like women talking back or challenging men; for doing so, they get labeled "contentious" as in "...a continual dropping in a very rainy day and a contentious woman are alike," Proverbs 27:15. For your Bible, women are evil: "Keep them from the evil woman, ..." Proverbs 6:24, and are seen as causing the downfall of men: "She hath cast down many wounded; yes, many strong men have been slain by her." How can we tolerate a religion that condemns nonconformist women and homosexuals to death? Your God? Your God is a cruel god. What does he do to Hagar, concubine of the patriarch, Abraham? Sends her and her son into the wilderness without any means of providing for herself I can't think of anything so cruel.

REV. JACK LEGGE: It's not for us to judge the ways of the Lord. We are just supposed to have faith and to obey like sheep.

ATTORNEY GENERAL: Think of the wars, the genocide. The hate crimes. The persecution of blacks, women, and homosexuals as a result of these ugly Biblical instructions. The massacres. The show trials. The lynching. Mass suicides at Jonestown, and the Order of the Solar Temple. And you had the nerve back there in the 1990s to accuse rappers of misogyny? No rapper ever stoned a woman to death because he read it in some crazy patriarchal book

REV. JACK LEGGE: You ought not to be saying these things. God will punish you.

ATTORNEY GENERAL: I'll take my chances. Your God versus mine.

REV. JACK LEGGE: (*Mutters*) Pagan savages. Look, I'm about fed up with this conversation. I demand that I be released. I'm not as influential as I once was, I admit, but I still have some powerful friends. When Mabel Johnson hears about this, you will have some explaining to do. She is one of the three Christians who still have a seat in Congress. (MABEL *is led into the cell, she has aged like all of the other characters who appeared in Act I. She wears a leopard-skin coat*)

MABEL: (*To guard*) Get your hands off me. I have congressional immunity. You can't . . .

REV. JACK LEGGE: Mabel, what you doing here?

MABEL: Some of these crazy Wicca police came to my house in the middle of the night. Turned the place upside down. Said they were looking for evidence.

REV. JACK LEGGE: Evidence. Evidence for what?

ATTORNEY GENERAL: She's been making a profit from illegal steak sales. She's raked in millions (PRESIDENT SUNG *enters with* AIDE).

PRESIDENT: I just wanted to see for myself the face of a person so vile as to sell steaks when I personally prohibited the marketing of such poison.

MABEL: You can't prove a doggone thing.

PRESIDENT: Oh! We can't, can we? All of your cohorts have confessed. They're making deals with the prosecutors. They said that you are the mastermind behind the whole scheme.

MABEL: They what? Those dirty low-down sneaks! (*Mutters*) Those disloyal motherfuckers.

REV. JACK LEGGE: That ain't the reason they're persecuting you, Mabel. Don't you recognize this man? It's Three Strikes.

MABEL: (*Shocked*) Three Strikes! That filthy-mouthed Rap singer?

ATTORNEY GENERAL: We're looking at some serious time here. And to think, you hauled me before a Congressional committee for singing Rap songs.

PRESIDENT: As much as I detest Rap music, no Rap music ever gave anybody a heart attack.

MABEL: Selling bad meat was the only way that I could stay in office. It takes a fortune to be a candidate these days.

PRESIDENT: You won't have to worry about running for office anymore.

ATTORNEY GENERAL: You can get ten years for raising the cholesterol level of the population.

MABEL: Ten years? That's ridiculous.

PRESIDENT: Ten years, my foot. I'm going to have to re-process these two. We must rid the nation's gene pool of characters like these.

ATTORNEY GENERAL: Re-processing. But, Ms. President, isn't that extreme?

PRESIDENT: You keep out of this. Oh! Now I get it. You're in cahoots with your fellow meat eaters. I knew it. You barbarian. Guard! Take these people to the reprocessing center.

ATTORNEY GENERAL: What? You would … me? You're asking for it. The Santeria party will have you impeached.

PRESIDENT: Let them.

REV. JACK LEGGE: Now wait a minute. Re-processing. Isn't that a little extreme? What is it, anyway?

ATTORNEY GENERAL: If you are such a loyal follower of your God, then maybe He will save you from the fate that awaits you.

MABEL: Re-processing. It's probably unconstitutional. I know my rights.

REV. JACK LEGGE: Yes. Good question.

ATTORNEY GENERAL: They're going to make us an example the way I was made an example by those Congressional hearings that took place in the 1990s.

PRESIDENT: Don't worry. You won't feel a thing. It's painless. We take you into a little room and-the Wicca way of execution is much more civilized than the crude and barbaric gas chamber, the electric chair. You'll die smiling with enlightenment.

REV. JACK LEGGE: Now hold on a minute. Ain't nobody said nothing about no execution. Let me out this place. Help! Help! (*Guard restrains him*)

MABEL: You won't get away with it. I knew I should have voted for the immigration bill barring these people from coming over here. These chinks have taken over the country. They are worse than white people.

PRESIDENT: Now look here, dearie. Don't try guilt tripping me. The Chinese never owned black slaves.

ATTORNEY GENERAL: Only yellow slaves. I suspect that this meat business is just a cover. She wants to use us to gain re-election. She wants to distract attention from her failed policies. The meat prohibition. The national quiet hour. Compulsory aerobics.

PRESIDENT: Nobody cares anything about you. Who would protest? A lowly high-fat peddler, wearer of animal skins and carnivorous steak thief, a has-been broken down colored preacher and a follower of (*contemptuously*) voodoo. The public will thank me. They're tired of your cult and its disgusting practices.

MABEL: You're just persecuting us because we're black.

PRESIDENT: Race. Race. Race. That's all you people think about. You can't tell us about oppression. We lived under the hated Japanese occupation. Your so-called servitude was a picnic in comparison to that. The slave master took care of all your needs. That's why you people developed a welfare mentality. You people are loafers.

MABEL: (*Lunges for* PRESIDENT, *stopped by guards*) Why you yellow slut. I'll wrap your sorry ass around my fist you motherfuckin' slope. (REVEREND *is shocked*) Excuse my French, Reverend (*sheepishly*).

PRESIDENT: That's it. That's it. Resort to violence. You people are the most violent in the world.

ATTORNEY GENERAL: When the Santeria hear about this, there will be a civil war that will make the one of the 1860s seem like a playground spat. I would advise you against proceeding with this madness. (*Guards begins to remove the* ATTORNEY GENERAL, MABEL, *and* REVEREND).

PRESIDENT: Let the Santeria try. I'm way ahead of you, my friend. I ordered raids on Santeria party headquarters on my way over here. Tonight I will make a speech to the nation. Tell the public what was going on inside those places. After that, whatever public support that you had will plummet.

REV. JACK LEGGE: Can't we talk this over? Please?

MABEL: (*To guards*) Get away from me. Let me go. Take your hands off me. (*Kicks one in the shins*)

REV. JACK LEGGE: Help me, Jesus! Please help me! I don't want to be re-processed. I want to live. Have mercy. Somebody help me.

(*We still hear the* REVEREND *screams for help from offstage.* PRESIDENT *checks to see if coast is clear. Sits down. Puts on Yankee's baseball cap. Removes a hamburger from a McDonald's bag. Begins to eat. Really enjoys it.*)


ACT 2: SCENE 2


(*St. John's Church.* SECRETARY *hears* REVEREND *screaming. Rushes in. She is played by the same actress who plays* MABEL. *He is seated at a desk. The TV is turned on to the* Oprah Winfrey Show, *no sound.*)

REV. JACK LEGGE: Help me. Please. Somebody. (*He's breathing heavily and sweating profusely. She wakes him*) Mabel—you're all right!

SECRETARY: Mabel? What's wrong with you? My name is Jacqueline. I'm your secretary, Reverend. You been hittin' the Scotch again?

REV. JACK LEGGE: Oh, yes! Of course ... I ... I ... had a bad dream (*calmly, thoughtfully*) "Thou scarest me with dreams and terrifiest me through visions." Job 7:14.

SECRETARY: What did you say, Reverend?

REV. JACK LEGGE: Forget it. Look, what is my sermon for Sunday?

SECRETARY: "Her Abominations Spilleth Over."

REV. JACK LEGGE: Change that. Make it something like: "Mary Magdalene: Holy Witness."

SECRETARY: But Mary Magdalene was a prostitute. Why preach a sermon about her?

REV. JACK LEGGE: There's not a scintilla of proof in the Bible that the Divine Person was a prostitute. For too long the role of women in the Bible has been denied. It's time to give them their due. After all, had there been no Magdalene, we would never have had a witness to the Resurrection, and without Mary, Christ's mother, there would have been no Christ. While the men betrayed our Lord, these women stood by him to the end and beyond. And daughter—

SECRETARY: Yes, Reverend?

REV. JACK LEGGE: I want you to put an ad in the *Amsterdam News* and the *City Sun*. We could use a new assistant pastor, a woman. All of the ones under me are men. I want you to get me a qualified woman who can handle pastoral duties. People get tired of looking at the same old hardheads every Sunday. We need some innovative approaches.

SECRETARY: Reverend, what's come over you? You once said that you'd die and go to hell before you'd share the pulpit with a woman.

REV. JACK LEGGE: (*Ignores this remark*) I want you to sell the two Cadillacs. We could use the money to set up a soup kitchen in the church here. Take .... take these rings (*removes them*) and cash them in. We could start a youth program. Keep kids off the street. And sister, call my maid. Tell her to give my three hundred suits and ninety shoes to the Goodwill. Don't look right. Our basking in luxuries while our people go hungry. As for my twenty-room mansion in Brooklyn, I want you to see about converting the place into a home for senior citizens. I'll move into an apartment.

Hell, Jesus didn't live in no palace. He moved from town to town, living in different people's houses. Another thing. That greedy Jezebel—I mean the daughter with whom I was supposed to have a private prayer in the home? Cancel that engagement indefinitely. Now what you got for me today?

SECRETARY: Connie Chung's show. You're supposed to debate Ice T, Dr. Dre, and this new Rap star Three Strikes.

REV. JACK LEGGE: Call it off.

SECRETARY: What?

REV. JACK LEGGE: I said call it off.

SECRETARY: But Reverend, this will give you an opportunity to harangue against this music that encourages violence and degrades our women. Besides, you know how you love photo opportunities. You've become the lightning rod for those who want to banish this music from the airwaves.

(MESSENGER *enters. Dressed in suit. Same actor who played the* POPE.)

MESSENGER: Reverend Jack Legge—

REV. JACK LEGGE: That's me (*hands him an envelope*). Haven't I seen you somewhere before? (*Opening the envelope*)

MESSENGER: I don't think so. (*Exits*)

SECRETARY: What is it, Reverend?

REV. JACK LEGGE: It's a subpoena from Congress asking me to appear before some committee that's out to do away with Rap music.

SECRETARY: That's a wonderful opportunity, Reverend. It'll probably be broadcast on all the networks. (REVEREND *rips up the subpoena*)

REV. JACK LEGGE: I'm not participating in no drive that would criminalize the free expressions of hip-hoppers, be-boppers, hard-rockers or anybody else. I may disagree with the music and the lyrics, but I can't subscribe to any proposition that would smack of censorship. Do you think that Martin Luther King, Jr., and I made all of those sacrifices so that words and music would be censored? That artistic expression would be criminalized? I doubt it. What would have happened had Jessssussss, the greatest rapper of them all, been reluctant to propose such radical ideas in his time had he lacked the nerve to speak out, to address taboos, to hold his tongue. The world would be quite different. I mean if we began outlawing groups whose expression we object to where would it end? (*Pause*) Who would be next? These kids are sending out a wounded shrill cry from those shut up in these festering inner cities. Police brutality, media harassment, unemployment, malnutrition, low birth weight, landlord exploitation. They didn't create these conditions, they are merely exhibiting them for us.

As for sexism and misogyny, the Church has plenty enough of its own to take care of without worrying about others. And if we can't straighten out the Lord's house, how are we going to straighten out the house of popular music? We would be hypocrites. Jesus Christ hated hypocrisy. Some of his strongest statements are against hypocrisy. "Ye also outwardly appear righteous unto men, but within ye are full of hypocrisy and iniquity." Mathew 23:28 or "What is the hope of the hypocrite, though he hath gained, when God taketh away his soul?" We don't want to be hypocrites like the Pharisees whom Jesus condemned to woe. Now daughter, I want you to take a letter. Address it to the Pope at the Vatican. (*She begins to take dictation*)

Dear Pope:

As a fellow Christian, I was ashamed of the way your organization clowned and carried on at the recent Cairo conference. Where do you get off telling a woman when she can and when she can't have a baby? You ain't no woman. Have you ever been pregnant? No, you haven't. Have you ever suffered morning sickness? No, you haven't. Have you ever had an accidental pregnancy and didn't know how you were going to feed the child? Or been raped by some man or by your own father, the height of iniquity? The answer is no. Until you have done these things, you should keep your mouth shut. And one more thing. I'd be real careful about trying to rule other people's morality. I read the newspaper. (*Lights begin to dim*) And it seems to me that you have plenty of problems yourself without going around condemning others. The Vatican debt is about $56 Million, ain't it? (*Dimmer*) You remember what Jesus said about the Pharisees in Matthew 23:27: "Woe to you, scribes and Pharisees, hypocrites! For you are like whitewashed tombs, which, outwardly, appear beautiful, but within are full of dead men's bones and all uncleanliness." Seems to me (*Rap music begins to come up*) this pretty much describes the condition of the Church, Pope. We put up a good front—with our swell edifices and rich congregations—but inside ... inside .... deep in the soul of the Church, there is rot and disease and the bones of dead men. Before we pretend to cleanse others, we should root out the evil in us. (*Lights down, music up, spotlight on Rapper*)

RAPPER:
*And so we conclude*
*the preacher and the rapper*
*our queer story and rhyme*
*about the hazards and drawbacks*

*of making art into a crime*
*you have your tastes and I*
*have mine and that's just fine*
*So give me one good reason*
*why we should fight all the time?*

*Some like Bach and others Mozart*
*the Count, the Duke, and the*
*venerable Earl Hines*
*Some like Cecilia Cruz*
*Willi Bobo and others, my man*
*Dr. Funkenstein*
*There's only good music*
*and bad music*
*Lenny Bernstein*
*was heard to say*
*That's a pretty good point*
*Why don't we keep it that way?*
*That's a pretty good point*
*Let's keep it that way*

CHORUS:
*The preacher and the rapper*
*One's dreadlocked, and one's dapper*
*A man of the cloth*
*and a man of the streets*
*The issues are old*
*and the passions run deep*
*and try as they might*
*will their minds ever meet?*

Ishmael Reed has taught at Harvard, Yale, and Dartmouth, and has long been on the faculty at UC–Berkeley. Reed is the author of more than twenty books, including novels, essays, plays, and poetry. He is a recipient of the MacArthur Genius Award and the Lila Wallace Foundation Award. He has been a finalist for the Pulitzer Prize and was twice nominated for the National Book Award. He lives in Oakland with his wife, Carla, and their daughter, Tennessee.

## A NOTE ON THE TYPE

The text of this book has been composed in a digitized version of Dante, a typeface designed by scholar-printer Giovanni Mardersteig (1892–1977). An active book printer and proprietor of the Officina Bodoni, Mardersteig's typographic creed stressed service to the author, followed by service to the reader and concluded with the tertiary aim of producing an elegant page without the trappings of idiosyncrasy. After many years studying and using the great Venetian and Aldine types, Mardersteig began work on his own interpretation of the Renaissance form. His efforts culminated in the drawings for Dante, which Mardersteig completed in 1954. To render his letterforms in metal type, Mardersteig commissioned Charles Malin, a renowned punchcutter with whom he had worked for many years. By 1955 the Dante types were complete and Mardersteig eagerly used them for an edition of Boccaccio's *Trattatello in Laude di Dante*, from which the type derived its name.

*Book design and composition by Mark McGarry,*
*Texas Type & Book Works, Dallas, Texas*